INTERNATIONAL POLITICAL ECONOMY
Managing World Economic Change

ROBERT A. ISAAK

Pace University

Prentice Hall, Englewood Cliffs, NJ 07632

Library of Congress Cataloging-in-Publication Data

Isaak, Robert A.
  International political economy: managing world economic change /
Robert A. Isaak.
    p.   cm.
  Includes bibliographical references.
  ISBN 0-13-472366-X
  1. International economic relations.   I. Title.
HF1411.I76 1991   90-30720
337—dc20   CIP

Editorial/production supervision
  and interior design: *June Sanns*
Cover design: *Ben Santora*
Prepress buyer: *Debra Kesar*
Manufacturing buyer: *Marianne Gloriande*
Page makeup: *Joh Lisa*

© 1991 by Robert A. Isaak
Published by Prentice-Hall, Inc.
A Division of Simon & Schuster
Englewood Cliffs, New Jersey 07632

Printed in the United States of America

10 9 8 7 6 5 4 3 2 1

ISBN   0-13-472366-X

PRENTICE-HALL INTERNATIONAL (UK) LIMITED, *London*
PRENTICE-HALL OF AUSTRALIA PTY. LIMITED, *Sydney*
PRENTICE-HALL CANADA INC., *Toronto*
PRENTICE-HALL HISPANOAMERICANA, S.A., *Mexico*
PRENTICE-HALL OF INDIA PRIVATE LIMITED, *New Delhi*
PRENTICE-HALL OF JAPAN, INC., *Tokyo*
SIMON & SCHUSTER ASIA PTE. LTD., *Singapore*
EDITORA PRENTICE-HALL DO BRASIL, LTDA., *Rio de Janeiro*

This book is dedicated
to Gudrun, Sonya, and Andrew
who shared time with it
for a decade.

CONTENTS

PART TWO   Domestic Sources of Multinational Behavior

CHAPTER FOUR

LIFE CHANCES, CLASS POSITION, AND EDUCATION   108

CHAPTER FIVE

STATE STRATEGIES AND STAGES OF DEVELOPMENT   128

CHAPTER EIGHT

EAST–WEST STRUCTURES AND STRATEGY   225

PART FOUR   Conclusions and Tendencies

PREFACE

The managers of the People's Republic of China attempted to initiate economic reforms without political liberalization, which led to corruption, inflation, and massive democratic rebellion by students and workers in 1989. Soviet managers tried to introduce political reforms without significant changes in the Russian economic market and pricing systems, resulting in widespread, outspoken demands for economic change and regional autonomy. Early in the 1980s, *The New York Times* buried the news that the nine largest U.S. banks had lent three times more to developing countries than they had to back it up with (and were unlikely to get it back) in the little-read Saturday edition, hoping to "manage" a potential crisis in the financial markets. These examples illustrate that economics, politics, and business cannot be separated into autonomous fields if one seeks to explain the management of international economic change in a global political economy. Indeed, errors by managers of nation-states, of multinational corporations, and of international organizations often stem from the inability or unwillingness to take political, economic, and business aspects into account simultaneously—or to hold at least two opposed ideas in the mind and still retain the ability to function (as novelist F. Scott Fitzgerald put it in *The Crack-Up*).

This book assumes that it is not possible to separate the fields of international political economy, international organization, and international business in seeking to explain how global economic change is managed. The basic thesis is that there are universal patterns of collective learning that go a long way toward explaining the asymmetrical positions of the developed and developing nations in the global economy. Collective learning is social learning with a specific organizational context and cultural gestalt: It involves specific patterns of emulating or modeling behavior picked up from a particular culture and organizational environment at a certain time—as if by osmosis. An example, with great historical portent, is the spontaneous collective learning among the peoples of Eastern Europe in 1989. As grass roots democratic movements spread from Poland and Hungary to Czechoslovakia, East Germany, Rumania and Bulgaria, one rebellion mimicked another as they positioned themselves in the power vacuum Gorbachev's policy opened up.

Effective international management is concerned with transforming such patterns of collective learning so that the people in the organization or state adapt to economic change while maintaining a sense of individual dignity and cultural integrity.

The notion of management refers to managers of economic change in both the public (government or international organization) and private (multinational corporation or individual) sectors. And the key concepts of the international management/collective learning model employed follow straightforward common sense with as little ideological baggage as possible attached (that is, "the defeatist," "the free-rider," "the maintenance," and "the entrepreneurial" strategies).

Ever since the 1973 OPEC oil crisis, my university teaching has alternated back and forth between post–World War II historical explanations of international political economy and multinational organization and international management courses anticipating trends to the year 2000. My seminars in comparative political economy and comparative management systems have no doubt given these pages a more comparative cultural emphasis than is usually the case. As a student of international political economy, my personal perspective is embodied in the title of a course I taught at the Johns Hopkins University School of Advanced International Studies (SAIS) Center in Bologna, Italy, in 1980 entitled "International Management and Social Justice." While the heart may be on the side of the disadvantaged for the sake of social justice, the head says that the strong can best help the weak, not the weak themselves initially, and that tough-minded, future-oriented management tools must be brought to bear in managing political and economic relations if the gap between the rich and poor in the world is to be narrowed.

This book represents a decade's work. It was conceived in Bologna between 1978 and 1981 while I was teaching at the Johns Hopkins SAIS Center. Bologna is a rich, well-organized city, sitting like a wagon wheel of medieval walls, arches, and avenues in the Po Valley. Over three decades ago, the managers of the Italian Communist Party established in Bologna what I call a "maintenance base"—a showcase of stability where little could possibly go wrong. It is a study of positive collective learning: The many wealthy people of Bologna adapted to the shift in organizational context by usually voting Communist locally—the party representing the "conservative," smoothly managed status quo—and non-Communist nationally. International political economy has transformed Italy into a kind of existential domain, where the masks that normally disguise the spectacle of reality are half lifted, making it hard to turn one's head pretending not to see.

While in Bologna I learned much from the German economist Wilhelm Hankel, who demonstrated that competent economics in rich countries can also be compassionate for developing nations (our collaboration there resulted in *Modern Inflation: Its Economics and Its Politics*). Also, I was stimulated by team-teaching with the late international relations theorist Hedley Bull, who persuaded me that the power of the United States is usually underestimated by most commentators on world affairs—particularly its economic power. Economic historian Vera Zamagni, with whom I team-taught "Postwar European Political Economies," illustrated what a gold mine economic history can be for those who want to understand where they are standing. And my friendship with Turkish Cypriot economist Ahmet Aker deepened my appreciation for the development economics perspective of poor countries. These influences may explain why this book has somewhat of a European flavor—a characteristic reinforced by the fact that I have spent more than half of the past decade living in Europe (in Spain, Switzerland, and West Germany as well as in Italy).

While this work was in progress, I was supported continually by Pace University (whose liberal leave policy helped to make such a long-term international endeavor possible), where I presently direct The German American Institute in the Graduate School. I am grateful to Professor Seweryn Bialer of the Research Institute for International Change at Columbia University and to Professor Susan Strange at SAIS Bologna for inviting me back to present initial versions of two of the chapters reworked here. And some may recognize parts of a paper on state strategies of development I delivered at the International Studies Convention in Atlanta and of an article published in *Business Journal* of Southern Connecticut State University in the spring of 1985 on corporate strategies and business cycles. Economics Professor Helmut Less of the University of Heidelberg and Schiller International University was kind enough to make useful comments on the chapter on the world monetary system. Economists Ghassan Karam and Walter Morris and Management Professor Larry Bridwell of Pace University were helpful sounding boards, while Karen Horton and June Sanns of Prentice-Hall smoothly brought the manuscript through editing and production.

My thanks also go to Peter M. Haas of the University of Massachusetts, John R. Freeman of the University of Minnesota, and Julie A. Erfani of Purdue University for their helpful comments and criticisms.

Finally, I am grateful to hundreds of students in the United States and Europe for helping me to pin down some of the ideas worked out in this book.

R.A.I.

INTERNATIONAL POLITICAL ECONOMY

INTRODUCTION

Ill fares the land with the great deal of velocity where wealth accumulates and there ain't any reciprocity.

O. Henry, "Supply and Demand"

O. Henry's short story "Supply and Demand" is the tale of a big white man who goes down to "Gaudymala" and uses force and his wits to turn an Indian tribe into slaves. The white man, Patrick Shane, sets himself up as king, takes the biggest house in the village for himself, and has the natives wash the streams for gold dust that they bring only to him. To keep this colonized political economy going, King Shane, or the "Grand Yacuma," gives the Indians a weekly sermon in the council-house (he is the council) on the law of supply and demand. He praises supply and knocks demand. Teaching them not to desire anything beyond their simplest needs, they bring him all the gold and remain contented on a bit of mutton, cocoa, and fruit. They even make their own clothes.

All goes well until a capitalist laden down with artificial jewelry and mirrors comes into the village on a mule and tempts the local population with Western luxuries in order to get at the gold that is rumored to be in the village. Enlightened by the marketing of the foreign salesman, the natives revolt against their ruler. The king and the capitalist flee for their lives, taking their trinkets with them but leaving behind the gold, which is not worth much if there are no goods to be traded for it.

O. Henry's tale illustrates key elements of the field called "international political economy": Some people have more than others to start with and they use their advantageous circumstances to speed things up, accumulating even more wealth and increasing the gap between themselves and the poor. But wealth does not seem to buy happiness. The hectic velocity of materialism combined with the lack of reciprocity in the community leads to a sense of meanness in the quality of life that can ultimately result in the undoing of those in power. The political ideology of pushing supply and knocking demand works only as long as the community can be isolated from the infinite variety of goods and services available to consumers on the global market. The collective learning of the native population in a community is a result of a number of factors, including: the resources and organizational structure of their political economy, the access of the population to external information and goods from the international environment, and the leadership interactions between the domestic community and the external world. Thus, *international political economy is the study of the inequality or asymmetry between nations and peoples and the collective learning and positioning patterns that preserve or change this asymmetry.*

What is striking in O. Henry's tale is not so much the inequality between the foreign elite and the natives—which is the nature of the world— but rather the specific ways in which this asymmetrical status quo is at first preserved and then eventually undermined. Nor are the natives necessarily better off when the foreigners leave, despite their freedom. Like Adam and Eve, they have been bitten by knowledge of the world and can never return to ignorant bliss. International political economy is a process of continual disenchantment. But by examining the collective learning patterns of other peoples as they cope with the conditions and rules of the global political economy, individuals can perhaps understand their own disenchantment as a fruitful learning process for themselves and their people. For there are strategies and tactics in this ceaseless struggle of the strong to keep what they have in conflict with the weak who seek to change the international system in their favor. Perhaps one can learn (as Antonio Gramsci suggested) to train the individual will to be optimistic despite the pessimism of the intellect when it is applied to the outcome of the collective behavior of human beings.

Ever since the Industrial Revolution there is no way that the field of international political economy can overlook the gaps or asymmetries between industrialized and developing countries as a central preoccupation. While the field as a whole deals with the interplay between international politics and international economics or business, or the process of international wealth acquisition and transfer, the key question concerns the essential dynamics that give rise to asymmetric distributions: Who gets what, when, and how among different players in the global economy? Because such asymmetric distributions are not immutable or frozen, the most fruitful focus is upon the ongoing collective learning and positioning processes as managers of nation-states, multinational corporations, and international organizations attempt to outmaneuver each other. This calls for paying attention particularly to nations or multinational companies in the process of making innovative breakthroughs—the newly industrializing countries (NICs) of East Asia, for example, or Japanese memory-chip companies. These Asian examples are not accidental when one realizes that in 1988 alone the national economic growth rate increased 11 percent or more in China, Singapore, South Korea, and Thailand. Such unusual rates of change in economic welfare and trade lead the student of political economy to ask: Which factors permit the development of such collective capacity for learning or adaptation in the global economy on the part of states or multinational organizations? Which breakthrough models of organization are most useful to emulate? Which structures block such innovative learning or adaptation and why?

The focus upon collective learning and positioning of asymmetrical actors in the global economy will be contrasted with a number of more conventional approaches or schools of thought: liberalism with its stress upon markets; Marxism's preoccupation with economic determinism and class conflict; economic nationalism or mercantilism's concern with state power; the structuralist school's advocacy of reforming the structures of global capitalism for the sake of the developing countries; the dependency theorists' conviction that the development of industrialized countries causes the underdevelopment of the nonindustrialized; and the world systems perspective highlighting the need to look at the globe as a single division of labor inequitably divided into core and periphery zones. As one observes how these perspectives illuminate the explanation of major phenomena in the global economy—such as the world trade and monetary systems—one also senses what has been left out or left in the dark. The observer can only wear one set of glasses at a time, and each set only permits the wearer to see what the lenses were designed to see. The student's suspicion that international political economy is a war of disciplines and ideologies over the same worldly turf is unfortunately accurate.

Yet the turf remains to be explained in some sort of universal and verifiable way—namely, the human use and abuse of the earth and the way people learn to position themselves to improve their collective life chances upon it. The political economist must separate universal (collective) cognitive patterns of learning from specific organizational and cultural modes of behavior. And in this process the picture of the whole earth or global context cannot be lost without ignoring the dominant revolutionary transformation of our times: the evolution of *one global market or economy* that will be managed one way or another by managers with transnational perspectives—whether they be managers of governmental institutions, multinational corporations, or international organizations.

POLITICS VS. ECONOMICS

The "whole earth" approach to political economy—a *world* view—remains the exception and not the rule.[1] Economists note that their discipline was traditionally called "political economy," the queen of the social sciences dating back at least to Adam Smith's *Wealth of Nations,* published in 1776. While more comprehensive than most visions of economists since, Smith's classical laissez-faire view was based on a Western society of small shopkeepers, anticipating the Industrial Revolution but hardly the global consequences of the multinational corporation or the nuclear superpower state. Nevertheless, Smith's classical tenets of economic liberalism—that minimal state interference in the economy and maximum reliance upon the market result in business productivity and social wealth—still predominate in Anglo-Saxon cultures today.

The sacrosanct value of individual freedom in the United States, for example, heavily depends upon the assumption that economics and politics can be kept separated, that the state should be kept out of people's private "business" lives as much as possible. That the Americans, "the people of plenty," have had difficulty maintaining clear boundaries between politics and economics within their own society, not to mention in their attempt to impose their liberal ideology upon other societies, is not surprising. For politics and economics overlap; they are logical spheres that can never be totally separated in the real world.[2]

One of the most influential critiques of the assumption that politics and economics can be separated was offered by the continental theorist Karl Marx in *Das Kapital,* published in 1867. Perhaps a third of the world's population have been taught that Marx's massive critique of laissez-faire capitalism—focusing upon class struggle as the prime mover—is "the economic truth." As American political economist Charles Lindblom noted in *Politics and Markets:* except for the distinction between despotic and libertarian governments, the greatest difference between one government and another is the extent to which market replaces government or government replaces market. Adam Smith understood this. So did Karl Marx.[3] Neither planned (or "control") economic systems, based on Marx, Lenin, and Stalin, nor market economies, based on Smith and Ricardo, can avoid key questions of governmental-market relations where politics and economics overlap. If the United States traditionally attempted to embody the ideology of Smith's market economy, the Soviet Union and the People's Republic of China sought to adapt Marx's economic vision to their own distinctive ideological purposes. The relationship between politics and economics thus became the ideological basis for cold wars between would-be superpowers.

Ideology involves falling in love with ideas that further a certain group's or state's concrete interests. Such action-oriented nests of ideas or worldviews serve to shore up the legitimacy of elites in power. The pragmatic individualism and empiricism of Anglo-Saxon thought in general and of Adam Smith's classical liberal doctrine of maximizing self-interest in particular served as preconditions for the birth of the Industrial Revolution in Britain. Students of international political economy often ask themselves concerning the origins of the Industrial Revolution: Why Europe first? Why England? While conditions other than economic ideology are necessary for a sufficient explanation in answering these questions, contemporary historical developments suggest that individual self-interest and organizational efforts to optimize what already exists, which are the engines of motivation behind industrial capitalism, are ideas without which no adequate explanation is possible. The notion of "industrial society" is an ideological objective of Western modernization rooted in ideas of individual and group self-interest, accumulation, and autonomy—with all the positive and negative implications of these priorities.[4]

The influence of Anglo-Saxon ideas upon the world economy deepened with the impact of John Maynard Keynes' *The General Theory of Employment, Interest and Money (1936)*, emerging as a therapy for the Great Depression that began in 1929. A father of the "mixed economy," Keynes focused upon the role of capital investment in providing for national economic growth and stability. In bad times the government was to intervene in the economy by increasing the money supply and government spending to stimulate the demand for production, which in turn would increase employment. In boom times government was to cool down the economy by intervening to tighten up the money supply, thus reducing demand to assure stable growth. Since government spending is more popular with democratic populations than are government austerity measures, Keynesian policy prescriptions, which have predominated in Western industrialized countries, have had an inflationary, debt-creating bias upon the structure of the world economy.

Anglo-Saxon ideology has "structured" much of the world economy since the British Empire dominated it in the nineteenth century and the American regime (partly a "colonial variation" of the British model) in the twentieth century. *Pax Britannica* was followed up with *pax Americana*. The compatibility of President Ronald Reagan and Prime Minister Margaret Thatcher on policies of political economy was no accident: It was the cultural outcome of a traditional "special relationship."

But the majority of the world's nations and peoples are not of the Anglo-Saxon culture. Yet they find themselves asked to play by its rules of the economic game and to speak its language. For British hegemony—or power domination—was replaced by American hegemony after World War II, epitomized by the system of Western monetary and trade agreements emerging in 1944 in Bretton Woods, New Hampshire. To the victors went the spoils. Only the United States had the military and financial power to enforce its economic will and to attempt to impose its classical liberal vision upon the world economy. As Louis Hartz noted in his classic work *The Liberal Tradition in*

America (1955), the United States skipped the feudal stage of history and the revolutionary reaction against feudalism. Americans, therefore, could never really understand the socialist left's rebellion against feudalism or the reactionary right's opposition to socialism. In short, rugged individualistic liberalism based upon Anglo-Saxon roots was all Americans knew, rendering their liberal ideology rigid and dogmatic. As a result Americans tend to define any form of socialist thought (much less fascist thought) as incomprehensible anathema and to see the world in terms of black and white categories of laissez-faire, liberal capitalism versus state-controlled, socialist communism.[5]

One could not blame the majority of the world's nations and peoples if they were to perceive the hegemony of the Anglo-Saxon culture and its incorporation in American economic liberalism to be self-serving. They look back to the nineteenth century and see colonial expansion by established Western nations, a time when mobility of labor and capital over state boundaries was much more taken for granted, and they discover unfair advantages seized by Western states in building up national wealth and power.[6] By the time that many of the world's nations became politically independent after World War II, most of the earth's prime real estate in terms of resources was already occupied and legal boundaries had been erected between states, which regulated and slowed down the flow of labor and capital among them. The doctrine of classical economic liberalism tracing back to Adam Smith and advocated by the Americans focused upon the more efficient use of the status quo allocation of existing resources, not upon their redistribution or radical restructuring for the sake of the disadvantaged. International law was defined as stable reciprocity in terms of protecting existing ownership and contracts. Classical economic liberalism's assumption that the world economy would become more prosperous and peaceful if each nation used its existing stakes or "comparative advantages" more efficiently did not permit for any redistribution of shares among peoples, more or less guaranteeing a widening gap between the wealth of the rich, established nations and the poor, developing countries.

By the end of 1988 the asymmetry in the distribution of income worldwide left 75 percent of the 5.1 billion people on the planet with 15 percent of the world's income to share in the developing countries. Meanwhile, Western industrialized nations, making up but 17 percent of the global population, lived on 66 percent of the world's income. Eastern Europe and the USSR, with 8 percent of the people of the world, divided up 19 percent of the total worldwide income of $18.4 thousand billion.[7]

THE PRIMACY OF GLOBAL LOGIC

The asymmetry or inequality among nations and peoples has become more pronounced in the postmodern world economy. Technological development and socioeconomic change have accelerated the tempo of modern life. The gap between the haves and have-nots has grown as those with property were positioned to benefit the most from the opportunities evolving from this historical transformation. As the logic of time seemed to speed up, the logic of space contracted with international communications, transportation, and financial flows. Major events such as the dropping of the gold standard, the 1973 quadrupling of oil prices by OPEC (Organization of Oil Exporting Countries), the rise of Japanese competitiveness, the debt crisis in the developing countries, the collapse of communist regimes in Eastern Europe, the nuclear arms race, and the nuclear accident at Chernobyl demonstrated that postmodern technological and socioeconomic events can only be fully understood in global terms.

The postmodern sensibility is one of no-nonsense disenchantment: The Industrial Revolution has come and gone, leaving uncompetitive manufacturers, perforated nation-states, impotent central banks, restructured conglomerates, miseducated youth, the proliferation of waste, and the still undigested split between the real economy (which produces goods) and the capital economy (which speculates on the spreads between borrowing rates and rates of return on investment). Postmodernism is postindustrialism never achieved, narcissism going sour, socialism approaching bankruptcy, and capitalism spreading fast throughout the globe—speeding up the socioeconomic tempo to the disproportionate advantage of the haves. The many parts of the globe that have yet to experience an industrial revolution are often told to forget about it by postmodern opinion-makers for the sake of ecology, if not for their own competitiveness. Quality of life is the postmodern preoccupation: Money is the means, a trophy, an indicator—not the end in itself. Postmodern language is that of "apolitical management"—transforming political and economic issues into technical or administrative black humor. A status job is more important than money, a safe home or maintenance base the prerequisite to entrepreneurial, existential risk-taking and world travel. The world is seen as a whole in postmodern eyes, but the differentiation between parts is more important than the wholeness.

The primacy of global logic does not go to the point of closure of Immanuel Wallerstein, who argues in *The Modern World System* (1974) that neither the sovereign state nor national society constitutes "a social system," that only the world-system constitutes a social system and that one can only speak of social change in social systems. Perhaps the primary characteristic of the postmodern world economy at the end of the twentieth century is its transitional nature between the modern nation-state system and the diffuse world social system that Wallerstein envisions. There *are* social systems that are less than global, but that may not be coterminous with the nation-state—the European Community, for example. Moreover, there are social systems of various sorts within nation-states—the Amish Mennonite community in the United States, for instance. And the anticipation of social change within discrete social systems within nation-states on the one hand and within regional organizations on the other is perhaps the critical task for the student of international political economy who wants to learn how to "manage" global economic change. Thinking globally but acting locally is what the human use of international political economy is all about.

The World Bank compares economic and social statistics of some 185 countries and territories ranging from 16 that have a gross national product (GNP) of $100 billion and more, to 95 with a GNP of under $10 billion. As no human being can keep 185 countries and territories in mind at once (much less numerous multinational corporations and international organizations with "autonomous" resources and influences), countries and territories must be grouped into collective categories to enable one to "see through" the world economy. As an illustration: the range between developing countries like Bhutan, with a GNP per capita of $150 and a life expectancy on average of 46 years, and advanced countries like the United States, with a GNP per capita of $18,430 and an average life expectancy of 75 years, is simply too great for citizens of either of these two nations to understand what it is really like to live in the other country.[8] How can one hold in one's head or picture the extreme economic differences between the richest and poorest countries?

TIERS

In economic terms, the world can be divided into a number of tiers or layers:

I. *OECD Nations:* members of the Organization for Economic Cooperation and Development (OECD), sometimes referred to as "the rich men's club": The United States, Japan, West Germany, France, and other members of the European Common Market (EEC), Switzerland, the Scandinavian countries, Canada, Australia, and New Zealand.

II. *Newly Industrializing Countries (NICs):* Spain, Portugal, Greece, Yugoslavia, Brazil, Mexico, Hong Kong, Korea, Taiwan, and Singapore (as defined by the OECD). These are the most upwardly mobile of the developing countries and are characterized by economic growth rates that are often higher than the more established rich countries of the first tier.

III. *Developing oil-exporting nations:* a nonhomogeneous group like the others ranging from Saudi Arabia (with the largest oil reserves in the world) to Nigeria and Venezuela.

IV. *Non-oil-producing developing nations:* numbering about 100.

V. *"Socialist" nations of the Eastern Bloc:* an increasingly heterogeneous mix as a number of them, such as Hungary and Poland, move rapidly toward market economy models.

Since the 1930s, about two-thirds of world trade has taken place within the first tier.[9] Compared with the early 1970s, the industrialized nations' share of world trade has shrunk a bit: In 1973 more than 70 percent of total world exports and imports was transacted by industrial countries compared to 68 percent for imports and 66 percent of exports in 1985. The Eastern bloc share of world trade fluctuated only slightly in this period, while the developing countries made an above-average contribution to the more than 40 percent rise in world trade since 1973.[10]

Nevertheless, the first tier of the wealthy OECD countries is where the overwhelming majority of the world's trade and investment takes place: More than two-thirds of foreign direct investment (that is, multinational companies setting up manufacturing facilities abroad) occur in this arena. And the radical transformation in the world economy toward the importance of financial instruments and away from manufacturing—toward the internationalization of capital—has been initiated by the OECD group. Notwithstanding the rise in manufactured goods originating in the second tier, the increase in oil revenues by the third tier, and the growth in direct bank lending to the fourth tier, the changes most responsible for the present global disequilibrium have come *within* the first tier in the past two decades.[11] The rich, in short, basically trade with and invest in the rich and are the prime movers in determining the direction of change in the postmodern world economy.

STATICS AND DYNAMICS: MANAGING CHANGE

The world political economy can be seen as a lopsided pair of scissors in which the global system represents a large, heavy blade while the individual country, international organization, or multinational corporation represents a thin "counter"-blade. Effective management of change involves human coordination so that the thin, more dependent blade functions in harmony with the predominant global reality.

The thinner and more dependent the small blade—as in the case of the poorest of the developing countries—the more the managers or elites seek control and stability, or the equilibrium that keeps them in power and makes their domestic economy appear predictable enough to merit foreign aid and investment.[12] The wealthier countries and multinational firms, in contrast, can more easily take equilibrium for granted. They can use this base of stability to take risks for entrepreneurship and technological innovation. Their managers can concern themselves with strategies of dynamic equilibrium in coordinating with the larger global reality.

Many of the wealthy, however, fail to take advantage of this dynamic management potential inherent in their privileged position, preferring instead to minimize their risks for the sake of preserving a status quo which is so friendly to their interests. Hence, there is an understandable conservative bias on the part of both rich and poor alike to seek out stability and to optimize the existing equilibrium they perceive in crisis rather than to take long-term risks in order to adjust effectively to the rapidly changing postmodern global political economy. The aim of this book is not only to explain the widespread human failure to take far-sighted risks for the sake of adjustment and global economic prosperity, but also to illustrate "break-through" models of collective learning and structural positioning that have led to economic and political success in the period since World War II.

In English, "crisis" implies a short-term juncture or turning point. In Italian, it derives from the word "process." And the Chinese symbol for crisis also signifies "hidden opportunity." To manage global change as-tutely requires a collective philosophy of viewing economic crisis as a long-term learning process in which one systematically takes advantage of hidden opportunities.

PLAN OF THE BOOK: ENVIRONMENT, BEHAVIOR, AND STRATEGIES

This book is divided into parts according to a collective theory of learning and structural positioning in the world economy, which is defined as the reciprocal interactions among global *environment*, domestic sources of multinational *behavior*, and the exercise of *collective cognitive strategies*. The asymmetry of the structure of the world economy in favor of the rich developed countries and to the disadvantage of the poor developing countries is taken as a given: It is the stage of international political economy upon which collective learning and positioning behaviors are acted out. In theory, world economic change can be managed in a "win-win" way, which serves to benefit the long-term collective interests of both the developed and developing countries and the multinational organiza-tions based within them. In practice, most cognitive strategies emerge from short-term perspectives conditioned by specific global environmen-tal constraints and habits of domestic behavior.

Part One of the study defines the collective-learning-and-positioning perspective and focuses upon the two key areas of global environment for managing organizational change: namely, the world monetary system and the world trade system. Part Two concentrates upon the domestic sources of multinational behavior—from the emergence of collective life chances, learn-ing, and socioeconomic positioning to state strategies of economic develop-ment to the direct investment behavior and incentives of multinational corporations. Part Three considers North–South and East–West structures, markets, and strategies. Part Four is the conclusion, summarizing principles and prospects for the future—a brief analytical overview that the reader may find useful to examine before reading the substantive chapters that follow. And preceding this final chapter is a summary of practical guidelines using the collective learning approach (pp. 258–261).

ENDNOTES

1. Notable among the recent exceptions who do take a global view of political economy are Wilhelm Hankel, *Weltwirtschaft* (Wien: Econ Verlag, 1977); W. Arthur Lewis, *The Evolution of the International Economic Order* (Princeton, NJ: Princeton University Press, 1977); Immanuel Wallerstein, *The Capitalist World-Economy* (Cambridge: Cambridge University Press, 1979); Independent Commission on International Development Issues (Brandt Commission), *North–South: A Program for Survival: Cooperation for World Recovery* (Cambridge, MA: MIT Press, 1983); Harold K. Jacobson and Susan Sidjanski, eds., *The Emerging International Economic Order* (Beverly Hills, CA: Sage Publications, 1982); Johan Galtung, *The True Worlds: A Transnational Perspective* (New York: Free Press, 1980); and Garret Hardin and J. Raden, eds., *Managing the Commons* (San Francisco: W.H. Freeman & Co., 1977).

2. See, for example, Charles E. Lindblom, *Politics and Markets: The World's Political-Economic Systems* (New York: Basic Books, 1977).

3. Ibid., p. ix.

4. See Richard J. Badham, *Theories of Industrial Society* (New York: St. Martin's Press, 1986).

5. Hartz's continuing relevance is demonstrated in Robert A. Packenham, *Liberal America and the Third World* (Princeton, NJ: Princeton University Press, 1973).

6. See, for example, Mahbub ul Haq, *The Poverty Curtain: Choices for the Third World* (New York: Columbia University Press, 1976).

7. Statistics from *Globus* as cited in *The Rhein-Neckar Zeitung*, Aug. 17, 1989, No. 188, p. 20.

8. Statistics from *The World Bank Atlas 1988* (Washington, D.C.: The World Bank, 1988), pp. 4–21.

9. André Frank, *Crisis in the World Economy* (New York: Holmes and Meier, 1980), p. 4.

10. "Structural Changes in World Trade from 1973 to 1985," Union Bank of Switzerland, *Business Facts and Figures*, September 1986, p. 3.

11. James M. Cypher, "Global Disequilibrium: The Instability of Interdependent Accumulation," *Economic Forum*, XI (Winter 1980–81): 23.

12. See Stephen D. Krasner, *Structural Conflict: The Third World Against Global Liberalism* (Berkeley: University of California Press, 1985).

CHAPTER ONE

COLLECTIVE LEARNING AND POSITIONING

Knowledge is the orderly loss of information.

Kenneth Boulding

The postmodern world economy is characterized by too much information to digest. "To know" has come to mean to lose as much of this information overload as possible in a systematic way in order to have a few basic principles or categories left over. The managers of the World Bank, IBM, or the U.S. Federal Reserve attempt to cut the quick from the dead in this thicket of data: "News" is some breakpoint in an expected trend or an habitual image of how things usually work. Significant news is often decked over by the superfluous. When it became apparent in the early 1980s, for example, that the nine largest U.S. banks had lent three times the amount they held in equity to developing countries, which had become incapable of paying back the interest on the loans, *The New York Times* published this sensitive news in a small article buried in its least-read Saturday edition. "Knowledge" that suggests "the sky is falling" could send the financial markets into a downward spiral and undermine the Western financial system.

This view of knowledge, however, has a conservative bias. Like Adam Smith's classical notion of capitalism, the motive behind it appears to be to understand the existing equilibrium and to optimize what already exists. In the asymmetrical international political economy, such viewpoints appear to be more compatible with the interests of the minority of the rich nations rather than with the majority of the poor: Optimizing what exists implies an inevitability in the status quo. Knowledge is limited to how things are. Classical liberal capitalism is concerned with the growth of things that exist, with maintaining them with greater efficiency, productivity, and effectiveness. What *could* exist, be created, or developed is excluded from the view of knowledge as systematically sifted left-over information or from Adam Smith's stress upon optimization.[1]

What is at stake here is the illusion that the classical economic liberalism of Adam Smith is always on the side of "progress." Initially, the private pursuit of self-interest is a powerful motivator, leading individuals and groups to accumulate great stores of private wealth through individual efficiency, rationalization, and productivity. But eventually a point is reached in a capitalist society where so many people have succeeded in creating plump private nest eggs that their interests shift from efficient productivity to risk-reducing maintenance of that which they have already accumulated. The state of rugged individualism becomes the affluent welfare state as risk-taking for future gains is overwhelmed by risk-reducing insurance against possible losses. Or, as economist Joseph Schumpeter suggested, capitalist societies succeed only to do themselves in: The very wealth and leisure that their economic success makes possible provide the means for counterculture life-styles and motives that undermine the work ethic and efficient rationality that led to the economic success in the first place.[2] From this perspective, the world political economy is characterized by a minority of old, rich capitalist societies conservatively attempting to preserve their past gains (OECD countries); another upcoming minority of "new rich" newly industrializing countries (NICs); a majority of "nonaligned" poor, developing countries without the capital or resources to get their own systems of dynamic economic growth started; and a mixed group of socialist states increasingly tempted by the economic successes of the old-rich and new-rich nations but ideologically or culturally blocked from moving too far in the direction of capitalism. The basic theme of this undertaking is the conflict between efficiently maintaining the old versus effectively creating the new in order to adapt to global economic change.

THE ARGUMENT

The argument of this study is that the only way that individuals, economic organizations, and states can cope effectively with global economic change (and the information overload it implies) is through a process of collective learning and structural positioning, which breaks beyond status quo-conditioned maintenance models to initiate targeted, innovative, strategic risk-taking and adaptation. Collective learning in international political economy is made up of three elements: the global and organizational *environment*, national and cultural *behavior*, and cognitive or managerial *strategy* and policy in the context of existing political and economic structures. In the course of Part One we will break down the global environment into its elements, focusing upon the international money and trade regimes, and spell out the dynamics of the collective learning approach in contrast with other approaches.

This collective learning perspective is grounded on a distinction between the organizational "maintenance base" (where people are preoccupied with efficiency, stability, and risk-reduction) and the external arena of entrepreneurship or global market (in which managers or entrepreneurs focus upon effectiveness, risk-taking, customer and niche creation, and export growth). The focus of the book from the viewpoint of corporations or states is upon the entrepreneurial "breakpoints" or developmental "take-off" points that result from effective collective learning and competitive positioning in the world economy. "Economic miracles" are assumed *not* to be miracles but collective adaptive responses to turbulent change.

In the post–World War II period, for example, West Germany and Japan can be viewed as "tight ships in a storm" in which the efficient reconstruction of the maintenance base of their political economies combined with targeted external policies of entrepreneurship and export-oriented economic growth resulted in their "economic miracles." That West Germany and Japan received an "asymmetrical opportunity" from their hegemonic "godfather," the United States, does not detract from their effective collective use of this opportunity. And to the extent these two states have become mini-hegemonies themselves in the global economy at the end of the twentieth century, the most fruitful focus is upon the recipes for hegemony that led to their prosperous condition rather than upon a passive lamentation of the injustices involved in the creation of such superior economic positions. The weak have more to learn from the strong than the strong from the weak if economic competitiveness and full employment are the social objectives. Mikhail Gorbachev's call for *perestroika* (restructuring) in the USSR is a case in point.

In the United States the maintenance base functions differently from that in West Germany and Japan. The ordered chaos of the largest domestic market in the world provides constant economic opportunities and new consumption choices through continuous restructuring within this entrepreneurial, newly rich society: The turbulence of the outside markets is brought home to create jobs through flexible investment opportunities and corporate reorganizations for both the American and global markets. The government serves as the gatekeeper and as a major customer, insuring the heavy debt structure of the society to keep up the cash flow. Dogmatic classical economic liberalism is the basis for the rugged individualism of the American political economy: It may be all the United States knows (as Louis

Hartz suggests)—but unlike all other societies, given the wealthy endowment of natural resources, it may be all the United States needs.

However, classical laissez-faire liberalism may be a wasteful, experimental approach to economic problem-solving in a technocratic global economy with resource scarcity and payoffs for tightly structured teamwork. The American assumption that each individual will learn mainly from his or her *own* experience (what can be called "learning by burning") implies a multitude of duplicate learning experiences and a host of failures in an uncoordinated trial-by-error approach. The question is whether or not the rest of the world can afford to continue to subsidize the wasteful individualism that is part and parcel of American liberalism. In *The Waste of Nations* (1989), economist Douglas Dowd documents U.S. consumer, military, industrial, agricultural, and human waste and characterizes the style of American hegemony as "an impulsive boyish recklessness."

* * *

"Collective learning" is social learning with a specific organizational context and cultural gestalt. Albert Bandura of Stanford University has defined *social learning theory* as the result of reciprocal interactions among person (cognition), behavior, and the environmental situation.[3] This stimulus-organism-response theory stems from a specific cultural context and derives its free-will aspect from the assumption that individuals can learn from others vicariously or from *modeling* their own behavior after others whom they have observed.[4] In other words, learning by burning—or from one's own experience alone—is not always necessary: It is often cheaper and wiser to learn from others to avoid making the same mistakes oneself. One can learn to manage well by watching other excellent managers in action, and so forth.

Collective learning theory is distinguished from social learning in that it presupposes a collective gestalt or organizational pattern that delimits the schemata for learning or for resistance to change. The "tight" neo-Confucian hierarchical pattern of Japanese society, for example, targets learning differently from the diffuse, loose individualism of the U.S. system.[5] Collective learning presupposes the legitimacy of specific learning models or structures and the exclusion of others. It involves the comparative study of what anthropologist Gregory Bateson termed *deutero-learning*—how people learn learnings. Bateson observed that democratic societies are based on specific learning contexts or meta-learning patterns in which people learn to decide in democratic ways, picking it up as if by osmosis from the structure of the culture in which they live.[6] If such cultures become "split" or "polarized" in terms of the dominant social learning models, a breakdown in political economic effectiveness results.[7] For example, the elites of highly developed societies may come to look down upon the mere wealth-creation or money-making function, free-riding upon its "bourgeois" industrial base while simultaneously undermining this hands-on management level by declassing its status, legitimacy, and motivation.[8] "High policy" learning models and life-styles thus become split off from "low policy" entrepreneurial and maintenance management functions.

When, eventually, the wealth of the upper class aristocracy declines and this group is declassed by socioeconomic change, as in the case of the downward mobility of the Balinese aristocracy or the samurai of Japan, aristocrats from a feudal tradition often resurrect their entrepreneurial capacities, turning to business to recover their sense of purpose, to create new wealth, and to reverse their decline in status.[9] Thus collective learning involves the shifting legitimacy of various learning modes or models over generations or even centuries with direct economic consequences for the life chances of those in the communities involved. Such generational waves of collective learning or adaptation transcend contemporary ideological movements (such as capitalism and socialism) and transcend Western dichotomies such as the politics of productivity versus the politics of redistribution, which have been used to characterize shifts in developed political economies during the last half of the twentieth century.[10]

Nevertheless, the world economic system today is overshadowed by global capitalism, which together with the nation-state system is the structural context for all collective learning that is aimed at economic competitiveness. Before the role of collective learning and socioeconomic positioning can be understood in terms of domestic sources and strategies for development, it is first necessary to understand the hegemonic political and economic structure of the global system and the international organizations for world trade and world monetary management that have resulted from this hegemonic structure.

CREATIVE DESTRUCTION AND WORLD SYSTEM LINKAGES

Joseph Schumpeter characterized capitalism as a process of "creative destruction" in which the new incessantly drives out the old. Technological innovation or development led by the dynamism of the entrepreneur is the engine driving this vision of capitalism. "Development" is defined as spontaneous economic change within a nation not forced upon it from without. Development goes beyond mere growth (or the optimization and expansion of what already exists): It implies that something new and distinctive is being produced by spontaneous design or planning that makes a nation (or organization) less dependent upon others. Producers are the agents that usually initiate development, whether they be private entrepreneurs in capitalist systems or apparatchik managers in socialist systems.[11] The dynamic for development emerges from some domestic or national base or other, not from the international system as a whole. Power is homemade.* However, for the overwhelming majority of nations of the world, the economic effectiveness of that power abroad depends upon how national development is managed to fit the markets of the capitalist world economy.

In 1979 Johan Galtung predicted that a new, profoundly capitalist world economy would emerge by the 1990s with the control center in the Orient, not in the West. Even more bluntly, Galtung noted: "Capitalism is not down and out. There is no crisis in capitalism. There is a profound crisis in the Western [read United States and Western Europe] position inside capitalism."[12] The rising economic power of Japan, Taiwan, South Korea, and Hong Kong makes Galtung's prediction ring true, not to mention the competitive difficulties of the United States and Western European economies. The British prepared the way for world capitalism with their Industrial Revolution and *pax Britannica.* The United States consolidated the heritage of Anglo-Saxon economic thought, institutionalizing global capitalism at the peak of American hegemony with the Bretton Woods system and *pax Americana.* That some scholars have been surprised that the institutional framework of Bretton Woods (in modified form) has survived as American power has passed its peak may be because they have focused too much upon "institutional inertia" from an American perspective rather than looking at the universal dynamism of capitalism from a global perspective.[13]

The increasing tempo of global social and economic change in the late twentieth century clarifies why international managers and students of international political economy seek some simplifying category or overarching theory to keep the turbulent process of creative destruction in perspective. Human beings are overwhelmed by future shock and a sense of loss—from the microelectronic revolution to the decay of Western status-order systems that gave hierarchical meaning to the economic world. Perhaps preoccupied with the sense of loss in global status of their own nation since its historical peak following World War II, American students of international political economy often focused upon what they called "hegemonic stability theory" in the 1980s to explain what was happening to them.

HEGEMONIC STABILITY AND IDEOLOGICAL BLINDERS

Hegemonic stability theory emerged from an interpretation of the Great Depression beginning in 1929, which attributed its width and depth to the absence of a leading country willing and able to bear a disproportionate share of the costs to discharge the responsibilities of a stabilizer. Or, to put the

---

*And goods, accordingly, should be "homespun" with capital remaining at home to benefit the nation and the nation's working class—argued John Maynard Keynes during the Great Depression. Cf. J.M. Keynes, "National Self-Sufficiency," *Yale Review* 22: 755–69.

theory positively, a stable world economic system requires the existence of a single great power state or *hegemon* willing and able to furnish an outlet for distress goods, maintain the flow of capital to would-be borrowers, serve as lender of last resort in financial crises, maintain a structure of exchange rates, and coordinate macroeconomic policies. The father of this theory, economist Charles P. Kindleberger, called the key stabilizer nation a "leader," not a "hegemon." He noted that "Political science has now transmuted the concept of leadership into 'hegemony,' a word that makes me uncomfortable because of its overtones of force, threat, pressure."[14] The clearest modern examples of such leaders or hegemons are Great Britain in the nineteenth century (to a limited extent) and the United States after World War II (the historical example *par excellence*).[15]

The hegemon provides stability by disproportionately subsidizing collective or public goods in the world political economy such as an open market economy based upon an open liberal trading regime, or a stable international currency or (more controversially) an international security system. A *public or collective good* is one that is not reduced for use by other potential consumers even after consumption by an individual, household, company, or state (a road, sidewalk, or ocean, for example). In addition to paying more than its share of the costs, the hegemon has to try to manage the "free-rider problem," namely, the dilemma of cheaters who free-ride upon collective or public goods without paying their "fair share." Thus, with America's decline in hegemony in the late twentieth century, it is little wonder that U.S. managers push their allies for "burden sharing" or picking up more of the economic and security costs of maintaining the global political economic system. From the perspective of the collective learning theory, however, the free-rider strategy is a rational, collective mode of behavior that certain individuals, companies, states, and international organizations utilize in historical situations where they have few other options: The poor, for example, often have little choice about being free riders.

What has surprised hegemonic stability theorists is that despite the apparent decline in American hegemony since the 1944 Bretton Woods agreement establishing the International Monetary Fund (IMF) for monetary cooperation and (ultimately) the General Agreement on Tariffs and Trade (GATT) for trade cooperation, the world economy has continued to remain basically stable and the institutions emerging from Bretton Woods have continued to perform their international stabilizing functions. This nest of American-driven institutional arrangements has been referred to as "regimes"—or "principles, norms, and decision-making procedures around which actor expectations converge."[16] And the continuation or effective residue of these regimes despite the relative decline in power of the U.S. hegemon provided the puzzle that seemed most to preoccupy American students of international political economy in the 1980s. That such a preoccupation may be ethnocentric, premature, or understate the actual American economic and military power position remains an often-neglected point of view.[17]

From the standpoint of theory, the hegemonic stability focus is but an unproven historical examination of one exceptional case before the story is over. No other nation will ever be likely to possess the nuclear monopoly enjoyed by the United States after World War II. Nor is it easy to imagine that another nation would have the abundance of resources and large domestic market of the Americans. Even the language of *hegemony* and *regime* has the flavor of a premature attempt to put historical distance between the analyst and the contemporary situation—a somewhat schizophrenic impulse to squeeze the unique quality out of the American case so as to explain continuity or decline in the world political economy. But the conservative bias of this perspective is unmistakable: Global information is being eliminated in an orderly manner to sort out the big fish (the U.S. hegemon) from the little ones (the other some 184 countries and territories for which the annual *World Bank Atlas* lists statistics) even if the big fish should turn out to be as rare as Moby Dick.

The word *hegemony* originated with the founder of the Italian Communist Party, Antonio Gramsci. Gramsci defined hegemony as a form of consciousness in which other social classes or the population as a whole accept an order in which one social class is dominant.[18] The "embedded" liberal economic order, embodied in the institutions, rules and habits of the Bretton Woods system dominated by the United States, is the case in point. The thrust for openness of classical liberalism has become "embedded" in the Bretton Woods hegemony of institutions because of the ongoing compromises this liberalism has made with domestic state demands for social stability and of full employment.

Hegemony usually designates a conservative bundle of habits or a world-view in the sense of philosopher Silvan Tompkins's view of right-wing ideology: The belief that human beings realize themselves only through struggle toward, participation in, and conformity to a norm, a measure, an ideal essence basically independent of man. Left-wing ideology, in contrast, considers a human being as "an end in himself, an active, creative, thinking, desiring, loving force in nature."[19] In sum, those who believe in sources of value outside of human beings—whether they be members of the "club" of U.S. elite universities, the French Communist Party, or the Catholic Church qualify as "conservatives."

Thus, hegemony has conservative implications when identified as the legitimate ideology of elite classes in the international system. The classic example is the balance-of-power ideology of the dominant European nations—the *ancien régime*—preceding the French Revolution. This balance-of-power hegemony broke down when the ideological elite of the *ancien régime* could no longer communicate with the counterhegemony ideology of Napoleon.[20] Napoleon's drafting of all male citizens and all-or-nothing objectives in war were incomprehensible ideas for the established balance-of-power elites who relied upon mercenary soldiers and limited rules of warfare. The rigidity of both these ideologies—anchoring value in standards outside human individuals in abstract ideals or rules—gave them a brittle, conservative quality, precipitating the breakdown of the equilibrium of the international system. Similarly, the cold war ideologies of neo-conservative *pax Americana* elites and the counterhegemony of the neo-Marxist socialist bloc threatened the stability of the 20th century international system, until Gorbachev's reforms seemed to provide a way to compromise. On the global economic level, this ideological conflict was embodied in the defense of the Bretton Woods regime by the developed countries against counterhegemony demands of developing nations for a New International Economic Order.

Both the ideological extremes of Western capitalism and Marxism-Leninism constitute different forms of conservatism, or varieties of economic determinism: The former argues that material self-interest is the engine of economic growth and progress, the latter that class structures and conflicts determine social life. Generally these competing cold war ideologies have served as legitimizing dogmas for established elites, as shields against change in the status quo, rather than as principles of adaptation or innovation. They have tended to function as top-down deterministic rules, outside of human individuals, used to mobilize more efficiency in the existing social equilibrium of the state, not as bottom-up instigators of grass-roots individualism and risk-loving dissent.

Gorbachev's political genius, from a collective learning perspective, was to see through the stalemate of this conventional hegemony—counterhegemony cold war logic and to *position* himself ideologically on the side of change and of the future (his "New Thinking"), leaving the defense of the old to his opponents at home and abroad. Ideologies are born radical, mature in pragmatism, and turn self-righteously inflexible in old age as those who heavily invested in them weigh the psychic and material costs of change. Gorbachev knew when to cut his losses and how to symbolize the collective learning his people would have to undertake to restructure their economy to compete in the 21st century. His policies of reform and reluctance to use force, in turn, stimulated the spontaneous collective learning of the peoples of Eastern Europe, permitting democratic movements from Poland, Hungary, Czechoslovakia, East Germany, Rumania, and Bulgaria to position themselves strategically in 1989 for radical political and economic change.

ECONOMIC NATIONALISM, LIBERALISM, AND MARXISM

The predominant ideologies that often function as blinders in the world economy of the late twentieth century are economic nationalism (or neomercantilism), liberalism, and Marxism. Each of these three ideologies or systematic worldviews represents a total belief system concerning human nature and society, which is not easily changed in the minds of true believers by logic or contrary evidence. As political scientist Robert Gilpin has demonstrated in *The Political Economy of International Relations*, while each of these ideologies or paradigms sheds some light or insight into the workings of the world economy, all of them are inherently incapable of being disproven empirically (such as the "truth" of the statement: "Chocolate ice cream *is* best because I *like* it best."). The collective learning approach used here attempts to transcend these ideological camps to focus upon which patterns or gestalts of human cultural organization have worked best to foster a harmony of dynamic economic growth on the one hand, and social equity on the other. Hypothetically, the identification of such effective collective learning patterns would benefit the objectives of any of these predominant belief systems—whether to help better target the protectionism of developing or developed countries in vital economic sectors, or to identify how to open markets domestically with least cost to the disadvantaged, or to restructure a socialist state using market incentives for economic and technological competitiveness without losing social consensus or governmental legitimacy. While the collective learning approach is biased toward successes and breakthroughs, it is indifferent as to whether these effective collective behaviors are uncovered in nation-states, multinational corporations, or international organizations.

Each of these three predominant ideologies is a reified or frozen set of beliefs used as a basis for political action in the world economy. Each, in other words, is like a spotlight in a dark amphitheater illuminating a limited part of the reality while inadvertently leaving other parts blacked out in the process.

Economic nationalism—otherwise known as mercantilism, statism, and protectionism—spotlights the economic and power interests of a single nation-state in competition with all others, viewing the world economy as a zero-sum game in which that not gained by the state will necessarily be lost to other competitive states. The modern nation-state system emerged from the breakdown of the unity of medieval Christendom and was first officially recognized as the European multistate system with the Peace of Westphalia in 1648 and the Treaty of Utrecht in 1713. The European conception of the sovereign state was one with a concentration of political power within it, which possessed a monopoly of the use of force within its borders.

Following the Industrial Revolution, this consolidation of political power normally corresponded with growing economic power. Economic nationalists are preoccupied with national security and the primacy of military power of the state in the international system, viewing political and economic power as a way to secure national survival. For nationalists or mercantilists, a favorable balance of trade is a prerequisite to national security, and a hard currency is a political weapon in the ceaseless struggle for status and advantage among states. Self-sufficiency, not economic interdependence, is their motto. If every economic system must rest on a secure political base, then in the terms of the collective learning approach used here, economic nationalists are preoccupied with the viability and security of this "maintenance base" defined in geographical and cultural terms. This search by the extreme realist for national unity is epitomized in a negative way by Machiavelli's observation that Italy is not a state but a mere geographical expression.

The lamp that shines from the ideology of *liberalism* looks for the maximization of individual interest and freedom, as often as not expressed in the form of economic profit. Rather than focusing upon the state, the liberal stresses the market. Critical of the zero-sum, conflictual stance of the economic nationalist, which can ultimately culminate in war, the liberal stresses the mutual gain that can come from international cooperation and interdependence: the creation of more economic pie for all through incentives for economic growth, rather than becoming bogged down in the distributional struggle for the pie that already exists (as besets the economic nationalists). The liberal position is critical of the amassing of both military and other forms of power, which can undermine economic efficiency. But the liberal preoccupation with economic success leads to a lopsided focus upon rational, economic individuals in free markets with full information to make their maximizing decisions. Social contexts, "irrational" cultural traditions, collective habits, hierarchical markets, and the normal absence of full information all become "exogenous" variables for liberal economists, variables too easily left out of their equations for not being easily quantifiable or explainable in terms of strict, individualistic, economic rationality. The state is understated, the market overmarketed.

Marxism spotlights the contradictions in the capitalist system that emerge from individuals rationally maximizing their personal interests without regard for the overall consequences for social equity and community well-being. Individual interest maximization leads to overproduction and subsequent economic contraction and unemployment, according to the Marxist thesis. Workers become impoverished and the growing gap between the bourgeois classes and proletariat or working classes will ultimately trigger a revolution and the overthrow of capitalism by a classless, socialist society of equity and solidarity. When he noted that workers within capitalist societies did not become poorer, Lenin argued in 1917 that the fault was in failing to view capitalism as a global phenomenon in which imperialism was the ultimate stage of capitalism: Financial capital in the core developed countries dominated industrial capital, and the law of uneven development assured that the capitalist, colonizing states reap the benefits of economic development, exploiting cheap labor and resources from the developing countries at the periphery of market interactions.

Modern World System theory (represented by Paul Baran, André Gunder Frank, and Emmanual Wallerstein—see Chapter 7) extends the Leninist interpretation of Marxism. It assumes that the modern world can only be understood as a global system with a single division of labor and multiple cultural systems forming an international hierarchy in the ceaseless struggle of states and classes: the advanced, dominant *core;* the newly industrializing *semi-periphery;* and the dependent, underdeveloped *periphery* (made up of most of the world's people). Modern World System theorists view state and market as epiphenomena of deeper social and economic forces that drive the world economy in a way that integrates the core and periphery so that the "metropolitan" core systematically *underdevelops* the dependent periphery areas both politically and economically.

The (Marxist) World System view, however, is often blind to political and strategic factors that can be as important in interstate relations as economic determinants. (On what basis could it have forecast the democratic uprisings in Eastern Europe in 1989, for example?) Modern World Systems theory is so preoccupied with the market processes of global capitalism—commercial growth, worldwide recession and the spread of trade and finance—that one could go as far as to suggest that without world capitalism (and its Anglo-Saxon liberal ideology) socialism as an ideology would not exist.

Each of these three ideologies or spotlights of consciousness—the state (economic nationalism), the market (liberalism), and the domestic and international economic development struggle between the haves and the have-nots (Marxism)—constitutes a different worldview of the same anarchical world. Historically, the anarchy of the international system has always been sufficient to undermine any particular oligarchy or imperial power group that has sought to impose its will upon the system.

The world has remained anarchical and oligarchical: anarchical given the absence of a monopoly of legitimate violence; oligarchical—or hierarchic—since without civil society, right depends mainly upon might.[21] The dominant oligarchy (or hegemon) is cast in a conservative and defensive role of trying to shore up its power and influence and to maintain the system's equilibrium against inevitable disintegration or entropy. Those outside the oligarchy attempt to change the asymmetrical system in their favor and to keep what autonomy they can. Or as Thucydides observed in ancient Greece: The powerful exact what they can, and the weak grant what they must.

The asymmetry between powerful oligarchies and weak, dependent peoples has become more pronounced in the era since World War II: Most of the advantages of the increasing tempo of technological and financial development have accrued to those best positioned to take advantage of these innovations. *Positioning* is the name of the game in political economy: Rich countries (or people) seek to hold their position while the poor attempt to position themselves more favorably (by joining the European Common Market, for example). *The initial starting position* carries profound importance in an anarchical world where physical and economic security are scarce commodities, not to mention the freedom of individual choice. Ever since the dropping of the first atomic bomb and the Bretton Woods settlement, the primary logics of political economy have been rendered increasingly global: the spatial logic of world power and world market shares on the one hand, and the temporal logic of the speeding up of global technological and socioeconomic change on the other.

THE LOGIC OF INDEFINITE INSECURITY

The struggle for world power or hegemony is focused upon the national security positions of the superpowers and upon their joint efforts to preserve their "minimum winning coalition" or "condominium" from dilution into multipolarity (a world of many or "multi"-power poles or nuclear players). This preoccupation with security at the superpower level of the United States and the Soviet Union has had the effect of creating a global milieu of insecurity—military, technological, economic, and psychological insecurity. Because the demands of these kinds of security appear to be insatiable in the postmodern era, a permanent perception of insecurity has been embedded in the world's population, heightened by the velocity of change and the world communication system (dramatizing disasters daily on television).

The primacy of insecurity—or of the infinite striving for security—inevitably makes the global perspective of political economy conservative. There are so many countries and factors involved, the first human task appears to be to order them into a system that is capable of being stabilized to prevent system breakdown in the form of world war. The nuclear powers and wealthy, developed countries with the most to lose in the event of system breakdown are structurally positioned to be on the side of maintaining the status quo. Organizations or individuals representing these countries can hardly escape the dominant conservative logic of this maintenance function.

Thus, in 1987 when the war between Iran and Iraq threatened to block vital oil shipments from the Persian Gulf, the United States and France sent warships into the Gulf to maintain the international shipping lanes (although it could be argued that this policy provoked instability more than assuring stability). As nuclear powers, the United States and France have also been at constant odds with New Zealand, which has led Pacific nations in advocating a nonnuclear zone, not permitting American warships that might be carrying nuclear weapons into its ports. As a result, the United States had New Zealand expelled from the ANZUS treaty. France went further and sponsored state terrorism in which secret French agents bombed the Greenpeace anti-nuclear boat, *Rainbow Warrior*, in a New Zealand port.

The heavy financial burden of the arms race between the superpowers for the sake of national security skews the entire world economy in its direction. The lack of trust and communication given the ideological polarity between the United States and the Soviet Union limits the possible disarmament and détente possible between them, even while the economic cost drives them to the bargaining table. While Gorbachev's peace initiatives have undermined cold war logic, they have not undone superpower structure. Indeed, their condominium status and superpower duopoly on the strategic chessboard depends upon the Soviet Union and the United States *not* fully succeeding at eliminating the nuclear weapons edge that keeps them "super."

National security issues are also useful to solidify the domestic power positions of superpower elites, who are wary of moving too far toward détente since this would leave a power vacuum on their right in a structurally conservative situation. These elites have an inherent interest in broadcasting the insecurity of the nation to help make themselves appear indispensable. The balance of terror has made security* difficult to achieve *technologically* and hence more desirable.

Elites of both developed and developing nations realize that the primacy of security is prerequisite to the continuation of the nation-state system and their own power position in it. But what management model can be used to analyze both the stability-maximizing and the high-risk expansion elements of such power positions?

THE MAINTENANCE MODEL OF INTERNATIONAL MANAGEMENT

Whether one steps into the shoes of military elites of the superpowers, management elites of multinational corporations, or of the *dependencista* elites of the developing countries, the existence of one world system is the primary reality (and insecurity the primary consequence of this reality—insecurity stemming from a permanent arms race and ceaseless technological and economic competitiveness). Global communications, financial flows, and nuclear accidents all serve to reinforce the perception of one world system. John Maynard Keynes may have been proven to have come up short domestically, where demand systems are as perforated as a Swiss cheese, only to have his theories substantiated globally, where supply and demand cycles are trapped in one world system.

Given the primacy of one world system, the key question for managing in international political economy is: Which organizational and individual

---

*Security is used here in Kenneth Boulding's sense of aiming for "unconditional viability"—a party that cannot be absorbed or destroyed as an independent source of decisions. That this ideal of absolute independence, freedom, or "sovereignty" is no longer achievable in the nuclear age does not mean it will not be sought. See Kenneth Boulding, *Conflict and Defense: A General Theory* (New York: Harper & Row, 1963), p. 58; also Robert Tucker, *The Inequality of Nations* (New York: Basic Books, 1977).

strategies serve best to cope with the creative destruction of global competition and the inevitable insecurity it engenders? Strategies, in turn, flow from the model of economic dynamism used by the strategist: What makes pieces of the world economy move, and how can cycles or trends be anticipated to enable the individual or organization to be positioned the right way at the right time?

* * *

Global economic dynamism begins with the technological innovation, financial power, and strategic position of the rich countries among whom nearly two-thirds of the world's trade and direct investment takes place. Each of these countries, as well as the multinational companies based in them, can be viewed as a system (actually, a subsystem of the larger world system), which needs to cope with the waves of creative destruction, of *syntropy* (the coming together of energies into a new order), and of *entropy* (the disintegration and diffusion of energies). In *Cybernetics*, mathematician Norbert Wiener demonstrated that all systems tend toward entropy: The role of the system manager is to sort out critical information or feedback from the environment to help the system adapt to change for the sake of the system's equilibrium—and ultimately its survival. In the high-speed postmodern world, managers coping with disintegrating systems have no choice but to be preoccupied with stabilizing their own subsystems, whether these be states or multinational firms or international organizations.

Technological innovation—the engine of creative destruction—is made possible by the creation of money or credit in political economies still at the traditional premoney barter stage of trading in agricultural and manufactured goods. Historically, financial innovation (via the creation of new forms of money and credit) precedes technological innovation (or productivity increases through industrial revolutions). Whereas in the traditional barter societies the same individuals perform the functions of producing, saving, and investing, the creation of money or credit financing through debt permits the splitting off of the producers and savers on the one hand, from the investors on the other. Individuals who have not earned, saved, or inherited capital can borrow it on credit to make dynamic, risky, innovative investments. Inflation is the inevitable result (more money chasing fewer goods), which serves as the lubricator for innovative investment and as the liberator of resources held by conservative property-owning individuals through the credit mechanism.[22] Money and credit creation thus lead to technological innovation, which leads to industrial revolution and a diffusion of power of the propertied classes. Societies are democratized through inflationary financing. In this environment, managers of organizations or states have to worry about reducing the costs of maintenance of their organization on the one hand, and about financing entrepreneurial innovation to keep up with the technological state of the art of the competition in the global process of creative destruction on the other.

The maintenance model of management is based upon the distinction between a boundaried *maintenance base* oriented toward internal stability and security "inside" the organization or collective system versus "outside" *entrepreneurship* oriented toward risky adaptation to global market innovation. Typically, the chief maintenance concern is for increasing *efficiency* or security and reducing risk within the home base or headquarters rather than with entrepreneurial *effectiveness* and risk-taking to adjust to changing outside markets and conditions.[23] (See Figure 1–1).

The maintenance model has great explanatory power at different levels of analysis and at various stages of development in international political economy. At the individual level of analysis, for example, the maintenance base in the traditional culture of France is the *foyer,* the family circle or quasi-sacred basis of French civilization. The duty of the head of the French household is to use his wits to take entrepreneurial risks outside the family in order to bring home the goods, much like the hunter bringing back his catch to his cave. In the process the Frenchman is traditionally supposed to keep clear of emotional extremes or entangling alliances that could undermine his will or render him vulnerable.[24]

At the state level, mercantilism—the philosophy of centrally steered economic nationalism—traditionally permits the French President to view France (or, even more accurately, Paris) as the maintenance base from which to take entrepreneurial risks elsewhere for the sake of maximizing French national interests. For example, the French government subsidizes the French company launching the Arian rocket abroad so as to help maximize French market share in the highly competitive commercial satellite launching business.

Strategic Behavior

An examination of individual, corporate, and state economic behavior in the 1970s and 1980s in terms of the maintenance model revealed at least four

FIGURE 1–1   The Maintenance Base

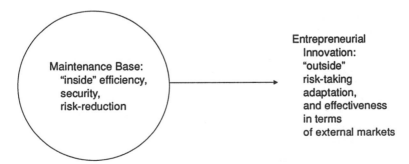

predominant types of strategic behavior* (expressed here as Weberian ideal types—or characteristic typifications of particular categories of behavior):[25]

1. *Defeatist:* takes as few risks as possible, cutting costs rather than risking assets; past-oriented, passive, defensive, plagued by a fear of loss and a neurotic conservative impulse; thrifty in consumption with a security-oriented, portfolio mix.

2. *Free-rider:* takes high risks at no cost or low cost, specializing in living at someone else's expense; present-oriented with active-passive motivation or *maximin*—*max*imizing individual gains and *min*imizing personal costs; high individual consumption when others pay, low otherwise; portfolio mix centered on cheap money or upon debt at low interest rates.

3. *Maintenance:* takes limited risks at moderate cost to keep up with the business cycle and inflation; present-oriented, short-term realism guided by passive-active motivation, seeking to co-opt change in order to assure stability; consumes high quality now before costs go higher; portfolio mix stresses stable returns, liquidity, diversity, and flexibility.

4. *Entrepreneurial:* takes high risks even at high costs; aims to come out ahead of inflation and present stage of business cycle; aggressive motivation stemming from tension between perception of handicap and potential advantage; seeks to thrust all energy and resources into direction of highest probable payoff; future-oriented; all-or-nothing consumption: "prince or pauper"; portfolio mix focused upon highest return through astute gambles on the business cycle.

These four types or categories of strategic behavior were derived by analyzing a large number of randomly selected cases of individual, corporate, and state behavior in reaction to the inflationary shocks to the world economy in the 1970s and 1980s (resulting, in no small part, from the OPEC oil price increases of 1973 and 1979). Initially, the behavior of individuals in coping with inflation during this period was observed and put into one of the four categories that best describe this behavior. Then the behavior of corporations and states during the same period was examined in black-box fashion, without concern for their inner structures, to determine what kinds of similarities the input-output behavior of these units had with the four categories of individual behavior.[26] Although these four categories are not exhaustive and most actual cases of behavior are a mix of more than one of these four types, in the majority of cases one type of strategy did seem to stand out or to predominate.

_____

*In terms of collective learning, a *strategy* is a personal or organizational cognitive blueprint or intentional plan for the future, whereas *strategic behavior* refers to patterns of observed individual or collective behavior *after* it has occurred, which is then categorized to whatever extent it is possible by the particular strategy or strategic mix it implies. Changes in the international *environment* presumably lead to adaptations of strategic behavior as collective learning takes place through the adoption of different strategies.

In many cases people or organizations did not *choose* a specific type of strategy as much as they *fell into it* as a result of the socioeconomic position and information sources in the global political economy at that historical moment. In other words, the maintenance model (and the four strategies deriving from it) is not a "rational actor model" (presupposing rational choices by rational individuals before the fact), but more of a socio-anthropolitical model of the psychology of economic behavior (dealing with the data after the fact—the result of social, economic, and emotional factors as much as it was the result of rational decisions).

Or, put concretely, the reason why rich individuals, corporations, and states overwhelmingly illustrated the *maintenance* strategy more than the other types was probably less due to rational choice (since maintenance was often not the best strategy) and more to the future-shock effect of being overwhelmed with more change than could be digested.[27]

Strategies, in short, are symptoms of structural positions in the world economy as much as they are constellations of choice. On the level of the individual, this is what Kierkegaard meant when he said, "I feel like the piece in the chess game that is not allowed to be moved." Decision-makers in Ethiopia and Bangladesh and other developing countries with little structural flexibility can identify with Kierkegaard's remark. Given that almost all human institutions and organizations are being "outpositioned" by the pace of technological and socioeconomic change in the late twentieth century, there are certain times when almost anyone can sense that the strategy they have chosen is the inevitable outgrowth of the structural position in which they find themselves as much as it is due to any freedom of will.

This does not mean that global structures *always* penetrate to individual cognition or that theorists *always* reflect the structural interests of countries from which they emerge. Free will exists, but not in a cultural or structural vacuum. The individual's *strategy* today—that is, his or her future-oriented blueprint or intentional plan—must be distinguished from individual or group *strategic behavior* tomorrow—the actual behavior performed in cultural, structural, and historical context. Effective collective learning can be measured by the extent to which groups of individuals overcome traditional patterns of behavior or habits that have become maladaptive and replace them with effective strategies of adaptation that result in more opportunities for the exercise of free will or autonomy by the company or state in the world economy.

The major American automobile companies, for example, found themselves outpositioned by foreign competition in the late 1970s—they were thrust into the defeatist category by the latest wave of creative destruction in the global economy. Rather than adopting entrepreneurial strategies to escape from their position of structural stalemate and noncompetitiveness, these U.S. companies fell back on defensive maintenance strategies, which blocked their potential adaptiveness. Chrysler even found itself in a free-rider position, accepting subsidies from the U.S. government, which also introduced "voluntary export restraints" (or tariffs by another name) to keep out the Japanese competition until the American companies had time to adapt. The automakers responded with more sophisticated maintenance strategies, forming joint ventures with Japanese car companies so as to be competitively positioned when the export restraints were removed: "If you can't beat them, join them."

The wave of mergers and joint ventures among multinational companies in the 1980s represented maintenance strategies of coping with the creative destruction of global competition. Smaller car companies (American Motors) were taken over by bigger ones.

A similar shakedown occurred in the airline industry with three major airline manufacturers emerging from the competitive trauma: Boeing, McDonnell Douglas, and Airbus. Airbus Industrie illustrates an astute blend between maintenance and entrepreneurial strategies. Founded in 1970 as a consortium of Western Europe's leading aircraft manufacturers (the maintenance base, supported by billions of dollars of state subsidies), the Airbus 320 became the fastest selling plane in aviation history during the 1980s given its technological edge with a fully computerized flight-control system (the entrepreneurial innovation side of the strategic mix).

Nor had the American competitors much grounds for complaint: U.S. government military contracts in the era of American hegemony after World War II enabled Boeing, Lockheed, and McDonnell and Douglas (which had not yet merged) to account for about 90 percent of all airline sales outside the Communist bloc by the late 1960s. Building on the mixed experience of the French–British *Concorde*, Airbus became the European symbol of a joint industrial policy of technological competitiveness to match the *Pentagon Inc.* industrial policy of the United States.[28] Such differences in industrial policy can only be explained by differentiating between the structures that define these political economies.

STRUCTURES AND DEPENDENCE

The structural position (and relative independence or dependence) of states and multinational organizations in the world political economy is made up of at least five primary structures:[29]

1. *The security structure:* the maintenance of order both within the organization or state and outside—within the international system at large.

2. *The money and credit structure:* the stability and relative value of the currency and the sources and flexibility of short- and long-term finance.

3. *The knowledge structure:* literacy rates, technological competitiveness, training systems, and the distribution of critical economic information and skills throughout the population.

4. *The production structure:* the way resources are organized and the knowledge structure is utilized to determine what is produced.

5. *The value structure:* a cluster of psycho-cultural beliefs and ideological preferences that transcend and color "the rational"—what the people predominantly *choose* to learn. In many cases traditional value structures block states from becoming what Karl Deutsch has called "adaptive-learning states" (post-1868 Japan, for example), which are able to change political and economic structures to cope with some major problem in the environment.[30]

Thus, political economy can be viewed as the collective capacity of a state or multinational organization to structure payoffs for effective learning or adaptation in the global system—or the study of learning by paying if such adaptation is blocked.[31]

The particular combination of these five primary structures determines the potential power of one state or multinational organization compared to others in the world economy. Power is the social capacity to satisfy human needs or wants relative to competitors: It is always increasing or diminishing.* Powerful states, for example, can perhaps best be described in terms of *surpluses in their structural assets.* What sociologist Max Weber might have termed the "ideal type" of Great Power state would be characterized by a surplus of security (nuclear deterrents, armed forces, military preparedness); a surplus of money and credit (a strong international reserve position, a creditor nation); a surplus of production (high gross national product growth, balance of trade surplus, a diverse, competitive industrial capacity); a surplus of knowledge (a deep and wide infrastructure of research and development, high productivity in innovative technologies, a national literacy rate higher than required for most job functions), and a surplus of value consensus (a widespread anti-inflation, pro-savings consensus; absence of ideological polarization; a community spirit that comes together to permit adaptation to new global challenges).

Thus, the world political economy can be envisioned as a hierarchy of states spread between structural surpluses and structural deficits, between relative independence and dependence.

The aim of the nation-state in the world economy is to use its potential power and influence to achieve self-sufficiency and independence with enough surpluses to serve as a buffer against global change. But absolute self-sufficiency or independence is no longer possible to achieve. As political scientist Richard Rosecrance put it: "To be fully independent, an aggressor would now need the oil of the Persian Gulf, the iron ore, bauxite, and uranium of Australia, the chromium of Zimbabwe and South Africa, and the granaries of Canada, Australia and the American West."[32]

---

*This definition stresses the ability of collective consensus to create solutions to adapt to change rather than power as mere materialistic distribution or authoritative allocation of values in the status quo. See R. Hummel and R. Isaak, *Politics for Human Beings,* 2nd ed. (Belmont, Calif.: Wadsworth, 1980), p. 34.

OLIGOPOLIES AND NEOMERCANTILISM

While American hegemony prevailed in the world system (roughly until about 1960), smaller states could pursue neomercantilist policies of export-oriented growth in order to increase their structural surpluses while free-riding upon the security structure and economic stability (maintenance base) provided by the *pax Americana*.[33] Indeed, following defeat of the Axis in World War II, the United States initially prohibited Germany and Japan from rearming, even writing into the Japanese Constitution that not more than 1 percent of that country's gross national product could be spent on defense. While the Americans reaped many commercial and political benefits from the "public good" of international stability that they provided, when American hegemony began to collapse the Americans found themselves ill-prepared for a more competitive, interdependent environment. Moreover, other leading Western industrial countries (such as West Germany, Switzerland, and Japan) were ill-disposed toward picking up the costs of the "public good" of international stability. The Japanese, for example, wanted nothing to do with nuclear weapons on their soil. And the West Germans and Swiss resisted having their currencies become international reserve currencies to supplement the dollar for fear they would lose domestic control over their own "money constitutions" (a fear justified by the increasing anarchy of the global monetary system, stimulated by the expansion of the "stateless" Eurodollar market).

With the shift from the hegemonic (*unipolar*) to the oligopolistic (*multipolar*) global system, it became problematic when the major states (or members of the oligopoly) focused upon export-oriented trade surplus policies at the same time. Someone, after all, has to import what the others export—or to accept trade deficits to permit others to have trade surpluses in the global system. In the 1980s the hegemonic role of the United States was radically transformed from surrogate world banker—providing international credit and liquidity—to major world debtor and borrower—and carrier of trade deficits that the borrowing helped to finance. In the process, the legitimacy of the dollar as the world's key reserve currency was undermined (in no small part by Pentagon-skewed federal budget deficits). Country elites scrambled to create their own exclusive buffer zones against the resulting international instability—from the OPEC cartel of oil-producing developing countries to the 1979 creation of the European Monetary System (or European float against the dollar). Multinational companies formed mergers and bought out competitors. Corporate executives of major firms demanded "Golden Parachute" clauses (giving them luxurious pension benefits in case they were fired in the creative destruction caused by merger buy-outs). Leaders of indebted developing countries threatened with instability (President Jose Lopez Portillo of Mexico, Ferdinand Marcos of the Philippines, and so on) built up private mansions and Swiss bank accounts with money borrowed from the International Monetary Fund. Human activity was focused upon shoring up the maintenance base of vested interests threatened by the inflation and uncertainty of the 1970s, then by the disinflation, deregulation, recession, and privatization trends of the 1980s.

The basic principle of oligopolies is to form minimum winning coalitions (that is, the fewest number of allies or club members required to succeed), since the greater the number of participants, the smaller the share of the economic pie for any one individual or group.[34] The shift away from multilateral to bilateral agreements between nations, for example, illustrates the belief that the payoff is greater and clearer for two partners than for more than two. And it is tempting to explain the crises of cooperation in the OPEC (over oil prices) and European Common Market (over agricultural subsidies) cartels on the basis of numbers alone: These clubs have too many members with too many diffuse interests to easily achieve the universal consensus needed within the organization for effective bargaining with the outside world.

COMPLEXITY, INTEGRITY, AND RESISTANCE

The complexity of the oligopolistic structure of the international political economy is so great that by the time students or policymakers or managers understand the rules and structures of the oligopolies at the top of the system they have little time or resources left over to analyze or identify with the majority of the world's developing peoples at the bottom. The conservative bias of conventional Western knowledge assumptions is in part the result of time pressures and the natural human tendency to focus on the two-thirds of the globe where most of international trade and investment take place. Westerners are often fully absorbed in the complexities of their own multiparty democracies and those of nations like their own. Since the managers of oligopolies at the top of the world economic system set both the terms of dialogue and the terms of trade and technological competitiveness, those at the bottom find themselves trapped in the language of dependence if they seek to adapt enough of the cultural integrity of their nations to attract capital investment and support from the developed countries. Third-World leaders lack the security conditions of developed countries and generally seek control over wealth, while aiming for both given their interconnection.[35] Whereas management texts in the Western industrialized countries put the planning function before control, planning is perceived as a luxury in most developing countries where control is the paramount concern.[36]

Not all developing countries are willing to mimic the industrial bias of knowledge typical of the Western countries, the IMF, and GATT. Some, like Papua New Guinea, seek to preserve the integrity of their cultural traditions, even if it means keeping "Stone Age" tribes frozen in a backward stage of development to prevent the extinction of their way of life. Three million people are split into a thousand tribes speaking 700 different languages, yet Papua has managed to create a form of democratic unity through decentralized administrative authority, preserving the integrity of the "large families" that comprise it. Nietzsche presumably once observed: "Character is neurosis." Individuals of character show the strength of their personalities by resisting change or status quo trends for the sake of principles and personal integrity. As with Antigone, who demanded to bury her brother even though it was against the law, their integrity depends upon resistance against what they believe to be unjust norms or conditions. The most idealistic of terrorists may view their armed struggle as a desperate effort on the part of the powerless to upset the rules of the status quo, which have permanently structured their people in a dependent position.

Even within the camp of the wealthy countries, not everyone accepts the priority of materialistic self-sufficiency and economic growth as values (preferences implicit in the dominant maintenance strategy). In his counterculture classic *Small Is Beautiful*, economist E.F. Schumacher argues that the "bigger is better" thrust of the corporate economies of advanced industrial states has contributed to the error of treating capital as income, particularly "natural capital" (such as fossil fuels) as if it were expendable without limits. Developing countries should not aim for this insatiable big business model of capitalist Westernization but wisely accept the limits of nature and the earth's resources, utilizing "intermediate technologies" targeted for their own unique capacities and situations. Economic growth per se is not a higher priority for Schumacher than is the concept of the dignity of man or the respect for the natural environment: "The substance of man cannot be measured by the Gross National Product. Perhaps it cannot be measured at all, except for certain symptoms of loss."[37] Or, to put the case another way, critic Ihab Hassan notes that in the postmodern age, order is rare and precious, but more precious and rare still is human dissent, the so-called crime that is actually the imagination diverging from "everything that is the case" and in the process creating and recreating all there is.[38] The dissent permitted by Western democracy may be an ultimate form of postmodern integrity providing the crucible for imaginative innovations that take us beyond the mere maintenance and optimization of what we already know exists.

IN CONCLUSION

Gross world product grew from about $600 billion in 1900 to over $13 trillion by 1987, spurred by a 12-fold increase in fossil fuel consumption. Even though four-fifths of all the oil discovered in North America has already been burned, energy consumption there remains profligate relative to per capita consumption elsewhere in the world. Free-riding upon the world's finite resources has become habitual despite the negative fallout of acid rain and cancer-causing pollution. Inflation-fighting and the maximization of economic growth remain primary policy objectives in the maintenance-dominated strategies of wealthy OECD countries whose numerous property-owning citizens stand to lose their asset value from inflation, and a sovereign sense of national competitiveness, and a theoretical "full employment" from a domestic slowdown in economic growth.

Following the end of World War II, American hegemony served as the international maintenance base for lending capital to rich (or former rich) countries, not to poor ones. Marshall Plan aid went to Western Europe, not Latin America or Africa. Nations already possessing the heritage of the knowledge and value structure for industrial modernization were given the additional asset of U.S. aid and credit for the sake of American security structure priorities in the cold war. By the time most developing countries had achieved political independence and demanded credit and aid to make economic independence possible, American hegemony had declined and the United States was no longer in a mood for altruistic lending: By the 1980s the U.S. position was reversed and the Americans became the world's largest debtor, not creditor, nation. Commercial banks stepped in during the late 1970s to lend capital to the developing countries to help pay for their higher (OPEC-inflated) oil bills, but the banks grew lending-shy in the 1980s when it became apparent that many of these countries could no longer afford to pay the interest on the debt, much less pay back the principal.

Thus, the rich developed countries benefitted most from the economic growth bonanza of the 1950s and 1960s: By the time the inflationary 1970s and disinflationary 1980s arrived the majority had become wealthy welfare states that sought to maintain and service what they had achieved more than to risk the pot on long-term entrepreneurial speculation. The result, epitomized by the experience of Great Britain prior to Margaret Thatcher, was a "stop (anti-inflation, tight-money) and go" (pro-economic growth through Keynesian government stimulation of demand) policy—a maintenance policy if there ever was one.

The rich have something to lose from inflation, not the poor who possess nothing of value. The deep-seated, conservative ownership characteristics that emerged as masses of people became property-owners in the developed countries via the credit innovations that split the savings/production function from the investment function set the stage for the conservative, risk-shy postmodern era in which inflation is perceived by the influential to be more of a problem than is unemployment even if the result should be stalemated growth or stagflation. When the peoples of the rich countries had accumulated enough material goods, leisure time became harried and the focus shifted to "positional goods"—status jobs or situations of security and prestige in the social hierarchy, which the elites sought to freeze once they were ensconced.[39] What trade the GATT tried to free up between countries was slowed down and regulated by the union and state hierarchies within them for the maintenance of their aging, position-holding citizens. Consolidation became more important than adjustment given the one-two punches or threats of inflation and disinflation in the world economy. Oligopolies emerged to preserve the advantages of the haves—through OPEC, the European Common Market, multinational corporate mergers—buffer zones against the economic waves of creative destruction of capitalism, with limited membership so as to preserve larger shares of the economic pie for those in "the club." Winners tried to take all and to keep others from positioning themselves to become potential winners.

Meanwhile, mismanagement of the developed political economies led to a breakdown in their status-order systems and authority structures. Old political elites were upset by young upstarts who promised to help those left behind or to perform the maintenance function even better for those established. Small young companies provided the majority of the new jobs with the spread of democratizing financial innovation and information technology. Merger strategies made multinational dinosaurs feel bigger but not necessarily better: The loss of entrepreneurial innovation was no longer made up for in economies of scale given the tempo of competitive change. IBM, for example, could no longer time the introduction of innovations in the computer market as the two-man, garage-spawned Apple Computer Company illustrated in no uncertain fashion.

The countries that performed best economically in the postwar period had a stable, predictable maintenance base from which to take entrepreneurial risks for the sake of export growth and international competitiveness. The prime examples are West Germany and Japan: The United States provided stability and capital for both, restricting their entrepreneurial energies to commercial activities (prohibiting them from diffusing their energies in the buildup of military capacity). The social market economy of West Germany was based upon a clear distinction between the limited, state-controlled *economic order* (or maintenance base) and the liberated business sector or *economic process* of the free market (or entrepreneurial innovation).[40]

Similarly, Japan's economic success was based upon a tightly knit, well-organized maintenance base crowned by the collaboration between the employers' organization, the *Keidanren*, and the Ministry of International Trade and Industry (MITI), which together targeted certain areas for national subsidies and development (from automobiles to microchips).[41] Both the West German and Japanese economies were dominated by the concentration of large firms, the superficial attempts of the Americans to break them up after the war notwithstanding. The keys to the West German and Japanese economic miracles were a stable and efficient maintenance base (a "tight ship in the storm" of creative destruction), an imposed free-rider component (the U.S. nuclear umbrella and American financing to shore up allies in the cold war), and well-targeted, entrepreneurial strategies to increase exports and create structural trade and economic surpluses. Low labor costs and a dynamic world economy were no doubt preconditions for this successful maintenance-entrepreneurial strategy mix. But one should not underestimate the astute blending of knowledge, value, and production structures to take full advantage of the free ride provided by the United States in terms of the security and credit structures that absorb most of the time, energy, and resources of less-fortunate countries.

The economic success of the United States was grounded upon the maintenance base of its largest domestic market in the world, refurbished by the technological development stimulated by the World War II effort. Nor should the economic hegemony of the United States be underestimated as the twentieth century comes to an end: Its financial innovations and subsequent ability to attract the lion's share of the world's capital have helped to subsidize a major technological revolution in information processing with unforeseen consequences for international economic competitiveness. Money and credit innovations precede technological revolutions, which make successful entrepreneurial economic developments possible.

Two major obstacles stand in the way of continued American economic dominance: the insatiable security drive of Pentagon spending, which skews the world political economy toward the buildup of armaments and utopian defense systems (i.e., the Strategic Defense Initiative); and the failure of the United States and other developed countries to create effective, growth-stimulating financial credit systems for the majority of the developing countries, which are supposed to serve as customers for the new services and products that the United States and other developed countries are producing. If the maintenance strategy so tempting to the developed countries overwhelmed with change becomes a rigid maintenance syndrome—a risk-shy, efficiency operation aimed just at keeping the status quo going—the world political economic organization may come to resemble a museum overseeing a declining, underemployed world economy in which ever fewer people can afford the price of admission. One way out of this stalemate is to understand how the world monetary system works in order to reform it, thus enabling the developing countries to have the means to participate fully in the world economy.

ENDNOTES

1. This conservative view of knowledge is derived from systems theory. See Kenneth Boulding's lucid, understated interpretation: *The Image: Knowledge in Life and Society* (Ann Arbor: University of Michigan Press, 1956). The associated view of Adam Smith's classical economic liberalism as an optimization of what exists goes back, of course, to Jean-Baptiste Say, only to be picked up in 1911 by Joseph Schumpeter in *Die Theorie der Wirtschaftlichen Entwicklung* (*The Theory of Economic Dynamics*), and recently contrasted with entrepreneurial innovation

in Peter Drucker's *Innovation and Entrepreneurship* (London: Heinemann, 1985). On the 'problem-solving' view of knowledge, see Robert Cox, "Social Forces, States and World Orders: Beyond I.R. Theory," in Robert Keohane, *Neorealism and Its Critics* (New York: Columbia University Press, 1986), pp. 208–10.

2. See Joseph Schumpeter, *Capitalism, Socialism and Democracy* (New York: Harper & Row, 1950) and Daniel Bell's recasting of the same thesis in *The Cultural Contradictions of Capitalism* (New York: Basic Books, 1976). What Bell sees as cause for conservative concern—system breakdown due to cultural and technological subversion—Jean-Francois Lyotard finds a cause for celebration in his *La Condition Postmoderne* (Paris: Les Éditions de Minuit, 1979): Paradoxical, cultural language games can lead to imaginative breakthroughs and innovative reconstructions. Compare Lyotard with the less euphoric *Legitimations Probleme in Spät Kapitalismus* of Jürgen Habermas.

3. Albert Bandura, *Social Learning Theory* (Englewood Cliffs, N.J.: Prentice-Hall, 1977), p. 194. "Reciprocal" here is used here to mean mutual action between events rather than referring to its narrower sense of similar or opposite counterreactions.

4. Ibid., pp. 16–53. Also see A. Bandura, "Influence of Models' Reinforcement Contingencies on the Acquisition of Imitative Responses," *Journal of Personality and Social Psychology* 1 (1965): 589–95.

5. See William Theodore de Bary and John W. Chaffee, eds., *Neo-Confucian Education: The Formative Stage* (Berkeley: University of California Press, 1989). The common Confucian culture of China, Japan, Korea, and overseas Chinese communities (and particularly the influence of "progressive" Chu Hsi, whose Sung learning principles were supported by the state) represents a dynamic force in the receptivity of the East Asian people to new learning and their collective capacity for cultural and economic development.

6. Gregory Bateson, *Steps to an Ecology of Mind* (London: Paladin, 1976), essay on *Deutero-learning*.

7. Ibid., See essay on "National Character."

8. See Charles Hampden-Turner, *Gentlemen and Tradesmen: The Values of Economic Catastrophe* (London: Routledge & Kegan Paul, 1983).

9. For the case of the samurai, see Everett Hagen, *On the Theory of Social Change* (London: Tavistock Publications, 1964), Chapter 14. For the Balinese, see Clifford Gertz, *Peddlers and Princes: Social Development and Economies in Two Indonesian Towns* (Chicago: University of Chicago Press, 1963).

10. For an example of an interpretation of developed Western economies in terms of the politics of productivity versus the politics of redistribution, see R. Isaak, *European Politics: Political Economy and Policy Making in Western Democracies* (New York: St. Martin's Press, 1980).

11. Some identify Schumpeter as a neoclassical economist, others as a neo-Marxist—evidence of his objectivity. He devotes a chapter to the concept of "creative destruction" in *Capitalism, Socialism and Democracy*, while his conception of development is detailed in *The Theory of Economic Development* (translated from the German by Redvers Opie. Cambridge, MA: Harvard University Press, 1934), pp. 63–65.

12. Johan Galtung made this projection at a conference in Ojai, California, in November 1979: transcribed in W.L. Hollist, "Continuity and Change in the World System," paper presented at the convention of the International Studies Association, Los Angeles, 1980.

13. An influential example of this American preoccupation is found in Robert O. Keohane, *After Hegemony: Cooperation and Discord in the World Political System* (Princeton, NJ: Princeton University Press, 1984).

14. Charles P. Kindleberger, "Hierarchy versus Inertial Cooperation," *International Organization* 40 (Autumn 1986): 841. This article expands the responsibilities of the would-be world stabilizer or "hegemon" initially set out in Kindleberger's *The World in Depression, 1929–1939* (Berkeley: University of California Press, 1973), Chapter 14. Kindleberger's concept of leadership is derived from Frohlich and Oppenheimer who argue that public goods will be underproduced (because of free-riders) unless a leader agrees to bear a disproportionate share of their costs. See Norman Frohlich and Joe A. Oppenheimer, "I Get Along with a Little Help from My Friends," *World Politics* 23 (October 1970): 20, 104.

15. The limitations to interpreting British leadership in the nineteenth century in terms of the hegemony stability thesis, particularly in regard to predicting tariff levels in international trade, are demonstrated in Timothy J. McKeown, "Tariffs and Hegemonic Stability Theory," *International Organization* 37 (Winter 1983): 73–91.

16. This is Stephen Krasner's definition in his "Structural Causes and Regime Consequences: Regimes as Intervening Variables," *International Organization* 36 (Spring 1982): 185.

17. The ethnocentrism implicit in the American fear of international instability due to the decline of U.S. hegemony is noted in Susan Strange, "Cave! Hic Dragones: A Critique of Regime Analysis," *International Organization* 36 (Spring 1982): 299–324. While team-teaching with the late international relations theorist Hedley Bull at The Johns Hopkins Bologna Center in 1980 he told me he thought American economic hegemony was being vastly underestimated. Others who find more continuity than decline in American power include Bruce Russett (Cf. his "The Mysterious Case of Vanishing Hegemony; or, Is Mark Twain Really Dead?" *International Organization* 39 (Spring 1985: 207–31) and, of course, Susan Strange (Cf. her "Still an Extraordinary Power: America's Role in a Global Monetary System," in Raymond E. Lombra and William E. Witte, eds., *Political Economy of International and Domestic Monetary Relations* (Ames: Iowa State University Press, 1982).

18. A. Gramsci, *Quaderni del carere* (Turin: Istituto Gramsci, 1975). For an application of Gramsci's notion of hegemony to the international political economy, see Robert W. Cox, "Production and Hegemony: Toward a Political Economy of World Order," in H.K. Jacobson and D. Sidjanski, eds., *The Emerging International Economic Order* (Beverly Hills, CA: Sage Publications, 1982), pp. 37–58. Cox, in turn, has been applied in James H. Mittelman, "Transforming the International Political Economy: A Crisis of Hegemony in the Third World," paper presented at the International Studies Association, Atlanta, Georgia, March 1984.

19. Silvan Tompkins, "Left and Right: A Basic Dimension of Ideology," in *The Study of Lives*, ed. by Robert W. White (Chicago: Aldine-Atherton, 1971, pp. 391–92. For the origins of "embedded liberalism," see John Ruggie, "International Regimes, Transactions, and Change," *International Organization*, 36, (No. 2), (Spring 1982): 379–415).

20. See Kyung-Won Kim, *Revolution and International System* (New York: New York University Press, 1970).

21. See Raymond Aron, *Progress and Disillusion: The Dialectics of Modern Society* (New York: Praeger, 1968), p. 160. Robert W. Tucker uses the point of departure

of the inevitable anarchy and oligarchy of the international system to defend the existing order or status quo over all else, in which the sovereignty and independence of states are presumably upheld by international law. See Tucker's *The Inequality of Nations* (New York: Basic Books, 1977).

22. See Wilhelm Hankel and Robert Isaak, *Modern Inflation: Its Economics and Its Politics* (Lanham, MD: University Press of America, 1983), Part Two; initially published in German: *Die moderne Inflation* (Köln: Bund-Verlag, 1981).

23. The distinction between efficiency preoccupation within the organization and market-oriented effectiveness in the outside environment is the basic dichotomy underlying Peter F. Drucker's *Management: Tasks, Responsibilities and Practices* (New York: Harper & Row, 1973).

24. Substantiated in R. Metraux et al., *Some Hypotheses About French Culture* (New York: Research in Contemporary Cultures, Columbia University, 1950). Also underscored in David C. McClelland, "French National Character and the Life and Works of André Gide," in *Roots of Consciousness* (New York: D. Van Nostrand, 1964) and R. Isaak, "France: An Administrative Economy of Cultural Supremacy," Chapter 3 of *European Politics: Political Economy and Policy Making in Western Democracies* (New York: St. Martin's Press, 1980), pp. 63–98.

25. *Modern Inflation*, R. Isaak, Part III: "Modern Reactions to Inflation: Private and Public Strategies," pp. 91–160.

26. This is Karl Deutsch's description of the methodology employed. See April 30, 1981, Johns Hopkins University Bologna Center Inflation Workshop Commentary transcribed in *Modern Inflation*, Part IV, pp. 198–99.

27. The conservative psychological impulse that results in the choice of maintenance strategies due to overwhelming loss or change is perceptively documented in Peter Marris, *Loss and Change* (New York: Pantheon, 1974); also see Isaak, *European Politics*.

28. "*Pentagon Inc*" is the description of contemporary U.S. industrial policy used by Yoshi Tsurumi in *Multinational Management: Business Strategy and Government Policy*, 2nd edition (Cambridge, MA: Ballinger, 1984), p. 8.

29. The primacy of security and then of money and credit among the first four of these structures is propounded by Susan Strange, "Protectionism and World Politics," *International Organization* 39 (Spring 1985): 234.

30. See Karl W. Deutsch, "State Functions and the Future of the State," *International Political Science Review* 7 (April 1986): 209–22.

31. Illustrated in *European Politics*.

32. Richard Rosecrance, "International Theory Revisited," *International Organization* 35 (Autumn 1981): 709.

33. See Paolo Guerrieri and Pier Carlo Padoan, "Neomercantilism and International Economic Stability," *International Organization* 40 (Winter 1986): 29–42.

34. See Mancur Olson, *The Rise and Decline of Nations* (New Haven, CT: Yale University Press, 1982), pp. 17–74.

35. Illustrated in Stephen D. Krasner, *Structural Conflict: The Third World Against Global Liberalism* (Berkeley: University of California Press, 1985).

36. The primacy of control over planning as a management function in developing countries is substantiated by comparing the cases in the *Columbia Journal of World Business* (Summer 1978), an issue devoted to comparative management. Also see Ramgopal Agarwala, "Planning in Developing Countries," *World Bank Staff Working Paper No. 576*, 1983.

37. E.F. Schumacher, *Small Is Beautiful: Economics as if People Mattered* (New York: Harper & Row, 1973), p. 20.

38. Ihab Hassan, "Desire and Dissent in the Postmodern Age," *The Kenyon Review* V (Winter 1983): 1–18.

39. The wealthy have more things than time to use them, making their leisure seem harried. See Staffan B. Linder, *The Harried Leisure Class* (New York: Columbia University Press, 1970). "Positional goods" are scarce in some absolute or socially imposed sense or are subject to congestion or crowding through more extensive use. See Fred Hirsch, *Social Limits to Growth* (London: Routledge & Kegan Paul, 1978), p. 27.

40. See Graham Hallett, *The Social Economy of West Germany* (New York: Macmillan, 1973), pp. 19–20; and "West Germany: A Social Market Economy," Chapter 2 of *European Politics*, pp. 27–62.

41. See Chalmers Johnson, *MITI and the Japanese Miracle, The Growth of Industrial Policy, 1925–75* (Stanford, CA: Stanford University Press, 1982) and Graham K. Wilson, *Business and Politics* (Chatham, NJ: Chatham House, 1975), Chapter 6, pp. 88–102.

CHAPTER TWO

THE WORLD MONETARY SYSTEM

Money has a life of its own which it properly should not have

Lionel Trilling

The status quo is no streetcar named desire

Wilhelm Hankel

Money or currency (*Bargeld* in German) is a form of *liquidity* or lifeblood that keeps the pieces of the world economy moving. Like a motor without oil, an economic system without sufficient liquidity slows down until it reaches an ultimate break-point—entropy. But although money was once a commodity in former times like gold or potatoes, it has become a fiat object of desire—a mysterious subjective phenomenon: The value of one national form of money or currency relative to another is literally changing every minute. The key question of the world's monetary system is whose currency carries the most weight, why, and for how long relative to other currencies and reserve assets (that is, gold)?

The asymmetry between the rich and poor nations of the world is reflected in their currencies: The rich are usually "hard" (appreciation-tending) currency countries, the poor are normally "soft" or "weak" (depreciation-tending) currency countries. The richest of the rich—the United States—had the hardest of the hard currencies at its peak moment of hegemony following World

War II. At this most sovereign moment of military and economic power, policymakers in the United States, in collaboration with those of the *pax Britannica* power structure whom they were replacing, symbolized the hardness of the dollar by guaranteeing that anyone who wanted to cash it in could do so for gold—at the 1934 rate of $35 an ounce. The dollar was declared as good as gold, and it became the world's chief *reserve currency*, meaning that individuals and foreign governments were willing to hold dollars rather than to cash them in for gold held in the U.S. Treasury. As long as the emperor (or hegemon) was clothed in untouchable power and could maintain the legitimacy he had imposed in victory, the credibility of the paper dollar I.O.U.'s he printed remained intact.

Led by the United States, the hard-currency countries since World War II have pursued a maintenance strategy of preserving equilibrium among the world's currencies before all else. Generally, stability has been promoted over economic growth, and the containment of inflation over the creation of credit. It is as if Western managers were overawed by Lenin's declaration that the best way to destroy the capitalistic system was to debauch the currency.[1] The stability of the world's money system makes great sense to those who happen to have money—*hard* money. That this priority should have overwhelmed others in the economic settlement at Bretton Woods, in 1944 (as World War II was about to end) should come as little surprise in the conservative atmosphere inevitably generated by military chaos and its aftermath. The longing for peace and order included the desire for some fixed and stable source of value.

ORIGINS

The history of money is the story of an evolution from commodity money— shells and gold—to credit (or fiduciary) money—paper currency and credit cards. This evolution was marked by the increasing demystification of money through the secularization of culture. For example, in the West African monarchy of Dahomey, cowrie shell money was considered a sacred currency lending divinity to the king.* When Dahomey was conquered by the French, the franc replaced the cowrie shell in the African money market, and the shells lost their sacred aura with the secularization of the society.[2]

Financial innovation transformed barter transactions to paper credit transactions with the creation of letters of credit and, following the invention of the printing press, paper money. As credit money expanded, the status imbued in the possessor of money was democratized: Suddenly one could

---

*In terms of etymology, the word *money* derives from the Latin words *monere* (admonish) and *moneta* (the mint in Rome: the temple of *Juno Moneta*, "the nagging Juno" who gave advice, warned, and admonished!).

be rich without owning land, and entrepreneurs could start enterprises on credit, not having a penny of their own to put down on the project. As the technical means to create credit exploded—epitomized today by plastic credit cards and quiet ticks in computer banking systems—the inflationary effects undermining the class status of commodity ownership by the "old rich" nobility surfaced: The established naturally began to resist the inflationary financing and the taxing of old rich estates, thus creating large numbers of "new rich" competitors. By this time the new rich of the developed countries had accumulated assets of their own to protect against the loss of value, and a stability-over-growth savers' mentality became widespread.[3] This conservative maintenance preoccupation was further stimulated by the inflation following World War I and by the stock market crash and Great Depression that began in 1929. In the United States, between 1929 and 1933 the GNP dropped from $103 billion to $56 billion, resulting in hardship, bankruptcies, bank failures, and political unrest. Stability was sought over all else. And those framing the post–World War II settlement remembered this. From 1945 to 1950, the United States gave Western Europe $20 billion in grants and loans—the Marshall Plan (or "the First Redistribution"). Beyond this the Americans worked to stabilize postwar economic chaos with the Bretton Woods Exchange-Rate System, the International Monetary Fund, and the International Bank for Reconstruction and Development.

The Bretton Woods System

The Bretton Woods system refers to the charter negotiated in July 1944 at Bretton Woods, New Hampshire, which established the International Monetary Fund (IMF) as well as the fund's sister institution, the International Bank for Reconstruction and Development (IBRD), or World Bank. This monetary system was fundamentally aimed to avoid the competitive exchange rate devaluations and "beggar-thy-neighbor" policies that led to the breakdown of the international monetary system in the 1930s following the Great Depression. The system was thus preoccupied with equilibrium or system maintenance, deriving from Anglo-American hegemony, heavily weighted toward the American position.

American Secretary of State Cordell Hull had set the stage for American predominance in the negotiations with Britain by using the Lend-Lease Act of 1941 to break the back of the British financial empire. Desperate for war matériels with which to fight the Germans, the British agreed to the loan conditions, which Hull knew would put the British in a structural position of financial dependence after the war: an example *par excellence* of *positioning* as the critical activity of international political economy.

The U.S. plan for the postwar economic order originated, however, not in the State Department but in the Treasury Department, under the supervision of Harry Dexter White.[4] An ambitious man with foresight, White produced a plan for the postwar international monetary system that was to bear his name before the end of 1941. Initially, the White plan aimed to prevent the disruption of foreign exchanges and collapse of monetary and credit systems, to assure the restoration of foreign trade, and to supply the large volume of capital needed throughout the world for reconstruction, relief, and economic recovery. These tasks were to be performed by a stabilization institution (the IMF) and an international bank for reconstruction (the IBRD, or World Bank).

White's plan went boldly against the predominant American public opinion trends of isolation and financial orthodoxy. The Stabilization Fund was to be made up of at least $5 billion (from contributions of member countries in gold, local currency, and government securities). This money would be used to help member countries overcome short-term balance-of-payments difficulties. The World Bank was to have twice as much capital stock as the Stabilization Fund in order to provide the liquidity needed for reconstruction, relief, and economic recovery for the "united" nations. It was to do this by making long-term loans at very low interest rates. However, in 1942 White's group in the U.S. Treasury made the Stabilization Fund the priority, letting plans for the World Bank languish—a decisive preference which was stimulated by the emerging conservative political milieu in the United States.

The British were represented at Bretton Woods by economist John Maynard Keynes for whom White had great respect. By late 1941 Keynes had developed a plan for an International Clearing Union based upon the centralization of exchange transactions through central banks in contrast to White's stress upon the restoration of competitive exchange markets with limited interventions by central markets to influence the exchange rate. The Keynes plan called for the creation of a new reserve asset, *bancor* (the forerunner of SDRs, or Special Drawing Rights, later adopted by the IMF), while White's design maintained the gold-exchange standard reinforced by a Stabilization Fund (the IMF). Keynes pushed for the symmetry in adjustment of exchange rate imbalances so that the creditor or surplus countries would share the burden with the debtor or deficit countries.

Anticipating a deflationary environment with a scarcity in demand after the war (a false prognosis as it turned out), the Keynes plan provided for overdraft rights of $26 billion, meaning that the potential U.S. liability could have amounted to as much as $23 billion—some $20 billion more than the final version of the White plan (calling for $5.2 billion with a U.S. contribution of $3.2 billion). And access to the credit under Keynes's plan was automatic, whereas White's plan called for strict lending conditions. Ultimately, the articles of the IMF reflected White's proposals rather than those of Keynes—a foregone conclusion given U.S. hegemony in 1944.

The Bretton Woods system, dominated as it was by the maintenance or stabilization bias of the IMF articles *a la* White, is perhaps most accurately seen as a system of macroeconomic management and microeconomic liberalism.[5] Paradoxically, this macromanagement, microliberalism mix was the intellectual position of Keynes preceding World War II—a position so influential that it had become the consensus epitomized by White at Bretton Woods. Keynes, meanwhile, had gone on to more farsighted ideas of creating techniques of credit and liquidity that would assist the countries most devastated by the war with the least capability of helping themselves. This would be achieved by soft, long-term interest terms (or a heavy dose of "illiberalism" for the sake of the disadvantaged). Believing that U.S. policies would predominate over all others, Keynes successfully negotiated for a passive IMF role in economic adjustment against the American internationalist, interventionist position. This was consistent not only with the primacy of national sovereignty but also with Keynes's interwar intellectual position (reflected in his *General Theory*) that exchange rates should be chosen with a view toward supporting domestic policy rather than using international exchange rates as a straitjacket to which domestic policy must conform (the position of some monetarists of the 1980s).

Keynes's position at Bretton Woods was not based merely on a short-term forecast of how he expected the world economy to go (into deflation). Rather, his economic perspective had an ethical base. Having studied the theory of probability under the influence of philosopher G.E. Moore's ethical system, Keynes was inspired by the obligation so to act as to produce by causal connection the most probable maximum amount of eventual good through the entire procession of future ages (as recorded in his *Two Memoirs*).[6] Keynes's long-term preoccupation was with the human suffering of unemployment, and he was determined to fight for sufficient international liquidity to stimulate demand in critical situations in order to bring depressed countries back on their feet, providing work through economic growth. As Lord Keynes put it in an address to the House of Lords in which he sought to win British support for the Bretton Woods charter: "Sometimes almost alone, in popular articles in the press, in pamphlets, in dozens of letters to *The Times*, in text books, in enormous and obscure treatises I have spent my strength to persuade my countrymen and the world at large to change their traditional doctrines and, by taking better thought, to remove the curse of unemployment."[7] The IMF, Keynes claimed, would help check unemployment by supporting three key Keynesian principles:

1. Domestic policies should primarily determine the external value of a country's currency, not the other way around.
2. Domestic policy should have control over domestic rates of interest to keep them as low as suits the national purpose, without interference from the ebb and flow of international capital movements or flights of "hot money".
3. While countries should aim to prevent inflation at home, they should not accept deflation dictated by outside influences.

Naturally, Keynes argued these principles in terms of British national interests, the "dictates from outside" presumably being American influences.

The United States opposed the larger amount of liquidity Keynes proposed because it wanted to limit its potential liability as the world's largest creditor nation in the postwar order and for fear that unmanageable inflation would be generated. Similarly, the Americans did not want as much flexibility in exchange rates as the British sought. Finally, the United States lightened the potential sanction on surplus nations to get them to move toward balance-of-payments equilibrium, leaving the weight of the burden for adjustment heavily on the debtor nations. By limiting the amount of liquidity that could be lent by the IMF and by establishing strict conditions (or *conditionality*) for such loans, American diplomats sought to win over a skeptical, conservative U.S. Congress that must ultimately approve how government money is spent. In sum, the Americans succeeded in establishing a blueprint for noninflationary, economic growth aimed at full employment and restoring competitive exchange rates at Bretton Woods. The fatal flaw, that was later to bring down the system, was that everything was based on the assumption that the dollar could forever be converted freely into gold—a flaw natural for a hegemonic power at its peak when both its dominance and legitimacy as reflected in the strength of its currency are taken for granted.

THE IMF. The International Monetary Fund officially came into being when representatives of forty-four nations signed the Articles of Agreement stemming from the Anglo-American negotiations in July 1944 in Bretton Woods, New Hampshire.[8] By the end of 1945 the critical number of countries had ratified the agreement. The Board of Governors first met in March 1946, adopting by-laws and deciding to locate the IMF's headquarters in Washington, D.C. A year later the IMF began actual exchange operations. Its objectives were to secure international monetary cooperation, stabilize exchange rates, and expand international liquidity for the sake of international trade and full employment.

To achieve its aims, the IMF initially tried to maintain fixed exchange values of currencies (linked to the given dollar–gold rate) and to eliminate exchange controls. To ease the transition to the new system, a one-time adjustment of up to 10 percent in the initial value of each currency was permitted. However, once the designated *par value* of a currency had been established, a member country could only make major changes with the fund's approval. Such approval depended upon whether or not the country's balance of payments was in "fundamental disequilibrium." In other words, the key criterion of the IMF in terms of exchange rates is the *maintenance of stability,* or the recovery of stability or equilibrium in the case of countries with deficits. Such stability was assumed to be the prerequisite for the collective goals of economic growth and steady investment.

Upon joining the IMF, a country is assigned a quota depending upon its position* in the world economy, which governs the size of its cash subscriptions, its voting power, and its drawing rights. Each member nation pays a quarter of its quota in SDRs and the remainder in its own currency. When a member country runs into balance-of-payments difficulties (that is, if more payments by domestic residents have been paid out than received from foreigners), it can automatically buy foreign currencies equal in value to a quarter of its quota—the equivalent of its gold subscription. Beyond this limit, the country must receive specific approval from the fund based on significant policy changes aimed to solve the balance-of-payments problems, such as by striving to control domestic inflation. The IMF is uniquely positioned to influence national policies of countries threatened with balance-of-payments deficits, for much of the time a needy country will have to borrow more than the first "gold *tranche*" or quarter of its quota. Countries borrowing from the IMF must repurchase their own currency (or repay the loan) within five years. The fund is geared to service short-term balance-of-payments adjustments, not long-term structural adjustments—the role of the World Bank.

The head of the IMF is the managing director who leads the meetings and negotiations. At Bretton Woods the parties agreed that the head of the IMF should always be a European, whereas the head of the World Bank should be an American. Given the shift of the world's liquidity to Japan in the late twentieth century, it would not be surprising if eventually a Japanese was made head of the IMF.

Formally, the IMF is governed by two bodies: the Board of Governors and the Executive Board. The Board of Governors is made up of one governor for each nation with voting power proportional to subscription quotas. That is, each member is given 250 votes plus one vote for each $100,000 deposited, assuring that the major subscribers maintain a dominant role. Initially the dominant countries numbered ten: the United States, the United Kingdom, Canada, France, West Germany, Italy, the Netherlands, Belgium, Sweden, and Japan. Saudi Arabia later joined this group following the OPEC oil price hikes of the 1970s. The Board of Governors deals with changes in the Articles of Agreement, with the admission of new members, and with the election of the managing director.

The other body, the Executive Board, is comprised of appointed and elected directors. Those appointed are nominated by the five members with the largest quotas, while those elected are nominated by particular groups of member countries. The votes of these directors cannot be split and must be cast as a unit. The Executive Board is permanently in session and handles the everyday operations of the IMF.

_____

*A member country's position is measured by its volume of international trade, national income, and international reserve holdings.

The initial quotas assigned to member countries were found to be inadequate and have been repeatedly increased to provide liquidity to cope with the increasing volume of transactions. A number of financial crises in the 1960s created a demand for additional reserves to be used in the settlement of international balances. The "management remedy" in 1969 was to introduce Special Drawing Rights (SDRs)—units of account that could be transferred between the IMF and national central banks to help resolve balance-of-payments problems. SDRs permit countries temporarily in deficit to draw supplies of foreign currencies according to predetermined quotas. The use of SDRs is not subject to negotiations or conditions, does not provide for repayment obligations if a member uses less than 70 percent of its SDR quota, and is accepted in final discharge of debts without being translated into any particular currency.

The first allocation of SDRs to IMF members in 1970 of $9.5 billion over three years represented the triumph of an American pro-liquidity policy over French resistance. American experts at the time argued that Keynes had been right after all at Bretton Woods and that the initial IMF system did not provide enough international liquidity. During the era of dollar scarcity after World War II, the dollar had been forced into the role of key international reserve currency. The Americans were moving to shift the international monetary system away from this overexposure by devising a new source of nonnational liquidity (although economist Robert Mundell later referred to the SDRs as "dollars in disguise"). The French, on the other hand, wanted less than the $3 billion to $5 billion in SDR annual liquidity advocated by the United States, demanding strict reconstitution obligations and that American deficits be put to an end before the SDR system went into operation. It was another instance of the recurrent classic debate in the history of the international monetary system of the need for expanded liquidity versus the need for IMF credibility and conditionality (that is, adjustments to IMF guidelines for non-inflationary economic growth by deficit countries seeking funds).

THE DECLINE OF BRETTON WOODS. The Bretton Woods system functioned to service economic growth throughout the world for two decades after its founding, less because of its design than because of the ability and willingness of the Americans to play the role of a world central bank, printing dollars to provide liquidity. The American balance-of-payments deficit allowed others to run surpluses, which was very convenient. As long as the Americans provided stable and responsible leadership in international economic policy and as long as the dollar was accepted abroad as a "legitimate" substitute for gold the system seemed to work. Yet Bretton Woods never functioned as Americans and the others had planned. After all, it was not the United States that was supposed to perform the role of a world bank but the International Monetary Fund and International Bank for Reconstruction and Development. This illusion had already dissolved by

1947 when the Americans realized how thoroughly World War II had destroyed the European economic system, a system based largely on trade that could not work with the sources of Europe's foreign earnings gone and with heavy European balance-of-payments deficits. So from 1947 until about 1960 the United States stepped in and assumed unilateral management of the international monetary system, appearing to use Bretton Woods as a veil of legitimacy for the liquidity provided by the outflow of American dollars.

However, the constant outflow of dollars from the United States undermined the very monetary system which it serviced.[9] In 1947 the United States held 70 percent of the world's official monetary gold stocks. Between the end of 1948 and the end of 1959 American gold holdings fell by 20 percent. In 1960 foreign dollar holdings exceeded American gold reserves for the first time. Many perceived the U.S. balance-of-payments deficit, which reached $3.7 billion in 1960, to be getting out of control. The weakness of the British pound and the speculative problems associated with European currency convertibility further served to weaken confidence in the dollar. From this point forward, it was no longer possible for the United States to manage the international management system alone, and thus an informal multilateral form of international management emerged with the United States still predominant but with less clout. As Europe and Japan recovered and prospered with American support, their bargaining power relative to the United States in international economic policy also increased: They lost the war militarily to win the peace economically. For example, European Common Market countries became more independent: whereas in 1958 only 29.6 percent of imports and 30.1 percent of exports by Common Market members came from other member nations, by 1970 imports reached 48.4 percent and exports 48.9 percent.

In 1961 the most important finance ministers and their deputies in the IMF created the Group of Ten—a club within a club that served together with the central bankers in the Bank of International Settlements of Basel, Switzerland, to help manage the international monetary system throughout the 1960s. Working Party Three of the Organization for Economic Cooperation and Development also assisted in this *ad hoc*, multilateral form of crisis management that substituted for U.S. hegemony. As previously noted, Special Drawing Rights (SDRs), or artificial international reserve units to be used among central banks outside the control of the United States and managed by the Group of Ten, were created as a new form of liquidity in the 1960s. Because the Europeans had a veto power on the creation of new SDRs they came to represent a dilution of American financial power mirrored by the rise of European influence. American financial power was further diluted with the rise of the Euromoney or offshore banking system, which originated after 1917 when the Soviets wanted to protect their dollars from being seized by the United States and put them in "friendly" European banks. These offshore dollars started to grow in volume in the 1960s and multiplied immensely after the 1973 OPEC oil crisis, ultimately reaching into the trillions by the 1980s.

The greatest crisis in the confidence of the United States came in the late 1960s when President Lyndon Johnson decided to wage war on Vietnam abroad and war on poverty at home without raising taxes—a destabilizing, inflationary decision that made the breakdown of the Bretton Woods framework imminent. This breakdown was indicated by three major currency turbulences—of the pound in late 1967, of the dollar in March 1968, and of the French franc and German mark in November 1968. French President Charles de Gaulle did what Frenchmen typically do in times of international crisis: buy gold. Already at his press conference of February 4, 1965, de Gaulle had argued passionately for "the supreme law, the golden rule": "Yes, gold, which does not change in nature, which can be made into bars, ingots, or coins, which has no nationality, which is considered in all places and at all times, the immutable and fiduciary value par excellence. Furthermore…it is a fact that even today no currency has any value except by direct or indirect relation to gold, real or supposed." So much for the French confidence in the dollar or acceptance of the legitimacy of American domination. The American government intervened, asking the German and British governments to buy up the dollars being sold off, temporarily stemming the crisis of confidence. But the Bretton Woods system based on a dollar fixed to gold (at $35 an ounce) was set up for self-destruction. It was only a matter of time.

From Gold to Floating

The shift from the fixed exchange-rate system, based on the dollar's convertibility to gold, to the floating exchange-rate system can be highlighted by tracing three permanent redistributions of wealth from Americans to others: the Marshall Plan of 1947, the OPEC oil price hike of 1973, and commercial bank lending in the late 1970s.

Because of the Marshall Plan (the first redistribution) American defense spending abroad, foreign aid, tourism, and foreign investment, a dollar scarcity following World War II was transformed into a dollar glut. Americans continued to spend more overseas than they earned from abroad. The United States shifted from being the world's principal short-term creditor to being its main short-term debtor. The willingness of the United States to run large deficits and thereby to provide the international money or liquidity to permit other countries to run surpluses undermined the discipline the Bretton Woods arrangement was supposed to instill, making the agreement increasingly irrelevant. As the United States functioned as a world central bank in promoting expansion by pumping up the world's money supply, developed Western countries were able to maintain currency convertibility without much domestic discipline, tight exchange controls, or protectionism. World trade and investment flourished. But the Achilles heel of the Bretton Woods system was the assumption that the dollar was convertible to gold.

For quite a while this weakness was successfully covered up. American experts advocated Special Drawing Rights—or "dollars in disguise"—as a new source of nonnational liquidity to supplement the dollar in its role as the key international reserve currency. Arguing that John Maynard Keynes had been right after all at the Bretton Woods Conference that the initial IMF system did not provide adequate sources of international liquidity, this shift by American advisors seemed to have an altruistic ring. But, in fact, it was consistent with the so-called policy of benign neglect (letting things go along as they are), taking politicians off the hook of having to decide whether to promote domestic recession on the one hand, or to restrict tourist, business, or military spending abroad on the other, so as to bring America's balance of payments back in line. The dollar's position as the key reserve currency allowed the United States to run deficits to finance "global responsibilities" without having to cut back on private outflow. Of course many American and European experts did honestly believe that SDRs could become the basis of a multilateral reserve system that might eventually replace the hegemony of the dollar. But the short-term effect was to provide another distraction from the problem of American deficits.

Observing that the United States had only a third enough gold in its coffers to cover the outstanding dollars and facing the certainty of another dollar devaluation, on August 15, 1971, President Richard Nixon did what perhaps any American president in that position might have been forced to do: Overnight he indefinitely suspended the dollar's official convertibility into either gold or foreign currencies. To put the best face possible on this move, Nixon called it his "New Economic Policy," simultaneously imposing a temporary surcharge of 10 percent on dutiable imports and freezing domestic wages, prices, and rents for ninety days, while cutting both federal taxes and expenditures. Using the outspoken Secretary of the Treasury, John Connally, as a lightening rod, Nixon managed to make the dollar's retreat appear to be an aggressive thrust to improve the U.S. trade balance. In an age when one person is considered to have almost no power, a single individual within twenty-four hours was able to shift the world economy from fixed exchange rates (the dollar fixed to the 1934 price of gold at $35 an ounce) to floating exchange rates (which officially emerged in 1973, signifying that any one country's currency is worth whatever people think it is worth at a particular moment). Characteristically, Nixon told no one of his intentions, including America's closest allies, thus deterring speculators and using the element of surprise to give drama to his decision. Much as Henry Kissinger, Nixon's national security advisor, used secret shuttle diplomacy to spring American–Chinese détente upon the world to distract public attention from American losses in Vietnam, so Nixon's New Economic Policy served as a red herring to shift attention away from the inherent weakness of the dollar. The very art of being a magician, after all, is to so dazzle the audience with the spectacle that the left hand is performing that no one notices the deceptive maneuvers of the right hand, which hide one's true intentions.

In the short transitional period between the fixed and flexible exchange rates in the early 1970s, Connally engaged in hard bargaining to assure acquiescence to the change by America's European allies and Japan. An understanding was reached in the Azores, which resulted in the Smithsonian Agreement of the International Monetary Fund in December 1971.

However, the Europeans and the Japanese were "reluctant allies" at this point. As an émigré from Nazi Germany, Kissinger was wary of the Europeans and argued that they and the Japanese had become free riders on the American security system, accepting the economic benefits of the post-war Western system without bearing their share of the burden. So Kissinger gave a cold shoulder to the Europeans, believing (probably correctly) that there was nothing to be gotten out of them. However, this "de Gaulle snubbing tactic" on Kissinger's part was to prove expensive later when the Americans found it increasingly difficult to obtain European cooperation for American objectives in the late 1970s. But perhaps what is most striking about the trilateral relationships of the early 1970s among the United States, Western Europe, and Japan are the similarities with some of the relationships existing in the 1980s: American policymakers, increasingly concerned with the U.S. trade deficit, desired to bring down the price of the overvalued dollar to increase the competitiveness of American exports abroad without losing American status in the process. They used hard bargaining tactics in trade and security negotiations with the Western Europeans and the Japanese, making use of the "free ridership" argument and protectionist threats, and they shifted the flavor of American policy toward a nationalistic mercantilism with the predictable strains in American–Japanese and American–European relations.

Alas, in human affairs, throwing all of one's energies to win in one arena often guarantees losing in another. In their total preoccupation with the chess games going on in the strategic triangle (among the United States, Soviet Union, and People's Republic of China) and in the trilateral trade triangle (among the United States, Western Europe, and Japan), Nixon and Kissinger neglected the "North–South triangle" (among the oil-producing developing countries, the non-oil-producing developing countries, and the developed countries).[10] In fact, evidence suggests that Nixon and Kissinger were willing to sacrifice the North–South game for the sake of the trilateral trade and strategic games. In June 1972 at a meeting of the Organization of Petroleum Exporting Countries (OPEC), a top U.S. State Department official, James Akins, made a famous "impromptu speech" maintaining that oil prices could be "expected to go up sharply because of lack of short-term alternatives to Arab oil" and that higher oil prices were "an unavoidable trend." Conspiracy theorists use this speech to argue that the Nixon White House wanted to have

OPEC raise oil prices in order to encourage domestic American production and to give the United States a competitive advantage over Europe and Japan, which were both more energy dependent upon OPEC oil than was the United States. At the very least Nixon and Kissinger appeared to be blind to the consequences of the 1973 oil price hike, a blindness encouraged with their preoccupation with the strategic stakes in the Arab–Israeli war on the one hand, and with trilateral trade competition on the other. These "maintenance men" failed to appreciate the main fulcrum of historical change, so absorbed were they in the *ancien régime* mentality of shoring up the status quo.

THE RISE OF OPEC: THE SECOND REDISTRIBUTION.   The quadrupling of oil prices by the OPEC oil cartel in 1973 would not have been possible without the rise in the price of gold, gold reserves, and foreign-exchange holdings due to the shift to floating exchange rates. For under the floating system, which officially went into effect in 1973, no mechanism existed for the international control over the quantity of international reserves. The international monetary system floated around the dollar, but the dollar no longer possessed the discipline of gold convertibility. Countries could simply buy reserves if they wanted them, and there was no check on the inflationary production of liquidity in the system. Paper gold became "paper paper" and commodities in the ground and tangible goods appreciated steeply in value with the onslaught of widespread global inflation in the 1970s. The Eurodollar (dollars outside the United States) and credit markets—that "stateless money" which was the international banker's vehicle for expansion throughout the 1970s—financed national exchange rate and interest rate disturbance after 1973 but at the cost of uncontrollable price rises.[11] Faced with this "inflation machine" and motivated to unite and act by the Arab–Israeli war, the oil-producing Arab nations were sufficiently motivated to use an oil embargo and then jack up their prices.

Naturally, OPEC could only get away with its huge price hike by (correctly) assuming that United States would choose to do nothing about it. Given the American debacle in Vietnam and U.S. domestic political difficulties at home, it was accurately assessed that America's national will, so necessary to support an invasion and occupation of Arab oil fields at the risk of a major confrontation with the USSR, was lacking. The OPEC nations shrewdly guessed what price increase their rich customers would bear and launched what some have called "the Arab decade." The Americans seemed collectively to have decided that their national power in the game of empires had peaked—at least for the moment. And history indicates that power vacuums are short-lived. Quite understandably, OPEC moved to fill the gap.

Leaders of OPEC prefer to view the oil price hikes of 1973 and 1979 as equitable "adjustments," not in terms of "revolution." They argue that up until 1973 the major oil companies largely dictated prices, even though oil was the critical developmental resource for many oil-producing countries.

After 1973 governments as well as oil companies had a hand in the price-setting. From the viewpoint of oil producers, the first oil shock of 1973 was certainly a "revolution." From the viewpoint of consumers it was a crisis. And from the viewpoint of most developing nations in the world, the OPEC "coup" was a symbolic victory for Third-World unity, demonstrating that cartel power could lead to a redistribution of wealth from the rich to the poor countries and help to create a "New International Economic Order."[12]

The OPEC wealth redistribution through oil price escalation in 1973 and thereafter was to have revolutionary implications for the structure of national economies in the world system, implications that were slow to be fully appreciated. Many advanced Western economies, and particularly the United States, had built cheap energy assumptions into their economic and industrial calculations. When energy costs skyrocketed in the 1970s—complemented by the inflation stimulated by global food shortages, a flood of international liquidity, and increasing labor costs—many basic industries in advanced Western countries became increasingly less competitive on world markets. After the 1973 oil price rises, the major industrial nations of the West overreacted with deflationary policies, thus helping to prolong the recession of 1974/75. Old Western policymakers overreacted to international change with stop-go economic policies: putting on the monetary brakes too heavily all at once, rather like a nervous, elderly driver trying to descend a steep hill in an old car, only to speed up too quickly at the bottom out of fear of losing momentum. And citizens began to accept as inevitable the jerky ride caused by the quick shifts between the fear of inflationary booms and deflationary busts, whereas actually it was often a case of widespread, short-term-obsessed mismanagement. Western policymakers used deflationary policies, recycling the $30-billion deficit they acquired from the OPEC price rises to the poor, developing countries of the Third World, and then expressed surprise in 1975 when these developing countries mobilized the "Group of 77" in the United Nations to demand economic justice.

THE DEBT TRAP: THE THIRD REDISTRIBUTION. The global economic crisis in the 1980s shifted from the inflationary liquidity surplus of the 1970s to a deflationary liquidity shortage and global recession. Private, commercial multinational banks were the institutions of adjustment in the 1970s, outbidding each other to lend money to developing countries at high interest rates, believing that if worst came to worst they might not get back their principal but they could at least survive on the interest. There was little regulation of this international banking activity, and the leaders of advanced industrial nations, which were themselves beset with economic and political problems, seemed relieved to have the private sector pick up the increasing burdens of international financial assistance. But both the developing debtor nations and the international banks falsely counted on the global inflation rate continuing at a level high enough to make the debts ever-cheaper from the perspective of the borrowers and to assure the repayment of the interest from the viewpoint of the banks. Conventional wisdom projected that oil prices would continue to rise, not fall.[*]

But in the early 1980s oil prices did fall. OPEC's share of the world market dropped below 40 percent and its cartel clout dissipated accordingly. Oil-producing developing countries suddenly found they could no longer pay back the interest on their debts. By January 1, 1983, the gross external debt of eight Latin American countries made up about 55 percent of the $550 billion that fifty developing countries owed to foreign creditors. And the debt of Argentina, Mexico, and Brazil alone amounted to more than $200 billion. The international banks and their Third-World clients discovered they had fallen into a debt trap: A third redistribution had taken place, not through a Marshall Plan or oil price hikes, but this time through indefinitely extended credit. Wealthy countries attempted to stem the crisis by increasing the resources of the IMF by almost 50 percent and by pressuring their major banks to continue lending to the deficit countries. But the world debt crisis, compounding the scarcity of liquidity so badly needed to stimulate a world economic recovery, appeared to be more than conventional government and private-sector strategies could cope with. It was not a time for the maintenance of the old as much as it was for reform and risk-taking to create new structures and strategies. The early 1980s tight-money, high-interest-rate policy of the U.S. Federal Reserve Bank—anti-inflation-over-everything-else—was part of the problem, driving up variable interest rates of foreign debts.

By 1987 the IMF had 151 member nations in its fold and was faced with a Third-World foreign debt of $1,080 billion. The 1987 increase in SDRs from $61 billion to $90 billion was not nearly enough to cope with the world debt problem. Given an American trade deficit of almost $160 billion, not to mention the large U.S. budget deficit, the U.S. Congress was in no mood to increase its funding to the IMF and World Bank significantly enough to have much effect. Rather, the American focus was upon persuading the key surplus trade countries (Japan with a positive balance of $106 billion and West Germany with one of about $62 billion) to stimulate domestic economic growth in order to help correct the trade imbalance. That such domestic stimulation might lead to excessive inflation, thereby causing Germany and Japan to raise their interest rates at a time when the world economy (and especially the U.S.) needed lower rates to stimulate economic growth, was a possibility neglected by the Americans.

The European Monetary System

The economic recovery of Western Europe and Japan after World War II coincided with the decline in American hegemony, calling for a shift in the

---

[*]Also see Chapter 7 under "The Debt Crisis" and "The Mexican Case."

fulcrum of managing Western monetary affairs. The creation of the Common Market, or European Economic Community (EEC) in 1958, symbolized the rise of Western Europe as a trading bloc, but coordination of regional monetary matters did not really follow suit until the breakdown of the system of fixed exchange rates and Smithsonian Agreement in 1971. At the beginning of 1972, the six members of the EEC, soon joined by the United Kingdom, Ireland, Denmark, and Norway, created the "Snake"—an exchange-rate regime that obliged its members to keep their currencies within a relatively wide "tunnel"; each currency was assigned a bilateral central rate with every other currency involved and each member government was required to keep its currency within a 2.25 percent margin either way of this rate, thus limiting the range of exchange-rate fluctuation. While only reluctantly joining the Snake—for fear of the Bundesbank's loss of control over domestic economic stability—West Germany quickly came to dominate the Snake as the strongest or key currency. Indeed, some referred to the arrangement as the "DMZ"—not "demilitarized zone" but "Deutschmark zone." Weaker currencies—the pound, lira, and Norwegian krone—soon left the system, given speculation against the dollar and pound in the new floating exchange-rate system. By 1974 the French franc, too, pulled out of the Snake.

The mid-1970s proved a time of great uncertainty for those who would manage economic and political affairs. The dollar devaluations of 1971 and 1973, the quadrupling of oil prices, and the escalation of grain prices drained purchasing power from most nations in the world, resulting in a deflationary impact. Nevertheless, the advanced industrial policies reacted with anti-inflationary policies, anticipating a global inflation fueled by the rise in oil prices, the expansion of world liquidity, and the absence of external restraint implied by the shift from fixed to floating exchange rates. This anti-inflation policy was based on an understanding among the United States, Japan, and West Germany, which broke down in the 1974/75 recession—partly the result of those deflationary policies. As the German mark rose 30 percent against the currencies of the Federal Republic's twenty-three major trading partners between 1972 and 1977, the pressure increased on the German authorities to permit the mark to be used as an international reserve currency. This pressure was strongly resisted, particularly by the Bundesbank, which feared losing control over domestic money markets. So while the Germans favored a moderately rising or revalued mark as a means to keep inflation out of Germany (provided that the mark did not rise too high and threaten the competitiveness of German exports), they were in the market for some external restraint or system to take the pressure of adjustment from their shoulders.

Meanwhile, at EEC headquarters in Brussels, President Roy Jenkins of the European Commission perceived the European economies to be overwhelmed with global change, leading inevitably to disintegration in the European Community unless some way could be found to stem the crisis.

His solution was to pick up the theory of European monetary union and to promote European unity as an "adventurous idea," which might help to make up for the threats posed by the expansion of the Common Market (enlarged in 1973 to include Britain, Ireland, and Denmark) and general economic uncertainty. In his Monnet Lecture at the European University Institute in Florence in October 1977, Jenkins spelled out five economic reasons for monetary union: (1) It would stimulate efficient rationalization of industry; (2) provide the European Community with the advantages accruing to "the issuer of a world currency" (buffering the Europeans somewhat against dollar instability); (3) contribute to the struggle against inflation; (4) help reduce unemployment; and (5) reinforce policies aimed at leveling out regional differences within the EEC.

Roy Jenkins, a professional politician of considerable skill, initiated his European monetary union strategy on two levels—at the "lower table" of public negotiations with others in the European Community bureaucracy and at the "higher table" of private talks with the leaders of key European currency countries—particularly West Germany, France, and Britain. At the lower table Jenkins, a British subject, had to confront his predecessor, F. X. Ortoli, a bureaucrat who had positioned himself well in the Central Bank Governors Committee with his typical strategy of small steps. Persuasion and co-optation were not in themselves sufficient means for Jenkins to sell his "wild idea" to Ortoli, who believed in achieving success by setting limited objectives. So Jenkins turned to the "high table" in 1977 to persuade the leaders of Germany, France, and Britain to join in his monetary crusade for the sake of European unity.

While at first appearing reserved, world events and his own perceptions caused West Germany's Chancellor Helmut Schmidt to come out strongly for European monetary union in early 1978. Schmidt's dislike for both President Jimmy Carter and America's volatile economic policies (culminating in the dollar crisis of November and December 1977) led him to the conclusion that it was vital for Europe to have a grand design to counter or at least buffer the impact of U.S. economic inconsistency upon the economies of the European Community. Schmidt was particularly critical of the "locomotive theory" of the Americans, according to which the West Germans and Japanese were pressured to stimulate demand in their domestic economies, thus acting as locomotives for world economic growth to counter the slowdown and stalemate of the U.S. economic situation.

Initially, French President Valéry Giscard d'Estaing stayed out of the controversial European monetary idea—until he safely steered his center-right coalition to election victory against a disunited left in the March 1978 French elections. Then Giscard d'Estaing, a former finance minister (as was his politically compatible friend, Helmut Schmidt), jumped on the German bandwagon, negotiating with Schmidt behind the scenes in order to announce the European Monetary System as a joint German–French plan. The

French president wanted to give the appearance that France was as strong, influential, and prestigious as West Germany, heading off domination of the European Common Market by one non-French country. The French also have a concern for monetary discipline and hoped that the European Monetary System (EMS) might provide an external restraint that could substitute for a return to the system of fixed exchange rates.[13]

The West Germans and the French proposed the "parity grid" system of exchange rates, expanding the Snake in which each country was bound to every other currency. While elastic, the parity grid system allowed currencies to move only 2.25 percent either above or below the bilateral par value before central banks of both the (over) high and (over) low currencies involved acted to bring their currencies back to the bandwidth permitted. The Germans liked this system, for the responsibility for exchange-rate adjustment fell equally upon both the strong currency (usually the mark) and weak currency involved. The weak-currency countries—particularly Britain and Italy—objected that it was unfair to put as much responsibility upon the weak as upon the strong.[14]

The weak-currency countries supported an alternative "basket system" based on a weighted average of all EEC currencies, called the European unit of account for central banks (ECU). The ECU is a reserve asset replacing part of the excessive dollar reserves. Some in the European Community see in the ECU the potential some day for a European currency.

The debate between the parity grid and basket system proposals was resolved with a Belgian compromise that combined the two systems: The basket system would serve as an indicator of divergence ("the rattlesnake") *within* the parity grid system, signaling central banks to start intervening at 75 percent of the 2.25 percent (× 1 – the percent of national currency in the basket) limit of flexibility allowed on either side of the central rate. West Germany, France, Denmark, the Netherlands, Belgium, and Luxembourg agreed to this system in late 1978. The ECU was approved for settling accounts among European partners as well as a $35-billion financial cooperation fund for stabilizing currencies. Italy and Ireland joined the EMS agreement by the time it went into effect in 1979 after receiving informal financial concessions (including a 6 percent range of flexibility rather than the normal 2.5 percent). While Britain agreed to have the pound in the basket-indicator system, the English did not join the system given the high rate of the pound and domestic political uncertainties.

In the early years of the European Monetary System (EMS) when the dollar was on a steady uptrend or downtrend and inflation was the primary concern of the eight member nations, participants were more or less content to go along with West Germany's dominant role as disciplinarian and paymaster. The Socialist government of France even reversed its Keynesian policy of public spending pursued from 1981–83 to adjust to EMS discipline rather than quitting the EMS. But by 1987, when the dollar's rate had become volatile and European countries had become more concerned with slow growth and unemployment than with inflation, the anti-inflation austerity of the Bundesbank and its power to crimp the national sovereignty of the non-German members had become unbearable. As Jean-Pierre Chevènement, a leader of the left wing of the French Socialist Party and presidential aspirant, put it: "We cannot accept forever that the EMS be no more than the camouflage of a mark zone." The non-German members received two concessions from the Germans: (1) West Germany would contribute more money earlier in necessary interventions for exchange-rate stability with fewer conditions and (2) West Germany would coordinate policies more frequently with other member nations (implying less autonomy for the German Bundesbank). In addition, the French pushed for Britain to enter the EMS to counter the power of West Germany in the system, but Prime Minister Margaret Thatcher held back, fearing for loss of national sovereignty over the British economy. And it remained to be seen how long West Germany would trust the other members to make their own economic policies while footing most of the bill for exchange-rate adjustments. But, all in all, the EMS provided for a tighter exchange rate system than the global one and a basis for the Common Market to work its way out of what political scientist Stanley Hoffmann called the European Community's "dark age" (1973 to 1984).

INTERPRETATIONS

Exchange-rate adjustments attributable to balance-of-payments deficits are epiphenomena on the surface of the world monetary system, typifying the political and money constitutions of the nation-states underlying them—the contemporary tips of old icebergs. These phenomena can be interpreted differently depending upon whether the observer is from a rich country or a poor one, or is a classical economic liberal, a monetarist, a structuralist, a neorealist, or merely someone who seeks to maintain the stability of the status quo. By looking at the alternatives a nation has for solving a balance-of-payments problem from these different perspectives, one can get a sense of the complexity and political implications of the kaleidoscope called the world monetary system.

Balance-of-Payments Adjustments

When the sum of all economic transactions between a state's residents and foreigners is greater than all receipts coming into the state and its residents during a year, that country is running a balance of payments deficit. Should the amount coming in exceed that going out, that country enjoys a balance-of-payments surplus. As the objective of conventional monetary theory calls for equilibrium rather than for surplus or deficit, international management efforts in the world monetary system can often be most easily explained by a maintenance model, which aims toward stability over all else. While stability undoubtedly benefits both rich and poor nations, the adjustment required to recover or to maintain balance-of-payments equilibrium often falls most heavily upon those who are least well off in the status quo, which is why conflicting perspectives emerge over the relative value of exchange-rate stability.

Three traditional methods exist for a country to cope with a balance-of-payments deficit:

1. *Internal economic policies:* typically deflationary policies to reduce the deficit such as a tighter budget or higher interest rates.
2. *External measures* to shift expenditures away from imports, securities, and other transactions that lead to payments to foreigners: typically involving import quotas, tariffs, or limiting the outflow of capital.
3. *Financing or raising liquidity:* typically cashing in gold or foreign-exchange reserves or borrowing through private markets or commercial banks.

In explaining these three adjustment choices to the U.S. Congress, Professor Richard Cooper of Yale used what has since become a classic diagram (see Figure 2–1).

Each point in the triangle in Figure 2–1 illustrates some mix of the three types of measures for managing an imbalance in the international payments of a country or region at a specific time under a fixed exchange-rate regime.

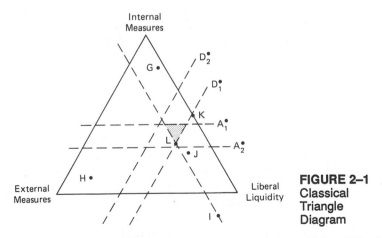

FIGURE 2–1
Classical
Triangle
Diagram

(*Source:* Richard N. Cooper, "Guidelines for International Monetary Reform," Hearings before the Subcommittee on International Exchange and Payments, Joint Econ. Comm., 89th Congress, 1st Session, Part 1: Hearings, July 29, 1965, pp. 109–113, 117, 119.)

Reprinted with permission from the publisher of Richard N. Cooper, *The Economics of Interdependence* (New York: McGraw-Hill, 1968), p. 18.

Each one of the three vertices of the triangle symbolizes the exclusive use of one of the measures or policy approaches: The closer a point is to one of the vertices the more the policy solution represents that particular type of measure. Point G thus signifies a heavy focus on internal measures: domestic deflation to reduce a payments deficit or domestic expansion to reduce a payments surplus. Point H, on the other hand, stresses external measures: exchange controls and import quotas. Point K could be a state within the United States where external measures are ruled out.

Point J represents a country awash with gold or reserves that can finance its deficit—or that has the capacity to borrow such liquidity easily from someone else without having to make many internal or external adjustments. The pressures upon countries with balance-of-payments deficits are clearly greater than those with surpluses—which can finance those surpluses indefinitely. Thus, in Figure 2–1, Keynes's focus at Bretton Woods was upon the liberal liquidity vertice of the triangle for the sake of long-term adjustment of deficit countries, while the American position of Harry Dexter White was upon internal and (to a lesser extent) external measures as preconditions for receiving short-term liquidity from the IMF.

Classical Economic Liberalism

Any actual national policy involves some mix of internal, external, and financing measures in adjusting a country's balance of payments. But classical economic liberals stress avoiding policy trade-offs that utilize external measures, arguing that the free flow of capital, goods, and services between nations is essential to increase both economic growth at home and global economic prosperity. Secretary of State Cordell Hull under President Franklin Roosevelt before and during World War II epitomized the classical liberal position. He argued that free markets and free trade would lead to global economic prosperity, that the rising waters would lift all ships (or nations, weak or strong), and that global prosperity would assure world peace.[15] Harry Dexter White represented a more developed extension of this perspective: Balance-of-payments adjustments must focus on internal measures, getting one's own house in order, so as to benefit from and qualify for financing or liquidity provided by the IMF or commercial banks.

While the Bretton Woods system was inspired from the American side by classical economic liberalism—which sought to deter obstructions to free trade and to head off competitive exchange-rate devaluations or external capital controls by providing a limited but reliable short-term source of liquidity to member states in need—the actual institutions of Bretton Woods represented a compromise, a manifestation that political scientist John Ruggie has termed "embedded liberalism." *Embedded liberalism* is the fusion of hegemonic political power (such as that of the United States after World War II) with social purpose agreed to by the parties involved (such as domestic state stability through full employment and anti-inflation policies) to yield a manifestation of political authority that was to transcend the decline in the hegemony of the United States in the 1970s and 1980s. American negotiators sought state self-sufficiency, economic growth, and free markets as ends—and credible, creditworthy, short-term loans supplementing free-market-oriented adjustments in the domestic economy as the means. But the IMF did not become a surrogate "invisible hand" (which Adam Smith hypothesized would steer private self-interest to the public good) as much as a collective, norm-governed balancing act between opening markets and international economic transactions on the one hand and protecting the domestic stability of the key states in the world economy from having to bear undue costs of adjustment to global economic change on the other. Indeed, it has been argued that discontinuity in the Bretton Woods agreements has been caused more by recent Anglo-Saxon efforts to dislodge this institutionalized liberalism to make it more pronounced than by efforts to overload Bretton Woods structures with domestic social objectives.*

Structuralism

From the perspective of the economic school called *structuralism* Adam Smith's "invisible hand" is too invisible: Nations must use external measures in making balance-of-payments adjustments in a world where the flow of finance, liquidity, and trade is *structured* against them. It is the rich states, after all, who could afford to purchase the most shares in the IMF and who have the largest quotas when it comes time to borrow liquidity (the United States, for example, is one of the top borrowers from the IMF).

Structuralists argue that the world capitalist system must be tilted or restructured toward the interests of the least-advantaged nations. Nobel laureate Gunnar Myrdal, for instance, suggested that the U.S. redistribution to Europe in the form of the Marshall Plan went to the wrong countries: The "old rich" Europeans were capable of recovering on their own and the historical moment of American good-will should have been targeted at the poorest countries in Asia or Africa without the training or tradition of economic recovery and development.[16]

Latin American economist Raul Prebisch argued that capital flows from poor countries to rich ones because the terms of trade are structured against the poor, who must live off the low price of commodities, while the rich countries benefit from the higher (and rising) prices of both manufactured goods and high-tech products and services.[17] The rich nations should therefore provide liberal liquidity for the poor countries and accept the

---

*"The foremost force for discontinuity at present is not 'the new protectionism' in money and trade, but the resurgent ethos of liberal capitalism": John G. Ruggie, "International Regimes, Transactions, and Change: Embedded Liberalism in the Postwar Economic Order," *International Organization*, 36, No. 2, (Spring 1982):413.

external measures the developing countries require to protect their limited markets and resources. Keynesian liquidity creation and long-term soft loans would suit the structuralist perspective of reducing the inequities between the rich nations and the poor ones—not the liberal classical priority of putting one's own house in order first to qualify for short-term, highly conditional credit.

Marxism

From the Marxist perspective, the IMF provides a "debt trap" for the developing countries, which renders them forever dependent upon external financing by the rich industrialized nations.[18] The world capitalist system is eventually set to self-destruct, breaking down in the contradictions of social and international class conflicts according to neo-Marxists. In the meantime, several intermediate Marxist strategies are available for countries with balance-of-payments deficits to follow. One—the Albanian and North Korean approach—is for such countries to isolate themselves from the world capitalist economy, creating import substitutes and attempting to become as self-sufficient as possible before once again opening the door to the outside world and to vulnerability. This is an extreme policy, one that emphasizes external measures over everything else.

Another strategy is that of the "Cambridge School." Many of the elites in the developing countries sent their children to study at Cambridge University in England. Partly as a result of this increasing influx of students from the developing world, a neo-Marxist economic wing developed at Cambridge, which Mexico called upon for advice in the late 1970s when Mexico was haunted by staggering balance-of-payments problems. Advisors influenced by Cambridge neo-Marxist thought persuaded Mexico to borrow as much as the Western commercial banks were willing to lend even though both sides knew the chances of paying back the principal on the loans were not good.* The Cambridge strategy was that even if the loans could never be paid back, Mexico would have the banks by their loans, a sort of reverse debt trap.

The banks, in turn, would have to continue to provide enough liquidity to Mexico to service the interest on the loans or risk a Western financial crisis by officially writing off the loans in reports to stockholders. And the banks ultimately had their governments by the debt. For if Citibank, for example,

---

*Not all of these advisors were neo-Marxists. Carlos Tello, for example, a key Mexican figure behind the borrowing (under President Luis Echeverria) and behind the bank nationalization (under President López Portillo) was educated at Cambridge and influenced by neo-Marxist thinking but often supported neo-Keynesian economic policies for Mexico. Still, the influence of the eclectic neo-Marxist Cambridge School of thought should not be underestimated. See Chapter 7 for details of the Mexican case.

or one of the other nine largest banks in the United States threatened to go bankrupt and trigger a financial crisis, the U.S. government would have to step in to bail them out. Mexico, with the threat of proximity to the U.S. border and the ability to allow unemployed Mexicans to drift across, thus was able to "restructure" global financial arrangements to create a permanent source of American liquidity. That David Rockefeller, chief executive officer of Chase Manhattan Bank, was one of the American elites strongly promoting this restructuring to make the Cambridge strategy successful is an historical paradox that Marxist theory alone might have a hard time explaining (not to mention the theory of classical economic liberalism!).

Monetarism

Monetarists, such as Nobel laureate Milton Friedman, argue that the money supply is the most important factor in a nation's economic policy and that only monetary policy can influence the course of the gross national product.[19] Monetarists usually assume that people tend to keep a fixed amount of money liquid, which they save (for example, the nonconsumed part of income held for convenience). Beyond this, if the nation's money supply provides citizens with easier access to money or credit, they will spend more. If, on the other hand, the nation's money supply is tightened the populace will consume and spend less. Moreover, if governments spend more, people or households will spend less since public spending presumably crowds out private and household spending. A nation with a balance-of-payments deficit, according to the monetarists, is probably living beyond its means and must focus upon internal (usually deflationary) measures to tighten up the money supply.

Monetarism is ultimately a free-market ideology advocating an anti-inflation policy above all else, and benefiting the most those who have something of value to lose from inflation—namely the wealthy. To the extent the IMF demands that countries reduce the money supply and adopt government austerity measures as prerequisites to IMF loans, it is adopting a monetarist policy.

Neorealism

Neorealism has its roots in the power precepts of Machiavelli and the nationalistic economic policies of mercantilism. The preoccupation with power—defined as control for the sake of the security, glory, and wealth of the imperial state—traces, in turn, back to Thucydides in his *Peloponnesian War*. The modern tradition of realism is, of course, epitomized by the nine "elements of power" of Hans Morgenthau: geography, natural resources, industrial capacity, military preparedness, population, national character, national morale, quality of diplomacy, and quality of government.[20] The neorealists of the 1980s picked up Morgenthau's concern with calculations of power and national interest in the United States as a reaction against the demise of the nation-state forecast by the global idealists of the 1970s. The inability of nation-states to control or to manage turbulent change in the 1970s was not attributed to the demise of the nation-state, according to the neorealists, but to the power vacuum resulting from the decline of American hegemony following America's defeat in Vietnam.[21]

The neorealist interpretation of optimum balance-of-payments adjustments stresses maximizing the power and internal controls of the state. For nations enjoying a surplus this means maintaining the surplus as a national security buffer or strong bargaining position and making only superficial compromises to the international community, striving not to weaken "the thing itself" (*Dinge an sich*)—the maintenance base of power and wealth. Deficit nations must use their weakness strategically to seduce stronger nations, banks, and international organizations into granting them financing on soft terms, and they must work to strengthen their power base at home, beginning, of course, with the power of the elites in charge. The maximization of national interest precedes international stability from the perspective of the neorealist: International agreements are nothing else than tough bargains struck between conflicting parties in which the strongest gets its way. Not to strive for hegemony is to lose the game.

IMPLICATIONS

While each of the interpretations considered in this chapter yields its own insights into the dynamics of the international monetary system, each has its drawbacks and blind spots. To use just one of these interpretations is like exploring a large dark house with a flashlight: One sees only where one has shone the light at any given moment, leaving most of the structure in the dark. Thus, classical economic liberalism sees free-market potential for economic growth and is often blind to global class-structured restrictions to opportunities for equal treatment. Both structuralism and Marxism spotlight inequitable distributions of the past, which discriminate against poor nations in the present, usually ignoring emergent technological innovations that recast the way money works in the future. Monetarists highlight money flows from the top of each national system downward, but neglect existing fiscal and class structures that funnel cash in certain directions rather than others. For the neorealists, the more things change the more they stay the same. They lack a positive vision for the future and underestimate those who act either for altruistic motives or who seek international system stability for its own sake. What is required is a comprehensive, systematic approach that focuses upon functional techniques of solving maintenance or stability problems efficiently on the one hand, and which anticipates emerging trends, cycles, and opportunities for innovation, growth, and future redistribution on the other hand.

* * *

In any international exchange-rate system of N nations there are only N-1 exchange rates, rendering one currency redundant.[22] If all N countries attempt actively to manipulate their exchange rates, the system is technically "overdetermined" and to that extent destabilized. Since, in practice, the redundant currency tends to be the key international reserve currency—today's dollar—the clear implication is that key-currency country policymakers should maintain a more or less passive policy except when it is necessary to intervene to keep their currency stable on world markets. To do otherwise not only "overdetermines" the system theoretically but also politicizes the existing international exchange-rate regime unnecessarily, thus undermining its legitimacy.

Simultaneously, the authority of the key-currency country is undermined when others accuse it of mercantilistic currency manipulations for the sake of national interests. Thus American allies protested in the 1970s and late 1980s when the dollar was undervalued, stimulating American exports at their expense, and they complained in the early 1980s when the dollar was overvalued, sucking their capital into the United States as it chased the higher interest rates. In the late 1980s, American policy was to devalue the dollar and to persuade West Germany and Japan to stimulate demand (for imports) domestically in order to help balance the United States trade deficit. But by 1990, this short-term policy led to a jump in global interest rates as Japan and West Germany raised their interest rates to dampen the inflation caused by their stimulation of domestic demand. The higher global interest rates hit the U.S. exactly when it needed lower rates to encourage economic growth and head off a recession. Interest rate roulette with the world's key currency is a precarious game. As a potential hegemon and superpower, the United States has the greatest stake in the stability of the existing dollar-dominated world monetary system and its more-or-less "apolitical" acceptance as *the* legitimate regime by other countries.

But the Americans mismanaged their position of privilege, overexposing their short-term national benefits and putting the very legitimacy of the monetary system in question. Erratic changes in economic policy under President Jimmy Carter undermined the system's stability and U.S. authority as the dollar fell 16 percent in value between the autumn of 1977 and the autumn of 1978, thus mobilizing the Europeans to create the European Monetary System—a joint float of European currencies intended to buffer European currencies from the dollar's instability.

In 1978 Carter appointed Paul Volcker as Chairman of the Board of Governors of the Federal Reserve System. Volcker applied the monetary brakes to bring down the U.S. inflation rate, which was about 13 percent. In so doing he "overdetermined" the international monetary system by refocusing Federal Reserve policy upon restricting the base of the entire U.S. money supply and not just upon interest rates. The Volcker policy of tightening the money and credit supply drove up U.S. interest rates to historically high levels and caused the dollar to be overvalued.

The high U.S. interest rates attracted capital from OECD and OPEC nations into American money funds and portfolio investment, draining the world market of liquidity where it was badly needed. American interest rates also helped to lock the United States into a structural trade deficit as the strong dollar made American exports less competitive on world markets. Since the Europeans and Japanese had planned on a strong American recovery to help their own domestic economies, not to mention the lesser-developed countries, the tight money policy of the Volcker regime had the effect of derailing yet another locomotive theory of economic growth. Late in the deep recession of 1981/82, Chairman Volcker then shifted to another extreme, loosening the money supply, ignoring M-1 (cash and checking account) fluctuations above his targets.

One reason for Volcker's "overmanagement" of the U.S. money supply was the creation of the *xeno* (foreign or "stateless") money and credit markets—usually known as the *Eurodollar* markets (any currency or dollar outside of its country of origin)—in the 1970s, which served to help recycle back into circulation the money flowing to OPEC for its oil. By the early 1980s the xeno or Eurodollar markets had expanded to *trillions* of U.S. dollars, none of which could be governed or controlled by the central banks of the key industrial countries. With their international control through currency monopoly and reserve requirements effectively diluted, to have the slightest impact upon international money markets the central banks such as the Federal Reserve were tempted to overreact or to oversteer—extreme tightening or extreme loosening of the domestic money supply. And while this form of defensive management might make short-term policy sense domestically, it served to undermine the legitimacy of the monetary system dominated by the dollar in the long-run when the United States oversteered or overly-politicized the exchange-rate regime. For it soon became obvious that American policymakers were exploiting their "privileged position" in the world monetary system either to manipulate exchange rates so as to attract capital to cover U.S. balance-of-payments and federal deficits or to make U.S. exports more competitive to ease the U.S. trade deficit.

As the dollar fell with the looser money supply and efforts of U.S. policymakers to turn their trade deficit around through competitive devaluation in the mid-1980s, capital flowed out of lower fixed-interest commitments into a speculative stock market, which was reaching record-level highs. Computer-programmed, futures hedging systems—or "portfolio insurance"—ratcheted up (and later down) these massive speculative investments worldwide. This was done faster than those who would control the world monetary system could keep up with. As the American policy of letting the dollar drop to help make U.S. exports more competitive failed to have any appreciable impact upon the U.S. trade deficit in 1987, the newly appointed head of the Federal Reserve System, Alan Greenspan, let interest rates rise to head off inflationary anticipations stemming from the lower dollar. Despite a February 1987 Louvre agreement among the key Western industrial countries (the Group of Seven) to hold the dollar and other key currencies within a specified (but secret) range of stability, U.S. policymakers again politicized the monetary management system by publicly accusing the West Germans and Japanese of not stimulating their domestic economies enough to help reverse U.S. trade deficits and to act as locomotives of world economic growth.* Disenchantment with U.S. economic policy became wide-spread as it became clear that Congress was making few significant steps to reduce the huge federal deficit and that not enough internal restructuring measures were being taken in the U.S. economy to reverse the large American trade deficit. When West Germany raised interest rates rather than lower them in accord with the wishes of the Americans that the Germans stimulate demand, U.S. Treasury Secretary James A. Baker openly criticized the Germans on October 16, 1987, stimulating a drop in the prices of U.S. stocks to be followed on October 19 by Black Monday—when the New York Stock Exchange saw its Dow-Jones average plummet 22 percent in a single day. The world's stock markets fell in tandem with the U.S. market, particularly given international, computerized portfolio systems. Baker's clumsy criticism appeared to undermine the agreement of industrialized countries to maintain exchange-rate stability since an anonymous, highly placed American official implied that if the West Germans did not lower their interest rates the Americans would push the dollar down further as an intentional policy (undermining German exports). The threat was another symbol of U.S. politicization of the monetary system for mercantilistic objectives, epitomizing massive disenchantment abroad with a U.S. economic policy that drained the capital of other countries to plug up American federal and trade deficits, which the Americans appeared unwilling or unable to do much about.

The residue of the Bretton Woods system—symbolized by the floating exchange rate-IMF-G-7 regime—assured that October 19, 1987, would not be a repeat of October 28, 1929 (Black Friday), in spite of the fact that in percentage terms the stock market actually dropped more on Black Monday than on Black Friday. Late in the day on October 19 the U.S. Treasury Secretary, the West German Finance Minister, and the head of the German Bundesbank (central bank) issued a joint statement from Europe assuring the

---

*Both the West Germans and the Japanese have been more concerned with keeping inflation low and their savings rate and export surplus high in the post–World War II period than have the Americans.

financial markets that the G-7 Louvre agreement was still operative and that they were doing everything to cooperate. On the morning of October 20, Alan Greenspan, head of the U.S. Federal Reserve System, publicly announced that the central bank would provide all the liquidity necessary for the American banking system to stem the crisis. This loosening of U.S. monetary policy was the opposite from that of the Federal Reserve after the stock market crash of 1929, when a tightening up of U.S. money policy led to an expansion of the stock market's fall to a run on the banks, thus helping to bring on the Great Depression. The fact that each individual bank account was insured for up to $100,000 (Federal Deposit Insurance) reassured the American public sufficiently in 1987 that they ran to U.S. banks to put money in this safe haven rather than taking all their savings out.

Once the stock slide started, computer-programmed trading increased the speed and volume of the fall to such an extent that the institutions of the stock exchange—much less federal government institutions—could not cope with what was happening. The managers of stock funds had protected themselves with dollar averaging: that is, as a stock declines, they sell in increments, and when it rises they buy in increments. But this process was stimulated greatly by the difference in the margin requirements in the New York and Chicago exchanges, thus increasing the arbitrage, or speculation on the differences between the exchanges. The Chicago Mercantile Exchange, which possesses the largest stock index futures market, had only a 7 percent margin requirement, meaning a buyer has only to put up 7 percent of his or her own money. But the New York Stock Exchange had a 50 percent margin requirement, which stimulated margin buying (a parallel between the 1929 and 1987 crashes), even though in this case the margin buying was in derivative products, not the main market.

Additionally, this process was stimulated because of the fashion of big traders to take out "portfolio insurance," automatically buying futures contracts in Chicago to hedge against a decline in the New York market. Thus the computer trading programs tend to push the market in a single direction, faster than money or institutional managers can cope with the change.

All that managers can do (to recover equilibrium according to the maintenance model of heading off entropy as fast as possible) is to try to slow things down in such a computerized market fall—what one could call a policy or strategy of *retardation*. John Phelan, chairman of the New York Stock Exchange, executed exactly this kind of strategy following Black Monday. He prohibited the use of the Big Board's order-distribution system on the New York Exchange for program trading, thus breaking the "financial meltdown" and stabilizing the market. He suspended trading on the ninety-one most volatile stocks, while approximately 1,500 kept trading. Yet his strategy showed moderation. He did not ban margin program trading entirely, but he took it off the computer system and told traders that they would have to do it by hand—a policy of retardation if there ever was one.

Nor did Phelan close down the New York Stock Exchange (NYSE) for the day, only a couple of hours early on days of the heaviest trading. Hong Kong's more extreme policy of closing its exchange entirely helped to stimulate the 33-⅓ percent drop in its stocks the day it reopened. John Phelan also went to major member-dealer firms (as well as to the generous Federal Reserve Bank) to ask them to provide the NYSE with liquidity in case of need.

When it was all over, Phelan saw the need for a more structural embodiment of what has been called here a strategy of retardation. Phelan noted that the major lessons learned were (1) to give everyone a little time so that people with knowledge can assess what can be done; (2) to pump liquidity in "so everything just doesn't dry up;" and (3) to figure out a better way to plug the lender of last resort into the system.[23]

* * *

Retardation alone is ultimately a self-defeating form of crisis management unless there is international cooperation among the industrialized countries to reform the unstable, private dollar-based world monetary system. Slowing down the entropy is not syntropy any more than slow death is resurrection. The consumption-oriented U.S. economy served as the world's central banker to provide the liquidity and import purchases, thus making the export-oriented strategies of other countries possible. But these neomercantilist strategies created worldwide overcapacity in a deflationary environment.[24] The competitive struggle of downward adjustment to match low-cost competition reached a point of diminishing returns. Still, the hard-currency countries, such as West Germany and Japan, attempted to use their currency revaluations (or upward floating) to keep inflation out of their domestic economies, to keep down costs, and to keep their exports competitive—an anti-inflationary policy in deflationary times. The stock market crash of 1987 revealed that this policy was not viable when confidence in the U.S. economy fell with the dollar's value. Inflationary-financed economic growth comes eventually by fiat if not by intentional policy coordination. The sharp drop in the American stock exchange of October 13, 1989 ("Friday the 13th") demonstrated that the globalization of stock markets both cushions the fall of individual markets and reduces the power of governments over their nation's economy (thus the self-confidence of the Japanese buffered the fall of the U.S. market as Japanese investors held on to their stocks, while risk-shy Germans sold and the German market fell 13 percent). Yet without systematic G-7 reforms of the international monetary system the liquidity will not flow to those countries that most need it since the global crisis in confidence discourages investment in high-risk areas. Ultimately, without liquidity, how will other countries be able to pay for German, Japanese, and American exports?

ENDNOTES

1. John Maynard Keynes noted: "Lenin is said to have declared that the best way to destroy the capitalistic system was to debauch the currency." Keynes, *The Economic Consequences of The Peace* (London, 1920), p. 220.

2. Melville J. and Frances S. Herskovits, *Dahomean Narratives* (Evanston, IL: Northwestern University Press, 1958). Also see Paul Einzig, *Primitive Money* (Oxford: Pergamon Press, 1966).

3. See Wilhelm Hankel, "The Causes, History, and Illusions of Inflation," Part Two of W. Hankel and R. Isaak, *Modern Inflation: Its Economics and Its Politics* (Lanham, MD: University Press of America, 1983), pp. 25–90. Or, in the German edition: *Die moderne Inflation* (Köln: Bund-Verlag, 1981), pp. 31–114.

4. The best history of the founding of the Bretton Woods System from the conflicting perspectives of Harry Dexter White and John Maynard Keynes is Richard N. Gardner, *Sterling-Dollar Diplomacy in Current Perspective: The Origins and Prospects of Our International Economic Order* (New York: Columbia University Press, 1980).

5. See John Williamson, "Keynes and the International Economic Order," in Chris Milner, ed., *Political Economy and International Money: Selected Essays of John Williamson* (Brighton, Sussex: Wheatsheaf Books, 1987), pp. 37–59.

6. Joan Robinson, *Economic Philosophy* (New York: Penguin, 1981—orig. published 1962), p. 16.

7. John Maynard Keynes, May 23, 1944 address to the House of Lords, in Gerald M. Meier, *Problems of a World Monetary Order* (New York: Oxford University Press, 1974), p. 34.

8. The history of the IMF is reviewed in J. Keith Horsefield, ed., *The International Monetary Fund, 1945–1965: Twenty Years of International Monetary Cooperation* (Washington, D.C.: IMF, 1969). For earlier monetary systems, see Robert Triffin, *The Evolution of the International Monetary System: Historical Reappraisal and Future Perspectives* (Princeton, N.J.: International Finance Section, Department of Economics, Princeton University, 1964).

9. See David P. Calleo and Benjamin M. Rowland, *America and the World Political Economy* (Bloomington: Indiana University Press, 1973), Chapter 5, pp. 87–117.

10. See Stanley Hoffmann, "Choices," *Foreign Policy* 12 (Fall 1973): pp. 3–42.

11. See, for example, Eugène L. Versluysen, *The Political Economy of International Finance* (New York: St. Martin's Press, 1981).

12. See Karl P. Sauvant and Hajo Hasenflüg, eds., *The New International Economic Order: Confrontation or Cooperation between North and South?* (Boulder, CO: Westview Press, 1977).

13. See Peter Ludlow, *The Making of the European Monetary System* (London: Butterworth, 1982).

14. See Luigi Spaventa, "Italy Joins the EMS—A Political History," Occasional Paper No. 22, Research Institute, The Bologna Center, June 1980.

15. See Cordell Hull, *Memoirs.* 2 vols (New York: Macmillan, 1948).

16. See, for example, Gunnar Myrdal, *Ökonomische Theorie und unterentwickelte Regionen: Weltproblem der Armut* (Frankfurt, 1974).

17. Raul Prebisch, *Towards a New Trade Policy for Development*, report by the Secretary-General of the United States Conference on Trade and Development, E/CONF 4613 (New York: United Nations, 1964).

18. See Cheryl Payer, "The Perpetuation of Dependence: The IMF and the Third World," *Monthly Review* 23, No. 4 (September 1971).
19. See, for example, Milton Friedman, *Tax Limitation, Inflation and the Role of Government* (Dallas: Fisher Institute, 1978). Also, Milton Friedman, ed., *Studies in the Quantity Theory of Money* Chicago: University of Chicago Press, 1956.
20. See Hans Morgenthau, *Politics Among Nations,* 3rd ed. (New York: Knopf, 1960).
21. J. Martin Rochester, "The Rise and Fall of International Organization as a Field of Study," *International Organization* 40, No. 4 (Autumn 1986): 799. Prominent American "neorealists" include Kenneth N. Waltz (see his *Theory of International Politics:* Reading, MA: Addison-Wesley, 1979) and Robert G. Gilpin (see his *War and Change in World Politics,* Cambridge: Cambridge University Press, 1981). Also see Richard K. Ashley, "The Poverty of Neorealism," and Robert G. Gilpin, "The Richness of the Tradition of Political Realism," both in *International Organization* 38 (Spring 1984).
22. The first part of this section was initially presented at The Research Institute of International Change at Columbia University, and an early version later appeared as R. Isaak, "The International Monetary Crisis and Economic Growth," *Working Papers in International Banking,* No. 4, Institute of International Banking, Pace University, New York, February 1983.
23. George Melloan, "Stock Slide Makes Phelan a Prophet...," *The Wall Street Journal,* October 28, 1987, Op. Ed Page.
24. See Winston Williams, "Waking Up to the Glut Economy," *The New York Times,* December 8, 1985; p. 1 of Business Section.

CHAPTER THREE

THE WORLD TRADE SYSTEM

Current-account surplus can't be achieved by all countries simultaneously. Moreover, no country should seek to run its economy and society in such a way as to entrench a massive and permanent trade balance in its favor.

British Prime Minister Margaret Thatcher

Every man who lives by supplying any want dreads anything which tends either to dry up that want or to supply it more easily and abundantly. It is to his interest that scarcity should reign in the very thing which it is his function to make abundant, and that abundance should reign everywhere else.

Philip H. Wicksteed (1910)

International trade is trade with foreigners—an idea that takes getting used to. For people are brought up in sovereign nation-states where they are socialized to believe in the superiority, if not the self-sufficiency, of their own culture. *Ethnocentrism*—the belief in the primacy of one's own people or way of life—is the ultimate motive behind protectionism and the formation of trade blocs: protective barriers separating "them" from "us" in order to assure one's own economic interests first. From the national perspective, if trade with foreigners is necessary for national prosperity then it seems natural to try to arrange it so that there is more money coming in than is going out, creating a trade surplus or buffer zone of wealth to protect one's people in case of a downturn in the turbulent world economy.

Of course there is more than one way to look at international trade. The British (followed by the Americans) came to look at a trade surplus as less important than a world system of free trade in which they could use their considerable, hegemonic power as a basis and their advanced economy as a means of expanding business worldwide for the sake of British prosperity at home. With the key international reserve currency backed by the British navy in the nineteenth century, they could run deficits without a short-run problem—unlike any other country. At its peak of power following World War II, the United States adopted the same classical liberal free-trade policy for much the same reasons. Therefore, it was natural for the British and Americans to scold smaller nations (which saw trade surpluses as their only long-term security) for not aiming at an equilibrium in their trade balance. That other up-and-coming economic powers did not always agree with this Anglo-Saxon free-trade position should come as no surprise.

Moreover, the developing countries found that the price of their agricultural commodities, upon which their economies were based, did not keep up with the price of manufactured goods or financial services, putting them increasingly behind the developed countries in their terms of trade. From their perspective the world trade system was structured against them, increasing the gap between their limited wealth and power and that of the rich nations. A banana republic with only bananas to export in exchange for everything else that it has to import can hardly be enthusiastic about a world system of free trade that permits wealthy, well-organized, multiresource nations to take advantage of vulnerable, single-commodity countries.

On the other hand, if borders shut down and each nation is forced to live off of what it has at home, the developed nations have most, the developing nations least. As uncertainty increases in the world economy, risk-shy, maintenance-oriented wealthy states are more tempted to trade with other stable well-to-do nations in their own image unless their governments or international organizations provide risk-insurance schemes to entice them to do business with less advantaged peoples. Financial crises, such as the stock crash of 1987, merely reinforce the natural conservative impulse and security consciousness of rich consumers, investors, and traders, making protectionism and trade war more tempting unless world leaders cooperate politically to create counter-incentives in the world trading system.

ORIGINS

"Buy cheap and sell dear" is the motto of all business, including international business. Mass production is one way to make things cheaper—through "economies of scale." The ancient Greeks were the first to use mass production.

International trade is furthered by stable, routinized relations among different peoples who can use a common currency in exchanges.

The Romans provided such international laws and stability—laws that gave even non-Roman citizens certain rights. And the Roman dinarius was the first international currency. The hegemony of the Roman Empire (even or *particularly* in its period of slow decline) provided a predictable basis for international commerce. When the empire broke down through the invasion of the German tribes, international trade languished. The Western World entered the Dark Ages.

The next hegemonic order in the West was that of the Catholic Church. However, the spirit of the Church was not conducive to stimulating commercial activity or the accumulation of material wealth. Much of international trade was still done by the barter system or exchanging goods for other goods (a system that was to shrink to about 5 percent of total world trade by the end of the 1980s). During the feudal period, either the Church or ruling lord granted a charter to merchants in one section of the castle, called the *faubourg*, in which limited commercial activities and international trade could take place.[1] Located in most castles, abbeys, and cathedrals beginning in the late eleventh century, the *faubourg* merchant settlements led to charters being granted by lords to merchants for towns. These charters often gave permission for merchants to form guilds or co-operative associations. The guilds were forerunners of modern trade unions.

Initially towns were often granted the right to a guild, commercial court, and a low form of justice, but rarely the powers of self-government. This power deprivation later led the French and Italians to create *communes*— sworn alliances of groups of people associated for a stated purpose, often in revolt against the local lord. Commune movements ultimately permitted villages to win special rights of self-governance.

Champagne, France, became the meeting place for traders from both the north and the south. In the twelfth and early thirteenth centuries, the Champagne trade fairs became the most important trade centers in Western Europe. The counts of Champagne provided booths, money-changers, police, and judges for the merchants. Modern trade fairs, which still play an important part in European commerce, thus originated in Champagne—not to mention a celebratory form of effervescent liquidity (Champagne wines— with one of the most fiercely protected brand names in history).

From the guilds thus arose the towns and trade fairs that stimulated the modern system of international trade. The guilds had social and religious functions. They paid for the funerals of their members and took care of widows and children. The weakness of the guild system, like that of the trade union system that grew out of it, was its inability to adjust to technological progress. The *faubourg*, guild, and contemporary trade union can all be seen as maintenance bases or traditional organizational buffers against the creative destruction of global capitalism; they seek to hold on to the rights of those already employed as members according to traditions of the past rather than to focus upon entrepreneurial adaptation to emerging technological and economic trends.

The great Crusades of the feudal era served to prepare the way for world economic change as military forces established major trade routes for the sake of ideological beliefs. Secularization was an inevitable trend as religious movements spent their legitimacy in bloody exhaustion.

The feudal order was displaced by national monarchic states at the close of the Middle Ages, customarily marked by the Treaty of Westphalia of 1648. Mercantilism, or the economic nationalism of states, flourished from the sixteenth through the nineteenth centuries and was exemplified in the writings and policies of men such as Colbert, Burleigh, Cromwell, and Frederick the Great. Nation-states wanted to increase their power in the world and such national leaders viewed trade as a means to this end. They accumulated gold and silver to hire mercenaries and equip fleets of ships. Each state aimed to maximize its share of the world's limited gold supply. Exports were promoted and productions costs were kept down so as to keep state competitiveness lean and mean in the trade struggle. A representative mercantilist pamphlet at the turn of the seventeenth century by Italian Antonio Serra was entitled *A Brief Treatise on the Causes Which Can Make Gold and Silver Plentiful in Kingdoms Where There Are No Mines*. Agriculture suffered hardships, for food prices were held down and luxury goods were considered taboo (enforced with heavy import duties). Foreigners were happily seen as customers, but not as suppliers.[2] It is little wonder that mercantilism often led to both military and trade conflicts.

If one flashes from mercantilism to the neo-mercantilism of the late twentieth century one notes great similarities in their aims: increase exports, reduce imports, and increase employment at home—regardless of the negative effects that these policies may have upon other nations. Indeed, these principles sound almost as if they could be the main platform planks in the electoral campaign in almost any contemporary democratic state. Export-oriented growth strategies are the panacea for the collective insecurity generated by turbulent world markets.

From Mercantilism to Classical Liberalism

In the eighteenth century a physician in the court of France's Louis XV, François Quesnay, propounded a school of economics called *Physiocracy*, even developing a *tableau économique*—a chart of economy. Insisting that wealth came not from gold and silver, Quesnay went against the tenets of mercantilism, arguing that wealth passed from person to person throughout the nation, replenishing the body politic like the circulation of blood. Quesnay's theory was not of much use for practical policy, however, for the production of "true wealth" was limited to the agricultural classes: The manufacturing and commercial classes were viewed as merely manipulating wealth in a sterile way.[3]

The French Physiocrats offered a doctrine based on free trade and competition to replace the nationalistic bias of mercantilism. Like certain late twentieth-century ecologists, they believed nature to be the only source of wealth and they (inaccurately) categorized manufacturers, artificers, and merchants as unproductive. Their list of proposals was topped by a call for a single tax on the net product of land—a list advising that industry and commerce be exempted from taxation. The phrase "Laissez faire, laissez passer" is attributed to an associate of Quesnay, Vincent de Gournay. The state was not to interfere with the authentic creators of natural wealth from whom society would ultimately benefit.

The classical liberal school of economics, enunciated in Adam Smith's *Wealth of Nations*, published in 1776, basically agreed with Quesnay and the physiocratic school apart from the doctrine that artificers, merchants, and manufacturers are unproductive. Gold and silver were asserted to be no more important than other commodities (in antithesis to the mercantilist assumption), having their price like the others. Adam Smith was concerned with the natural laws of wealth. According to these laws of the market, the drive of individual self-interest in an environment of similarly motivated individuals would result in competition; competition, in turn, would provide society with wanted goods at acceptable prices. The market should be left alone: Its productivity would then spill over to the advantage of the public good as if by "an invisible hand." As long as a man does not violate "the laws of justice," he should be left perfectly free to pursue his own interest in his own way, bringing both his industry and capital into competition with those of any other men or order of men.

Smith's view was an optimistic, although realistic, economic philosophy: Increased competition would lead to increased productivity and increased wealth, making social progress through economic growth inevitable. It was, of course, a doctrine devised in a nation of small shopkeepers with limited factories in mind—not a world of giant multinational corporations, which Smith would probably have found abhorrent to the extent that they stifled competition. Nor did Smith foresee that his so-called "invisible hand" might indeed be totally invisible, leading to societies characterized by private wealth and public poverty (to use John Kenneth Galbraith's description of the United States in *The Affluent Society*).

The Politics of Comparative Advantage, Or, Anglo-Saxon Ideology Applied

By the 1830s the Industrial Revolution had started to disrupt the comfortable mercantilism of the landed gentry in Great Britain, who found themselves at odds with the emerging industrialists. Economist David Ricardo, representing an industrial constituency in Parliament, proposed the theory of *comparative advantage* as a rationale for opposing the "Corn Law." The Corn Law was designed to protect British grain from cheaper continental competitors—particularly imports from France. The industrialists wanted to keep down food prices so that they could keep wages low in England. Ricardo argued that differences between production costs on soil of maximum fertility and those on less fertile soil give rise to a differential income in favor of the owners of the more fertile soil. He pointed out that according to the theory of comparative advantage, even if England had an absolute advantage in producing both woolen products and wine compared to Portugal, for example, each nation would benefit more if England specialized in producing woolen goods, in which the English were particularly efficient, and if Portugal specialized in producing wine, at which the Portuguese were comparatively more efficient than in making woolen products, and if both nations traded. The key was that the less efficient country, Portugal, was not equally less efficient in producing both wine and woolen products. The *cost ratio* (or opportunity costs) of producing the two products within the *same* country compared to the cost ratio in the second country is the decisive factor in determining whether or not a comparative advantage exists. The phrase *terms of trade*, in turn, refers to the exact exchange rate at a particular historical moment of British woolen products in terms of Portugese wine, or vice versa.

For Ricardo, as pointed out in the first chapter of his *Principles of Political Economy* (1817), the value of a commodity depends on the relative quantity of labor necessary for its production—the labor theory of value (which most modern economists, including many Marxists who favored it, have deserted as inadequate).[4] But, on the other hand, the terms-of-trade concept growing out of the theory of comparative advantage is critical for explaining the widening gap between the rich industrial nations and the poor agricultural countries in the nineteenth and twentieth centuries.

Perhaps the most persuasive explanation for the occurrence of the Industrial Revolution in Great Britain as opposed to any other country is that Great Britain was the country with the highest agricultural productivity at the end of the eighteenth century. As Nobel economist W. Arthur Lewis has shown, the Industrial Revolution did not create an industrial sector where none had been before, but transformed an existing industrial sector by introducing new ways to make the same old things. Thus, according to Lewis, the principal cause of poverty in the developing countries and of their poor factoral terms of trade is that about half of their labor force produces food at very low productivity levels, limiting the domestic market for manufactures and services, keeping the propensity to import too high, reducing taxable capacity and savings, and bringing forth goods and services for export on unfavorable terms.[5] Even by the middle of the nineteenth century Britain was the only country in the world where the agricultural population had fallen below 50 percent of the labor force, signifying a very slow industrial learning process even among developed countries. Throughout the world, landed classes well understood the benefits of cheap imports whereas the advantages of displacing their own power with that of emerging new industrial classes were more mysterious. Resistance to industrial change was for the landed classes a rational polit- ico-economic form of behavior.

In addition to the resistance to industrialization from the top, another reason for the slow impact of the Industrial Revolution upon the volume of world trade was that the leading industrial countries—Britain, the United States, France, and Germany—were almost self-sufficient. Except for wool, these core countries had the raw materials they required for their industrial- ization—coal, iron ore, cotton, and wheat (for food). (So much for the theory that the Industrial Revolution depended upon raw materials from the Third World.) In short, the mercantilist era had provided these core developed countries with the maintenance base (typified by agricultural efficiency and relative self-sufficiency) that served as the take-off platform for their industrial development. National trade patterns are shaped by relative self-sufficiency, the stage of agricultural development, and indus- trial capacity. These factors, in turn, determine the *absorptive capacity* of the nation—the extent to which a nation *can* absorb the products of another nation (either because of its own satiation in such products at home or because of a backward stage of development that limits the domestic market for industrial or technological products).

The spread of the Industrial Revolution and the resultant increase in the volume of world trade also depended, of course, upon the financing and developing of railroads and lines of communication. As these increased so did the volume of trade in the nineteenth century. London served as the chief source of financing for these "trade tracks" in North America as well as in Europe—part of the package of "invisible services" that made up for the British balance-of-payments deficit and kept British hegemony afloat.

The Heckscher-Ohlin-Samuelson (HOS) Theorem

While the industrialization and trade patterns of the nineteenth century clearly divided the world into the developing agricultural states and the industrializing developed nations, it remained for economists in the twentieth century to refine Ricardo's theory of comparative advantage to try to explain emerging trade patterns within the context of classical economic liberalism. In 1919 Swedish economist Eli F. Heckscher argued that international trade altered factor prices (that is, the prices for land, labor, and capital) and therefore redistributed income within a country. Heckscher's student, Bertil Ohlin, went further in his 1924 thesis *Handelns Teori* (rewritten as *Interregional and International Trade*—the book which won Ohlin the 1977 Nobel Prize in economics). Ohlin argued that certain countries were disproportionately favored with certain factors that led them to produce those commodities that were most to their advantage. Countries with lots of land produce lots of wheat, for example, or those with a great supply of labor might produce a great number of machines. Put another way, capital-abundant nations hold the comparative advantage when producing capital-intensive products for international trade, whereas labor-abundant countries hold export competitiveness in labor-intensive products. Countries, in short, should capitalize upon those factors in which they had a particular abundance in order to produce specialized products with a comparative advantage in world trade. American economist Paul Samuelson later extended the work of Heckscher and Ohlin to describe the conditions necessary for a full equalization of factor prices in international trade, which would presumably eliminate the need for migration from over-populated to underpopulated countries.[6]

In sum, the classical theory of free trade assumes that national living standards are raised through the international specialization of production and international trade—even in a country rich in natural resources like the United States. From this viewpoint, *absolute advantage* refers to a situation when one country can produce an item better and more cheaply than another: coal production in the United States or sugar production in Puerto Rico, for example. *Comparative advantage* is the principle that answers the following question: Supposing that a nation could produce everything more cheaply than any other nation, why should it buy anything from abroad? The answer is that the nation stands to benefit by specializing in those products in which its advantage is the greatest. David Ricardo illustrated the principle of comparative advantage with a classical example:

> Two men can both make shoes and hats, and one is superior to the other in both employments; but in making hats he can only exceed his competitor by one-fifth, or 20%, and in making shoes he can excel him by one-third or 33-1/3%. Will it not be for the interest of both that the superior man should employ himself exclusively in making shoes, and the inferior man in making hats?[7]

To take another example, Babe Ruth began his career in baseball as a pitcher and was an excellent one. But he was even a greater hitter. Knowing that pitchers cannot play in every game, he gave up pitching to specialize in his greater comparative advantage in batting. Thus, it is the *ratio* between domestic advantages that counts.

If economic growth is the main value priority of a society, comparative advantage is a fairly persuasive theory. But how, exactly, did this "Anglo-Saxon ideology" come to be institutionalized in the world political economy?

GATT

The General Agreement on Tariffs and Trade (GATT) is a modified organizational embodiment of the classical Ricardian theory of comparative advantage (and its reformulation in the Hecksher-Ohlin-Samuelson theory), which makes adjustments in principle for domestic stability.* GATT is a voluntary commercial treaty that came to represent the third pillar of U.S.-British hegemony after World War II—the other two being the International Monetary Fund and the World Bank (or IBRD). This multinational organization monitors 90 percent of world merchandise trade and has served to stimulate industrial countries to reduce their tariffs more than 40 percent to an average of less than 5 percent since its founding.[8]

The origins of GATT must be traced back to the Stock Exchange crash of 1929 and the ensuing Great Depression. While nearly 45 percent of the world's production of manufactures was concentrated in the United States in 1929, and U.S. exports made up 20 percent of world exports, exports represented only 6 percent of the U.S. gross national product. The relative self-sufficiency of the American economy, backed by its unique natural resource base, encouraged Congress to enact the Smoot-Hawley Tariff Act of 1930, expanding the protection of the domestic market to cover an additional 900 items. This legislation set off a chain reaction of import restrictions in other countries, leading to a 40 percent decline in the volume of world trade in manufactures by 1933.[9] *protectionism reduces world trade*

Convinced that world peace depended upon the reduction of trade restrictions rather than upon their increase, U.S. Secretary of State Cordell Hull lobbied Congress to amend the Smoot Hawley Act of 1930, resulting in the passage of the Reciprocal Trade Agreements Act of 1934. Thus, the President was empowered for three years to initiate trade agreements based upon the reciprocal reductions of tariffs. This principle became known as "most favored nation" (MFN) treatment and led to reciprocal agreements with twenty-nine countries before World War II—agreements with little overall impact on tariffs but with value as precedents for GATT rules.

The trade surplus of the United States with the rest of the world at the end of World War II made reciprocity a convenient policy for the objective of establishing U.S. hegemony. While John Maynard Keynes argued before Bretton Woods for an International Clearing Union in which countries in surplus would disproportionately increase imports to ease the burden of those in deficit, the American position ultimately adopted, which became the trade plank of *pax Americana,* was that strict reciprocity should be the basis for the GATT treaty with an American benefit in exports to other countries for each concession on reducing U.S. import

---

*See Charles Lipson, "The Transformation of Trade: The Sources and Effects of Regime Change," *International Organization* 36, No. 2, (Spring 1982): 417–55, where Lipson goes so far as to claim that "The GATT regime does not contemplate a world in which commercial policies are based on the austere pursuit of comparative advantage" (p. 424). The doctrine of classical liberalism, in short, has been modified by multilateral GATT negotiations that take into account the need for political stability and domestic economic adjustment to tariff cuts on the part of participating states—particularly in the case of mature, basic industries (i.e., steel, textiles, shoes, and autos).

restrictions, regardless of the significant advantages of the United States at the starting line. This principle contrasted with unilateral trade reductions made by the British under the *pax Britannica*.[10]

The development of trade agreements or rules is particularly subject to domestic political pressures in the United States, for the President needs congressional approval for any trade accord. While international monetary and financial issues tend to be left in the hands of the elite (that is, central bankers, finance ministers, and exchange rate experts), trade issues are more broadly politicized and democratic, involving the livelihoods and pressure groups of the butcher, the baker, and the computer-maker. It is but a slight exaggeration to say that the world trading system that emerged after World War II was a product of the constitutional balance of power between the executive and legislative branches of the U.S. governmental system. Congress, not the President, is granted the constitutional power to levy tariffs and regulate foreign commerce.

The executive branch at the close of World War II was dominated by Cordell Hull's liberal vision and the willingness of American elites to use the economic surplus and security monopoly of the United States to establish a postwar commercial order based upon free trade. This vision was articulated in the Havana Charter, the set of provisions to create an International Trade Organization (ITO), which was to be the trade equivalent of the IMF in the field of international monetary management.

The vision of the ITO was based upon an Anglo-American consensus as World War II drew to a close: Tariff reductions and the free flow of trade were essential to maintain high levels of domestic employment and income, quantitative restrictions on trade must be eliminated, and an automatic tariff-reducing formula should be found to assure "substantial" tariff reductions and the "elimination" of discriminatory treatment.[11] In 1945 the United States proposed a plan based on these principles for a multilateral commercial convention, providing for the ITO to oversee the trade system. However, the United States and Great Britain were not able to dominate in the international trade negotiations as easily as they had been able to in setting up the monetary system. European countries demanded safeguards for balance-of-payments problems, and even Britain insisted on maintaining its Imperial Preference System. The developing countries pressed for attention to economic development issues. Although the executive branch under both the Roosevelt and Truman administrations provided strong U.S. leadership for the ITO proposal, congressional opposition proved to be stronger: Protectionists opposed the arrangement for being too liberal, and liberals were against it for remaining too protectionist. In 1950 the Truman administration was forced to withdraw the proposal before it faced certain defeat in Congress. Without U.S. support the ITO was dead. *imp.*

When the ITO failed to come into being, GATT took over its international trade function by default even though GATT was designed as a

maybe reason for collapse

commercial treaty between contracting parties rather than as an international organization that states join (such as the IMF). Negotiated by twenty-three countries in 1947, the General Agreement on Tariffs and Trade came into force in 1948 with a minimum of institutional arrangements. About once a year the Session of Contracting Parties is held, where decisions are generally taken by consensus rather than by vote. When voting does take place, each contracting party (or member country) has one vote—in contrast with the weighted voting system of the IMF. For most decisions a simple majority vote suffices. But for "waivers" or authorization to depart from specific contractual obligations a two-thirds vote of more than half the member countries is required (to approve an import surcharge, for example). Amendments to the key principles of GATT (expressed in Part I and Articles XIX and XXX) can only be made with unanimous agreement.

The first principle of GATT is that of *most favored nation* (MFN) treatment—the clause in Part I committing all parties to conduct trade on the basis of nondiscrimination. Accordingly, all parties are bound to grant treatment to each other as favorable as they give to any other country in the application and administration of import and export duties and charges. For example, if the United States reduces a tariff on machine tools from West Germany by 10 percent, it is then obligated to reduce the tariff on machine tools from all other GATT countries by the same amount. The MFN principle creates a spill-over effect, helping to make free trade contagious. It is based upon the assumption that no country within GATT should give special trading advantages to another country or to discriminate against another: All countries are in theory put on an equal basis, sharing in the benefits of any move toward lower trade barriers. The status of MFN is the motivator aimed to move nations from bilateral alliances to a cooperative multilateral system of world trade.

The second principle of GATT is *reciprocity*. Because GATT is a commercial treaty, nothing requires countries to reduce or abolish tariffs automatically. Tariffs are negotiable: Countries reduce tariffs in exchange for reciprocal reductions from other countries or trading partners. Without such an agreement, a contracting party is not obligated to make a reduction, and without reciprocity, examples of unrequested, unilateral tariff reductions are few in twentieth-century commercial history.[12]

The third GATT principle is *nondiscrimination*. Once foreign goods cross the border into another GATT country, they are to be treated as domestic goods in terms of equal rights of competition. According to Article III such "national treatment" means that foreign goods from other GATT members are not to be subject to discriminatory measures, such as higher taxes, compared to those produced domestically. It is the principle of nondiscrimination that was violated most often in the turbulent 1970s and 1980s through "Voluntary Export Restrictions" (VERS), "Orderly Marketing Agreements" (OMAs), and other forms of discriminatory nontariff barriers (such as state subsidies and inspection regulations). State subsidies and obscure nontariff barriers are often difficult to detect, thus violating GATT's *principle of transparency:* namely, that all producers and their governments should be aware of existing trade barriers.

Finally, although the developing countries failed to achieve the inclusion of a separate chapter in the GATT treaty specifically devoted to problems of economic development (which they had sought in the Havana Charter), they did succeed in Article XVIII in addressing development needs in the context of post–World War II reconstruction. This article recognizes that special government aid may be needed to promote the establishment, development, or reconstruction of particular industries or branches of agriculture and that in "appropriate circumstances" the grant of such assistance in the form of protective measures is justified. Later, developing countries assumed that Article XVIII "reflected the predominance of the import substitution approach to economic development."[13]

As the convertibility of their currencies was restored after World War II, the major developed countries successfully used the principles of GATT to reduce quantitative restrictions on their trade. This was accomplished in the first seven rounds of multilateral trade negotiations in GATT: Geneva, 1947; Annecy, 1949; Torquay, 1950–51; Geneva, 1956; Dillon Round in Geneva, 1960–62; Kennedy Round, 1964; and the Tokyo Round, which began in 1973, made possible by the 1974 Trade Act. The first five rounds represented renewals of the Reciprocal Trade Agreements Act of 1934, while the Kennedy Round represented the international counterpart of the Trade Expansion Act of 1962. American hegemony is thus still alive, if not well, in GATT, which initially seems to be the international extension of U.S. tariff policy.[14]

The first seven rounds of trade negotiations cut import tariffs for ninety-five countries from an average of over forty to 4 percent and served as a line of defense for governments against demands for protection from domestic interest groups.[15] As a result of the Tokyo Round alone, the weighted average (the average tariff measured against actual trade flows) on manufactured products in the world's nine major industrial markets declined from 7.0 to 4.7 percent—a 34 percent reduction in customs collection. The eighth round, or Uruguay Round of negotiations launched in 1986, sought to extend the GATT framework to parts of the service sector and to shore up the shift from bilateral alliances to multilateral systems, which GATT represents, particularly in the area of *nontariff trade barriers* (that is, quotas, customs, export subsidies, "voluntary" restraints, and domestic bureaucratic standards and rules). GATT is seen as needing shoring up by its supporters given that trade in textiles and clothing (vital to many developing countries) has been taken out of the GATT, agricultural trade has not been submitted to GATT discipline, and strong factional pressures for increased subsidies and protection against imports have risen given the slowdown in world trade and output growth since the 1960s. The salient features of the most protected products include standardized labor-intensive processes; mature, price-competitive markets, and local producers: steel, textiles, and clothing are predominant examples.

INTERPRETATIONS

While the importance of international trade for economic development is affirmed by most schools of economic thought, the degree to which such trade should be "free" or regulated by the state is perhaps the decisive issue in distinguishing between schools. An equally important subsidiary issue related to this one is the degree to which a domestic economy should attempt to maintain self-sufficiency or autonomy over other policy objectives, often implying protectionism or even temporary isolation from parts of the global trade system. Whereas democratic mass publics usually appear to be willing to leave "esoteric" issues of international money and exchange rates to elitist experts (in noncrisis situations) such is not the case with trade issues that are politicized worldwide by their dependence upon the whims of the U.S. Congress (not to mention European and Japanese laws) and which are closely tied to the survival and growth of particular economic sectors and to the unemployment rates in every country of the world.

Neoclassical Theories

The neoclassical vision flowed from Adam Smith through David Ricardo to Heckscher-Ohlin-Samuelson and the founding of GATT. The Anglo-American hegemony of ideas after World War II focused on the notion that each country should specialize in and export what it could produce more cheaply in exchange for goods and services produced comparatively more cheaply in other countries. International trade thus makes possible the division and specialization of labor on which the productivity of the capitalist global economy is based—trade being an engine of economic growth as much as investment and technological progress are. Collective learning takes place as specific nations or locales or producers discover which of the various products or services of those with advantage can be produced and exported with *most* advantage compared to the other options: Comparatively, this is where the optimal return lies, or the least "opportunity cost." The neoclassical model suggests that from a global perspective, costs will be reduced and economic growth increased in a free trade system without tariffs blocking the normal shift of production factors in the world market. Economic growth, in turn, fosters global prosperity and increases the chances of world peace (according to Cordell Hull's interpretation). GATT's embedded liberalism is skewed toward the ideology of free trade and comparative advantage despite its compromises for the sake of domestic economic adaptation and political stability among its member states.

In the language of game theory, the neoclassical perspective interprets world trade generally as a variable-sum, cooperative game (or, more precisely, a version of the "prisoners" dilemma* in which everyone will be better off if all countries decide to maximize their long-term mutual interests by reducing tariffs and conforming to the rules of reciprocity and nondiscrimination set forth by GATT). While policymakers are constantly tempted to adopt programs of short-term expediency for the sake of national interest, setting the GATT rules aside, this assures a better outcome only on the condition that everyone else (or at least almost everyone) continues to observe the rules. Otherwise, to use a metaphor, one person's advantage in standing on tiptoes in a crowd to better see the parade is canceled out as the whole crowd follows suit and stands on its tiptoes too. Infractions of the rules, in short, set precedents—or models of collective learning for others—who are also then tempted to take shortcuts and break the rules, undermining the entire trading order of intricately specialized but coordinated activity.

The thrust of the neoclassical vision of world trade is that if tariffs are dropped and the exchange of goods and services kept free among national borders, a more productive use of given resources (or "factor endowments") will result with gains in consumption, production, economies of scale, price stability, competitiveness, economic growth, and employment.[16] The GATT rules serve as a code of behavior adding predictability and cooperative incentives for the long term to the anarchy of international markets.†

Nor is the neoclassical position unaware of the need for protection—*temporarily*—in certain circumstances, such as sheltering infant industries until they are strong enough to compete internationally. The infant-industry argument goes back to John Stuart Mill (see Book V of Mill's *Principles of Political Economy*, [1848]) in which he maintains that the only case where protecting duties can be defensible is when they are imposed temporarily (particularly in a young and rising nation) in hope of "naturalizing a foreign industry" found to be suitable to the circumstances of the country. For, Mill continues, the superiority of one country over another in a sector of production often arises only from having begun it sooner, and it cannot be expected

---

*The "variable-sum game" refers in economics to a situation in which two or more players have an option that permits them to cooperate for a greater mutual payoff (or the creation of additional "economic pie") than either would gain alone in making a choice that did not permit or involve cooperation. This contrasts with the "zero-sum game" (i.e., chess or checkers) in which cooperation is not "rational" since each choice with a positive payoff for one player has exactly the same negative payoff for the other player (thus summing to zero): The focus is upon the distribution of the existing pie (protectionism?) rather than upon the creation of new pie (free-trade capitalism?). (See John von Neumann and Oscar Morgenstern, *Theory of Games and Economic Behavior*, 2nd edition. (Princeton, NJ: Princeton University Press, 1947).

†Significantly, the neoclassical vision does not dwell upon questions of distribution (i.e., gains in consumption and production *for whom?*).

that individuals, risking almost certain loss, will introduce a new manufacturing product, bearing the burden until producers have refined their processes up to par with the competition.

While the neoclassical school allows for temporary protection for certain infant industries for the sake of innovation, experimentation, or "vital
economic interests" (such as protecting the nation's ability to become agri-
culturally self-sufficient), there is an underlying assumption that all nations
are potentially equals and can be brought quickly up to the standard of
competitiveness in the world economy set by the leaders. A few short-term
concessions in a few critical sectors should patch things up for the sake of all
nations' becoming equally competent to participate in the free-for-all of the
creative destruction of world capitalism.

On the one hand, the neoclassical school advocates a form of economic
Social Darwinism for the sake of economic efficiency and technological
progress (only the strong should survive in each economic sector, forcing the
weak out of business until they find a niche in which they were meant to
succeed given their natural, factor endowments). On the other hand, this
perspective assumes that globally *everyone* will be better off if free markets
and free trade prevail everywhere. The policymakers in a country like Honduras, which sustains itself on two basic industries (bananas and rents
received from U.S. military bases), must scratch their heads in wonder as to
how the global prosperity promised by neoclassical economic theory is
supposed to trickle down to them.

Structuralism

The collective learning through tariff reductions for the sake of free
markets and world economic growth advocated by the neo-classical school
and GATT ideology was perceived to be blocked by many developing nations
because of the way they were structurally positioned in the global economy.
In the 1950s two development economists proposed interpretations of world
trade that became the basis of the "structuralist school" and reforms in the
GATT—Raúl Prebisch, executive secretary for the Economic Commission for
Latin America (ECLA), and Hans Singer.

Prebisch and Singer argued that the world economy was structured
or tilted against those countries that depended upon the production of
primary commodities for their economic survival (that is, structured
against the interests of most developing countries). Rather than an equitable system of comparative advantage in which all countries benefited
by maximizing production in those products most appropriate to their
factor endowment, the structuralists found an asymmetrical system of
trade in which the demand for manufactured and industrial goods produced by *the center,* or developed countries, was much greater than the
demand for the agricultural and basic mineral commodities in which *the*

periphery, or developing countries, specialized. Therefore, *the terms of trade* were systematically structured against the position of the developing countries and in favor of the position of the developed industrialized countries.[17] This unequal structural position between the center and dependent periphery countries resulted in a *trade gap* between them (that is, a persistent disequilibrium in the trade balance of countries relying primarily upon prime commodities). The trade imbalance, in turn, meant that the periphery countries could not earn enough through exports to cover the cost of the imports they so badly needed for their development.[18]

Initially, the structuralists believed that industrialization was the key to development for the periphery. When it became clear that the center or developed countries would continue to trade predominantly among themselves and, therefore, limit the export earnings that the developing countries could expect from the developed world, Prebisch advocated that periphery countries create their own trading system or bloc until a certain "takeoff" point of modernization was reached, perhaps eventually to result in a regional or subregional common market made up of preferential agreements for dependent countries.[19] To achieve this takeoff position, the structuralists usually advocated a *strategy of import substitution* in order to reduce developing countries' dependence upon exports from the industrialized countries: Brazil's policy of producing automobile fuel from sugar cane to cut down on oil imports is a typical example. Both the neoclassical and structuralist schools assumed that international trade was an engine of growth. But whereas the neoclassical school stressed leaving things up to the markets alone, the structuralists advocated Keynesian controls, so convinced were they that unregulated markets would not change inequities among countries anymore than this economic philosophy solved inequities within them.[20]

The structuralist position was persuasive to the managers of developing economies since export earnings accounted for about three-fourths of their foreign-exchange resources. And primary products, in turn, accounted for about three-fourths of the exports from developing countries. Not only did the value of the primary products decline relative to the value of the manufactured products that dominated the trade of the developed countries, but productivity increases in advanced industrial states put a continual upward pressure on wages and other input costs, keeping prices constant or pushing them up. However, Prebisch noted that in developing countries productivity increases do not translate into wage increases or constant prices given weak labor organizations and disguised unemployment. Rather, increases in productivity in the poor countries lead to the decline of prices—a savings passed on largely to consumers in the rich nations. Other factors put a downward pressure on the prices or demand for primary commodities as well. As income increases, the percentage spent on food declines, not to mention the percentage of primary products of the total factor inputs necessary to produce industrial goods. Furthermore, technological innovation provides synthetic substitutes at lower prices for many primary products.[21]

From the structuralist perspective, the game rules of GATT were tilted to the advantage of the multi-resource, rich developed countries and to the disadvantage of the dependent developing countries: It was, in short, a "rich man's club"! The most favored nation principle (MFN) prevented rich nations from giving poor nations preferential treatment in importing their manufactured goods for the sake of fostering their development. Reciprocity sounds good in principle as long as there is a wide enough diversity of products to have something to exchange for concessions. But if bananas is all you have, you have nothing to negotiate with: You have to protect your bananas with all your might. The American principle of strict reciprocity meant that poor countries would have to make a concession to the United States for each tariff the United States agreed to lower: Clearly the rich countries had much more room for bargaining than did the poor countries when it came to making *quid pro quo* concessions. Thus, the initial GATT regime was a subtle maintenance system of preserving the asymmetrical structures of the status quo, giving most of the payoffs to the rich industrialized countries most able to take advantage of the GATT rules. (All boats might rise with the world economic growth stimulated by global trade but the big boats would stay big and the advantages of those most highly developed at the start of the voyage would be structurally consolidated, their relative position confirmed.)[22]

The "principal supplier rule" of GATT negotiations was also seen by the structuralists to discriminate against the developing countries. Briefly, according to this rule, negotiations begin bilaterally with requests (not offers) for tariff reductions on a particular product made only by the exporter of the largest volume of that product to the market of a second country. Most developing countries were not in this position and were, therefore, not able to request reductions. Their best hope was the "splashing effect" from the MFN clause allowing them to benefit from tariff reductions between developed countries that dealt with products of concern to them. But this "splashing effect" cut two ways: It also precluded developing countries from negotiating concessions just among themselves. The multilaterization process of GATT negotiations was dominated by the strongest trading countries, taking into account the competitiveness and capacity of these countries to overflow their home markets.[23] As the Indian representative noted in regard to the original GATT rules in 1955: "Equality of treatment is equitable only among equals."[24]

A key complaint concerning GATT by developing countries viewed sympathetically by the structuralists was that agriculture, one of the largest sectors of commodities, was excluded from the GATT and was, therefore, protected. The United States had received an exceptionally broad waiver for strategic, political, and social reasons.[25] And when the Treaty of Rome creating the European Common Market came into force, the Common

Agricultural Policy of the Europeans was similarly protectionist. Later, with the expansion of these exclusions from the GATT to include textiles and footwear—products of particular importance to the developing countries— salt was added to the wound.

The acceptance of the Anglo-American hegemony of neoclassical assumptions behind the GATT was increasingly undermined when large numbers of colonies became politically independent in the 1950s and 1960s and sought economic independence as well. Provided that the colonizing power that had supervised them was a member of GATT, these nations were treated as *de facto* members and permitted to vote even though all the GATT regulations did not apply to them. In 1958 the Haberler Report by the well-known economists Gottfried Haberler, James Meade, Jan Tinbergen, and Roberto Campos (a Brazilian) provided a fulcrum for building pressures among the developing countries through its conclusion that the dilemma of the developing countries was in large part due to the trade policies of the developed countries. Committee III of the GATT was set up as a result of this report to examine the obstacles faced by developing countries in getting their exports into developed countries, but nothing concrete came of the committee's recommendations.

Still, the Haberler Report and Committee III provided information and motivation for collective learning on the part of developing countries, stimulating the formation of a collective strategy to improve their position in the asymmetrical world trade regime. A year after the Haberler Report, fifteen developing countries got together to issue a *Note on the Expansion of International Trade* within GATT, pointing out that developing countries were limited in their capacity to initiate negotiations and asked for negotiations on nontariff trade measures that discriminated against exports from developing countries.[*] In the early 1960s, some of the same fifteen nations combined with others to form a group of twenty-one, which proposed a *Programme of Action* calling for the unilateral reduction of tariffs and nontariff barriers affecting the exports from developing countries.[†] The stage was set for a major collective effort on the part of developing countries to pressure GATT for reform of existing rules and for enforcement of rules on the books of particular interest to the poorer nations.

UNCTAD

The structuralist perspective of Raúl Prebisch served as the ideological consensus behind the collective movement of developing countries to establish in 1964 the United Nations Conference on Trade and Development

---

[*]These countries included Brazil, Burma, Cambodia, Chile, Cuba, Federation of Malaya, Federation of Rhodesia and Nyasaland, Ghana, Greece, India, Indonesia, Pakistan, Peru, and Uruguay.

[†]The twenty-one included Argentina, Brazil, Burma, Cambodia, Ceylon, Cuba, Chile, Nigeria, Federation of Malaya, Ghana, Haiti, India, Indonesia, Israel, Pakistan, Peru, United Arab Republic, Tanganyika, Tunisia, Uruguay, and Yugoslavia.

(UNCTAD) as an organ of the United Nations General Assembly. If GATT was "the rich man's club," UNCTAD was "the poor nations' pressure group" designed to change the GATT rules concerning trade and development for the sake of the developing countries and for a new international economic order.[26] A pressure group is just that, having no institutional power of its own. Indeed, some quipped that UNCTAD actually stood for "Under No Condition Take Any Decisions." But this understates the influence of an organization from which the well-known "Group of 77" (developing countries in the United Nations) emerged, not to mention GATT reforms such as the Generalized System of Preferences (GSP).

UNCTAD, in effect, is a series of conferences sponsored by the United Nations, which can make proposals or suggestions but which cannot force compliance. Prebisch, a dynamic Argentinian, was appointed the first secretary-general of UNCTAD, which he wanted to use to summon developed nations unilaterally to extend preferential treatment to less developed nations for their exports of manufactures and semimanufactures. However, the motivating force behind the initial creation of UNCTAD was not so much Prebisch as it was Wladek Malinowski, who was previously associated with the United Nations. Malinowski believed that the only hope for bettering the position of the developing countries in the world trading system was if they could unify under the prestigious umbrella of the United Nations. The enthusiasm of Malinowski for this strategy, combined with the intellectual leadership of Prebisch in the context of the proliferation of developing countries because of decolonialization, resulted in UNCTAD. Collective learning emerged from the influence of these spiritual and intellectual models, not to mention the influential role of Chile, whose delegate to GATT in the early 1960s, Federico Garcia Oldini, proposed that the developing countries be granted "concessions without compensation" and challenged the principal-supplier procedure.

The environmental context in which the "learning and positioning"* by developing countries occurred was marked by a doubling in world trade from 1950 to 1960. But the leaders of developing countries noted that their share of world trade dropped from 41 percent in 1950 to 30 percent in 1960.[27] Diplomats from the East European countries and less developed nations joined forces at UNCTAD I in Geneva, which established UNCTAD as a permanent organ of the United Nations, and pressed for preferential trade agreements and special financial resources for developing countries from the advanced industrialized nations of GATT.

The founding of UNCTAD aimed to improve institutional arrangements and the machinery of the world economic order; to reduce or eliminate all barriers restricting exports from developing countries; to expand export markets for these countries; to create financial circumstances to more easily

---

*See final section of Chapter 8 on "Collective Learning."

enable developing countries to increase imports, and to seek better coordination in world trade policies. From the UNCTAD perspective, the GATT market system was structured against the developing nations from the outset, buoyed by tariff barriers, protectionist policies, and discrimination on the part of the developed countries that worked to the detriment of their poor neighbors. The northern industrial countries were not only "the center" but were self-centered. And GATT was their greenhouse.

UNCTAD II in New Delhi in 1968 continued the focus upon Third-World exports; it dealt with shipping, trade among developing countries, the food problem, and the special difficulties of the land-locked countries. UNCTAD III in Santiago, Chile, in 1972 was preoccupied with the economic implications of the Suez Canal, disarmament, and environmental policies. In the early 1970s the first concrete fruits of "Prebisch pressure" became visible: The developing countries succeeded in getting the industrialized nations to adopt a *Generalized System of Preferences* (GSP) for ten years, eliminating tariffs on manufactured and semimanufactured goods exported by the developing countries. No tariff concessions were asked for in return, significantly modifying the reciprocity principle of GATT. The purpose of GSP was to help promote the industrialization of the developing countries by stimulating their exports.

In addition, in 1974 the developing countries used the impetus of UNCTAD to push for the *Integrated Program for Commodities* (IPC) to control both price fluctuations and average prices of commodities negotiated on a case-by-case basis by exporters and importers. The IPC sought to better the terms of trade structured against national economies that depended upon the export of primary commodities for the lion's share of their exports earnings in a world of falling commodity prices. The IPC identified ten of the eighteen agricultural and mineral commodities that make up three-fourths of the primary commodity exports of developing countries, commodities that could be stockpiled, thus creating a buffer zone against price instability. And the IPC called for a $6 billion Common Fund made up of contributions from exporters and importers to help finance the buffer stocks.

UNCTAD IV at Nairobi in 1976 set target dates for the IPC, including a system that would commit to the purchasing and selling of commodities at agreed prices, another that could cover short-term balance-of payments problems, and a program to further the processing of commodities by producing countries.[28] Western countries, and particularly the United States, were wary of any automatic, universal system of price control such as that implied by the IPC, fearing they would lose flexibility and control and that such a system would result in continual inflation. The Americans preferred case-by-case, market-oriented arrangements.[29] The philosophies of both structuralism and neoclassical economic theory were clearly at loggerheads in the IPC proposal. UNCTAD IV also dealt with issues related to duty-free entry, domestic production, technological capacity, and socialist countries.

UNCTAD V in 1979 and UNCTAD VI in 1983 both dealt with the stabilization of commodity goods. UNCTAD V in Manila focused on the export earnings of the developing countries, the flow of aid, protectionism, technology transfer, the brain drain from the developing to the developed countries, and discriminatory air fares between countries. UNCTAD VI followed up with a stress upon export earnings and the effects of stable commodities but came to no concrete conclusions.

No doubt part of this diffusion of energies and disappointment in the results of UNCTAD conferences is attributable to the group system according to which UNCTAD is organized. For purposes of elections and voting, UNCTAD member states are classified into four groups: Group A: Afro-Asian states and Yugoslavia; Group B: developed market economies, or the West; Group C: Latin American states; Group D: states with a centrally planned economy, of the East European bloc. Cross-group alliances are rare except for the steady coalition of the countries of Groups A and C—the well-known "Group of 77."

Conventional wisdom holds that the UNCTAD conferences, which meet about every three years, have had but a minor impact on restructuring the world trade system to the advantage of the developing countries.[30] But this misses the point: UNCTAD is but part of a long-term process of delegitimization of Anglo-American (and particularly American) hegemony in the world economy. Such a process does not have to sharply revise GATT decisions in the short-term to succeed. UNCTAD is but one form of strategic behavior illustrating a collective learning and Third-World positioning process in the world trade system in which great numbers (seventy-seven if not the absolute majority of the United Nations state membership) may lose through diffusion in the short run only to win by creating the groundswell or momentum for a global political economy sea change in the long run.

The decline of Western hegemony in the world economy is manifest in the 1980s shift in world capitalism to the Pacific-rim countries. For example, to the extent Japanese models of trading competitiveness replace Western models, Western hegemony may be in long-term jeopardy. Could it be that UNCTAD is but the forerunner of a blueprint or a shadow cabinet for a trade regime that will replace (or diffuse) GATT in the twenty-first century?

Trade Blocs: The EEC and OPEC

The archetype model of collective behavior of which UNCTAD is such a diffuse and imperfect example is the *trade bloc*—an organized group of nations of limited membership that attempts to create a buffer zone of import, export, and protectionist strategies to maximize the collective economic benefits of its members at the expense of those outside the bloc. Given the increasing tempo of technological innovation, communication, and transnational exchanges in the "creative destruction" of the global capitalist system, it is a natural, human, and conservative impulse to band together with nearby friends to try to structure scarcity to mutual advantage and to protect one's own group from the competitive abundance of the production of others outside the group.

The ultimate examples of the trade-bloc model of collective learning and positioning, which nations have tried to mimic in various forms in the post–World War II world trade system, are the European Economic Community (EEC), or European Common Market, and the Organization of Petroleum Exporting Countries (OPEC). By limiting the size of their membership to much less than the size of GATT or UNCTAD these organizations have reaped greater proportional rewards for their members and have at times demonstrated a bargaining cohesiveness that has surprised the rest of the international community.

THE EUROPEAN ECONOMIC COMMUNITY (EEC). The European Economic Community emerged from efforts of European businessmen and politicians to put the disintegration of World War II behind them, to cooperate in key economic sectors for their mutual advantage, and to protect themselves from future American and foreign competition. Specifically, a continuing Franco-German "axis" is the engine of the European integration movement in terms of trade and industrial cooperation.[31] Konrad Adenauer, the first chancellor of the German Federal Republic, viewed political and economic integration with the French as a strategy for reducing occupation restrictions upon Germany after its loss of the war and for creating a stable basis for future economic and strategic development. In 1950 French Foreign Minister Robert Schuman proposed the "Schuman Plan" for pooling German and French coal and steel production. Steel and coal are vital strategic industries. Schuman saw the advantages of controlling the rich resources of the Ruhr in northern Germany (which had serviced the German war machine in the past), while Adenauer perceived the Schuman Plan as a vehicle whereby the Germans might ease the French occupiers out of the Ruhr through future economic cooperation. The result was the founding of the European Coal and Steel Community (ECSC) in 1952, made up of six member states: West Germany, France, Italy, the Netherlands, Belgium, and Luxembourg.

The ECSC abolished customs duties, restrictions, duel pricing systems, and transport rates for coal, coke, iron ore, steel, and scrap for all community members and set production target and investment programs. To head off the dismantling and nationalization of German industries tainted by Nazi leadership, Adenauer promised the unions major participation in the running of private companies. As a result the workers in the ECSC coal and steel industries were allowed to elect 50 percent of the supervisory boards (the policy of "co-determination") as compared to 33 percent in the rest of German industry. Moreover, the four institutions of the ECSC became the precursors of similar European Common Market (EEC) institutions: the High Authority (the EEC's Commission), the Council of Ministers (EEC's Council of Ministers), the Common Assembly (the EEC's European Parliament), and a Court of Justice (the EEC's Court of Justice).

The six original members of the ECSC founded the European Common Market, or European Economic Community (EEC), in the Treaty of Rome in 1957, led by the Franco-German dynamism and institutional framework of the ECSC. The Common Market, or EEC, succeeded in its basic objective of initially reducing all trade barriers among its members and then essentially eliminating them within twelve to fifteen years. Armed with a common customs tariff—the corollary of an internal customs union—the EEC greatly increased its external trade policy clout with its solidarity. Faced with this economic competition, in 1959 British paymaster-general Reginald Maulding led the way to create a second European bloc, the European Free Trade Association (EFTA), made up of "the Seven": Britain, Austria, Denmark, Norway, Portugal, Sweden, and Switzerland. This was the first clear example of collective learning from the EEC model for the sake of bettering the collective economic position of a group of allied countries. However, unlike the EEC, the EFTA did not aim to establish a common policy toward the outside world but merely to reduce and eventually abolish tariffs and other trade restrictions among EFTA members. Plagued by Britain's Commonwealth ties with former British colonies, EFTA was not nearly as successful as the EEC, and Britain soon applied for EEC membership.

The small Benelux countries—Belgium, the Netherlands, and Luxembourg—supported British membership in the EEC, calculating that Britain might offset the power of the Franco-German axis. The Germans also favored British entry, hoping it would end the division of Europe into competing trade blocs and knowing that Germany would stand to gain a great deal from trade with Britain and the Commonwealth. Indeed, West German trade with EFTA amounted to three times the sum of French trade with these countries. France, under the leadership of Charles de Gaulle, initially opposed British entry—which could dilute French power in the EEC and make decision making more difficult given Franco-British cultural differences (especially since England carried the baggage of the Commonwealth). De Gaulle also resented "special" British ties with the United States (that is, Anglo-Saxon hegemony). By holding out the longest against British membership, the French managed to tilt the European integration process toward the French position.

Nevertheless, in 1973 the United Kingdom, Ireland, and Denmark entered the European Common Market, following difficult negotiations. In the 1980s Greece, Spain, and Portugal followed suit, and "the Nine" became "the Twelve." By 1984, imports and exports of the Twelve (excluding trade among themselves) represented an average of 12.5 percent of their gross domestic product. This can be compared to 7.5 percent for the United States and 13.5 percent for Japan in 1984. According to GATT figures for that year, the EEC's share of world trade was 18 percent in contrast to 17 percent for the United States and 9 percent for Japan. By 1985 the developing countries absorbed 34 percent of EEC exports.[32] Some 130 countries have diplomatic relations with the EEC as such, and the EEC has observer status in the United Nations and in some of its specialized agencies. Trade between EFTA and the Twelve makes up about 21 percent of all EEC trade (a little more than EEC–U.S. trade). As of 1987, there were 322 million people living in the European Community, compared to 237 million in the United States and 275 million in the USSR. Between 1957 and 1986 trade among EEC countries increased sevenfold while EEC trade with the rest of the world tripled.

As Figure 3–1 illustrates, by 1985 the EEC was the largest trading bloc in the world in terms of exports and was barely surpassed by the United States in terms of imports. As a percentage of gross domestic product (GDP), the average external trade of the EEC in terms of both imports and exports was greater than that of either the United States or Japan.

In 1985, a second wave of EEC bloc dynamism was initiated when the European Council (made up of the heads of the twelve member states) agreed to constitute a single market by 1992. This initiative was aimed to break down national regulations within the bloc on things such as transportation, banking, copyrights, borders, industrial subsidies, professional certification and health requirements. A White Paper specified 300 areas for such deregulatory action complete with deadlines for EC* Commission proposals to deal with them. In 1986, EC members signed the Single European Act amending the Treaty of Rome by permitting decisions in most areas to be made by a qualified majority instead of unanimously (although still leaving the European Council with the most authority). In principle, the unification of the market has been based upon (1) granting of "mutual recognition" of each others regulations and standards by members, and (2) home-country control, or the right of a company to operate throughout the community if licensed in one member country.

Such pragmatic principles eliminated the need for the commission to lose energy in "harmonizing" or adopting a single European standard or in pushing for "European companies." As political scientist Stanley Hoffmann noted: "There will be instead a kind of free market of competing national standards."[33] Nor do the member nation-states seem to "lose" what the European Community "gains" in power since governments and bureaucracies remain the chief players. Still, like de Gaulle before her, British Prime Minister Margaret Thatcher remained convinced that her nation's sovereignty was at stake and resisted any nibbling away of her authority, particularly when it came to issues such as the creation of a common central bank or one European currency. But in terms of collective learning, the persuasive power of Commission President Jacques Delors on these monetary matters

---

*EC refers to "European Community"—all political, legal and economic institutions of the European Common Market (an updating of the more *economically* focused "EEC").

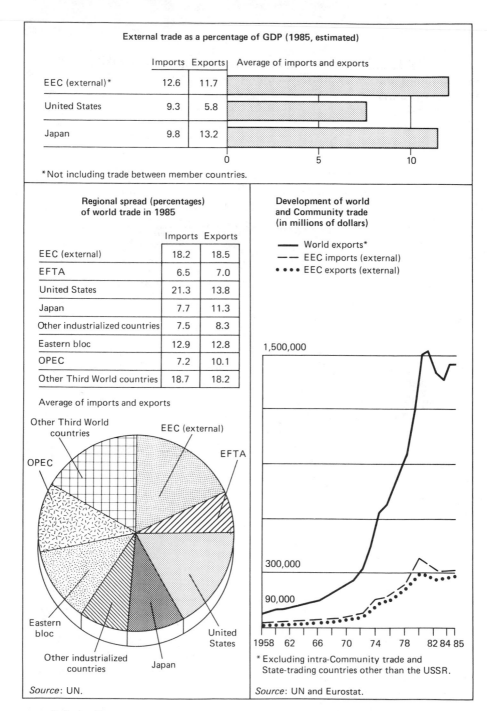

External trade as a percentage of GDP (1985, estimated)

	Imports	Exports	Average of imports and exports
EEC (external)*	12.6	11.7	
United States	9.3	5.8	
Japan	9.8	13.2	

*Not including trade between member countries.

Regional spread (percentages) of world trade in 1985

	Imports	Exports
EEC (external)	18.2	18.5
EFTA	6.5	7.0
United States	21.3	13.8
Japan	7.7	11.3
Other industrialized countries	7.5	8.3
Eastern bloc	12.9	12.8
OPEC	7.2	10.1
Other Third World countries	18.7	18.2

Average of imports and exports

Development of world and Community trade (in millions of dollars)

—— World exports*
– – – EEC imports (external)
• • • • EEC exports (external)

* Excluding intra-Community trade and State-trading countries other than the USSR.

Source: UN.

Source: UN and Eurostat.

FIGURE 3–1[34]

Source: "The European Community in the World," *European File* 16/18 (October 1986), Brussels: Commission of the European Communities, pp. 3–4.

Reprinted with permission of the publisher.

was such in the late 1980s as to suggest that monetary union might evolve on the continent with or without Britain on board.

By the end of the 1980s, the "marketing" of 1992 Europe—the world's largest market of over 320 million people and $4 trillion in purchasing power—was so successful that investments from all over the world flowed into Europe. In 1989 alone, for example, the stock markets rose 20 percent to 50 percent in France, Denmark and the Netherlands. The fall of the Berlin Wall and possibility of German unification stimulated the French to push the pace of European integration even faster, hoping to anchor West Germany quickly before her energies were distracted to the East and desiring to make the EC rather than NATO the fulcrum of European power in the Europe of the Gorbachev era. This stimulus was behind the agreement of the twelve EC members and six European Free Trade Association (EFTA) members (Austria, Finland, Iceland, Norway, Sweden, and Switzerland) to form a free-trade zone at the end of 1989. This agreement created an eighteen nation "European economic space" giving the EFTA six a special relationship with the EC, which may become the basis for future expansion to include Eastern European countries, or even the USSR, without the necessity of letting them into the EC proper. The EFTA six countries accounted for a full 25 percent of the $880 billion value of European Community trade (exports plus imports) by 1989 compared to 19 percent for the United States, 14 percent for newly industrializing countries (Argentina, Brazil, Hong Kong, Israel, Philippines, Singapore, South Africa, South Korea, Taiwan, Thailand, and Yugoslavia), 8 percent for OPEC nations, 8 percent for Japan, and 6 percent for Eastern Europe.[35]

The undisputed success of the EEC as a regional trade bloc can be contrasted with all other regional integration efforts—such as LAFTA—the Latin American Free Trade Association founded in 1960. The long history of European roots and regional trade traditions gives the EEC a tremendous "learning by doing" advantage, based on the experience of centuries. (The first ideological proposal for a federated Europe was advanced by Pierre Dubois in 1306.) Moreover, when the highly developed Western European infrastructure was destroyed by World War II, the necessity for immediate reconstruction and modernization was clear. In addition, the cold war heightened the perception of the Soviet threat as seen from the American position, thus stimulating Marshall Plan aid for the sake of Western economic and military hegemony.

In contrast, the impulse for Latin American integration in LAFTA was strongest in times of world economic crisis when the Latin Americans adopted inward-looking policies. And while LAFTA countries also benefited from "learning by doing" in diversifying their export products first in a regional context, as soon as world economic growth was resurrected national interests in global markets displaced regional bloc preoccupations, weakening LAFTA's potential bargaining position immensely.[36] The only truly successful trading bloc among developing countries is OPEC.

ORGANIZATION OF PETROLEUM EXPORTING COUNTRIES (OPEC). While OPEC is often referred to as a commodity producer cartel rather than as a trading bloc, the effect in terms of the world economy is similar: A limited group of member nations strive to cooperate to increase their internal development benefits, shifting the costs to those outside the club wherever possible through joint pricing policies. The rationale for calling OPEC a trading bloc is increased when one notes that world economic data are usually broken down into "oil-producing" versus "non-oil-producing" developing countries, reflecting the continuing importance of the OPEC bloc.

Functionally, OPEC serves like the EEC as a buffer zone against the creative destruction of turbulent change of global capitalism—an effort at cooperative management by individual states or organizations in order to cope with change to their mutual benefit. Buffer zones can be seen as arenas of opportunity for collective learning and structural positioning, which succeed through solidarity and joint traditions of learning by doing and fail to the extent solidarity and such mutually beneficial learning traditions break down.

After World War II the global economy was characterized by excess oil supply over demand, dominated by "the Seven Sisters"—the major multinational oil companies of the West: Exxon, Texaco, Mobil, Standard of California, Gulf, Shell, and British Petroleum. These seven companies controlled both production levels and prices throughout the 1950s and 1960s, more or less dictating management policies to the host developing countries whose oil provided the basic resource for the business. Given the surplus of supply over demand, oil prices were kept low, thus providing a cheap energy basis for the extraordinary economic growth rates of Western nations through the 1960s. In 1959, the Seven Sisters even went to the extreme of lowering oil prices, triggering the formation of OPEC by developing nations who defensively banded together in an initially impotent gesture in 1960 to try to hold the line on the price of the commodity upon which their economic survival seemed to depend.

OPEC was first made up of Iran, Iraq, Kuwait, Saudi Arabia, and Venezuela. Later, Indonesia, Algeria, Libya, Nigeria, Ecuador, Qatar, Abu Dhabi, Dubai, Sharjah, and Gabon joined them. Thus, one could say that OPEC was symbolically created from the threat imposed by a cartel of multinational corporations who overplayed their dominant hand to the point of making economic injustice patently blatant.

As the decade of the 1960s drew to a close, major shifts were occurring in the global oil industry. Independent oil companies—such as Occidental Petroleum—sprang up alongside the Seven Sisters, establishing their own sources of supply and diffusing the power of the major oil firms. High growth rates in the Western economies increased energy consumption to such an extent that the international oil market became tight as demand came in sight of matching supply. The dollar—the currency in which oil is priced—was devaluated, increasing the inflationary pressures already hitting the oil-producing developing countries hard. Col. Muammar el-Qaddafi, the unpredictable leader of Libya, correctly perceived an unusual bargaining opportunity in the changed world economy. He demanded a higher price from Occidental Petroleum for Libyan oil than the price asked in the Middle East, arguing that Occidental's transport costs for Libyan oil were cheaper and that the low sulfur content of Libyan crude gave it a special value to ecologically minded Western consumers with their rising environmental standards. Because Occidental Petroleum depended almost solely upon Libya as a source of supply, this independent company was eventually pressured to give into Qaddafi's demands despite counterpressures brought to bear by other oil companies.

Anticipating that Libya's success would lead to similar demands upon oil companies by other Middle Eastern states, which in turn would stimulate Qaddafi to raise Libyan prices even more—resulting in a vicious circle—the major oil companies got the oil-producing nations of the Middle East and North Africa to agree to the Teheran and Tripoli Agreements of 1971, which were designed to manage world oil price increases in a stable structure of multinational cooperation. Alas, the major multinational companies had "learned" too late.

OPEC's breakthrough, largely inspired by Qaddafi, was based upon the willingness of major OPEC members to take concrete and concerted actions in the event that negotiations should fail.[37] Libya cut back its oil output to convince oil companies to lower their prices—at a moment when Libyan oil (supplying about a quarter of Western Europe's needs) was in great demand. When Occidental Petroleum agreed to Qaddafi's demands, other companies followed suit and that set the stage for the Teheran negotiations of February 1971, largely tilted in favor of the oil-producing countries.

However, global economic and political events quickly outstripped the Teheran and Tripoli Agreements—the 1971 and 1973 dollar devaluations, the outbreak of war in the Middle East in October 1973, and the resulting oil embargo by the Arab oil-producing states against the United States, the Netherlands, and Portugal for their support of Israel. Afraid that their vital oil-supply lines could be disrupted, Western nations bid up the price of oil. OPEC took advantage of this great uncertainty in the world oil markets to quadruple the price of petroleum. Given domestic political uncertainties in the United States (of which the Arabs were no doubt well aware), the Americans were in no position to follow political scientist Robert Tucker's risky advice to invade and occupy the Saudi Arabian oil fields until oil prices came down. OPEC's world energy "revolution" was thus a *fait accompli*.

From the perspective of the developed oil-importing countries, the quadrupling of oil prices in 1973 and the subsequent doubling of oil prices in 1979 following the revolution in Iran were seen as "crises." But from the perspective of the oil-producing states these price rises were perceived as "adjustments of imbalances" long overdue. As Dr. Fahil

Al-Chalabi of Iraq, the second in command at the OPEC Secretariat in Vienna, noted in 1980, given the dollar devaluations and inflation of the 1970s, if the same quantities of oil continued to be pumped at the same low prices, the oil reserves would be depleted much sooner than anticipated, not giving oil-producing developing countries the time to use their oil revenues to invest in infrastructure development and alternative industries to complement their lopsided oil economies.

Financially, the oil-producing countries would be better off to leave their oil in the ground than to deplete their lifeblood resources at low prices in an inflationary environment when developed Western countries were anxious to stockpile all the oil they could in case their supply should be cut off. Moreover, Dr. Al-Chalabi argued that a consistently rising price of this finite fuel was in the interest of Western economies, which desired to become less dependent upon OPEC oil and needed higher oil prices to stimulate the search and development of alternative sources of energy.[38]

OPEC's 1973 and 1979 price rises had a *deflationary* rather than an inflationary impact on the world economy of the 1980s for a complex set of reasons. Most of the OPEC oil-producing nations had an absolute preference for liquidity in their investment strategies, putting their petrodollars into short-term (usually off-shore) bank accounts where they could not be easily taxed or frozen by governmental authorities. This liquidity preference meant that the OPEC states served as a transformer of real investment capital into short-term liquidity, creating a worldwide liquidity surplus. Meanwhile, in the rich developed countries, inflationary fears led to anti-inflation policies and austerity measures, resulting in tight money policies and high interest rates. Inflation was subdued at significant social costs (for example, the severe U.S. recession of 1981–82). Conservation measures in the energy field and massive oil stockpiling by governments and companies led to an oil glut in the disinflationary environment of the mid-1980s. Paradoxically, this temporary situation of oil abundance diluted OPEC's power. By 1988 OPEC found it necessary to invite non-OPEC oil producers to their negotiations in order to consolidate the petroleum trading bloc and reduce production enough to keep prices rising. But these efforts were mixed given that OPEC members did not carry out all the promises made at the negotiations (that is, producing more oil than they were supposed to), particularly given the uncertainties of the war winding down between Iran and Iraq. And if OPEC members themselves refused to abide by their own agreements, compliance by non-OPEC oil producers was also undermined.

However, during the last three years of the 1980s the demand for oil steadily grew, along with the exports of crude oil by OPEC members. Moderates, such as Saudi Arabia's Oil Minister, Hirsham Nazer, saw to it that oil prices were kept stable and relatively low in order to take away the incentive for Western countries to develop their own new sources of energy. And to prevent other OPEC members from attempting to outposition Saudi dominance in the cartel, the Saudis threatened to pump oil freely if any other member tried to reduce its 25 percent share of total OPEC output. As the country with the largest proven untapped oil reserves, Saudi Arabia would like to extend the dependence of others upon its oil for as long as possible in order to have time to modernize and create non-oil sources of wealth. With the greatest to lose in case of revolutionary change, the Saudis seek to stabilize the oil markets just as the Japanese, who have the greatest amount of liquid cash and financial clout, seek to stabilize the financial markets after any stock market crash. Those who have the best position in a particular strategic sector of the global economy naturally seek to maintain that position.

The extent to which global environmental factors can affect the bargaining power of cartels such as OPEC was illustrated by the fall of oil exports by the Soviet Union accentuated by Soviet occupation of Azerbaijan (a Soviet republic bordering Iran) in 1990. As the world's largest oil producer, Soviet policy had been to use Russian coal and nuclear power at home and export oil to earn hard currency. But the Chernobyl nuclear-reaction accident of 1986 led to Soviet shutdowns of other reactors to improve their safety, causing the Soviets to burn more oil. Labor strikes in the coal mines also stimulated this trend. And although Azerbaijan produces only about 3 percent of Soviet oil, two-thirds of the nation's oil service industry is located there. The bloody conflict between the Muslim Azerbaijani and the Christian Armenian workers reduced the production of this critical oil equipment. Consequently, both Soviet oil production and oil exports were reduced, increasing the dependence of Western nations upon OPEC for oil and making it easier for OPEC members to agree to reduce their pumping in order to raise prices.[39] And while the United States raised its share of nuclear-produced energy from 10 percent to 20 percent of domestic energy consumption during the 1980s, despite anti-nuclear protests at home, its dependence upon foreign oil increased, giving OPEC greater bargaining power in the process.

IMPLICATIONS

Trade blocs may perhaps be best understood as buffer zones in the turbulent process of creative destruction that characterizes global capitalism. Such buffer zones provide time for politico-economic adjustment for member nations inside the zone and to coordinate policies in order to maximize the advantage of members in the economic competition with nations outside the bloc. The extraordinary successes of the European Economic Community (EEC) and the Organization for Petroleum Exporting Countries (OPEC) were preconditioned by unusual sets of fortunate historical circumstances. In the case of the EEC, a long and deep educational, cultural, and technological infrastructure was not difficult to resurrect after World War II, particularly given Marshall Plan aid aimed to shore up Western Europe against the cold war threat from the Soviet Union. Moreover, the Americans and British had learned from the settlement of World War I not to break the back of Germany economically after a war, but rather to help the country reconstruct in order to find an acceptable and positive role again in the family of nations. In this sense, West Germany (and thus the EEC) certainly benefited from the Anglo-Saxon hegemony predominating in the West in the second half of the twentieth century (a French-Soviet hegemony, in contrast, would undoubtedly have been much more harsh upon the Germans).

In the case of OPEC, a producer cartel was formed based on an indispensable commodity by raw material producers who owned enough of the basic resource to be able to seize effective control over the market at a critical historical moment. After 1973, producer organizations in copper, bauxite, iron ore, bananas, and coffee were stimulated by the OPEC example, but they lacked the favorable prerequisites that assured OPEC's success. The very high levels of economic growth in the 1950s and 1960s made the developed Western countries increasingly dependent upon oil as a source of energy supply. Demand was high and oil supplies tight. Moreover, in the medium term, the inelastic price of oil favored OPEC—that is, merely increasing the oil price does not automatically lead other new producers to enter the market, given the long lead-times, investment, and development efforts required. OPEC also benefited from the reluctance of many developed Western countries to shift heavily to nuclear energy to substitute for their dependence upon oil (given political resistance stemming from the possibility of nuclear accidents like Chernobyl). And the feasibility and economics of solar power in many regions of the world limited the use of the sun as an energy source alternative to oil.

However, even to analyze the efficacy of trade blocs it is necessary to go from the global and regional level of analysis to that of domestic sources of international behavior. Such is particularly the case in exploring why certain nations and national companies have been successful in exploiting the weakened but continuing GATT trade regime. Japan, for instance, succeeded in exporting semiconductors and computers through temporary protection of the home market to permit local producers to achieve competitive, low-cost production.[40] The risks to the Japanese domestic maintenance base of such hothouse production are minimized by an export-oriented corporate culture. Significantly, the success of this Japanese strategy depends upon asymmetrical access to foreign markets— upon nationalistic positioning.

A domestic analysis of the newly industrializing countries (NICs) of Latin America and East Asia presents a more mixed picture. On the one hand, these NICs have been quick to exploit the export opportunities made possible by the Generalized System of Preferences of the GATT, using state subsidies to target high technology and other "sunrise" sectors. On the other hand, given the asymmetries of national resources among these developing countries, they are particularly vulnerable when a weakening GATT regime fails to stop discriminatory protectionism in steel, shoes, clothing, textiles, and other vital sectors.[41] To discriminate adequately between effective strategies at various phases of national development given the sectorial differentiation of the trade regime, one must look for sources of international behavior within the domestic boundaries of particular states.[42]

ENDNOTES

1. Sidney Painter, *Mediaeval Society* (Ithaca, NY: Cornell University Press, 1951), pp. 72–73.

2. See, for example, Jan Penn, *A Primer on International Trade* (New York: Vintage Books, 1967), Chapter 1.

3. See Robert L. Heilbronner, *The Worldly Philosophers* (New York: Simon and Schuster, 1986), p. 49.

4. David Ricardo, *Principles of Political Economy* (London: Everyman's Library, 1911), Chapter 1.

5. W. Arthur Lewis, *The Evolution of the International Economic Order* (Princeton, NJ: Princeton University Press, 1978).

6. See Charles P. Kindleberger, "The 1977 Nobel Prize in Economics," *Science* 198 (November 25, 1977), pp. 813–14, 860.

7. Ricardo, *Political Economy*, p. 83.

8. Arthur Dunkel, Director General of the GATT, "GATT at 40: It's More Needed Than Ever," *International Herald Tribune*, October 30, 1987, Op-Ed page.

9. W. A. Lewis, *Economic Survey 1919–1939* (London: Allen & Unwin, 1949), p. 50.

10. See F.V. Meyer, *International Trade Policy* (London: Croom Helm, 1978).

11. See Richard N. Gardner, *Sterling-Dollar Diplomacy*, 2nd ed. (New York: McGraw-Hill, 1969), pp. 101–109.

12. See Diana Tussie, *The Less Developed Countries and the World Trading System: A Challenge to the GATT* (London: Francis Pinter, 1987), p. 19, fn. 4.

13. Kenneth Dam, *The GATT: Law and International Organization* (Chicago: University of Chicago Press, 1970), p. 227.

14. See Meyer, *Trade Policy*, p. 126.

15. Arthur Dunkel, "To Put the Theory to Work: From Bilateral Alliances to Multilateral Systems," *Innovation* 11/12 (1987): 32.

16. See Richard Blackhurst, Nicolas Marian, and Jan Tumlir, *Trade Liberalization, Protectionism and Interdependence: GATT Studies in International Trade No. 5* (Geneva: General Agreement on Tariffs and Trade, 1977).

17. The first structuralist works of Raúl Prebisch: United Nations, *The Economic Development of Latin America*, E/CN. 12/89/Rev. 1, New York: U.N., 1950 (Spanish edition, 1949) and United Nations, *Economic Survey of Latin America, 1949*, E/CN.12/164/Rev. 1, New York: U.N. 1951. The seminal article of Hans W. Singer: "The Distribution of Gains between Investing and Borrowing Countries," *American Economic Review, Papers and Proceedings* II, No. 2 (1950).

18. See Tussie, *Less Developed Countries*, pp. 22–37.

19. Raúl Prebisch, "Five Stages in My Thinking on Development," Washington, DC: World Bank, 1982 (mimeographed), p. 8.

20. Tussie, *Less Developed Countries*, p. 22.

21. Prebisch's viewpoint is summarized in Albert O. Hirschman, "Ideologies of Economic Development in Latin America," *Latin American Issues* (New York: Twentieth Century Fund, 1961), pp. 14–15.

22. See John W. Evans, "The General Agreement on Tariffs and Trade," in *The Global Partnership*, edited by R. Gardner and M. Millikan (New York: Praeger, 1968), pp. 92–93.

23. See S.B. Linder, "The Significance of GATT for Underdeveloped Countries," in Proceedings of the U.N. Conference on Trade and Development (New York: UNCTAD, 1964), p. 527.

24. As cited in Tussie, *Less Developed Countries*, p. 25.

25. See Dam, *The GATT*, p. 260.

26. See Joseph S. Nye, "UNCTAD: Poor Nations' Pressure Group," in Robert Cox and Harold Jacobsen, eds., *The Anatomy of Influence: Decision Making in International Organization* (New Haven, CT: Yale University Press, 1973), pp. 334–70.

27. Michael Zammit Cutajar, *UNCTAD and the North–South Dialogue, the First Twenty Years* (Oxford: Pergamon Press, 1985), p. 13.

28. Ibid. p. 106.

29. See David H. Blake and Robert S. Walters, *The Politics of Global Economic Relations*, 2nd ed. (Englewood Cliffs, NJ: Prentice-Hall, 1983), pp. 38–39.

30. For example, Joan Spero concluded, "The UNCTAD 'victories' had led to only minor revisions in Southern dependence," Spero, *The Politics of International Economic Relations*, 3rd ed. (New York: St. Martin's Press, 1985), p. 239.

31. This Franco-German axis thesis as the basis of Common Market integration is demonstrated in "The Common Market: Organizing for Collective Bargaining Power," Chapter 6 of R. Isaak, *European Politics: Political Economy and Policy Making in Western Democracies* (New York: St. Martin's Press, 1980), pp. 151–85.

32. These statistics are from "The European Community in the World," *European File* 16/86 (October 1986), Brussels: Commission of the European Communities, pp. 3–4.

33. Stanley Hoffmann, "The European Community and 1992," *Foreign Affairs*, Fall 1989, Vol. 68, No. 4, p. 35.

34. UN and Eurostat statistics as compiled in "The External Trade of the European Community," *European File* 1/87 (January 1987), Brussels: Commission of the European Communities, p. 4.

35. European Community statistics for 1988 as cited in *The New York Times*, December 8, 1989, p. D5.

36. See Tussie, *Less Developed Countries*, Chapter 5: "The Oscillations of Regional Economic Integration in Latin America: LAFTA-LAIA," pp. 104–35.

37. Karl P. Sauvant and Hajo Hasenpflug, *The New International Economic Order: Confrontation or Cooperation between North and South?* (Boulder, CO: Westview Press, 1977), p. 369.

38. Fahil Al-Chalabi, Deputy Secretary General of OPEC, "OPEC's View of the Second Oil Crisis," paper presented at the Johns Hopkins University, School of Advanced International Studies Center, Bologna, Italy, June 2, 1980.

39. See Thane Gustafson, *Crisis Amid Plenty: The Politics of Soviet Energy under Brezhnev and Gorbachev* (Princeton: Princeton University Press, 1989), and Matthew Wald, "Azerbaijani Strife Expected to Lift Oil Prices Throughout the World," *The New York Times*, January 25, 1990, p. 1.

40. *Business Week*, June 1, 1981, p. 80.

41. See, for example, Patrick Smith, "The Fibres of Protectionism," *Far Eastern Economic Review*, May 15, 1981, pp. 74–76.

42. See Charles Lipson, "The Transformation of Trade: The Sources and Effects of Regime Change," *International Organization* 36, No. 2 (Spring 1982): 417–55.

CHAPTER FOUR

LIFE CHANCES, CLASS POSITION, AND EDUCATION

Crisis, the Greek term that has designated "choice" or "turning point" in all modern languages, now means "driver, step on the gas"...understood in this way, crisis is always good for executives and commissars, especially those scavengers who live on the side effects of yesterday's growth: educators who live on society's alienation, doctors who prosper on the work and leisure that have destroyed health, politicians who thrive on the distribution of welfare which in the first instance was financed by those assisted.

Ivan Illich, "Useful Unemployment and Its Professional Enemies"

Although collective learning is conditioned by the global and organizational environment (and particularly by whether or not it is benign or malign), its most distinctive characteristics derive from domestic or cultural sources of multinational behavior within specific nation-states. It is necessary to descend from the macro-global-level of analysis to the microlevel of life chances, class position, educational structure, stage of national development, and specific economic and investment cycles and corporate strategies in order to understand and anticipate contrasting patterns of multinational behavior in the late twentieth century.

No human being can choose where or when to be born. Each individual represents a collective throwing of dice at this starting position, a cluster of probabilities born into a particular culture, family, and historical set of circumstances. Life chances are first born, then made. Those born rich naturally try to maintain their position: They can never really understand those in poverty without experiencing poverty themselves. Thus, the human condition is inherently tragic from the outset: Individuals are arbitrarily thrown into different cultures, classes, languages, and historical conditions that are exceedingly difficult to transcend if they are to understand those born otherwise. Collective learning for the sake of the interests of a national or global community involves a lifetime of unlearning parochial habits, languages, and ways of seeing with which one is inevitably born.

By 1987 there were 5 billion people on the planet—double the population of 1950 and a billion more than in 1974. If all 5 billion stood shoulder to shoulder they could fit into Hong Kong: It is more the relative distribution of people upon the earth's surface that determines their life chances than the absolute quantity of people. Globally, the population is growing too rapidly in the wrong places, creating dense pockets of poverty and deprivation. Some scholars—all living in the rich developed countries—have argued that the world's poor are materially better off in the late twentieth century than they were in earlier times.[1] The majority of the world's population no longer earns its living from agriculture, for example.[2] But what if I as a human being believe that I am worse off in a situation where I am no longer able to live off the land as a self-sufficient farmer? The industrial process of modernization works to homogenize life chances worldwide, rendering people impotent to satisfy their own basic needs independently.[3] Global industrialization makes the masses of the world population increasingly dependent upon ever-accelerating *global* market processes—creative destruction turned on high speed.[4]

Out of a population of 5 billion people, about 100 million of them (2 percent) are estimated to be in danger of starving to death, and 700 million (14 percent) to be seriously malnourished.[5] These estimates are measures of the extent to which an overabundant global food supply is mismanaged and maldistributed: As with any domestic economy, the global economy cannot depend alone upon the "invisible hand" of surplus production automatically to spill over and satisfy public needs. From a global perspective, life chances are indeed chancy for most people if left merely to laissez-faire markets. Poor nations provide few opportunities for those with talent to develop. Of course, the argument that the world economy in no way approaches a total laissez-faire free-market system is also valid. Still, the collective management implied by the doctrine of global Keynesianism seems more hopeful to the disadvantaged of the earth than the winner-take-all premise of Adam Smith's laissez-faire capitalism. The creative destruction of global capitalism in the late twentieth century is more of a threat to those down the class scale without the resources to buffer themselves from the uncertainties of change than it is to the wealthy minority, which may well perceive such change to be more of an opportunity than a threat. Sociologists have noted that those in the underclass tend to perceive life chances merely as a matter of "luck," whereas those up the class scale have the resources and educational tools to give them the self-confidence that their life chances can, at least in part, be "managed."[6]

ORIGINS

The notion of "life chances" can be traced back at least to Aristotle's conception of the human being as a political animal inclined to live in cities or states and who often wants more than he or she needs, but is constrained by existing social and economic conditions and the competition of others. Early in the twentieth century, sociologist Max Weber used the concept of life chances to imply a competitive struggle for survival among individuals or types of people.[7] In the late twentieth century, sociologist Ralf Dahrendorf interpreted life chances as the odds of fulfilling the full range of human possibilities given the individual's social ties and options.[8] Weber's vision has a pessimistic tone of Social Darwinism, stemming no doubt in part from the social struggle for the survival of the fittest in the wake of the Industrial Revolution. Dahrendorf's more positive view of life chances, on the other hand, grew out of socioeconomic conditions created by the abnormally high economic growth rates in advanced developed countries in the 1950s and 1960s when it was sometimes assumed that affluence could be taken for granted—along with lower-level material needs. By the last decade of the twentieth century this assumption did not seem to hold except for a wealthy minority of the world's population.

Life chances, in short, is the concept that allows one to locate an individual in the class structure or stratification system of his or her society at a particular historical moment. From a materialistic point of view, *class* refers to how much you have got of what your society considers it important to get. *Status* is how much others *think* you have got or the degree of deference others give to you based on how you got the goods or go about getting them. Social class constrains or supports an individual's life chances. If you are born rich, you usually sense social support for your efforts to maximize your life chances, whereas if you are born poor, your daily experience is more apt to be one of constant constraints. Of course if the capitalist society into which you are born has a socialist revolution, you may find the rules of the game reversed, leading to social discrimination against the rich. Ever since the French Revolution one could argue that the importance of equality as a social value in Western democratic countries has become ingrained in public consciousness to such an extent that the wealthy (in northern Europe, at least) often find it more comfortable to understate their wealth and social standing in order to reduce envy and potential social and political animosity from the majority down the class scale. The French Revolution served to delegitimize the aristocratic upper classes of the *ancien régime* once and for all, and we are still experiencing its social effects.

Class position depends to no small extent upon how many people are living together on how much space under which economic conditions. Before the Industrial Revolution, life for the majority of people was more often than not as philosopher Thomas Hobbes described it—"nasty, brutish and short." The Industrial Revolution of the eighteenth century introduced technologies that were soon to lift the life standards of the masses way beyond the expectations of pessimists such as Karl Marx, who projected (wrongly) that the poor would become increasingly worse off. Indeed, despite the pockets of poverty and deprivation still remaining, by the 1970s much of the population of the United States lived as well as did the wealthy of the colonial era.[9] Such technology did little to sweeten the fate of those born in Bangladesh rather than the United States, however: In Bangladesh some 110 million people survive on one of the smaller gross national products per capita in the world, and two-thirds of the country was flooded in 1988, causing rampant medical and malnutrition problems. Numbers, space, and natural resources (or disasters) are all determinants of class position in the world economy, not to mention the level of technological and educational development.

The impact of numbers on personal welfare is notable in the differences in the sizes of generations *within* countries as well. The coming of mass production and mass consumption in industrialized countries did serve to diminish the importance of being born high or low on the class scale. But in the period between the world wars, industrial society brought on a new form of economic uncertainty in the form of periodic recessions (or depressions) in which mass unemployment could undermine an individual's life chances overnight. Fortunately, since that time unemployment insurance has been provided in most developed countries (such as the 1946 Employment Act in the United States). Nevertheless, if one is lucky enough to be born in a generation when the birthrates are low, one will find oneself to be relatively much better off than a generation in the same country born when birthrates were high. Thus, between the end of World War II and 1960, individuals born in the low-birth rate 1930s found their services in high demand given labor shortages (aggravated, of course, by losses of manpower during the war): They prospered and tended to have large families—the baby-boom generation of the 1950s, who, in turn, found the competition keen, their standard of living under financial pressure, and the temptation to limit the size of the family they intended to have an accepted social reality. Baby-bust generations tend to bring baby-boom generations into the world, and vice versa, creating an economic cycle of life chances unforeseen a century ago.[10]

Social Class and Educational Level

While it is true that the higher the social class, the higher the educational level for most people in the world, there are increasingly important economic and political implications of this correlation in an emerging high technology–high information global economy. *Nam et ipsa scientia potestas est*—"Knowledge is power," wrote Francis Bacon in 1597. Today this has been reduced to "information is power" in an age of uncertainty when people are distrustful that such a thing as objective knowledge truly exists. Hence, Kenneth Boulding's definition of knowledge as the systematic loss of information makes modern sense of Bacon's proposition in a postmodern world. The key question in terms of social class is: Which kind of information is an individual from the lower class most apt to "lose"—or, more important, to keep and cling to—compared to someone from the upper class? And what is the difference in lower-class and upper-class time horizons?

The short answer to these questions from psychologists and political sociologists is that people from lower classes tend to lose the abstract and to cling to the concrete, focusing upon the present at the expense of thoughts about the past or the future.

Low-status or working-class individuals are typically characterized as lacking an adequate frame of reference or general perspective—or of possessing a fixed, rigid one. Such a mind-set renders them open to suggestibility in terms of participation in extremist movements.[11] The lack of education of lower-class individuals means that they do not have a sophisticated worldview nor the ability to form abstractions from concrete experience, and they demonstrate an absence of imaginative flexibility. They lack a prolonged time perspective, without an historical sense of continuing tradition reaching toward the past and without a cultivated ability to make imaginative, strategic plans to shape their own future. Typically, they react immediately to the present, absorbed by its daily routine business.[12] They feel driven to adjust to the outside world rather than to cultivate their own impulses by fantasy and introspection, at least according to studies of lower-class children.[13] Working-class people are not as apt as middle-class people to see the *structure* of an object, but are characterized in their perception by an action-oriented behavior in reaction to an object's *content*.[14] American attitude surveys over time show that elites are interested in abstract values such as freedom and stability in foreign affairs, whereas the masses focus upon simple, concrete values such as improving their own income, housing, and schools.[15]

Extending the correlation between social class and educational level from the national to the international level, a direct relationship is apparent between high national economic status or economic growth and levels of primary and secondary school enrollment and national literacy. For example, the ten nations with the highest percentage of children aged between six and seventeen enrolled in primary and secondary schools in the mid-1980s—Denmark, France, New Zealand, Finland, the United States, Norway, Canada, Spain, the Netherlands and Japan—were all among the top fifty countries in the world in terms of GNP, and six of the ten with highest enrollment percentages were among the top fourteen nations in terms of GNP.[16] A comparison of country literacy rates in Europe in the mid-nineteenth century reveals a strong correlation with rates of economic development in the same countries a century later.[17] And Emmanuel Todd's 1970 data on literacy rates in various areas of civilization rank those areas highest in literacy from which a number of the most dynamic newly industrialized countries appear to be emerging in the late twentieth century: (1) Buddhist and Confucian Asia (Taiwan, China, Vietnam, and Korea): 83 percent average literacy; (2) "Indian" America (Peru, Ecuador, Bolivia, Paraguay, Mexico, Venezuela, Colombia, El Salvador, Honduras, Guatemala, Nicaragua, and Panama): 70 percent literacy; (3) "Small Vehicle" Buddhist Asia (Sri Lanka, Thailand, Burma, Laos, and Cambodia): 63 percent literacy; (4) South India (States of Kerala, Tamil Nadu, Karnataka, Orissa, Andhra Pradesh, and Maharashtra): 37 percent; (5) Central and Western Moslem world (Syria, Tunisia, Egypt, Algeria, Iraq, Morocco, Sudan, Iran, Afghanistan, Pakistan, and Bangladesh): 35 percent; and (6) Northern India (Indo-European) (Gujarat, Punjab, Uttar Pradesh, Rajasthan, Bihar, Madhya Pradesh, and West Bengal; Nepal): 26 percent.[18]

Studies done of individual countries, such as France, reveal that only half of the economy's post–World War II growth rate can be accounted for by changes in capital and labor: The other half is ascribed to "residual" factors, the most important of which is education.[19] Powerful group learning potential is enhanced in countries like China, Japan, Korea and overseas Chinese communities where the common Confucian culture represents a dynamic force in the receptivity to learning and in the collective capacity for cultural and economic development.[20] In Japan, for instance, neo-Confucian respect for knowledge and teachers extends basic learning throughout the life-cycle; information gathering becomes focused and "takes on a special campaign-like intensity when an organization recognizes an issue as preeminently important."[21]

In the 1980s, data in the United States showed a heavy correlation between high levels of education and high lifetime earnings: The average eighteen-year-old male graduating from college was projected to earn more than $250,000 compared to $170,000 for those graduating only from high school, or $120,000 for those not completing high school. Education, of course, provides only a potential power basis or springboard for socioeconomic clout. The richest Americans explain their wealth overwhelmingly in terms of entrepreneurship, to a much less extent in terms of inheritance, with financial acumen and invention being even less weighty factors.[22]

The critical question in terms of national competitiveness—the transformation of an efficient maintenance base into dynamic, export-oriented entrepreneurship—is not merely the level of education and literacy in the country, but the degree to which this education is entrepreneurial (pro-economic growth and technology-friendly) in orientation and group-consensus building in terms of social equity and cultural values. Not surprisingly, there are conflicting interpretations of this so-called efficiency-equity trade-off that can lead to such ideological polarization in a national culture that the political economy can make little headway toward either more economic growth or toward greater social fairness.

INTERPRETATIONS

Societies, and Western societies in particular, develop cultural splits or polarizations that undermine economic effectiveness and are rooted in the educational and class structure. Knowledge itself has no *edge* to it: It is infinite, overwhelming, diffusing, forgiving, and unforgiving. The individual—guided by class and culture—must give knowledge an arbitrary edge—a slant or niche to render it useful for specific purposes.

The Gentleman versus the Craftsman or Tradesman

Within the industrial society—particularly in its British manifestation, which served as the model for so many countries*—the archetype of educational success is the gentleman. According to economist Thorstein Veblen in his classic *The Theory of the Leisure Class* (1899), this role model of leisure-class life was characterized by a conspicuous exemption from all useful employment. Typically the occupations chosen by "gentlemen" symbolizing this characteristic are government, war, sports, and devout observances.[23] Clearly Veblen did not have a high opinion of the ability of these occupations to contribute to a society's economy. The solution, as he saw it, was to resurrect the status of the craftsman and technician (or engineer), demoting "proper" or "useless" occupations to their appropriately low rank of contribution to productive enterprise. In the process the "invidious distinctions" created by the leisure class to shore up their status—their pecuniary trophies of material success and ownership and conspicuous consumption of unnecessary luxuries—would be shown up for the decadence they symbolized.

While Veblen was international and historically wide-ranging in his examples of decadence embodied in gentlemen of the leisure class, the decline of the British economy in the twentieth century is often attributed to the gentleman's narrow invidious distinctions, which are the soul of elitist British education.

The essence of British elitist education is marked by the values of exhibition, symbolization, self-expression, sociability, and consumption—as

---

*Another example of the worldwide influence of Anglo-Saxon ideology capped with English as the global language of business.

opposed to spectatorship, the management of things, social utility, task, and production. This being-before-doing culture of sociability and polite behavior looks down upon entrepreneurship and mere money-making. The gentleman looks down on the mere tradesman, and in the process the basis of the British economy is slowly undermined as the hard-working producers are discriminated against socially.[24] This class-based snobbism is epitomized by a story told by British journalist Claude Cockburn about his father, who had a first-class upbringing, following World War II. "A friend said there was a position available as chief of an interallied financial mission to oversee the finances of Hungary. My father replied that he knew almost nothing about Hungary and absolutely nothing about finance. Would this not be a disadvantage? The friend said that this missed the point: They had a man doing this job who knew all about Hungary and a lot about finance, but he had been seen picking his teeth with a tram-ticket in the lounge at the Hungaria Hotel and was regarded as socially impossible. My father said that if such were the situation he would be prepared to take over the job."[25]

The British model of elitist education has had more than its share of influence as elites in the developing countries have sent their children to Oxford and Cambridge to study and "ape the British gentleman" before coming home to manage their own societies. By socially discriminating against pragmatic, mundane, "hands-on" models of the mind, the traditional British priorities undermined the will to self-sufficiency so important for the autonomous development of the developing countries. As British writer C.P. Snow noted, literary intellectuals are often "natural Luddites"—a reference to a band of workers in the early nineteenth century who tried to prevent the use of laborsaving machinery by destroying it and burning down factories. As Snow observed:

> Industrialisation is the only hope of the poor. I use the word "hope" in a crude prosaic sense. I have not much use for the moral sensibility of anyone who is too refined to use it so. It is all very well for us, sitting pretty, to think that material standards of living don't matter all that much. It is all very well for one, as a personal choice, to reject industrialisation—do a modern Walden, if you like, and if you go without much food, see most of your children die in infancy, despise the comforts of literacy, accept twenty years off your own life, then I respect you for the strength of your aesthetic revulsion. But I don't respect you in the slightest if, even passively, you try to impose the same choice on others who are not free to choose.[26]

The Two Cultures and Educational Consequences

The passage above is from C.P. Snow's influential 1959 Rede lectures, published as *The Two Cultures and the Scientific Revolution*. Deploring that academia was divided into two mutually incomprehensible intellectual camps—the literary intellectuals versus the scientist/technologists—Snow went on to argue that this cultural divide split societies and helped to explain why the Soviet Union was training so many more engineers than were being trained in the West. The higher status of literary intellectual studies in traditional British centers of elitist institutions of education drew many highly qualified minds away from careers in science and engineering, diminishing the technological power base of Great Britain compared to the USSR. Critics accurately noted that Snow's controversial thesis applied particularly to Anglo-Saxon cultures and was not as universal as Snow implied. Yet given the domination of the British Empire followed by American hegemony and the residual status of British and American universities as educational models, the consequences of the cultural split between the humanities and scientific technology should not be underestimated.

During the 1980s, the United States was still graduating many more lawyers and liberal arts graduates than required for existing job positions in the information-processing, technological economy, and too few electrical engineers and computer scientists for existing slots—particularly on university faculties. By the late 1970s, Japan was graduating 21,090 electrical engineers annually, compared with 14,085 for the United States, 6,649 for West Germany, and 1,749 for France.* Computers and electronics represented 4.3 percent of the gross domestic product in Japan, compared to 2.7 percent of the U.S. GDP, 2.1 percent for West Germany, and 2.3 percent for France.[27] This educational mismatch with the job market presumably signifies a lack of competitiveness in the United States compared to Japan. Perhaps the major educational debate of the late twentieth century is to what extent high-technology developments will further aggravate structural unemployment and underemployment and what the training policy implications are for the sake of international competitiveness and social well-being.

A 1983 Data Resources study noted that high-tech workers represented only 3 percent of the U.S. nonagricultural work force and were likely to rise to just 4 percent by 1993. Only about 200,000 of the 700,000 new jobs created during this period by high technologies are apt to require science and engineering preparation. Most job slots will be for machine operators, managers, and clerical personnel. And the number of new high-tech jobs generated by 1993 are apt to be less than half of the 2 million U.S. manufacturing jobs lost between 1980 and 1983. This paradox may in part be explained by the shift of the U.S. economy away from manufacturing (about 25 percent of workers employed) toward the service sector (75 percent of workers). Many information-processing jobs in the service sector may not require high-tech skills. Yet if American educational institutions aim merely to satisfy the needs of the existing low-skill job market with vocational, pragmatic curricula to

---

*There are trade-offs for democratic freedom of course: The Japanese administrative bureaucracy allows only 2 percent of applicants to pass the bar exam each year, reducing the number of lawyers compared to the United States.

boost their enrollments in the short term, the long-term needs in terms of theoretical and experimental research and development will be short-changed and the United States will pay the price in global competitiveness with the Japanese and other rivals. What is at stake here is not just a college "major" nor a professional goal portfolio but the educational *structure* of the entire society: Short-term entrepreneurship does not always result in long-term economic competitiveness nor necessarily in social respect for the work required for such competitiveness.

At the secondary, high school, and university levels, educators are deeply polarized about the extent to which curricula should be radically retooled with computers for the high-tech future. During the 1980s, for example, at Vassar College in Poughkeepsie, New York, the debate turned on whether computer facilities should be expanded to attract more students in a declining market, or whether limited resources should rather be used for other objectives—such as the hiring of new faculty. At the same time a nationwide debate raged in West Germany as to whether it is desirable for every student to learn how to use computers at school. While computer science was first introduced in 1972 in German high schools, there is controversy about "computer illiterates" who may have mastered reading, writing, and arithmetic but not this fourth "basic" skill. In the West German educational system, the computer market pressure (and opportunities) are apt to be enormous in the 1990s. And there is a shortage of trained teachers as well as computers—a situation that exists not only in the United States but in all other countries of the world. Student frustration with the existing educational system in West Germany extended to the point that the share of *Abitur* (the high school passport to the almost totally subsidized university system) graduates planning to go to the university dropped from 90 percent in 1972 to 62 percent in 1983 according to the German Federal Bureau of Statistics. Instead, by 1984 nearly a fourth of the *Abitur* graduates opted for job-training programs in an apprenticeship system that brings the workers in Germany to the highest technological level in the world.

With one of the highest percentages worldwide of high school graduates going on to study at the university level, the United States inadvertently declasses the value of high school education and those in American society who perform low-skill jobs not requiring academic qualifications. Not surprisingly, high school is thus seen as a mere transition to a higher-level education and is often not taken seriously. What is worse, those individuals (with or without high school degrees) desperately needed to perform blue-collar and low-skill white-collar jobs do not receive sufficient respect in American society, making their job functions socially unattractive. This class discrimination effect exists also in West Germany, but not nearly to the extreme that it does in the United States, largely because of the apprenticeship system that receives high respect from most people in German society. Ranging from glass-blowing to high-tech robotics to training to become a bank teller, the apprenticeship system in West Germany permits students of about 16 to divide their time for 2–3 years between on-the-job training and theoretical studies (regulated by the state but paid for by firms including training salaries for students).* The *structure* of the German society allows respect for blue-collar and low-skill white-collar workers and for those who have no university education—the majority. The system structures everyone "in" and almost no one "out" in terms of social respect. One senses this in meeting people socially where it may be months or years before one person finds out what another does for a living, whereas in the United States one usually finds out within ten minutes. Social respect, in short, is accorded to the *human being per se* first and to his or her status in a job hierarchy only in retrospect. While the West Germans have a well-articulated social class structure, basic social politeness calls for understatement concerning one's job status and for sensitivity in asking what could be embarrassing questions of another in terms of how he or she earns a living. Politeness implies that social solidarity or equal human dignity overshadows social competitiveness or divisive class discrimination—at least formally. And social consensus is indispensable for an efficient national maintenance base that provides a reliable take-off platform for effective global export-oriented entrepreneurship.

Equality and Efficiency?: The Swedish Model

The commonplace Western assumption is that an inverse relationship necessarily exists between equality or solidarity and efficiency or economic competitiveness. According to this premise, the Western society with the highest taxes and greatest percent of government spending compared to gross domestic product (that is, welfare spending for the sake of solidarity) should not be an efficient or economically competitive society. But, in fact, this society—Sweden—is remarkably efficient and competitive given its unquestionably expensive welfare system.

The Swedish model assumes that whether equality is compatible with efficiency or not is a question of organization. If the society is overwhelmingly committed to full employment, equality, and democracy as basic values, *work* can be used as a proxy for efficiency instead of profit or money.

---

*By 1990, these dual German training programs had been "exported" to sixteen other countries including a two-year applied international banking studies program in New York City sponsored by eight German and Swiss banks for local American B.A. students. This program involves twenty months of practical training and four months of classroom instruction as well as three and one-half hours per week of economic German language (and pays $20,000 the first year and $22,000 the second year to the student, as well as providing a 3–6 month stay in a European bank and a job to follow). For the origins, see Stephen F. Hamilton, "Apprenticeship as a Tradition to Adulthood in West Germany," *American Journal of Education*, Vol. 95, No. 2, February 1987.

In other words, if efficiency is defined as the optimal use of resources, a maximum amount of work performed in a competitive market economy approximates an efficient situation (that is, a situation when the benefit or value of production cannot increase anymore).[28] Sweden's commitment to full employment is demonstrated in an unemployment rate of less than 2 percent in the late 1980s—a period in which most Western economies had an unemployment rate six to eight times higher. In a country characterized by a strong labor and Social Democratic movement (typical, by the way, of all the Scandinavian countries), the apparently dispassionate Swedes seem to have a passion for work, which they believe is vital for individual welfare. Work brings self-esteem, a sense of a significant social role, a means to create social prosperity and self-respect. The work ethic in Sweden appears to be almost universal, transcending the motive for profit maximization and permitting the society to limit the income gaps between people (that is, equality for the sake of solidarity).

In Sweden, the life chances of all citizens are given higher priority than extraordinary salaries for competent superstars. Sweden has the highest labor force participation rate among Western industrialized countries—82 percent (compared with 76 percent in the United States, 73 percent in Great Britain, 65 percent in France and 64 percent in West Germany).[29] This high participation rate may partly be a result of more than 80 percent of Swedish blue-collar workers belonging to unions, and even more telling—70 percent of white-collar workers. The assumption of the Swedish unions is that even a small amount of unemployment signifies great losses in potential production and wealth, thus undermining the welfare state as it is forced to distribute money for unproductive unemployment benefits.

The inequality of family income is lower in Sweden than in other industrialized countries. In order of least dispersion, family income spread is as follows: Sweden, Norway, United Kingdom, Canada, West Germany, and the United States (with the most market-oriented wage structures having the greatest dispersion). The Scandinavian welfare system is universal, giving all children (not only the poor) an equal right to good, free education and all people (not only the poor) access to free medical care—the best available. The aim is to restructure society toward becoming a classless society by organizing the public sector for everyone: the most needy stages of the life cycle—those of children, families, and the aged—are supported, while the most prosperous phases—those of the young adult and middle-aged—are tapped for progressively greater contributions.

But what does all of this cost?

Lots! The Swedes hold a world record in terms of public expenditure as a percent of GDP—65 percent. And the volume of Sweden's GDP increased 35 percent between 1970 and 1986, compared to an average of 47 percent for European OECD countries and 59 percent for all OECD (developed) countries. During the 1980s, inflation in Sweden was higher than the overall

OECD average and higher than in European OECD countries (averaging 9 percent compared to 3.5 percent in West Germany, one of Sweden's most important competitors). And tax rates in Sweden are also among the highest in the world. The average full professor earns $32,000 in gross income and $17,000 net income after tax, for example. But given Sweden's generous welfare system, the professor has more disposable income than this indicates and does not need as much income as a professor in a country with a greater market orientation such as the United States.[30]

What is striking in the Swedish equation is that despite the high costs in taxes and government spending, the Swedish economy remains competitive, the unions remain responsible, and the system delivers a GDP per capita that is higher than that of West Germany, Denmark, Finland, France, the Netherlands, Belgium, and the United Kingdom (and is just behind Japan, Norway, and the United States)—all with close to full employment! Even unemployment among Swedish youth was down to 6 percent in the 1980s—substantially below the corresponding figure for the OECD countries as a whole. So while Sweden may not deliver the highest abstract growth rates in the world and spreads taxes as thick as peanut butter, hardly anyone is out of a job, education is free, health and pension benefits are among the best in the world, the average wealth level is significant, and the companies are heavy with liquidity. During the 1980s, the Swedish stock market outperformed that of almost all other industrial countries.

This stable, work-oriented welfare state forms the basis of an unusual program for the handicapped as well. In 1980 the Swedish government centralized employment for the handicapped under the Samhall Group—an amalgamation of all sheltered workshops and industrial relief work facilities in the country owned by the government. Based on the principle that meaningful work is more important than meaningful products, twenty hours of work are demanded per week in this group of twenty-four companies made up of 350 factories. But no one is fired for absenteeism or low productivity. Of the 34,000 workers in the Samhall Group, 29,000 are handicapped. The centralization provided more equality for the handicapped all over the country, more equal competitiveness, and a more equal cost structure, lowering the support necessary from society. Beginning with a 70 percent level of government support in 1980, by 1988 the Samhall Group had lowered the subsidy level to 50 percent, making up more than a half billion dollars in savings for the government. The Samhall Group has become the biggest producer of Swedish furniture and a large producer of textiles, with 20 percent of their products exported. The 1980 centralization resulted in 7,000 more people obtaining jobs by 1988 at less expense per employee (despite a 12 percent rate of employees leaving the group each year). Thus, a universal commitment to full employment and equality of opportunity in Swedish society provides a framework for self-respect and economic competitiveness for even the most disadvantaged groups in the population.[31] The Swedish case demonstrates that equality and efficiency need not be mutually exclusive: Indeed, the former may ultimately be a prerequisite to the latter in a society with a social conscience.* The economic and government crisis of 1990 can be viewed as a temporary structural adjustment to lower welfare costs that had too long been taken for granted in a more competitive global economy.

Collective Learning as Unlearning in Kenya

Equality versus efficiency is not the only polarity that must somehow be brought into synthesis in the process of collective learning. "Work smarts" versus "school smarts" is another such split to be overcome, particularly in developing countries like Kenya, which is undergoing a rapid process of modernization. In the case of Kokwet, a rural farming community in Kenya, the natives found themselves having to unlearn traditional models of child-rearing, and educational development focused upon training children to work in the home economy at a tender age for the sake of adapting to compulsory schooling introduced with the modernization process. Whether the loss of traditional cultural values is worth the sacrifice for the sake of Western modernization goals is an open question.

Given the differences in physical settings, Kokwet babies sleep less than their American counterparts: Americans have more rooms and Kokwet children sleep with their mothers, not in separate places. By the time the Kokwet child is seven years old, half of its time is spent in work activities in the household economy—processing food, cooking, tending the fire, taking care of animals and siblings. In contrast to the emphasis upon play in the development of the middle-class Western child, work is considered the main task of the traditional Kokwet childhood.[32] Language development for the natives of Kokwet is minimal, stressing commands and socialization for obedience and responsibility in contrast to the focus upon expressive verbal individuality in the American culture.[33] A traditional concept, *ng'om*, translated as intelligence, implied responsibility to group obligations. But after compulsory schooling was introduced, which meant that work time had to be sacrificed to homework and test preparation, this concept had to be "unlearned" or differentiated into *ng'om en ga* ("intelligent at home") and *nq'om en sukul* ("intelligent at school"). Moreover, these two kinds of "intelligence" are generally agreed to be uncorrelated.[34] Whether such language differentiation, which is absolutely necessary for modernization toward the Western industrial model, makes the individual human being "more whole" than the old traditional model (or a better citizen, for that matter) is clearly a question worth pondering.

---

*Of course if all equality risks are "hedged" this can lead to bureaucratic stalemate, motivational malaise, and social instability. For a more critical view of Sweden, see Hugh Heclo and Henrik Madsen, *Policy and Politics in Sweden* (Philadelphia: Temple University Press, 1987).

IMPLICATIONS

Each society has its relevant fictions or utopias, to use the terms of German sociologist Karl Mannheim, which guide its educational system, structure its class system, and condition the life chances of its citizens.[35] In Sweden, equality through full employment is the predominant vision. In the United States, individual freedom through various checks and balances of prevailing governmental powers is the ideology. The market dominates the United States, and extreme disparities of income mark its socioeconomic structure. The state is the largest actor in the Swedish system, and organizations within it usually tend to work to lower disparities of income as much as they can for the sake of equality, while still maintaining competitiveness.

Game theorist Anatole Rapoport did a comparative study of values in the United States and in Denmark (which is similar to Sweden in its tilt toward equality) using the famous "Prisoners' Dilemma" as a tool. The Prisoners' Dilemma gives two people, who cannot communicate, the option of maximizing their own interest at the heavy expense of the other person or the choice of settling for a more moderate payoff, which would be better for both people and maintain the basis for long-term cooperation. Two-thirds of the American students in Rapoport's experiment opted for maximizing their own interests (the tilt toward freedom whatever the social costs), whereas the Danes overwhelmingly selected the more moderate reward for the sake of cooperation (respecting equality despite the individual cost to themselves). Value frameworks or structures are passed on as if by osmosis in each society, predisposing individuals to behave in one way rather than another and to strive for socially acceptable goals. In Kokwet, Kenya, as we have seen, "work intelligence" shifted to "school intelligence." Collective learning begins with individual adaptation to specific social norms, whether or not these norms are the best for the society as a whole or are helpful in national adaptation for the sake of competitiveness in the world economy.

As a society is industrialized, knowledge is organized for the sake of certain human interests over others.[36] In Great Britain, the values of the gentlemen have traditionally been ranked above those of the craftsman or merchant, and the most prestigious universities have cultivated a certain disdain for the mere man of affairs. This ideology was a contributing factor in the decline of the British economy in the late twentieth century.

In contrast, the strong work ethic in Sweden has helped to keep that country competitive economically despite its heavy government spending and tax burdens. The freedom *not* to work was savored in old England; the equal opportunity *to* work is the guiding motivation of the Swedish economy. And a shift away from work responsibility in the household characterizes modernization in rural Kenya.

The Collective Work Ethic and a Sense of Calling

The collective work ethic seems to have waned in Great Britain and waxed in Sweden, resulting in that country's greater relative success in producing sufficient economic development to service its welfare state while maintaining its competitiveness in the world economy. This interpretation, of course, is based on German sociologist Max Weber's *The Protestant Ethic and the Spirit of Capitalism*. In this classic work, Weber argues that the Industrial Revolution occurred first in Western Europe (and then America) not because of accident but because the asceticism of the spirit of Protestantism had prepared European society psychologically for this form of economic development. Weber derived the spirit of capitalism from the development of rationalism as a whole: Capitalism is a special form of rationalism in which the individual is dominated with acquisition and action in rational pursuit of more acquisition as the ultimate purpose in life. Idle pleasure and spontaneous enjoyment are not "rationally" part of this Protestant asceticism in which both uncontrolled consumption and spending are regarded as sinful; acquisition and profit-making become a *calling* or vocation, causing the capitalist to be a constant innovator in order to be better positioned for new acquisition and material achievement.

According to Weber, "The most important opponent with which the spirit of capitalism...has had to struggle was that type of attitude and reaction to new situations which we may designate as traditionalism."[37] Innovative action in pursuit of profits and acquisition regardless of the impact upon the status quo is the calling of the capitalist. The future-oriented, business entrepreneur is set into conflict with historical traditions or mere maintenance thinking. If a whole society is socialized and taught in this tradition, a collective capitalism can emerge based upon an ethos of "workaholics" who define collective economic growth, efficiency, and international competitiveness to be the main sources of their international pride (as in the case of post-World War II Japan). A nation sets people up for certain kinds of collective learning, which may or may not encourage the calling of "aescetic, accumulative entrepreneurship" over the callings of roles that maintain existing traditions of the past. But if certain nations become tightly integrated "hit teams" of efficiency, information-gathering and competitiveness regardless of the social consequences at home or abroad they can set the tone of international competition in the world economy, setting the standards to which other nations must adapt or else pay the price: The threat of Japanese displacement of American economic power in the late twentieth century is a case in point.

The significance of Weber's distinction between entrepreneurial capitalism based on the work ethic and the maintenance of traditions of the past in terms of economic development must be separated from Protestantism for a number of reasons. Critics have pointed out that the spirit of capitalism was not the creator of capitalism as much as the emerging class of businessmen, and that people need not be "called" to riches to devote themselves fully to their pursuit without stopping to enjoy them.[38] In fact, the capitalist spirit appears to have existed long before the Reformation, and Protestantism was more of a product of intellectual, social, and cultural changes toward a more secular, rational worldview than it was a father of this secular shift. Indeed, although the economic development of the Netherlands, England, France, and Germany, as well as other European countries, can be correlated with Protestantism, it could well be that prosperity leads to Protestantism rather than the other way around.[39]

One must avoid throwing the baby out with the bathwater, however, and realize that Weber's contribution was to stress the *psycho-cultural* bases or prerequisites involved in dynamic industrial development and to focus upon the importance of the cultural milieu in preconditioning individuals' selections of one "calling" and educational path over other possible options.

For Weber a social event was an empirical or existential occurrence *plus* the significance with which it was imbued. One must go beyond Marx and the proposition that existence precedes and determines consciousness to recognize that certain ideological, religious and value constructs precondition occupational and economic choices. One is, in other words, not just "called" *from* but "called" *to*. Certain societies are more apt to raise the status of the calling to become an electrical engineer or technician than others and these will reap collective economic benefits in the high-tech global economy of the twenty-first century. The West German apprenticeship system is a case in point. Moreover, research has demonstrated that crafts or occupations create their own states of consciousness (or what Thorstein Veblen termed "habits of mind") that are independent from other bases of knowledge such as an individual's social origins, the market position of a person's occupation, or even someone's own economic interests.[40] The logics of an individual's national milieu are becoming increasingly differentiated in the world economy. Family, class, occupation, craft habits, tax incentives, religious and ideological affiliations all can play independent roles in influencing economic behavior. To maintain national competitiveness, the state must "call" the individuals into certain fields over others, if they can, to become collectively more effective in targeted niches of the increasingly differentiated world economy. Otherwise, the mismatch between traditional educational paths and emerging economic and technological opportunities will grow worse rather than better.

In looking at the emerging needs of the world economy as a whole, Dr. Nancy J. Needham, president of the Institute for Corporate and Government Strategy, Inc., identified five technological trends related to training needs:

1. *Trends of reversal*—no longer beginning with the material and then asking what can be done with it, but beginning with a need and going back to the lab to perfect a material to address that need.
2. *Specificity*—sharpening the ability to pinpoint on an ever-more minute level.

3. *Explosion and implosion in terms of scale*—things are being done on an ever-smaller (microelectronics) *and* an ever-larger scale, thus increasing the number of projects that cannot be handled by a single company, institution, or government.

4. *Acceleration*—high tech has increased the speed at which things are done.

5. *Growing recognition of the need for cooperation*—this despite our ability to specialize and to be specific.[41]

Equality of opportunity must be combined with a collective sense of competitiveness targeted at such emerging trends as those cited above and structured into occupational niches that make sense in terms of a country's comparative advantage if a nation is to experience efficient collective learning. It may help to explore briefly the typical phases of national economic development and to identify viable strategies at each stage in order to better understand how one can differentiate educational structures for the sake of optimum life chances for the citizens of a nation in an uncertain world economy. This will be the focus of the following chapter.

ENDNOTES

1. See, for example, Raymond Vernon, "Global Interdependence in a Historical Perspective," in *Interdependence and Co-operation in Tomorrow's World* (Paris: OECD, 1987), pp. 22–35. Also, Jonathan Power, "Population: Don't Be Frightened by the Numbers," *International Herald Tribune*, April 27, 1987.

2. Karl Deutsch dwelled on this point in a lecture at the University of Mannheim, Germany, June 7, 1988.

3. See Ivan Illich, *Toward a History of Needs* (New York: Pantheon Books, 1978).

4. See Theodore Levitt, "The Globalization of Markets," *Harvard Business Review* 61, No. 3 (May–June 1983).

5. Power, "Population."

6. See, for example, Frank Parkin, *Class Inequality and Political Order: Social Stratification in Capitalist and Communist Societies* (New York: Praeger, 1975), pp. 76–77.

7. See Max Weber, *Wirtschaft und Gesellschaft* (Tübingen, 1956), p. 20.

8. Ralf Dahrendorf, *Lebenschancen* (Frankfurt: Suhrkamp, 1979), pp. 48–50.

9. Lance E. Davis et al., *American Economic Growth: An Economist's History of the United States* (New York: Harper & Row, 1972), p. 84.

10. See Richard A. Easterlin, *Birth and Fortune: The Impact of Numbers on Personal Welfare* (New York: Basic Books, 1980).

11. Hadley Cantril, *The Psychology of Social Movements* (New York: Wiley, 1941), Chapters 8 and 9, and Seymour Martin Lipset, *Political Man: The Social Bases of Politics* (New York: Doubleday-Anchor, 1963), Chapter 4.

12. Richard Hoggart, *The Uses of Literacy* (London: Chatto and Windus, 1957), pp. 158–59. For the American case, see E.D. Hirsch, *Cultural Literacy* (Boston: Houghton and Mifflin Co., 1987).

13. B.M. Spinley, *The Deprived and the Privileged* (London: Routledge & Kegan Paul, 1953), pp. 115–16. Also see W.T. Grant, "The Forgotten Half; Non College Youth in America," *Phi Delta Kappan*, Vol. 69:408–14, February 1988.

14. B. Bernstein, "Some Sociological Determinants of Perception," *The British Journal of Sociology*, 9 (1958): 160. Also see: Harry C. Triandis, *Variations in Black and White Perceptions of the Social Environment* (Urbana: University of Illinois Press, 1976); and Christine Oppong, ed., *Female and Male in West Africa* (London: George Allen and Unwin), 1983, esp. pp. 10–5 and 223–235.

15. Philip E. Converse, "The Nature of Belief Systems in Mass Publics," in *Ideology and Discontent*, edited by David E. Apter (New York: Free Press, 1964), pp. 206–61.

16. "School Enrollment Ratio, 1984," in *The World Bank Atlas 1987* (for 184 countries and territories) (Washington, DC: The World Bank, 1987), pp. 24–25.

17. C.M. Cipolla, *Literacy and Development in the West* (London: Penguin, 1969), p. 115.

18. Emmanuel Todd, *L'enfance du monde*, as cited in Jean Boissonnat, "World Economic Development: Some Observations," in *Interdependence and Co-operation in Tomorrow's World* (Paris: OECD, 1987), p. 38.

19. Boissonnat, "World Economic Development," p. 36.

20. William Theodore de Bary and John W. Chaffee, eds., *Neo-Confucian Education: The Formative Stage* (Berkeley: University of California Press, 1989).

21. Ezra A. Vogel, *Japan as Number One: Lessons for America* (New York: Harper and Row, 1979), p. 31.

22. *Forbes* (Fall 1983).

23. Thorstein Veblen, *The Theory of the Leisure Class* (New York: The New American Library, orig. 1899, 1953 Mentor ed.), p. 44.

24. See Charles Hampden-Turner, *Gentlemen and Tradesmen: The Values of Economic Catastrophe* (London: Routledge & Kegan Paul, 1983, especially Chapter 2.)

25. *The Autobiography of Claude Cockburn* (Harmondsworth, Middlesex: Penguin, 1967), pp. 37–38. Also see R. Isaak, "Great Britain: A Socialized Economy in Crisis," Chapter 4 of *European Politics: Political Economy and Policy Making in Western Democracies* (New York: St. Martin's Press, 1980), pp. 99–125.

26. C.P. Snow, *The Two Cultures* (London: Cambridge University Press, 1969), pp. 25–26.

27. James Botkin, Dan Dimancescu, and Ray Strata, *Global Stakes: The Future of High Technology in America* (Cambridge, MA: Ballinger, 1982), p. 13. Also: R. Isaak, "Mismatches Between Jobs and Education: Collective Learning Across Cultures," a paper presented at the International Studies Association meeting April 12, 1990 in Washington, D.C.

28. Anna Hedborg (Director of Swedish Association of Local Authorities), "The Swedish Model—A Happy Marriage between Efficiency and Equality," paper presented at the "Sweden: Equality and Efficiency?" Conference at Indiana University, Bloomington, September 30–October 1, 1988. This section draws heavily upon insights derived from this conference organized by Professor Tim Tilton of Indiana University.

29. Ibid., p. 4. Statistics from 1987.

30. The above statistics (except for the 65 percent public expenditure as percentage of GDP figure, which is from the OECD) are from "The Swedish Economy: Facts and Figures 1988," published by the Swedish Institute of Stockholm.

31. Based on a personal interview with President of the Samhall Group, Gerhard Larsson, on October 1, 1988, in Bloomington, Indiana.

32. Sara Harkness and Charles M. Super, "The Cultural Structuring of Children's Play in a Rural African Community," in K. Blanchard, ed., *The Many Faces of Play*. (Champaign, Il: Human Kinetics, 1986), pp. 96–103.

33. S. Harkness and C.M. Super, "Why African Children Are So Hard to Test," in L.L. Adler, ed., *Cross-Cultural Research at Issue* (New York: Academic Press, 1982), pp. 145–52.

34. Charles M. Super and Sara Harkness, "The Developmental Niche: A Conceptualization at the Interface of Child and Culture," *International Journal of Behavioral Development* (North Holland: Elsevier Science Pub.; Dec. 1986), Vol. 9, No. 4, pp. 545–69. Also see R.H. Munroe, R.L. Munroe, and B.B. Whiting, eds., *Handbook of Cross-Cultural Human Development* (New York: Garland, 1981), particularly pp. 181–270.

35. See Karl Mannheim, *Ideology and Utopia: An Introduction to the Sociology of Knowledge* (New York: Harcourt, Brace and World, Inc., 1936).

36. For an analysis of the victory of positivism in this process of development, see Jürgen Habermas, *Knowledge and Human Interests* (Boston: Beacon Press, 1972).

37. Max Weber, *The Protestant Ethic and the Spirit of Capitalism*, translated by Talcott Parsons (New York: Scribner's, 1958), pp. 58–59.

38. See H.M. Robertson, *Aspects of the Rise of Economic Individualism: A Criticism of Max Weber and His School* (London: Cambridge University Press, 1933).

39. See Kurt Samuelsson, *Religion and Economic Action*, translated from the Swedish by E. Geoffrey French, ed. by D.C. Coleman (New York: Basic Books, 1961).

40. See Joseph Bensman and Robert Lilienfeld, *Craft and Consciousness: Occupational Technique and the Development of World Images* (New York: Wiley, 1973).

41. Paper presented at the "Training for a High Technology Future" Conference of the German American Institute of Pace University, New York City, April 19, 1985. See "Quality and Competitiveness" and "Where to Target Training," in *The German American Trends Letter* II, No. 1 (Winter 1985): 1–2. in R. Isaak, *German American Trends: 1984–1989*, Published by The German American Institute, Pace University, Pleasantville, NY 10570.

CHAPTER FIVE

STATE STRATEGIES AND STAGES OF DEVELOPMENT

Let the chips fall where they may.

Anonymous

From the global perspective, the striking success stories in the world economy in the late twentieth century appear to be Japan and the newly industrializing "dragons" of Asia, namely Taiwan, South Korea, Hong Kong, and Singapore. These are tight ships in a storm of economic turbulence, which set the standards for manufacturing competitiveness in many key areas. Other looser, more democratic communities may enjoy more freedom individually at home only to find that their individualism has a high economic opportunity cost in the trade conflicts with other nations. Japan was permitted by others to rise quickly economically following World War II, using protectionism to cultivate many "infant industries" until the Japanese could compete as equals on the world market partially because it was the only newly industrializing country systematically using these strategies at the time. Had Japan and the four dragons risen simultaneously, they might well have been slowed down, if not stopped, by the key countries in the world economic community. Japan benefitted by a strategy out of sync with most other states.

The Japanese example of turning a situation of wartime defeat and dependence into one of economic competitiveness and independence shone through the world economy like a lantern in the dark. Somehow the Japanese mastered the principles of the world economy, organized themselves collectively to be effective in it by targeting their efforts, and converted weakness into strength, poverty into wealth. It was not a matter just of strategies but of structures—educational structures for setting up the most effective systems in which collective learning could take place; industrial structures of close government-business cooperation; financial structures of long-term local financing for firms; job structures of lifetime employment and commitment for that portion of the working population employed in key sectors of manufacturing competitiveness; and value structures of group solidarity and community loyalty, which encouraged short-term savings and sacrifice for the sake of long-term collective gains and security.

Theories of international political economy are usually abstract; the astonishing Japanese results are concrete. This chapter will attempt to relate the theoretical abstraction to comparative concreteness in state strategies at various phases of economic development. In the process, polarizations of Western thought—capitalism versus socialism, short-term versus long-term, homogeneity versus duality—seem to collapse.

As striking as the successes of the Japanese and Far Eastern "dragon" economies is the unraveling of industrial economies in processes of deindustrialization, deregulation, and cutbacks in welfare-state development. The linear Western assumption of progress has more often than not been turned on its head with regressive taxes replacing progressive taxes, disintegration replacing integration, illiteracy replacing literacy, economic dualisms of various sorts replacing any single homogeneous standard of national economic development in so-called developed countries. The "postindustrial" society has been shown to be a misnomer: The competitiveness of the "service economy" depends upon the efficacy of its manufacturing base much as the competitiveness of industrial development depends upon the efficiency of the agricultural sector. The deindustrialization of both Great Britain and the United States in the second half of the twentieth century demonstrates that imperial economic designs have points of diminishing returns—as the Soviet economy has demonstrated in no uncertain terms in the Eastern bloc with its desperate *perestroika* program. In 1989, *perestroika* released grass-roots democratic revolutions from below throughout Eastern Europe—from Poland and Hungary to East Germany and Rumania—making a shell of the one-party Communist state, which broke up as mass movements demanded political freedom and market-oriented reforms. But efforts of socialist states to move toward market incentives were not always one-way streets: In the late 1980s the People's Republic of China rolled back its free-market strategies after price increases outstripped wage increases and a 50 percent inflation rate and economic corruption caused disenchantment among the masses of the Chinese population. National student demonstrations for reforms were crushed with the massacre at Tiananmen Square in Beijing June 3, 1989.

Despite the discontinuities stemming from the linear, progressive sequence of development posited by Western theorists, it is useful to summarize briefly the origins of these assumptions as a point of departure. To the extent that the dynamic of the late twentieth-century world economy is capitalism, competitive strategies of "state capitalism" are vital to understand, regardless of where one happens to stand ideologically. And, as indicated in the last chapter in the case of Sweden, it is not at all clear that the supposed opposites of capitalistic efficiency and social equity cannot be brought into a successful dynamic harmony given the right preconditions for such a cooperative national consensus.

ORIGINS

Conventional Western theories of national economic development focus upon an assumption of a universal process of modernization, rationalization, secularization, and democratization. This focus is Eurocentric insofar as most of the social theorists came from the European tradition (and its American extension) and stressed the events leading up to the Industrial Revolution and its aftermath as this transformation was illustrated in the European experience. Put simply, the conventional modernization paradigm is the story of how the agrarian, feudal societies of Europe were transformed by the Industrial Revolution and the applied techniques of capitalism into modern, industrial societies of expanding markets, secular values, and institutions of democratic pluralism. The universality of this paradigm was taken for granted by Westerners—it was just a matter of time until other fortunate parts of the world would undergo European modernization, flavored with the egalitarian ideals of the French Revolution and the worldly aims of export-oriented, economic growth using the manufacturing sector as the engine and trade as the means. That everyone would be better off for this transformation was also taken for granted as the prosperity of free markets supported and stimulated the growth of democratic political institutions, thus increasing individual rights and autonomy.

Modernization and Purposive Rationality

Modernization as understood in the Western tradition is a process of disenchantment in which reason, science, and technology systematically undermine traditional belief systems, mythologies, and spontaneous ways of doing things. Knowledge itself involves a process of disenchantment: The knower tests hypotheses against empirical experience, learning what the truth is as false assumptions are displaced in the process. Western modernization, however, turns this scientific testing process into a systematic ideology of applied reason or purposive rationality.

Modernization involves a certain cooling-off process in collective learning as people learn to detach themselves from their traditional habits and opinions and to test their behaviors for efficacy in the real world. To be modern is to be cool. Science and technology reign; superstition and emotion are edited out. Armed with reason—or technology, which is but reason applied—the individual becomes more autonomous and free of traditional social bonds even as the state bureaucracy becomes more powerful and centralized in order to keep individuals from spinning out into chaos or violence against the law. But how does this process of modernization get going and take off?

In 1861 Sir Henry Maine suggested that progress entailed a shift from a "status" society to a "contract" society. An individual in a status society is accorded rights and duties on the basis of family and kinship ties, whereas a contract society relies upon contractual relationships between individuals, grounded upon territorial ties and enforced by the acceptance of a universally defined code of ethics.[1] In 1887 Ferdinand Toennies elaborated upon Maine's distinction, contrasting *Gemeinschaft* (community) with *Gesellschaft* (society). *Gemeinschaft* is characterized by human association based on affective, non-rational, emotional ties of kinship, community, and neighborly spirit. *Gesellschaft*, in contrast, is marked by neutral human relations of rational, calculating individuals whose relationships are distinguished by contractual arrangements aimed at maximizing an individual's strategic goals. Belongingness was displaced by cool, contractual exchange as a society was modernized by the Industrial Revolution.[2]

In his *De la Division du travail social* of 1893, sociologist Emile Durkheim stressed the positive advantages of modern society (which he termed "organic") in terms of its potential for individual development in contrast with the repressive and "mechanical" nature of traditional society. Rather than seeing the danger of class conflict in greater role differentiation in a modern society, Durkheim perceived greater individual opportunities and a social solidarity based upon diverse but authentic interests in contrast to the more authoritarian form of solidarity imposed by traditional societies.[3]

At least three distinct phases of modernization can be identified—the traditional, the legal-rational, and the technological. After creation, a society hardens into routines and traditions—the *traditional* phase. The traditional phase is based on affective or prerational community relationships (blood ties), diffuse role structures (jack-of-all-trades), and ascriptive notions of social and political authority (that is, deference for being the son of the king or a witch doctor). Eventually, the traditional society becomes so encumbered with routines and rites that people are obstructed from satisfying their needs—the original purpose of the society. At this point, sociologist Max Weber notes that a social crisis usually occurs: Political authority flows away from traditional roles (such as the king) to a charismatic leader who symbolizes the solution to the crisis. For Weber, the key to modernization was the shift in authority patterns from the traditional to the legal-rational, with the charismatic performing the function of transition.[4]

A *legal-rational* society is one made up of contractual community relations (work prescribed by legal contracts), specific role structures (specialization rather than jack-of-all-trades), and achievement-oriented modes of social and political authority (deference given on the basis of accomplishment rather than blood ties to the king or the witch doctor). Of course legal-rational societies retain some of their traditional aspects, for no pure legal-rational societies exist anywhere in the world. The "traditional," "legal-rational," and "charismatic" are what Max Weber called *ideal types* of authority patterns—abstract theoretical constructs that represent or typify certain kinds of social realities.

Traditional societies become modern when their cultural norms of legitimacy are undermined and overwhelmed by the forces of rationalization (and, Weber would add, bureaucratization). Social thinker Jürgen Habermas defined this Western process of rationalization as the proliferation of *subsystems of purposive-rational action.* And far from being "value-free" or neutral, Habermas stressed the ideological nature of the uses of science and technology in this process of modernization.[5] Such forces of rationalization are marked by new bureaucratic reorganizations in legal-rational societies and by the dominance of applied scientific technology in technological societies.

In *technological societies* technologically exploitable knowledge undermines both traditional cultural norms and the social cooperation made possible by the legal-rational framework. Traditions are overwhelmed by scientific techniques, monarchs are replaced by technological maintenance professionals, roles dominate personalities, conditioning steers socialization: Humans as traditionally cultured beings are overwhelmed and dominated by the so-called apolitics of scientific technique and expertise. When Habermas in the late 1960s first pointed to purposive-rational action as being destructive of existing social bonds and community ties, the counterculture student rebellion (which latched on to his work) prevented him from being taken too seriously. But considering the displacement of foreign-language requirements (the study of at least one other traditional, cultural world) with computer science "literacy" in American high schools and colleges in the 1970s and 1980s, Habermas' insights have become almost conventional wisdom. Technological societies tend not toward technological limits but toward technological satiation as an ever-greater percentage of the population clamors to get on board.

The ideological nature of purposive-rational action or the transformation into a technological society is manifest in the unwillingness to see social reality in any *other* way without identifying this alternative as "old-fashioned" or "archaic."* Technology is ideology insofar as it becomes a way of life, displacing other ways that may be more humanly satisfying.

In sum, the modernization process from the agricultural, traditional society to the industrial, legal-rational society and finally to the technological, high-information society presupposes a process of systematic rationalization and a cooling down of values—sometimes in abstract, dehumanized forms. That there is often cultural resistance to this linear assumption of economic development or "progress" is hardly surprising and may, indeed, be wholesome. There is something in human collectivities that demands a balance between the "hot" (emotional belief) and the "cool" (rationalization and industrialization). To neglect this need for balance is to invite another Iranian Revolution—a case in which a Westernized, technocratic Shah attempted to modernize his people too quickly on the Western model and was totally insensitive to the resistance on the part of the traditional segments of Iranian culture until fundamentalist leaders struck back with a vengeance from which the world still reverberates.

INTERPRETATIONS

Although the origins of the Western sequence of modernization are not difficult to sketch, the multitude of interpretations of the process of state economic development and effective strategies involves a literature so

---

*For example, some of the world's greatest poets (perhaps the least economically motivated of people) insist on writing first in long-hand rather than composing on a typewriter. Similarly, they might be expected to keep to an old typewriter rather than switch to a modern computer. Each of these technological innovations speeds up the writing process, but the poet wants to slow down the process for the sake of quality and tone; some of the best poems require as much as ten years of quiet incubation! But modern technological society pays no one to slow down; quite the contrary—even when it may be in society's best interest. The author recalls being annoyed when first arriving in Bologna, Italy, from Manhattan to discover that the mail was not picked up each day (much less several times each day as I was used to) at the Johns Hopkins University Center where I worked. For six months I lambasted this lack of efficiency, this hopeless lack of modernization as my letters sat for three days before they were taken out. By the end of my three-year stay I found that I either withdrew or changed one-third of my letters, greatly increasing their quality and efficacy. Now, back in the United States, I miss the slower pace and opportunity to retrieve my flawed work before it officially becomes "an anonymous product." Similarly, in Spain I was amazed to see a plumber use the palm of his hand in a pumping fashion to unclog a bathtub drain. Without the modern technology of a "plumber's helper" nearby I'd forgotten many of the original uses of the hand. It may be that the failures of the technological society will eventually teach us to slow down and to become more human.

immense as to make any summary or synthesis almost impossible. The best one can do, perhaps, is to highlight a few basic themes as they relate to the fundamental thesis of the book—that there are universal patterns of collective learning which go a long way toward explaining both the developed and developing nations in the world in terms of their asymmetrical position in the global economy. "Universal" here clearly transcends "Western": Japan and the four dragons have illustrated that it is more an astute blend of Western and Eastern techniques that makes for extraordinary collective competitiveness than it is the contribution of any one region or culture. "Universal" also has the scientific promise of getting beyond the idiosyncrasies of any particular culture or ideology in terms of effectively managing collective change.

Neoclassical versus Transformational Schools

Perhaps the main "civil war" between schools of thought on economic development since World War II has been the debate between the neoclassical and (roughly) transformational schools. Derived from Adam Smith, neoclassical models stress the linearity of economic growth with collective learning most effectively triggered by market mechanisms (as opposed to being imposed by state intervention). In contrast, the transformational school argues that the neoclassical argument is far too simplistic and that successful modern capitalist societies involve major restructuring of sectors, social relations of production, investment targets, and institutional frameworks conducive to entrepreneurial risk and innovation. Indeed, Charles Lindblom's *Politics and Markets* could be seen as a response to this debate in which Lindblom suggests that the most useful political economy question is: How much state and how much market? This either/or framework, however, leads him to a rather typical American liberal stress on the antagonism between the state and the business sector, with the nontypical surprise ending: Big companies have won the struggle in the American economy by out-positioning every other potentially threatening interest group.[6] The oversimplifying abstraction—state versus market—of this analysis, however, underestimates the subtleties of mixed economies in the late twentieth century.

Rather than asking "How much state and how much market?" it may be more compelling to ask "How much capitalism is necessary for modernization?" And "How much modernization is possible without undermining cultural integrity?" In the late twentieth century many developing countries headed by governments publicly "anticapitalist" privately sought financial and technological support from developed capitalist nations. Ideological compromises were made to achieve the "takeoff" from agricultural to industrial stages of economic development—as in the de-Maofication of China and the early 1980s emphasis there upon private economic incentives and "zones".[7] The intelligence of Mao Tse-tung permitted him to see that "purposive rational action" was overwhelming his socialist agenda, thus causing him to try to turn back the clock with his Cultural Revolution (against the intellectuals and technocrats) in the late 1960s. But it was too late. Once the forces of technological society have been released from the bottle, no magician can wish them back into it again by merely waving an ideological wand. Nevertheless, the leaders of the People's Republic of China reversed themselves again in 1988, fearing that entrepreneurial individualism, soaring inflation, and economic corruption were getting out of hand in Chinese society.[8] Their question must have been: "How much capitalism is really necessary for the modernization of China?" In Eastern Europe the question was reversed in the revolutions of 1989: "How much socialism can we afford to keep if we are to become autonomous and competitive nations in the postmodern world economy?"

Capitalist Incentives and Economic Growth

The historical evidence of the post–World War II era suggests that "the inevitability of capitalism" is less of a passing phase of modern development than either Marx or Lenin supposed. On the one hand, socialist economies have been forced to introduce capitalist or private-market incentives to stimulate economic growth and industrial production; on the other, the postindustrial phase has proved to be elusive for many developed Western economies, which have resorted to fiscal austerity and tax-cutting measures to rekindle falling growth rates in productivity and to raise stalemated national growth rates and national competitiveness in world markets.[9]

Economic growth depends upon the effective collective motivation of human activity—ultimately on a large scale. But human motives start small.[10] Economic motives necessarily address the self-interest of the individual. Noneconomic, social, or ideological motives may spark unusual individual initiative at certain critical, charismatic phases of historical development and revolutionary transformation, but as passions abate so does the efficacy of this "selfless" collective form of motivation in the economy.[11] The stick replaces the ideological carrot and when the stick no longer works, the private market incentives of Adam Smith are (re)introduced through the back door—as in the private garden plots promoted to reverse agricultural stalemate in the Soviet Union and the capitalist economic zones set up in the People's Republic of China to attract foreign investment and technology.

STAGES OF ECONOMIC GROWTH: A CAPITALIST MANIFESTO. Perhaps the best-known historical summary of the vision of inevitable capitalist stages of economic development in the modern state is W.W. Rostow's influential book *The Stages of Economic Growth: A Non-Communist Manifesto* (1960). Rostow, an economic historian and economist, describes states as interacting organisms whose development is marked by social, political, and economic motivations (in contrast to mere economic determinism, which he attributes to Marx). According to Rostow, all modern societies since about 1700 can be located within one of five categories in terms of their economic dimensions: the traditional society; the preconditions for takeoff; the takeoff; the drive to maturity; and the age of high mass-consumption.

While not static, the initial traditional phase is limited in attainable output per head by "pre-Newtonian science and technology and pre-Newtonian attitudes toward the physical world." Given this limitation on productivity, traditional societies generally devote a high proportion of their resources to agriculture, which, in turn, involves an hierarchical social structure with relatively narrow scope for vertical mobility.

Rostow compares the second stage, "preconditions for takeoff," to the process of building up compound interest in a savings account by leaving in interest to compound with principal: that is, growth normally proceeds by geometric progression, and this requires a transition involving education, increased receptivity to modern science, and the assumption of the necessity of growth; increased investment in transportation, communications, and raw materials; and the emergence of entrepreneurs in the private sector and in government willing to mobilize savings and to take risks in pursuit of profit or modernization. The scope of commerce expands as modern manufacturing evolves using new methods. Still, the socioeconomic pace remains traditionally slow with low-productivity methods predominating. A decisive feature at this stage is the political development of an effective, centralized state with a new nationalism creating coalitions in opposition to traditional landed regional interests and colonial power or both.

The third stage of economic growth, the "takeoff phase," is the watershed of modernity: Growth becomes the society's normal condition as old ways and resistances are overcome: "Compound interest becomes built, as it were, into its habits and institutional structure."[12]

In the terms of *this* book, a collective learning or adaptation process has taken place and becomes part of the infrastructure of social institutions and the motivational milieu of the citizenry. Rostow maintains that the main stimulus for takeoff in the Anglo-Saxon countries (Britain, the United States, and Canada) was technological. Not only is there a buildup of social overhead capital and technological development in agriculture and industry, but also a group comes to political power determined to make economic modernization a high priority item on the government's agenda. Typically, the rate of effective investment and savings may double and new industries expand rapidly, plowing back a large share of their profits into new plant and equipment. The new class of entrepreneurs expands, channeling investment funds into the private sector. Agriculture as well as industry are marked by new production techniques, particularly given that revolutionary changes in agricultural productivity are a precondition for takeoff. Within a decade or two the political, economic, and social structures are so transformed that self-sustaining growth can be sustained thereafter. Rostow pinpoints the takeoff phases in Britain: the two decades after 1783; France and the United States: the several decades preceding 1860; Germany: the third quarter of the nineteenth century; Japan: the last quarter of the nineteenth century; Russia and Canada: the quarter century preceding 1914; and India and China: the decades starting with the 1950s.[13]

The fourth stage of economic growth, the drive to maturity, involves a 10 percent to 20 percent investment of the national income, allowing output to keep ahead of population increases and stimulating the spread of technology throughout the nation's economy. Fluctuations in progress and ceaseless shifting in economic sectors lead the society to discover its role in the world economy. About sixty years after the beginning of the takeoff phase, maturity is usually attained, involving refined and technologically complex economic processes. At this point the economy demonstrates the capacity to move beyond the key industries that powered its takeoff to apply modern technology and efficiency to managing the resources throughout the nation. The society shows that it has the technology and entrepreneurial skills to produce whatever it decides to produce (although it may lack the resources or preconditions to provide all kinds of outputs).

Finally, the economy moves into the fifth and final stage of economic growth, the age of high mass-consumption, where the leading sectors stress durable consumer goods and services. Basic needs have been met and a high percentage of the population works in offices or in skilled factory positions. In this "postmaturity" phase, the further extension of technology is no longer accepted as an overriding objective. Social welfare and security emerge as primary areas of state spending in the society where consumer sovereignty reigns. Beyond this mass-consumption phase, Rostow envisioned the possibility of a value shift, subsequently termed "postindustrialism", in which basic material satisfactions could be taken for granted and most people would seek higher-level satisfactions.[14]

Rostow called this hypothetical future "the pattern of Buddenbrooks dynamics" after the novel by Thomas Mann that traces several generations of the Buddenbrook family: the first seeking money; the second taking money for granted and desiring social and civic position; and the third, born of both comfort and family prestige, looking toward music for satisfaction. The "Buddenbrooks behavioral dynamics" epitomized the changing aspirations of succeeding generations as they give low value to that which they take for granted while seeking newer sources of satisfaction.

As the late twentieth-century world economy shifted back towards pro-market, pro-capitalist models, Rostow's influential stage-model appears somewhat prophetic, which is why his theory is given detailed coverage here. Yet one must be wary of its oversimplification, pretense of universality, and Eurocentric (if not Anglo-Saxon) bias. The experience of

Latin American industrialization illustrates that takeoff stages were never really reached because of production bottlenecks, the saturation of domestic markets for consumer nondurables, and the difficulty that countries discovered in graduating to the manufacturing of consumer durables without foreign corporate ownership of such manufacturing enterprises. As a recipe grounded in various interlocking forms of collective learning, Rostow's sequence appears to be more attractive as a blueprint than as a forecast. But it pinpoints key factors in the collective coordination of economic growth that should not be underestimated.

SOCIAL COSTS OF CAPITALIST GROWTH.   Every recipe has its opportunity costs: One may not like the taste of the meal that results, no matter how abundant it may be. Capitalist growth has social and environmental costs. Most of the negative social effects of capitalism are well known. Indeed, they are too often taken for granted by those in the "capitalist habit of mind" and too often underestimated by developing societies that hunger for the material luxuries of advanced Western nations. The free pursuit of individual self-interest creates a society of winners and losers. Moreover, capitalism appeals to those with a winner's instinct; socialism to those with a loser's. Assuming he or she will win, the capitalist wants the greatest share of the economic product that he or she had a hand in producing, paying as little as possible to the government umpire in the form of taxes. However, assuming one will sooner or later lose leads one to desire social insurance and security provided by the state even if the cost in taxes of this risk-reducing insurance keeps going up. Thus, the priority of economic growth accentuates the distance between the winning and losing social groups, constantly redirecting resources to the winners in order to make them self-fulfilling prophecies and "locomotives" for the economy. To the extent capitalist incentives are inevitable, so are manifestations of social inequality.[15]

Karl Marx, of course, took this as his point of departure, saying that the winners in capitalism were few and the losers many: Eventually he anticipated a point in economic development and polarization in which quantity would be transformed into quality as the many rejected a system in which they, as the absolute majority, were structured to be the losers. However, rather than the many becoming increasingly impoverished, they have become at least marginally better off in capitalist societies, undoing the collective motivation that Marx believed would lead to revolution. And, when interviewed, even those who are not better off in capitalist society are against turning over the system, for they seem to be confident that their children or grandchildren will be better off: They want a better shake and a larger share rather than a revolutionary transformation. Perhaps these attitudes can be explained by the findings in the previous chapter on education and class, which demonstrated those down the class scale are more likely to focus on concrete values today rather than upon abstract ideological convictions: mass consumerism *ad absurdum.*

Thus the classical liberal ideology of maximizing national economic growth over all other values is inherently unlimited. The increase of anything is equal to the additions minus the subtractions: More additions mean growth. Growth tends to expand until its ecological niche is filled—and the niche is ever-changing. The concept of equilibrium is thus a fiction—it is a mere temporary state when an ecological niche has momentarily been filled. Even the earth is an open system of disequilibrium in that when fossil fuels are exhausted, solar energy from outside the terrestrial sphere provides an alternative. Because everything is either in growth or decline—in a normal state of *dis*equilibrium—the natural, democratic political appeal has to be for more growth (not decline). The crucial political economy question is: *Whose growth is it or who will it belong to?* And further, *At what social and ecological cost will this growth take place?* The natural tendency is for each nation to run an export-oriented growth policy in order to maximize domestic wealth even at every other nation's expense, using the rest of the world in free-rider fashion as a dumping ground for industrial waste, unemployment, inflation, wars, and so on. Because there is no international police force, there is nothing to prevent the most powerful nation from maximizing its own growth at everyone else's expense and distributing the benefits of this growth to a small minority of its people. In a world economy that has become a global village, any one nation's growth has social and ecological implications for every other nation.

However, even the successful state that is operated like an economic growth machine needs to keep its legitimacy going to maintain itself. The crucial question for the legitimacy of the state is whether or not the marginal inequality necessary for economic growth incentives is based upon an "open" meritocracy or upon a "closed" concentration of resources. The development of democratic institutions fosters openness. Even if one does not go as far as to accept Marxian class analysis, which argues that the appropriation of surplus labor in the form of surplus value by the upper classes will undermine legitimacy, a process of "delegitimization" does appear to accompany the progressive "rationalization" of society as scientific and technical development is institutionalized. Sociologist Jürgen Habermas observed that the technical and organizational conditions under which social wealth is produced by industrially advanced capitalism make it increasingly difficult to assign status in an even subjectively convincing manner through the mechanism for evaluating individual achievement.[16] In other words, as the "rational" status-hierarchy of achievement of the industrial stage of development is undermined by technological advances in the "casino capitalism" of the high-tech, high-information economy, profit and social status often seem less associated with greater productivity than with successful speculation (through corporate takeover efforts or computer stock arbitrage, for example). As the old industrial class system is undermined, individuals shuffle between social categories more loosely in society—particularly in the United States where status, not class, is the measure of social significance and the cash nexus has become the driving force behind the achievement of status.[17]

The classical liberal ideology of growth assumes that capitalism will generate enough opportunities so that the disadvantaged can pick themselves up by their own bootstraps, thus eliminating the need for extensive redistributions of wealth by the state. The bootstrap theory of growth as a surrogate for redistribution has failed exactly to the extent that most existing forms of capitalist society shortchange open meritocracy or opportunity for the sake of established concentrations of resources and interest groups.[18] Democratic institutions have become too abstractly representative and technocratic, if not oligarchical.

Greater economic production does pull up the entire society and provides for employment, but usually at the social cost of creating greater gaps between the rich and the poor and of sharpening the social competition for access to meaningful jobs.[19] If the gap between the high earners and low earners becomes too great for the legitimacy of the social system to bear, as in the case of pre-Mitterand France (where this gap was among the widest in OECD countries, surpassing even Spain), a political shift to the left for the sake of fairer redistribution is a probable result. If, on the other hand, the pendulum swings too far to the other end of the spectrum in providing and redistributing more social services than the economy can bear, a deficit-cutting austerity policy and shift to the political right tends to result (as citizens living in northern European countries in the 1980s made clear).[20]

Such pendular extremes in societies heavily reliant upon capitalist incentives have helped to lead some analysts to conclude that capitalism has a tendency to create a social context in which it "self-destructs."[21] According to this interpretation, capitalist growth results in such a level of affluence that an overdose of leisure time and overeducated citizens are spawned—forces that undermine the bureaucratic rationality of industrial efficiency with counterculture life-styles and that stimulate socialist attacks by intellectuals. Antigrowth, antibusiness, antitechnology constituencies emerge in this "destructive" Buddenbrooks behavior scenario, undermining the legitimacy of the economic growth as the highest priority in society.

The challenge confronting the postmodern political economy is to find a way to structure the inevitable capitalist incentives and inequalities necessary for economic growth in a socially acceptable framework of meritocracy and opportunity so that both social equity and prosperity are being furthered, thus making legitimacy self-sustaining as well as growth. Full employment is not possible without economic growth, but economic growth is quite feasible without full-employment. And as if it were not difficult enough to find out how to establish social limits for the sake of legitimacy without killing the goose that lays the golden egg, different rates of economic growth in different sectors of the economy turn the problem into a complicated puzzle.

Dual Economies and Engines of Creative Destruction

Capitalism is a philosophy of winners who become self-fulfilling prophecies of success, consolidating their positions and attracting resources sometimes to the point of monopoly. Successful centers of development thus tend to draw off resources from peripheral areas where they may be more badly needed. It has become clear that early development literature limiting the concept of the dual economy to developing countries was overdrawn: Dual economies operate at many levels during all phases of a nation's economic development. Indeed, to the extent that the world economy is driven by capitalist incentives and that technological progress is permitted to drive out the old with the new at an ever-increasing tempo, any existing economic sector in any society could be considered "dual" in that what exists will soon inevitably become obsolete and be displaced by a more dynamic and adaptive development. State strategies may be most effective in assuming themselves to be obsolete upon birth, barely permitting national institutions to cushion their infancy and to pay back their "opportunity costs" before ploughing themselves under with their own self-spawned technological replacements. But if efficacy is the only social criterion, vast regions of the country may be left temporarily unemployed, in the dark, as it were, as the limelight shifts to the newest technological development. Few are in the economic sunshine at any one moment, while the majority exist in some kind of shadow economy.

The reality of dualism and discontinuity in even the most developed of industrial or technological economies shatters the conventional myth that one homogeneous national economy can be managed with supply-and-demand tools from a centralized cockpit and that macroeconomic trends can be projected only "from the top." While some centralization and use of supply-and-demand tools are necessary, they are not sufficient to explain, control, or project national economic trends. "The system" is a composite of systems.

Dualism and discontinuity are most obvious in developing countries predominated by small domestic markets and industries that produce low output over time. The emerging modern sector in these countries is almost by definition high output over time, composed of enclave economies directed toward large metropoles (metropolitan centers of large, developed economies) or toward the world market. And given the larger sizes of these developed or extensive markets, the modern sector tends to consist of large, capital-intensive enterprises. While dualism in both developing and developed economies results from factors relating to the market, the division of labor, and productivity, the specific causes of dualism are usually different in the two cases. In the case of the lesser-developed country, dualism usually emerges because of industries of different sizes. In the developed country, on the other hand, dualism most often stems from the varying degrees of the stability of markets within the same industries.[22]

In *Modern Capitalism*, John Cornwall demonstrates that the dual-economy model can be a powerful mode of explaining growth-rate differences in the more advanced OECD (developed) market economies in the period since World War II. Based on the work of economists Ingar Svennilson and Joseph Schumpeter, Cornwall stresses the importance of entrepreneurship and investment in manufacturing technologies as catalysts in bringing about qualitative changes or structural transformations.[23] Cornwall underscores the importance of demand and of the opportunity of absorbing less productive workers in a traditional sector (say agriculture) into a more productive manufacturing sector without unduly raising their wages. The beginning of the development process entails the enlargement of the advanced sector (usually but not necessarily the industrial). At this stage there is no emphasis upon wages, for the backward sector has a backlog of underemployed workers who can be released for the advanced sector—workers who demand only slightly higher salaries due to their marginal productivity. Thus the industrial sector can be widened without the deepening of capital through hefty wage increases (due to investment in the same workers) expanding employment. At a certain point the backward sector becomes so small that stable wages cannot be maintained and intense structural change results.

Virtuous versus Vicious Circles and Learning by Doing

Cornwall's explanation takes Engel's law into account: that at different levels of income people have an elasticity of demand that differs (for example, in becoming richer at a certain point you cannot continue to buy more steak instead of chicken for dinner and shift your money somewhere else). Accordingly, various sectors of the economy grow at a different pace. In the process of structural change, technology gaps emerge in different areas in different countries. But the manufacturing sector is "the engine of growth." And following Verdoorn's law (the "learning-by-doing approach," roughly speaking), there are numerous advantages that are derived from a fast-growing manufacturing sector due to learning-by-doing as workers go through new technological steps.

The learning-by-doing approach depends upon a distinction between *static* and *dynamic economies of scale* in the manufacturing sector. A *static* economy of scale refers to a reduction of unit costs (and a rise in average productivity) as output over a given production period goes up. Typically, static economies of scale come from increases in plant, firm, or industry size. Longer production runs in the same production time reduce unit costs since production does not have to be stopped and started up again, less inventory has to be kept, and there is less loss of downtime to make adjustments for running through different models. The Deming principle of increasing quality by reducing variation seems to be at work here.* In contrast, *dynamic* economies of scale are referred to as "learning economies" since they involve continuous reductions in unit costs and increases in productivity attributable to continuous increases in output of a corporation, industry, or economy over time. The key of Verdoorn's law is the stress on the growth of output in determining the rate of growth of productivity rather than the level of output determining the average level of productivity.[24] Consistent with this approach, economist Kenneth Arrow argues that productivity growth results from a learning process, particularly in the capital goods industry, a process that can be maintained only by constant new investment.[25] The industrialization of Japan and the de-industrialization of Great Britain since World War II provide two illustrations of learning-by-doing in the context of economic dualism.[26]

Thus, the manufacturing sector acts as an engine of economic growth (or creative destruction) in having not only backward but also forward linkages as it propels the dynamic-learning economy in a *virtuous economic circle* and demonstrates positive learning reactions. The strategic nature of manufacturing output becomes clear in the links between domestic economic conditions and external export and monetary results.

The dual-economy structure sets the state up for either vicious or virtuous circles, which are critical for international competitiveness. In the post–World War II period, Britain, for example, often slipped into a *vicious circle* of sluggish productivity, which led to difficulties in exports, problems in the balance of payments, lower productivity growth, excessive wage increases, and a decline in competitiveness in world markets. Typically, a vicious-circle strategy involves devaluing the currency in order to stimulate export sales in the short term by making them cheaper; but this has the effect of increasing inflation at home, thus causing workers to demand higher wages to match rising living costs, driving up the costs of production, and making exports less competitive until the government intervenes with another devaluation to start the circle anew. An economy in a virtuous circle such as West Germany after World War II, on the other hand, shows a steady or improving level of productivity at home, leading to competitiveness abroad with export growth resulting in opportunities for employment and investment, which, in turn, help to stimulate productivity, revalue the currency upwards to head off inflation, maintain competitiveness, and lead to an avoidance of balance-of-payments problems.

---

*W. Edwards Deming's essential fourteen points for managers aim to create constancy of purpose toward improvement of product and service by ceasing dependence on inspection to achieve quality by eliminating the need for inspection on a mass basis by building quality into the product in the first place, moving to minimize total costs by awarding business on the basis of price tag, and moving toward a single supplier with long-term trust and commitment. See Bruce Serlen, "W. Edwards Deming: The Man Who Made Japan Famous—For Quality," *New York University Business* (Fall 1987/Winter 1988): 18.

Neo-corporatism

Another interpretation of successful capitalist economies since World War II stresses not the underlying economic factors of production, labor cost, inflation, investment, and learning-by-doing but the institutional relationships among major business, labor, and governmental interest groups, which are conducive to harmonious collective management on the one hand, and equity in representation by various levels of workers in society on the other. This approach has been called *neo-corporatism*. The original notion of *corporatism*, or "state corporatism," stems from a belief in political representation through functional, occupation-related institutions (not geographically defined electoral units) as embodied in the right-wing Fascist regimes of Mussolini in Italy and Franco in Spain. The "new" or "neo" or "liberal" corporatism is used to describe post-1945 Western economies that still guarantee certain functional labor, management, and employee interest groups more or less a monopoly right to represent their part of society in government negotiations but without the coercive aspects of state corporatism negatively associated with the Fascist governments.[27] Free elections, democratic rights, and the ability to withdraw from negotiations voluntarily as an interest group are political characteristics of neo-corporatism, as contrasted with corporatism, while still maintaining integrated, functional "peak" organizations as the chief labor-management bargainers in the government—labor organizations for workers, business federations for employers, agricultural organizations for farmers, and so forth. Each worker or employer is automatically a member of the organization relevant to that economic sector in government policy-making. Neo-corporatist states can thus be contrasted with non-corporatist states with fragmented economic interest groups without such widespread membership that are only intermittently consulted by the government and where such interest groups rarely carry out administrative duties on behalf of the state.[28]

Neo-corporatist states tend to have large working-class movements, a heavily unionized labor force, and a social democratic tradition. The neo-corporatist states of Norway, Sweden, and Austria, for instance, have a unionized labor force making up more than 80 percent of the work force. The Social Democratic Party has also done well in these countries, particularly in Sweden, where it has dominated the government for the past half century (although the 1990 austerity program freezing wages, prices, rents, local taxes and stock dividends plus a two-year ban on strikes will undermine the Social Democratic image of the "Swedish model"). And in West Germany, often identified as having many neo-corporatist characteristics, unionized labor plays a strong role in labor-management-government relations, and the Social Democratic Party is one of the two major parties to be reckoned with (and on the rise given integration with the companion Social Democratic Party in East Germany). A country with strong corporatist traditions is one in which the trade union leadership and employers' associations are committed to an ideology of social partnership and where the trade unions, employers, and the state cooperate in some economic policy areas. Usually the number of labor strikes is low in such states and "authoritarian" incomes policies are not imposed by the state. Switzerland is sometimes interpreted as a liberal form of corporatism—with comparatively low state involvement.[29] And Japan is sometimes described as "corporatism without labor" or "private corporatism"—a consortium of big business and government with labor largely co-opted in unions organized *within* specific firms that often promise lifetime employment.

Typically, distinctions are made in state strategies among *corporatist* modes of policy coordination, resting upon a "balance of class forces" among labor, capital, and the state (described above); *pluralist-sectoralist* modes of policy coordination with low degrees of policy coordination across policy areas but not precluding tri-partite (union, employers' associations, and the state) networks in certain policy areas; and *pluralist* modes in political economies dominated by "the non-socialist tendency" and where integrated policy networks and an underlying consensus among labor, employers, and the state are largely absent.[30] The countries with the corporatist modes of policy coordination, whether of the liberal (meaning less state) or more heavily social democratic versions—Austria, Japan, Norway, Sweden, and Switzerland—managed to maintain relatively low levels of unemployment from 1974 into the 1980s compared to the mass unemployment that plagued all other OECD countries during this period.[31] So if full employment is the number-one policy priority, corporatist or neo-corporatist modes of policy coordination appear to be useful, if not necessary, preconditions for successful anti-unemployment strategies. The consensus on social cooperation reinforces the stability of the maintenance base of these welfare states. The key question raised is: To what extent can these societies afford the trade-off costs in terms of economic growth and entrepreneurial innovation implied by state-centered as opposed to more pluralistic market-oriented economies? Or could it be that this whole notion of "trade-off" is a short-term, polarized Western black-and-white interpretation of phenomena that can be subtly integrated into a tight state strategy that provides both high levels of employment and high levels of economic growth and entrepreneurship (Japan?)? Perhaps it is useful to identify the dominant types of state strategies that emerged in the 1970s and 1980s in order to determine which mixes of these types are possible and most fruitful in terms of maximizing both the objectives of full employment and dynamic economic growth.

A Typology of State Strategies

An empirical examination of the strategies of both hard and soft currency states in the 1970s in order to discover which strategies were most effective in coping with inflation resulted in the derivation of four ideal typical strategies at the individual, corporate, and state levels.[32] Each strategy was broken down into risk orientation, time orientation, guiding motive, consumption pattern, and characteristic policy or portfolio mix. The four types are the modes of conduct of the Defeatist, the Free-rider, the Maintenance Man, and the Entrepreneur—"pure" (Weberian) types of strategies that in any concrete situation are usually mixed. Figure 5–1 summarizes them.

Rather than starting with preconceptions, these types were derived by observing the various reactions to the global inflation of the 1970s and then sorting these into their common characteristics, with four categories emerging as predominant. The *Defeatist strategy* is past-oriented and defensive, designed to take as few risks as possible, while seeking out bargains. Defeatist policies typically focus on security and passive attempts to head off the worst possible outcomes. Total ideological rigidity or total compromise out of fear of loss are not uncommon to this type.

Free-rider strategies, in contrast, are present-oriented with a more active than passive set of policies aimed at high risk as long as someone else is paying or the cost today is low. Free-rider policies aim to export domestic costs to others, to take on debt, to postpone repayment of debt, to devalue currency for short-term export growth (postponing the costs of the "vicious circle" until tomorrow), to subsidize lame-duck industries, to index wages of existing workers to inflation increases, and to use selected protectionism when advantageous.

Maintenance strategies are grounded in present-to-middle-range-future time perspective, strive for limited risks at moderate cost, and try just to keep up with the economic or business cycle. Maintenance policies stress co-opting change to keep costs and benefits in balance for the sake of stability or equilibrium: co-determination between unions and management, for example. The thrust of the maintenance strategy is to manage the status quo efficiently, anticipating change in order to adjust the political economy in time to maintain its stability.

Entrepreneurial strategies, in contrast, are future-oriented, aimed at taking high risks even at high costs in order to put most of one's chips in the *avant-garde,* high-growth sectors that will permit one to come out significantly ahead of the short-term business cycle or economic average. The focus is upon outwitting the future with extraordinary achievement, creative high-risk investment for boosting productivity, and effective innovation for the sake of competitiveness. This involves shifting support from declining, or sunset, industries to sunrise, or emerging, high-tech and high-information sectors, creating payoffs for research and development, and stimulating both productivity and export-oriented growth. Targeted state subsidies for long-range technological breakthroughs are an example, while subsidies for lame-duck industries, agriculture, and declining sectors are apt to be cut.

The next step in theory-building using this approach is to hypothesize into which priority the types are most apt to fall in the typical strategic mix

FIGURE 5-1

Ideal Types of State Strategies	Time Perspective	Risk Orientation	Characteristic Policies
DEFEATIST	Past-oriented	As few risks as possible: fear of loss and bargain-hunting	*Focus* on security and defending past policies and values Passive and defensive policies to head off worst outcomes Rigid adherence to past ideologies or total compromise Aid requests at lowest interest rates for decaying infrastructure and to meet daily food and energy needs
FREE-RIDER	Present-oriented	High risks at low cost	*Focus* on exporting domestic costs to others, on loans, postponing payments, on exploiting the international arena for short-term benefits (i.e., devaluations) Indexation; agricultural subsidies Government subsidies for lame-duck industries Periodically tapping IMF and others for loans Wage and price controls when necessary Selected protectionism when advantageous
MAINTENANCE	Present-middle-range future	Limited risks at moderate cost	*Focus* on co-opting change to keep costs and benefits in balance for stability Use of voluntary wage and price guidelines Tight monetary and fiscal policies as needed Preservation of steady exchange rate Stress on bringing federal budget more into balance Simultaneous cuts in taxes and government spending Elimination of excessive imported labor, immigration limits Co-determination policy with unions and management
ENTREPRENEURIAL	Future-oriented	High risks even at high costs	*Focus* on outwitting the future with extraordinary achievement, productivity, innovation Elimination of indexation Elimination of subsidies for lame-duck industries, farms, agriculture Payoffs to stimulate productivity and export-oriented growth (through tax cuts, stimuli, etc.) Eliminate double-tax on corporate gains, encourage long-term capital investment and research and development Support accelerated depreciation based on replacement cost State subsidies for long-range technological breakthroughs Antitrust legislation and seed money for starting small businesses

or constellation at different stages of state development. Such clusters of hypothetical priorities are illustrated in Figure 5–2.

An approach emphasizing strategy clusters or portfolios has the advantage of articulating the choice menus available to state managers at different phases of economic development. Typically lesser-developed states find themselves locked into defeatist and free-rider strategies without the financial or technological resources to break out and to modernize. The precondition for this takeoff is an entrepreneurial strategy applied initially to increasing agricultural productivity and efficiency and secondarily to uncovering manufacturing niches in which the lesser-developed country has significant potential comparative advantages in the global economy. Modernization away from the traditional, agricultural economy is therefore measurable in terms of the extent to which entrepreneurial strategies displace defeatist and free-rider strategies targeted toward agricultural self-sufficiency and the emergence of industrial competitiveness.

When India and the People's Republic of China became self-sufficient in food, their next step was to use targeted entrepreneurial strategies aimed at the global economy both in terms of agricultural and manufactured products. India, for example, targeted machine tools in niches of the U.S. market, which had become too small to interest large American manufacturers any longer. But in addition to these openings led by entrepreneurial strategies, both China and India were heavily preoccupied with maintenance strategies aimed to increase the efficiency of their domestic economies, to ensure domestic political stability, and to create an atmosphere attractive to future foreign investment and technology transfers. Nor were these countries beyond using free-rider strategies in efforts to secure development loans from abroad—whether from the World Bank, commercial banks, or foreign governments interested in better diplomatic relations.

In the case of China, the maintenance base is a centrally planned economy within which entrepreneurial free-market islands are targeted to make the political economy more flexible and to increase individual initiative. Outside China, international organizations and the experiences of smaller newly industrialized Asian countries are used as free-rider opportunities of surrogate experience and potential sources for hard currency and

FIGURE 5–2   Hypothetical Priorities Among Strategies at Different Stages of State Development

Agricultural	Newly Industrializing	Industrial– Super-industrial	Postindustrial or Postmodern
1. Defeatist	1. Entrepreneurial	1. Maintenance	1. Free-rider
2. Free-rider	2. Maintenance	2. Entrepreneurial	2. Maintenance
3. Entrepreneurial	3. Free-rider	3. Free-rider	3. Defeatist/Entrepreneurial

technological innovation—what some have called the "Greater China" strategy of letting other Asian countries be the pilot tests for China's long-term positioning. The Chinese maintenance base remains as a vertical, centralized structure, not comparable with the horizontally structured market economies of the West—what the Chinese see as "institutionalized chaos."[33]

As we move to the industrial–super-industrial* phase of development, efficient maintenance strategies become the dominant preoccupation supplemented by entrepreneurial export-oriented growth and stimulation for innovation, research, and development at home. Free-rider strategies are used as icing on the cake whenever opportunities arise to reduce costs at home or to exploit unusual exchange-rate and financing opportunities abroad. Japan is the clearest example of this combination of industrial–super-industrial strategies, which might be summed up as *maintenpreneurial*: the overwhelming efficiency concentration at the maintenance base providing the opportunities for entrepreneurial effectiveness at home and abroad, or, using the maintenance base as a launching pad for entrepreneurial risk. This strategy synthesis is probably the optimum strategic structure for the "learning economy" or "learning state" in the world economy: always reducing costs and increasing efficiency at home and using the resources this frees up to take growth-oriented, market-share expanding, targeted risks for the long term. The sophistication of the Japanese maintenance base takes years of study to understand fully. An extremely hierarchical educational and social structure with Confucian value elements of humility, respect for knowledge and one's elders provides the basis for a society that smothers problems with targeted information, uses group decision-making processes to increase motivation, cuts costs and reduces errors, and relies upon a neo-corporatist interrelationship between government ministries and big business to give priority to collective learning and economic adaptation.[34] From an economic and competitive business viewpoint, Japan's learning culture is formidable in no small part because it integrates simplistic Western polarities (centralization and decentralization), prefers the pragmatic and concrete to the intellectually abstract, and focuses upon improving existing innovations by cutting costs and increasing quality rather than aiming to discover something new under the sun.[35]

Another, more maintenance-oriented maintenpreneurial strategy is represented by West Germany with its *social market* economy, which presupposes a delicate but dynamic balance between social stability and free-market entrepreneurship.[36] Social stability results from widespread consensus on a maintenance base of fundamental social rights and duties protected by the government. Recent efforts to decode the meaning of "social" in the social

---

*"Super-industrial" refers to the large size and scale of modern enterprise and its social and environmental impact. See Herman Kahn and J.B. Phelps, "The Economic Future," in F. Feather, ed., *Through the '80s* (Washington, DC: World Future Society, 1980), pp. 202–09.

market economy resulted in conceiving social as the collective efforts within a market economy to create a situation where ideally everyone in the society is involved in the market forces and is thereby guaranteed a direct share of the product of the market economy.[37] From this maintenance base of social consensus, corporate teams of aggressive entrepreneurs are given the freedom to operate worldwide, knowing in advance their range of domestic responsibility. The stable "apolitical" social base, in short, provides the predictability that makes long-term economic planning and investment possible on the part of the private sector. The social market economy is grounded on the German distinctions between *economic order* (the state-stabilized structure or maintenance base) and *economic process* (free-market entrepreneurship) and between state intervention (*Marktbeeinflussungen*) and state *control* of the market. For instance, if the policy objective is to lower the cost of housing for the poor, the payment of a housing allowance is consistent with a free market in housing (and free-market assumption of social economy), whereas rent control is not. The principles of the "social market economy" appear to be the guidelines for the economic side of the ongoing reunification of East and West Germany.

Since 1973, the emergence of the floating exchange-rate regime, the volatility of oil prices, and the policy-linked distortions of the value of the dollar warped the context of global economic development and severely limited the strategy options available to all nation-states, rich or poor. Still, the hard-currency maintenpreneurial countries had much more flexibility than did the majority of the world's soft-currency nations whether the fashionable policies were inflationary or (more commonly) anti-inflationary. Able to take their maintenance domestic frameworks for granted, these hard-currency countries were able to pursue entrepreneurial strategies using the Eurodollar markets as free-riders to reduce the cost of imported inflation. The successful West German strategy in the "floating game," for example, was to appreciate the value of the mark to push down imported inflation, but not to the level of global inflation, thus preserving West German export markets.[38] Hooking their own currency to the value of the West German mark, the Austrians maintained a hard-currency policy, using foreign-exchange-rate subsidized capital imports to finance domestic restructuring and development.[39] Both in the industrial–super-industrial category of development, West Germany and Austria used the priority of stable maintenance strategies as a base for secondary entrepreneurial and free-rider strategies in order to protect themselves from inflation and to maintain their international competitiveness.

The Swiss had another effective brand of maintenpreneurial strategy: using monetary policy to neutralize foreign inflows through a wide range of controls and using their effective federal Export Risk Insurance scheme to protect Swiss exporters from all sorts of risks stemming from transfer, bad debts, production, politics, and particularly the threat to their prices and profits resulting from the appreciation of the Swiss franc.[40]

The strategies of weak-currency countries in the agricultural development category, on the other hand, aimed for mere maintenance as a goal by using depreciation to improve their balance of current accounts and to substitute for imported depression or unemployment. Taking economic advice from the Cambridge School, developing countries in Latin America, such as Mexico, took all the credit they could get from private commercial banks (the OPEC-dollar recycling agents of the 1970s)—a consummate free-rider/defeatist strategy blend. But such vicious-circle strategies are expensive in terms of stimulating world inflation and creating burdens for future domestic development when the foreign debt mortgages must be repaid. Carefully timed, one-shot free-rider strategies (suspending payments on international debts) combined with short-term, anti-inflation shock treatment (deep cuts in wages and state spending) may work to break states out of vicious, inflationary cycles if democratic populations are patient enough—as in Bolivia in 1985 and (hopefully) in Poland in 1990.[41]

Another weak-currency-country strategy variation is the free-rider indexation* scheme used by nations whose credit is good because of their strategic importance, such as Israel and Iceland. But the Italians discovered that the unarguable benefits of redistribution to those down the class scale resulting from such indexation schemes can reach a point of diminishing returns: To attempt to restore international competitiveness and to break free of vicious circles, the Italians began in the 1980s to dismantle their system of indexation. After all, the free-rider has to know when to get off since the status quo is no streetcar named desire.

The United States used yet another version of a complex free-rider strategy, manipulating dollar exchange rates and high U.S. interest rates in order to keep international money flowing into the United States to offset the crowding out of U.S. private investment by government borrowing that was feared due to the large federal deficit. The shift in the mid-1980s to use a falling dollar to make American exports cheaper and to ameliorate the large U.S. trade deficit appeared to many critics to be another free ride on the world economy—a potentially vicious-circle-strategy of devaluation that permitted the Americans to postpone inevitable internal (budget cuts or tax increases) and external (protectionist tariffs to match competitors subsidy for subsidy) adjustments that are politically unpopular at home. Such free-rider preoccupations threaten to move the United States precipitously from the super-industrial to postmodern or post-industrial phase in which a nation hangs onto maintenance by burden-sharing or attempting to shift more of the costs to other states.

IMPLICATIONS

In a global capitalist economy, rational choice for the individual citizen is apt to be maximized in a free-wheeling, deregulated domestic market like that

---

*Indexation refers to automatic, indexed hikes in industrial wages linked to inflation or rises in consumer prices.

of the United States. But as a consequence, a small minority of individuals in the national community—the professional speculators—are positioned to make the most rational use of available choices given the information overload of a system in which the set of available choices is the greatest in the world. That is, a political economy maximizing laissez-faire entrepreneurship pays off in terms of the great range of freedom or the range of choice in professional work, investments, and so forth.

By the same token, the overwhelming majority of citizens at any one historical moment are structurally in a position where they will most probably make less than rationally optimal decisions or even make irrational decisions, thus increasing the gap between their own life chances and those of the rational few (a sort of "reverse Donald Trump effect"). Such nonadaptive, ill-informed decision making, in turn, risks undermining the basis of the large middle class, which Aristotle believed to be the prerequisite to his ideal form of balanced, democratic-aristocratic state—the *politea*.

As a contrast, the trade-off of neo-corporatist political economies is to give citizens a more limited range of freedom of choice for the sake of greater social stability and coverage of the risk of social failure (falling to the bottom, "down-and-out"). Governmental bureaucracies tend to make routine decisions concerning health, old-age pension, unemployment insurance benefits, and educational structures, leaving citizens with less routine decisions (and less decision stress), thus freeing time for the kinds of decision making they most enjoy.

Sociologist Philip Slater, in *The Pursuit of Loneliness*, argued, for example, that Americans have to make more decisions than do people in any other culture in the world.[42] The opportunity cost of this freedom is to be overwhelmed as an individual and having to make more decisions than one wants to in any one day, eating up time with "busyness" and leaving the individual autonomous but lonely as he or she has to sort out everything individually. The neoconservative solution of Alan Bloom in *The Closing of The American Mind* is to reduce this "openness" for the sake of cultural calculability.[43] Or, in W. Edwards Deming's terms, by reducing the amount of variation, the quality of any process can be increased. The problem, of course, is whether in an antistate liberal society such as that of the United States the majority of citizens would tolerate the arbitrary closing down of options or openness by the state for the sake of increased predictability collectively desired.

Americans, for example, typically, want improvements in public services, but no increases in taxes to pay for such improvements—a free-rider strategy of improving the maintenance base grounded on borrowing from others, a policy that may not be able to last indefinitely. Indeed, in 1990 national opinion polls suggested a shift toward tolerating a marginal tax increase if the money were spent to fight drugs and to improve the environment.

The problem, as we have seen, lies not just in getting the majority of people in a nation to choose differently at any one moment, but in restructuring the society so that all individual choices are perceived as social choices, and that the individual and community learn to work in harmony for the sake of long-term social adaptation and economic competitiveness. Structure, in short, seems to precede strategy rather than the other way around. In the United States, individual freedom has been structured as primary in the social system no matter what the cost in social or economic distance between individuals or groups. In the neo-corporatist economies, autonomy for the "peak" interest groups of labor, management, and government bureaucracies is structured to predominate over individual choice, limiting individual freedom somewhat but increasing social harmony and decreasing social distance between individuals and groups.

Still, we have seen that at certain transitional phases of economic development, nations collectively appear to have strategic choices between strategy mixes that can restructure their economies toward more industrial competitiveness or not (see chapters 7 and 8). One concrete measure of the existing political economy strategy mix in a society is the amount of the nation's economic product devoted to government spending.

State Spending as a Measure of Political Economy Constitutions

To compare how different national political economies are structured, economists Joseph Schumpeter and Rudolf Goldschied maintained that the nature and amount of government spending is the best point of departure. The OECD publishes these data annually under the title "Total Outlays of General Government" in which government outlays include goods, services, public investments, interest payments on debts, and the cost of social (welfare) transfer payments. These comparative data show how limited the room for political flexibility since 1960 has become. The states most heavily burdened with government spending (note the correlation with *social democratic neo-corporatism*) are Sweden, the Netherlands, Denmark, Belgium, and Luxembourg. Between 1960 and 1985, government outlays as a percentage of the annual total GNP rose for Sweden from 31 percent to 65 percent (the government outlay as a percentage of the GNP is called the *state quota*). Similarly, the state quota for the Netherlands and Denmark rose to 60 percent in the same period. West Germany's state quota—somewhat representative of the average for Europe—rose from 32 percent in 1960 to 48 percent in 1985. In contrast, consider the *liberal neo-corporatist* states such as Japan and Switzerland, which have much lower state quotas—about 30 percent in 1985. And the state quota of the most liberal of nations, the United States, rose only from 27 percent to 36 percent between 1960 and 1985.[44]

The key empirical questions in terms of the range of strategic choice available for restructuring of a political economy are (1) Why are the differences between the state quotas so different—from 30 percent to 60 percent, and (2) What are the consequences of a large or small state quota for international competitiveness and social welfare? While a number of hypotheses respond to the first question (including the distinction between social democratic and liberal forms of neo-corporatism), two hypotheses are particularly well-grounded empirically. One of these is the "openness-of-the-economy hypothesis." Political scientist David Cameron of Yale University demonstrated that political economies that were more strongly integrated in the world economy in terms of international trade have higher state quotas, whereas nations with a small portion of their GNP made up of foreign trade have much smaller state quotas.[45] Thus, European countries that are heavily integrated into the world economy have high state quotas, whereas the United States and Japan, which are heavily oriented domestically in terms of their political economies (foreign trade making up some 15 percent of the U.S. economy and 20 percent of the Japanese), have low state quotas.

The second well-grounded hypothesis explaining the differences in state quotas is the "power-and-party-division hypothesis." Political scientist Manfred Schmidt of the University of Heidelberg has shown that since 1960 the countries with the smallest state quotas—the United States, Japan and Switzerland—have been dominated by bourgeois right-wing parties, whereas Denmark and Sweden, with high state quotas, have been dominated by Social Democratic parties. This Social Democratic tradition has seeped into the cultures of Denmark and Sweden to the point where politicians take social democracy for granted, while in the United States and Switzerland the state plays a more restrained role. In strategic terms, one could say that political economies with high state quotas are more maintenance-bound, whereas those with the more liberal, less Social Democratic tradition are more entrepreneurial in orientation (self-help versus state-security).

Coming to the second question—the consequences of high state quotas for international competitiveness—the empirical findings appear to be less conclusive and dependent upon changing global economic conditions. In his book *Sozialdemokratische Krisenpolitik*, political economist Fritz Scharpf showed that Sweden, Austria, West Germany, and Great Britain developed successful Keynesian recipes for coping with the world economy dilemmas of the late 1970s: There was a consensus among their unions not to push for wage hikes to match the rising inflation rates, thus enabling their governments to carry on state-deficit economic politics with low interest rates. Austria had full employment with a low inflation rate. Sweden maintained full employment as unemployment declined. West Germany held the world record for fighting inflation, but lost jobs in the process. And for two years Great Britain slowed down unemployment and inflation only to have the government lose control over the unions, which raised their demands.

However, in the 1980s these successful Keynesian recipes no longer worked. The high real dollar interest rates transformed the international capital market, which had become so globally integrated that money flowed toward the highest real return wherever that happened to be in the world. Consequently the incomes of taxpayers stagnated while the profits of investors soared. Given the high interest rates and loss of domestic capital, governments had to pay more money to cover their budget debts and thereby nearly lost the flexibility to use the Keynesian instrument of intervention in the domestic economy.[46] Thus the high-real-interest-rate strategy of the United States to attract the money needed to service its rising deficits skewed the world economy toward the American position—a policy perceived by Europeans as a free-rider tactic on the part of the United States, which delayed the inevitable long-term economic adjustment domestically in America at the cost of making mere maintenance in European economies more expensive.

Finally, the ability of a nation in the 1980s to deal with such exogenous (or foreign/external) shocks and to achieve a successful maintenpreneurial strategy mix depended on both the collective learning capacity of the political economy (and particularly of the governmental institutions) to make inevitable adjustments and on the strength of the bargaining position of the economy in the global context. And this ability depended in part upon major multinational companies headquartered in the nation, and upon corporate strategies and direct investment targeted to take advantage of economic cycles.

ENDNOTES

1. Henry Maine, *Ancient Law: Its Connection with the Early History of Society and Its Relation to Modern Ideas* (London: Lardon J. Murray, 1861).

2. Ferdinand Toennies, *Gemeinschaft und Gesellschaft* (1887), translated by Charles P. Loomis, *Fundamental Concepts of Sociology* (New York: American Book Co., 1940).

3. Emile Durkheim, *De la Division du travail social* (1893), translated by George Simpson, *The Division of Labor in Society* (Glencoe: The Free Press, 1949).

4. See Max Weber, *The Theory of Social and Economic Organization*, translated by A.M. Henderson and Talcott Parsons (Glencoe: The Free Press, 1947).

5. Jürgen Habermas, *Toward a Rational Society* (Boston: Beacon Press, 1970).

6. Charles Lindblom, *Politics and Markets: The World's Political-Economic Systems* (New York: Basic Books, 1977).

7. See, for example, Christopher S. Wren, "China's Courtship of Capitalism," in *The New York Times*, December 25, 1983; and C. Wren, "China Turning Back to Its Educated for Help," *The New York Times*, March 4, 1984.

8. See, for example, Edward A. Gargan, "China Explains Policy Shift Retightening Economic Grip," *The New York Times*, October 28, 1988.

9. See Sylvia Ostry, "The World Economy in 1983: Marking Time," *Foreign Affairs*, "America and the World," Vol. 62, No. 3, pp. 533–60.

10. According to an MIT survey of 5.6 million firms between 1968 and 1976, 80 percent of the jobs in the United States were created by companies that were four years old or less and employed 100 or fewer workers. See David L. Birch,

"Who Creates Jobs?" *The Public Interest* 65 (Fall 1981). On the theory of motiva-
tion in the welfare state, see Kenneth E. Boulding, *The Economy of Love and Fear*
(Belmont, CA: Wadsworth Publishing Co., 1973), and Thomas C. Schelling,
Micromotives and Macrobehavior (New York: W.W. Norton, 1978).

11. Economist Albert Hirschman has identified alternating cycles of public involvement and return to private interest maximization: see A.O. Hirschman, *Shifting
Involvements: Private Interests and Public Action* (Princeton, NJ: Princeton University Press, 1982).

12. W.W. Rostow, *The Stages of Economic Growth: A Non-Communist Manifesto* (London: Cambridge University Press, 1960), p. 7.

13. Ibid., p. 9.

14. For other interpretations of "postindustrial" values, see Ronald Inglehart, "The
Silent Revolution in Europe: Intergenerational Change in Postindustrial Socie-
ties," *American Political Science Review*, 65 (December 1971); Fred Hirsch, *The
Social Limits to Growth* (London: Routledge & Kegan Paul, 1978), and Daniel Bell,
The Coming of Post-Industrial Society (New York: Basic Books, 1973) and Daniel
Bell, *The Cultural Contradictions of Capitalism* (New York: Basic Books, 1976).

15. See, for example, Frank Parkin, *Class Inequality and Political Order: Social Strati-
fication in Capitalist and Communist Societies* (New York: Praeger, 1975); and
"Social Liberalism: A New Political Economy," Chapter 11 in R. Isaak, *American
Democracy and World Power* (New York: St. Martin's Press, 1977), pp. 172–86.

16. Habermas, *Rational Society*, p. 122. For a Marxian class analysis, see Stephen
Resnik, John Sinisi, and Richard Wolff, "Class Analysis of International Rela-
tions," in *An International Political Economy*, International Political Economy
Yearbook, Vol. I, ed. by W. Ladd Hollis and F. LaMond Tullis (Boulder, CO:
Westview Press, 1985), pp. 87–123.

17. See Part III: "The Loose Individual" of Robert Nisbet, *The Present Age:
Progress and Anarchy in Modern America* (New York: Harper & Row, 1988),
especially pp. 122–25.

18. See Charles S. Maier, "The Politics of Inflation in the Twentieth Century," in *The
Political Economy of Inflation*, edited by Fred Hirsch and John H. Goldthorpe
(Cambridge, MA: Harvard University Press, 1978).

19. See Hirsch, *The Social Limits of Growth* and Staffan B. Linder, *The Harried Leisure
Class* (New York: Columbia University Press, 1970).

20. See R. Isaak, *European Politics: Political Economy and Policy Making in Western
Democracies* (New York: St. Martin's Press, 1980).

21. See Daniel Bell, *The Cultural Contradictions of Capitalism*, Joseph Schumpeter,
Capitalism, Socialism and Democracy, and Fred Hirsch, "The Ideological Underlay
of Inflation," in Hirsch and Goldthorpe, *Political Economy of Inflation*, pp. 263–84.

22. See Suzanne Berger and Michael Piore, *Dualism and Discontinuity in Industrial
Societies* (New York: Cambridge University Press, 1980), p. 69 ff.

23. See Ingar Svennilson, *Growth and Stagnation in the European Economy* (Geneva:
Economic Commission for Europe, 1954); Joseph Schumpeter, *The Theory of
Economic Development* (New York: Oxford University Press, 1961); and John
Cornwall, *Modern Capitalism: Its Growth and Transformation* (Oxford: Martin
Robertson and Co., 1977).

    Certain important qualifications apply to Cornwall's model at certain stages
of development: In less developed nations the key emphasis which Cornwall
gives the manufacturing sector as a means to achieve the take-off stage to
industrialization can also result in growing unemployment and a failure in

agricultural and domestic market development. Cornwall also neglects an important exogenous variable, namely the country's effort to borrow or develop technology, which is not insignificant in a theory driven by technical progress.

24. See N. Kaldor, *Strategic Factors in Economic Development* (Ithaca, NY: Cornell University Press, 1967) and N. Kaldor, "Economic Growth and the Verdoorn Law: A Comment of Mr. Rowthorn's Article," *Economic Journal* (December 1975).

25. Kenneth Arrow, "The Economic Implications of Learning by Doing," *Review of Economic Studies* (June 1962).

26. See Cornwall, pp. 152 ff. and R. Minami, *The Turning Point in Economic Development: Japan's Experience* (Tokyo, 1973).

27. See Philippe Schmitter, "Interest Intermediation and Regime Governability in Western Europe and North America," in Suzanne Berger, ed., *Organizing Interests in Western Europe: Pluralism and the Transformation of Politics* (Cambridge, England: Cambridge University Press, 1981); P. Schmitter, "Still the Century of Corporatism," *Review of Politics* 36 (January 1974): 85–131; and Gerhard Lehmbruch, "Consociational Democracy, Class Conflict and the New Corporatism," in Philippe Schmitter and Gerhard Lehmbruch, eds., *Trends toward Corporatist Intermediation* (London: Sage, 1979), pp. 53–62.

28. See Chapter 7, "The Neo-corporatist Nations" of Graham K. Wilson, *Business and Politics* (Chatham, NJ: Chatham House Publishers, Inc., 1985), pp. 103–13.

29. See, for example, Peter J. Katzenstein, "Capitalism in One Country? Switzerland in the International Economy," *International Organization* 35 (Autumn 1980): 507–40. And, for a contrast of Switzerland as a form of "liberal corporatism" and Austria as an example of "social democratic corporatism," see P. Katzenstein, *Small States in World Markets: Industrial Policy in Europe* (Ithaca, NY: Cornell University Press, 1985).

30. See Manfred G. Schmidt, "The Politics of Labour Market Policy: Structural and Political Determinants of Rates of Unemployment in Industrial Nations," in *Managing Mixed Economies* edited by Francis G. Castles, Franz Lehner, and Manfred G. Schmidt (Volume 3 of *The Future of Party Government*, edited by Rudolf Wildenmann) (Berlin/New York: Walter de Gruyter, 1988), p. 17 fn.

31. Schmidt, "Labour Market Policy," p. 6.

32. See R. Isaak, "Modern Reactions to Inflation: Private and Public Strategies," in Part II of Wilhelm Hankel and R. Isaak, *Modern Inflation: Its Economics and Its Politics* (Lanham, MD: University Press of America, 1983); in German: *Die moderne Inflation* (Cologne: Bund-Verlag, 1981). The initial version of the application of the typology to stages of development was presented as a paper, "State Strategies and Stages of Development: Shards of a Theory," at the 25th Annual Convention of the International Studies Association at Atlanta, Georgia, March 27–31, 1984. When first presented at a conference at the Johns Hopkins University SAIS Center in Bologna, Italy in 1981, Professor Karl Deutsch summarized the methodology used to derive the typology as follows: "He observed what certain individuals did to try to cope with the inflation of the 1970s and organized the results in four categories. Then he examined the behavior of corporations and states during the same period in black-box fashion, without concerning himself with their inner structures, to determine what kind of similarities the input-output behavior of these units had with the four categories of individual behavior. Larger systems can be exactly as aggressive in their behavior as the individuals are who lead them. Hitler's Germany is a perfect example. Both the behavior of the individual and the state he governed were nasty and aggressive. Such a distribution of psychological types that can be

applied at different levels may take us methodologically beyond the complicated theories of Erik Erikson, enabling social scientists to do a kind of market
research analysis: for example, a state or corporation might be in the market for
a maintenance man in a certain historical phase—supported by people who,
themselves, may not be conservative." (Karl Deutsch's conference commentary
in taped transcript, *Modern Inflation*, pp. 198–199.)

33. Guy Kirsch and Klaus Mackscheidt, "Western Ideas about China's Economic
Direction Are mostly Wrong," *The German Tribune*, No. 1266, March 15, 1987,
p. 8.

34. See Ezra F. Vogel, *Japan as Number 1* (Cambridge, MA.: Harvard University
Press, 1979); Chalmers Johnson, *MITI and the Japanese Miracle, The Growth of
Industrial Policy 1925–75* (Stanford, CA: Stanford University Press, 1982); and
T.J. Pempel and Keiich Tsunekawa, "Corporatism without Labour," in
Schmitter and Lehmbruch, eds., *Corporatist Intermediation*, pp. 231–70.

35. See R.G.H. Siu, *The Tao of Science* (Cambridge, MA: MIT Press, 1957), T.S. Lebra,
Japanese Patterns of Behavior (Honolulu: University Press of Hawaii, 1976), and
Richard Tanner Pascale and Anthony G. Athos, *The Art of Japanese Management*
(New York: Warner Books, 1981).

36. See R. Isaak, "The West German Industrial Model Under Seige," *Adherent*
(Spring 1983); Graham Hallett, *The Social Market Economy of West Germany* (New
York: Macmillan, 1973), pp. 19–20; and "West Germany: A Social-market Econ-
omy," Chapter 2 in *European Politics*, pp. 27–62.

37. See Klaus Peter Krause, "In Search of the Meaning of 'Social' in a Social Market
Economy" (originally in German in the *Frankfurter Allgemeine Zeitung*, October
8, 1988), *The German Tribune*, No. 1344, October 23, 1988, p. 7.

38. See Part II of *Modern Inflation*. Also see Wilhelm Hankel, "Germany: Economic
Nationalism in the International Economy," in Wilfred Kohl and Giorgio Basevi,
eds., *West Germany: A European and Global Power* (Lexington, MA: D.C. Heath,
1980), pp. 21–43.

39. See W. Hankel, *Prosperity Amidst Crisis: Austria's Economic Policy and the Energy
Crunch* (Boulder, CO: Westview Press, 1980), p. 149. Originally published as
Prosperität in der Krise (Vienna: Molden, 1979).

40. Katzenstein, "Capitalism in One Country?," p. 511.

41. Robert E. Norton, "The American Out to Save Poland," *Fortune*, Vol. 121, No. 3,
Jan. 29, 1990, pp. 129–134.

42. Philip Slater, *The Pursuit of Loneliness* (Boston: Beacon Press: 1976).

43. Alan Bloom, *The Closing of the American Mind* (New York: Simon & Schuster, 1987).

44. R. Isaak, "Die Politik der Umgestaltung in Europa: Währung, industrielle und
parteiliche Orientierungen," paper presented at the Fakultät für
Sozialwissenschaften, Universität Mannheim, Mannheim, West Germany, June
21, 1988. The implications that follow are based upon this paper.

45. David Cameron, "The Expansion of the Public Economy: A Comparative Analysis," *The American Political Science Review* 72, (December 1978): 1243–61.

46. Lecture by Fritz Scharpf on *Sozialdemokratische Krisenpolitik in Europa* at the
University of Heidelberg, June 9, 1988.

CHAPTER SIX

MULTINATIONAL STRATEGIES, ECONOMIC CYCLES, AND DIRECT INVESTMENT

Giant organizations are nothing new in international trade. They were a characteristic form of the mercantilist period when large joint-stock companies, e.g., The Hudson's Bay Company, The Royal African Company, The East India Company, to name the major English merchant firms, organized long-distance trade with America, Africa and Asia. But neither these firms, nor the large mining and plantation enterprises in the production sector, were the forerunners of the multinational corporation. They were like dinosaurs, large in bulk, but small in brain, feeding on the lush vegetation of the new worlds (the planters and miners in America were literally Tyrannosaurus rex).

Stephen Hymer, *The Multinational Corporation and the Law of Uneven Development* (1972)

As the twentieth century winds down, the nation-state often appears to be an antique, if not obsolete, structure from the perspective of global economic change: To shore up its overloaded maintenance base, national leaders seek to use multinational corporations as the vanguards of economic growth, development, and employment. The locus of economic dynamism has shifted from the state to the global company, which offers more flexibility and higher salaries to its managers than does any government. Given normal geographical fixity, the world of nation-states often seems like an ice-cube tray with global liquidity flowing over it or not depending upon the capriciousness of external trends.

While multinational companies can invest or disinvest, merge with others or go it alone, rise from nothing or disappear in bankruptcy, the state seems stodgy and stuck in comparison, glued more or less to one piece of territory, fighting off entropy and budget crises, the national community usually assessing the latest foreign attacks upon a condition of declining competitiveness and the vulnerability in its domestic markets. Thus, it may be beneficial to examine briefly the sources of dynamism behind the strategies of multinational companies and the ways in which these strategies are targeted to take advantage of shifts in economic or business cycles.

The changing nature of multinational corporations and direct investment in a global era of high technology and instant information flows makes it ever more important to understand the nature of economic cycles and the strategies available for coping with them. For no small part of the asymmetry between rich and poor nations is due to the collective learning capacity of multinational companies based in different countries in terms of responding effectively to shifting business cycles. While national resources, state structures, and access to foreign capital are significant constraints, the collective learning ability of the private sector in cooperation with public-sector support may well be the cutting edge in turning a political economy around from a dependent, deficit-ridden condition to a more self-sufficient, surplus-bound situation where efficient maintenance strategies are not a dream but a daily habit. This, in turn, suggests that the factors contributing to the bargaining power of the multinational corporation (versus that of both the home and host governments) are the essential elements of competitiveness in international political economy and the extent to which the economic fruits of this competitiveness are reinvested in long-term infrastructure (industrial plant and equipment) for the sake of employment and social prosperity, or are diffused in short-term accumulation strategies of private investors.

ORIGINS

Generally a "multinational" corporation in a strict sense refers to a company owned by stockholders in several countries that is also based in two countries—Royal-Dutch Shell and Unilever (in Britain and the Netherlands), for example. But these are the exceptions, not the rule. Usually multinational corporations are based and owned in one country with manufacturing facilities in two or more other countries that repatriate profits that are not reinvested. Such firms based in one country are sometimes called "transnational" corporations to distinguish them from the purer, two-country-based companies. But everyday usage suggests that it is wiser to retain the term "multinational corporation" although few firms qualify in the "pure" sense, much as Max Weber's ideal type of "charismatic" is used to describe authority figures who may not be charismatic in all senses of the word.

In terms of size, multinational corporations are traced back to the East India Company, chartered in London in 1600, which established "outposts of progress" or branches overseas. Ultimately, the British East India Company had its own private army to protect its stakes and employees in unpredictable environments abroad. From the nation of small shopkeepers (and local pin factory) of Adam Smith, to the national corporation, to international representation for trade abroad, to direct investment in manufacturing and the emergence of multinational corporations with global strategies, the development of multinational strategies has been evolutionary, often catching contemporary government policymakers by surprise. Business managers are compulsively future-directed (although not necessarily long-term oriented); technology is inherently unpredictable (although not necessarily always absorbable); and foreign competitors are enigmatic (but not undecipherable). Thus, to get at some of the universals in multinational development despite historical or cultural differences is not a simple matter. A brief comparison of business systems emerging from significantly different cultural traditions illustrates the possibility and complexity of the task of pinning down such principles.

The Emergence of U.S. versus Japanese Multinational Corporations

From the English, French, and Dutch mercantile families of the seventeenth century, the Americans learned that to succeed at international trade it was necessary to have representatives overseas. Typically, the Americans would either send independent agents or family members abroad to represent their businesses as foreign commerce grew in the colonial era. Up until the time of the American Revolution, American business development was conditioned by the control of British mercantile policy: This policy aimed to keep a favorable balance of payments for the home (mother) country, to discourage manufacturing within the colonies, and to constrain the colonists to trade within the British Empire.[1] True to their independent nature, the Americans openly disregarded such restrictions.

Individuals Go Abroad: Entrepreneurship Multinationalized

At the turn of the nineteenth century, cotton became the greatest American export and the basis for establishing an important American textile industry (relying, of course, upon inexpensive slave labor). In the early third of the century, canals were built to link the interior of the country with the coast. The mood became one of "Manifest Destiny." However, perhaps due to the tradition of rugged, laissez-faire individualism, many of the businesses started abroad by Americans in the middle of the nineteenth century lasted only for their lifetime or that of their sons. They found themselves heavily under pressure in the developing countries by host governments, and their concessions were often cancelled—as opposed to more benign treatment in countries like Canada. The Panama Railroad and Nicaraguan carriage-steamboat line were the most important American direct foreign investments preceding the Civil War.

American experience in Nicaragua and elsewhere taught U.S. business people that they had to vary their plans for different cultures. In the second half of the nineteenth century American business abroad came into increasing competition with the British, particularly in third-country regions such as Mexico and Central America. Transportation and communication developments within the United States increasingly made it possible for companies to become *national* enterprises—the first step toward becoming multinational concerns. When a U.S. company decided to go abroad, true to the laissez-faire tradition of American liberalism, the government usually had little involvement, leaving the company on its own. In the late nineteenth century, surplus output and the desire to benefit from economies of scale led many U.S. companies to seek export markets. However, again true to the American belief in free trade, there is little evidence of "dumping" by American businesses; rather, there was a rough adherence to the principle of comparable prices. Communication innovations led to automatic international extensions as the Western Union Telegraph Company was founded in 1856 and the International Ocean Telegraph Company installed the first cable to Latin America between Florida and Havana in 1866. By the 1880s, Tropical American Company had acquired the telephone rights in South America and was selling parts to Latin American telephone companies. At the same time, the Edison Electric Light Company was exporting to Brazil, Chile, and Argentina and started installing lighting systems in Latin America. But after reaping few profits, Edison withdrew from foreign markets in disappointment.

By the last decade of the nineteenth century, American inventors, manufacturers, and marketers were involved in international business, led by men such as Isaac Singer, Alexander Graham Bell, Thomas Edison, George Westinghouse, George Eastman, John D. Rockefeller, and J.P. Morgan. What Mira Wilkins has termed the "American Invasion" era was in full swing.[2]

The thrust of American international business activity was directed toward forward integration into sales or into horizontal integration—generally in the industrial or industrializing countries. The American government, in turn, was pulled into becoming more involved—passing the Sherman Antitrust Act of 1890 (forbidding agreements that restrained trade) on the one hand, and conquering the Philippines (which government policymakers thought would become a base for U.S. trade in the Orient) on the other. In the chaotic Third-World markets, the U.S. government was particularly likely to provide American businesses with information and assistance. Rather than directly competing with the Americans, the Europeans preferred a policy of "negotiated environments." For example, American and European gunpowder industries negotiated market boundaries, some exclusive, some shared, and some free. In coming to terms with European traditions, many American businesses found they had to cooperate with European companies rather than act independently as they were naturally inclined to.

German hostility to foreign enterprise at the time, not to mention high tariffs and restrictive patent laws, led American firms to set up manufacturing facilities there (much as Japanese were motivated out of similar concerns to make direct investments in the United States a century later). For somewhat different reasons (but including high tariffs), American companies also started local manufacturing in France. In Russia the American multinational ran into a stiff nationalism: Businesses operated under close government scrutiny with the Finance Minister monitoring almost every deal and with the Russian government serving as virtually the exclusive customer for some companies (such as Westinghouse Air Brake Company). To cope with nationalism abroad, American multinational strategies focused on incorporating in a joint venture with host companies, shifting from sales operations to manufacturing and refining so as to bypass tariffs, hiring local people, buying locally, taking on "national" titles and, if necessary, making security deposits (in the case of insurance companies).

In the American political economy, multinational corporations emerged primarily from an entrepreneurial strategy—businesses and families sending their agents abroad to make foreign trade possible; innovations in transportation and communication facilitating the emergence of national companies that sought export markets *on their own* for surplus production and economies of scale; and protectionist international relations leading to high-risk direct investments to avoid tariffs and cultural obstacles. The state or government followed with supportive policies long after entrepreneurs had led the way, many businesses going bankrupt abroad within one or two generations for lack of assistance and continuity. Contrast this with the way Japanese multinational companies emerged, something we will now examine.

Zaibatsu and Sogoshosha: How Japanese Maintenpreneurial Multinationals Emerged

The rise of Japanese corporate groups, the *zaibatsu* (literally "financial clique"), stemmed from the Meiji Restoration of 1868. Prior to this radical change in government form toward centralization (which helps to explain the "tight-ship-in-a-storm efficacy" of "Japan Inc." in the world economy today) Tokugawa Japan possessed a government (the *bakufu*) of decentralized personal bonds that linked the shogun, the daimyo, and the samurai, bonds that were more important than institutions. The impetus for changing the governmental structure came largely from abroad. In 1853 and 1854 U.S. Commodore Matthew Perry forced open Japanese ports to the West. Foreign trade interests began to invade the country, imposing a 5 percent limit on the tariffs the Japanese could put upon imports. The foreigners went so far as to demand the right to "extraterritoriality" so that their citizens could be governed by their own laws rather than those of the Japanese while they resided in Japan. The resentment of the Japanese helped to bring down the shogun who ran the country, theoretically returning power to the Emperor—Meiji— whose name is used to identify the 1868–1912 consolidation of the Japanese political system.[3] In *Imitation and Innovation* (1987) sociologist Eleanor Westney details how Western organizational forms were emulated in Meiji Japan: "collective learning" at work.

As in Great Britain and the United States, a number of mergers characterized business restructuring in Japan in the second half of the nineteenth century. Many of the largest businesses in the early to mid-Meiji era were single-industry businesses. By 1896, of the fifty largest manufacturing and mining companies, twenty-eight were cotton textile companies—firms that were to become even more dominant because of the merger movement. At the very beginning of the twentieth century, the number of cotton-spinning companies fell from seventy-eight to forty-six.[4] Such Japanese industrial companies were less integrated than American firms and were more comparable to British companies. The insular state depends upon companies abroad for sources of raw materials and markets for finished goods, resulting in a relative lack of vertical integration. Japan had a reasonably well-developed marketing system dating back to the early nineteenth century so that manufacturers did not have to set up their own marketing networks. Foreigners (to this day) have found it difficult to penetrate this marketing arrangement.

Thus, huge diversified companies—*zaibatsu*—soon assumed a hegemonic position over the industrial and other business sectors in Japan. More diversified than American or British multinational companies, the *zaibatsu* typically included manufacturing, a bank to finance manufacturing activities, and a trading company to market the products abroad (the *sogoshosha*). By 1914, Japan was dominated by eight major *zaibatsu*, three of which (Mitsubishi, Mitsui, Sumitomo) are still among the largest of the nine main *sogoshosha* (trading companies) that help to steer Japanese business in the late twentieth century. By the early 1920s, a great deal of the mining, shipbuilding, banking, foreign trade, and industry of Japan was controlled by the *zaibatsu*.

Almost all Japanese firms specialize in a single sector—a specialization nurtured in part by MITI—Japan's governmental ministry of industry and trade, which seeks to create appropriate conditions for the competitiveness of the country's major companies over the long run. This specialization contrasts with the loose American conglomerate, made up of businesses from different sectors that may be added or dropped depending upon short-term market fluctuations. Either companies from a single industrial sector organize for collective learning and clout, or one strong firm from each sector is incorporated into a *zaibatsu*, which is centered around large banks and linked to non-*zaibatsu* groups. The twentieth-century tradition of the *zaibatsu* was to have a holding company at the top, directly controlling the specialized firms in the *zaibatsu* group. Although these holding companies were forbidden and dispersed during the occupation following World War II, the *sogoshosha*, or trading companies, remaining still operate along the lines of the *zaibatsu*, much as the large companies supposedly broken up in Germany after the war have been recast and predominate in the German economy.[5] The five largest of the nine major *sogoshosha* in the late 1980s are not just trading companies but utilize a strategy aimed at securing sources of basic raw materials and maintaining world market share. For example, the largest of the five (Mitsubishi, Mitsui, C. Itoh, Marubeni, and Sumitomo) alone account for about one-third of the energy (gas and oil) imported by Japan.[6]

The *sogoshosha* serve not only the big organizations but also the small: They eliminate difficult barriers to entry into new foreign markets for small manufacturing firms that would not normally have the financial or managerial resources to support international ventures. Brazil, Korea, and the Southeast Asian political economies have developed their own forms of *sogoshosha* based upon the Japanese model, so convinced are they that these organizations are engines of export-led economic growth. Overcoming the static concepts of comparative-advantage theories of international trade, the *sogoshosha*'s key strength is to gather foreign marketing intelligence from all over the world, to sift through the information, and target it for the right company at the right place at the right time.

As information increasingly becomes the basis for power and competitiveness in the international economy, the Japanese trading company intelligence networks are strategically placed and traditionally cultivated to be highly efficient information processors for both Japanese multinational companies and the Japanese nation. Using something of a "tribal clan mode of organization," the *sogoshosha* serve as large and loyal clearing houses for companies offering diverse goods and services, hooking ultimately into the *senmonshosha*—thousands of specialized, wholesale distributors trading in specific sectors. The *sogoshosha* are flexible organizations, highly leveraged (in terms of debt-equity ratio), and thrive on both dynamic and static economies of scale given a national and worldwide network of market contracts. They are able to barter goods and services among themselves for significant savings and can move in and out of specific markets quickly with the effective collective learning capacity made possible by territorial knowledge bases cultivated over decades.[7]

Perhaps the most significant contrast between the American and Japanese multinational management cultures is the traditional laissez-faire antagonism between the (government) maintenance base and the entrepreneurial company on the one hand, and the maintenpreneurial cooperation between big government and big business in Japan on the other. Early in the twentieth century, American antitrust legislation led the U.S. government to break up Standard Oil of California, for example, into eleven parts (each of which ultimately became larger than the initial company). In comparison, MITI and the *Keidanren*,* the government trade and industry bureaucracies, actively cultivate mergers between weaker companies to consolidate firms into large, competitive units to make Japan more effective in international trade. The laissez-faire system encourages individualism and entrepreneurial innovation, whereas the maintenpreneurial approach stresses long-term targeting and collective adaptation with an institutional structure that assures follow-through on national strategies.

INTERPRETATIONS

Regardless of which culture one observes, the trend in multinational organization or global direct investment in the twentieth century has been one of mergers organizationally and towards foreign direct investment led by oligopolistic industries (that is, those controlled by a few competing sellers). Not only did the influence of the state on national political economies grow greatly in the twentieth century, but the impact of multinational corporations also expanded: The turnover of the ten largest multinational companies is greater than the GNP of some eighty countries. What made this national and international growth of corporations possible is the growing importance of *imperfect* competition. In a world of perfect competition—the utopia of Adam Smith—there would be many small competitors in each nation supplying all the goods and services demanded and no impetus for direct foreign investment. But in the real world economy, the imperfection of competition provides irresistible payoffs for companies with special access to scarce resources or specialized knowledge or technology for which there is great demand. The chaos of imperfect markets, reasserted incessantly by the creative destruction of capitalist innovation, creates the motivation for oligopolistic organizations to maximize their global market share and to merge or form cartels with their counterparts to make entry into their markets difficult through economies of scale and cooperative pricing. In the process, observers have noted that the world economy has become increasingly structured into developed and uneven developing regions—metropoles and peripheries epitomizing the asymmetry between rich and poor nations in the late twentieth century.

---

*The *Keidanren*, the peak industrial association made up of the 700 or so largest companies, works closely with MITI.

Direct Investment: Oligopoly and the Law
of Uneven Development

In tracing the development of companies from workshop to factory to national corporation to multidivisional corporation to multinational corporation, economist Stephen Hymer not only argued that oligopolies were the leaders in direct investment but that such direct investment is concentrated in the metropolitan centers (or metropoles) of advanced developed countries leaving everywhere else—the periphery—underdeveloped.[8] It is not just a question of increase in size: Corporate growth is qualitative as well as quantitative, evolving increasingly complex administrative and communication systems, or "brains." By the early 1980s, of the top fifteen recipients of direct investment only four were generally not classified as developed countries: South Africa, Brazil, Mexico, and Hong Kong. The less developed countries (LDCs) accounted for only about 31 percent of foreign-owned affiliates, 54 percent being in Europe.[9] Thus, the statistics support Hymer's argument. The thrust of his interpretation is that money and new plant construction from the rich nations will continue to flow disproportionately to the most developed sections of the rich countries, financing technological and economic innovation and development there at the expense of all the other peripheral areas of the world where the investment could have gone but did not. Because of the "learning-by-doing" effects of this deepening of capital, two different worlds of education and economic sophistication emerge as the gap between them grows.

Hymer's vision is one of an emerging imperial economic hierarchy headed by oligopolistic multinational corporations that eventually reach an "oligopolistic equilibrium" following an accute competitive phase aimed at increasing global market share. This "Imperial System" will follow the "Law of Uneven Development" as it creates poverty as well as wealth, underdevelopment as well as development. The division of labor between geographic regions corresponds to the vertical division of labor within the company. High-level decision making in the system will be centralized in the metropoles—a few key cities in the advanced countries. The metropoles, in turn, are surrounded by a number of regional subcapitals. The rest of the world (the periphery) is confined to low levels of activity and income—having the status of villages or towns in the Imperial System. The metropoles monopolize income, status, authority, and consumption, sharing some with the regional subcapitals but with declining curves of these values as one moves from the (metropole) center to the periphery, perpetuating a pattern of inequality and dependency. Thus, New York, London, Tokyo, Bonn, and Paris (and eventually Moscow and Beijing) become the major centers of high-level strategic planning in the Imperial System, while lesser cities deal with day-to-day operations. And the "best" and highest-paid professionals—administrators, doctors, lawyers, scientists, educators, government officials, actors, and servants—will be concentrated in or near the metropoles.

Again, Hymer's vision is astutely prophetic in terms of the concentration of economic and political power in the asymmetrical world economic system of the late twentieth century. Statistically, the metropoles (and their suburbs) are even responsible for being the greatest producers of new patents—the indicator of cutting-edge research and development. Corporate, government, and academic institutions in the metropoles often have a lead-time of at least six months in receiving information on new technological and economic innovations, giving them an often decisive competitive edge in a fast-moving global economy and perpetuating their dominance over subsidiary and lesser institutions located in the periphery. If information is power in the emerging high-tech/high-information global economy, then sitting at the source of new information is a prerequisite to political and economic competitiveness. And the most sophisticated technologies for processing information—for sorting out the quick from the dead—are often concentrated in the metropoles in such quantity as to make a qualitative difference in the levels of information flows received by inhabitants of these privileged areas. Collective learning happens faster here and in a concentrated, high-tempo manner, thus intensifying the learning and experience curves hypothesized by economist Kenneth Arrow and the Boston Consulting Group.[10] The metropoles, in short, are staging grounds for static and dynamic economies of scale that propel institutions there ahead of others.

Host Country versus Home Multinational Bargaining Power

Having one's headquarters in one of the world's key metropoles can help maximize the bargaining power of a multinational corporation in dealing with host countries in the periphery where it makes direct or portfolio investments. Theodore H. Moran identified three other variables perhaps even more crucial in determining the negotiating balance of power between multinational corporations and host countries: (1) the extent of competition in the industry (or, How unstable are the oligopolies?); (2) the changeableness of the technology (or, How fast is it changing?); and (3) the importance of marketing and product differentiation. Bargaining power for the multinational corporation is high relative to the host country if competition is low, if technology is changeable, and if the importance of marketing is high. On the other hand, host countries can be expected to have high bargaining power if competition is high, if technology is stable, and if marketing is of little importance. Moran projects increasing power for Third-World host countries as bargaining power changes over time, as the host countries move up a learning curve, and as the viability of economic nationalism in Third-World countries increases.[11]

The shift in bargaining power from First-World-based multinationals to Third-World host countries began in the 1970s with the success of OPEC.

Stimulating Third-World economic nationalism and largely frustrated efforts at forming other commodity cartels, host governments became more sophisticated in their bargaining conditions. However, with the widespread debt crisis in developing countries in the 1980s, bargaining power shifted back the other way. Desperately in need of new capital, many developing countries had to make major concessions—particularly on initial corporate tax rates—in order to lure First-World multinational companies into uncertain political and economic environments. Standing to gain from more optimum utilization of production factors and idle resources and the possibility of upgrading resources and production with new technology and investment, developing countries bent over backwards to attract foreign companies to their soil.

The risks involved—the exploitation of their prime resources, the replacement of local firms by the multinationals, and the potential destruction of local entrepreneurship—not to mention increasing dependence upon foreign influence—were often understated for the sake of short-term economic and employment gains that could bolster the power position of elected officials in the Third World.

In the late 1980s and 1990s a strategy is emerging in the Third World aimed at consolidating the gains in bargaining power of the nation-state made in the 1970s with the economies of scale made possible through organizing large multinational enterprises by subsidizing the creation of Third-World-based multinationals.[12] The success of such efforts to use home-grown multinationals as arms of the state's economic policy depends not just upon obtaining start-up financing but upon the previous success of critical transfers of technology relevant to the product cycles involved.

The Product Cycle and Technology Transfer

That which has been called "the product cycle" almost always begins in the developed countries where high-income market economies provide an environment conducive to both technological innovation and the ad hoc flexibility and maintenance risk insurance facilitating the commercial applications of such technological change. The United States is the prime example. Its large domestic market, loose, flexible labor structure, high-income consumption, and collective tendency to try out, develop, or purchase "the new" make it an optimal testing ground for new products. The entrepreneurial culture spawns new product innovation. It also serves as a basis for the hegemonic role of the United States (as the entrepreneurial culture *par excellence*) in the world economy since World War II, attracting direct foreign investment and portfolio investment with some combination of a multitude of inventive investment options, political stability, attractive interest rates, receptiveness to innovation, a skilled and mobile labor pool, and multiple sources of capital and technology.

The product life-cycle theory—sometimes called the *neotechnologist school*—is divided into four stages: introduction or innovation; growth; maturation; and decline. At the *introductory* stage, a new product is created in a developed market economy where the cost of innovation is not a problem and the innovator does not have to worry about the product having a high initial price. Then, if the product has a certain amount of success, the *growth* stage commences and the product becomes widespread in the national market. When the product reaches the *maturity* stage, its production has become standardized and, therefore, cheaper to produce with unskilled labor. At this stage the product is exported, having satiated the domestic market. But given the standardization of production it soon becomes cheaper to produce the product in developing countries where the wages are lower than in the home country. Competition emerges as the technology is copied or adapted or bought. The foreign developing country then starts exporting the same product back into the home, developed country where it was born—the final phase of *decline*.[13]

Product-cycle theory assumes that information does not flow freely across national borders, but that key technological processes related to production and marketing are concentrated and protected in certain developed countries—at least initially. Moreover, it assumes that each country has its own peculiar milieu, which is more or less conducive to technological change and which steers the direction of that change. Finally, the theory assumes that international trade is often directed by the particular stages that products happen to be in during their life cycles combined with the changing matrix of international marketing opportunities for the product.

Empirical testing of the product life-cycle theory indicates that it applies to many but not all products.[14] For example, the fashion industry moves so quickly, the creative destruction occurs so fast, that the product life-cycle theory hardly applies as the new is constantly replacing the old.[15] But if it can eventually be established that the theory covers most products, a major cause for the asymmetry between the developed and developing countries will have been discovered. For the rich, developed countries where the innovations initially take place get the most profits and mileage out of the products in the early phases of their life cycle. And by the time the products are in decline, the multinationals in the metropoles have more innovative replacements ready to launch on the markets in order to maintain market leadership, if not domination. One has the sense that the developing countries are given recycled technologies by the developed countries after quite a bit of the juice has been drained from them.

Benjamin Franklin argued that technological innovations of any kind should be shared freely with mankind. But that was in the eighteenth century when he could hardly dream that the United States might one day attempt to live more off of selling the patents for technological innovations and their servicing than from producing agricultural or manufactured goods. In service-sector-dominated developed economies, the control of technology transfers to potentially competitive economies has become a key to maintaining their economic, if not political, hegemony.

To understand the dynamics of the multinational corporation in a global context, it is not sufficient just to focus upon the product cycle and technology transfer. Longer-term economic and business cycles are significant as well for managers who seek to cope effectively with change by systematically reducing uncertainty into calculable risk. A failure to understand these cycles—or the error of mistaking one for another—tempts corporate managers to become preoccupied with mere maintenance strategies rather than those of the dynamic entrepreneur. And the larger the corporation, the more tempting it is to be predominated by maintenance strategies. The U.S. manager, for example, is shackled with the short-term scrutiny of stockholders (unlike longer-term bank-financed Japanese managers) who block him from "going for broke" with everything in terms of innovation or the direction of the highest long-term payoff. So the American manager "satisfices"—maintaining low risks in some areas while taking high-risk gambles in others.*

Short-term, Intermediate, and Long-term Business Cycles

Corporate plans and strategies succeed or fail depending upon the accuracy of assumptions that managers make concerning the frequency and nature of business cycles. Such cycles, together with power transitions, can also be used to anticipate wars between states.† In everyday usage, the concept of "business cycle" refers to three- to eight-year patterns of rising and falling economic activity, of expansion and recession, peaks and troughs. However, many economists have found these short-term, fluctuating modes of behavior alone to be insufficient to explain and predict business patterns. Therefore, they have combined short-term "business cycles" with intermediate-term (fifteen to twenty-five years) "long-swing" investment (or Kuznets) cycles, and long-term or "long-wave" (forty-five to sixty years) Kondratieff cycles.

Expansionary economic phases can be viewed as part of a *syntropic* process, a building up of production, employment, incomes, stock market prices, and construction. Periods of recession or decline, on the other hand, may be seen as a form of *entropic* process, of obsolescence and

---

*Economist and Nobel laureate Herbert A. Simon used "satisficing" to combine "satisfy" and "suffice": the tendency to choose an alternative that looks like it will make do, rather than the best one.

†For political management perspectives on the relationship between economic cycles, power transitions, and wars, see "Special Issue: The Economic Foundations of War," *International Studies Quarterly* 27, No. 4, (December 1983), particularly the article by Raimo Yäyrynen, pp. 389–418.

disintegration. Business or corporate survival literally depends upon accurately anticipating syntropic and entropic shifts in the economy, at least in terms of the key sectors upon which the lifeblood or cash flow of the business depends. But such economic forecasting is a precarious undertaking. It depends upon where one is standing and upon whether one is preoccupied with short-term, intermediate-term, or long-term cycles when analyzing socioeconomic change.

For example, focusing upon the interconnection between short-term and intermediate-term cycles, Harvard economist Alvin Hansen concluded that from 1795 to 1937 in the American economy there were seventeen cycles of an average duration of 8.35 years. One to two minor peaks occur regularly between the major peaks of these eight-year cycles, each minor cycle lasting less than half the duration of the major or "normal" business cycles. However, in looking at the key sector of building construction, Hansen noted that the cycle in this area averaged between seventeen or eighteen years in length, or about twice the length of the normal business cycle. He concluded: "American experience indicates that with a high degree of regularity every other major business boom coincides roughly with a boom in building construction, while the succeeding major cycle recovery is forced to buck up against a building slump....[T]he depressions which have fallen in the interval of the construction downswing are typically deep and long. And the succeeding recovery is held back and retarded by the unfavorable depressional influence from the slump in the building industry."[16]

In illustrating the interconnectedness of short-term business cycles and intermediate-term Kuznets cycles (referring to the 1971 Nobel laureate and economist Simon Kuznets, who discovered them in 1930), Hansen makes clear that a corporate strategy dependent upon the building construction sector would most likely come to grief if it failed to consider the perspective of the intermediate-term cycle, if it focused, for example, only upon short-term cycles. But what about the opposite danger? It is also possible to go wrong in strategic planning by unduly stressing long-term cycles lasting half a century or so at the expense of neglecting short-term fluctuations.

Russian economist Nikolai D. Kondratieff fathered the concept of the long-wave cycle in capitalist economies of some fifty years in length, only later to die in solitary confinement in one of Stalin's concentration camps.[17] Kondratieff discovered two-and-a-half cycles in a series of price, wage, interest rate, and value-affected data, with troughs in 1790, 1844–1851, and 1890–1896; and peaks at 1810–1817, 1870–1875, and 1914–1920.[18] Although production data do not always fit well into Kondratieff's framework, the "idealized" Kondratieff Wave approximates the actual behavior of U.S. wholesale prices closely enough to suggest to long-wave observers that the American economy may be descending into a depression, as Figure 6–1 suggests.

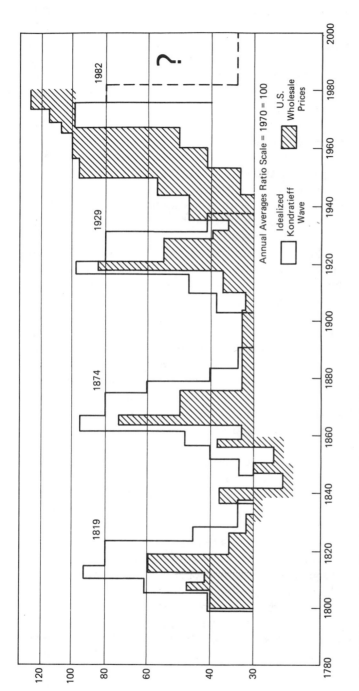

FIGURE 6–1 "The Kondratieff Wave" and U.S. Wholesale Prices

Source note: This line drawing is the author's rough conception of the original "Kondratieff Wave." The original chart was published in the international MONEYLINE, a financial newsletter.

The Forrester Model

The case for a coming depression based on Kondratieff's long wave has been made most thoroughly by Jay W. Forrester, a professor of management at M.I.T. Forrester and his colleagues developed a National System Dynamics Model with the use of computers, built up from policies followed in major sectors of an industrial economy. Flows of people, information, money, prices, and goods connect sectors in the model such as consumer durables, capital equipment, energy, agriculture, and building construction. These sectors are constructed to represent a typical company, and production processes are represented in detail, with adjustments made for inventories, prices, costs, order backlogs, growth rate, marginal productivity, liquidity, profitability, return on investment, and regulatory restraints. Each production sector has an accounting system, and the model also provides for a labor mobility network for the movement of people between sectors, a banking system, the Federal Reserve, household consumption, government, and demography.

Using this replica of the actual American economy, the Forrester group concludes that short-term business-cycle behavior arises basically from management of inventories, backlogs, and employment, in contrast to the dominant view of government policymakers that focuses on the importance of the role of capital investment in such fluctuations. The significant implication here is that the manipulation of interest rates, credit availability, and investment tax incentives has little effect on short-term business cycles given the lead times required for capital construction and depreciation.[19]

The Forrester model indicates that the intermediate Kuznets cycle is concerned with policies in consumer durables and, most likely, agricultural sectors in the ordering of capital equipment. Whereas short-term cycles arise from interactions between the market and employment policies in the durable sectors that try to manage backlogs and inventories of durables, the intermediate cycles arise from interactions between the durables sectors and employment policies in the capital sectors that try to manage backlogs and capital equipment. In relating this view of the intermediate Kuznets cycle to the Kondratieff cycle or long wave and the probability of economic depression in the late twentieth century, Forrester concludes that the Kuznets cycle is apt to appear as "shoulders," that is, an accentuated peaking of the long wave. For example, a drop in the Kuznets cycle could account for the greater severity of the 1958 recession, as well as for the accentuated capital-investment peak of 1971, not to mention the plateau that typically follows a peak in the long wave.

Forrester believes that the long wave, which is apparently related to capital investment, is more important in explaining economic behavior than either the business cycle or the Kuznets cycle. The long wave represents "a massive expansion of the capital sectors followed by a relatively rapid collapse in their output. It is usually described as a peak of economic activity followed by a 10-year plateau, then a drop into a depression period for about a decade, and a long climb over some 30 years to the next peak." Such long-wave behavior appears to account for the great depressions of the 1830s, 1890s and 1930s, and may be crucial in explaining the U.S. economic situation of the late twentieth century. Forces arising from the long wave may explain many present economic cross-currents, raising the spectre of a coming depression.[20]

There were a number of similarities between Forrester's National Model at a peak in the long wave and the economic situation in the United States in the 1980s: lower capital investment, rising unemployment, a flattening out of productivity, lower return on investment, increasing amplitude in business cycles, and less innovation given the maturity of the technological advance of the last wave. The crux of Forrester's anticipation of the probability of a depression is that capital construction peaked in the last wave in the 1970s, leaving the United States with fully developed technologies of the type relevant to the last long wave and with saturated capital markets, meaning a decline in opportunities for attractive investment in capital equipment and building. In terms of excess capacity or idle factories, some economic data support Forrester's depression scenario thesis *if* he is correct about the key prime mover of long-term waves (for example, capital equipment/production and buildings) and *if* he is right that the United States will suffer from a hiatus between the ending of the present technological wave and the beginning of a new one: Whereas the utilization of American manufacturing capacity ran as high as 90 percent in the mid-1960s, it declined to an average in the low 80 percent range during the 1970s, and fell to 74.8 percent by the end of 1981.[21] However, by 1988 plant capacity in the United States was back up to its maximum, close to 85 percent.

Several critical objections can be raised to Forrester's complex articulation of a probable depression. First and foremost, his preoccupation with entropic processes of long-wave decline may blind him to counter-cyclical syntropic processes of economic growth and technological innovation, which may well balance out the entropic processes sufficiently to keep what might have become a depression within the bounds of what may be a series of limited recessions. Forrester's model may also suffer from what Karl Popper called the "poverty of historicism" by basing future projections upon past behavior, whereas we can never know what people in the future will know and therefore cannot predict what their options will be. Another objection to Forrester's gloomy thesis is that it could become a negative self-fulfilling prophecy, having a reverse Pygmalion effect—increasing the odds of extraordinarily bad economic outcomes by projecting such negative expectations.

The difficulty for the corporate strategist who overemphasizes the long-wave is the tendency to miss the healthy trees by taking a distant view of the dark forest: Not all sectors decline in any particular recession. The astute entrepreneur may be far better off looking for hidden positive opportunities in familiar territory in a situation of economic turbulence than he or she would be by accepting a fatalistic, cyclical determinism that implies going bankrupt waiting for a decade or more to pass to catch the next long wave as it begins to make its "inevitable" ascent. For example, by ignoring market cycle timing and by focusing on specific company situations he knew from interviewing or personal experience, Peter Lynch was able to maintain the highest average returns for his Fidelity Magellan Fund portfolio of stocks throughout the 1970s and 1980s, transforming it into the largest American mutual fund (see Lynch's *One Up on Wall Street*). Forrester's model has the flavor of the material determinism against which Benedetto Croce warned us two years after the onset of the Great Depression of 1929: "The sterility of matter will not bring forth and cause to blossom either morals or religion or poetry or philosophy, and not even economics itself, which requires the glow of life, keen intelligence, and eagerness."[22]

In sum, in using short-term, intermediate-term, and long-term business cycles as a basis for corporate or business planning, one must be wary of the errors that result from overemphasizing any one time-frame or cycle or from assuming that a general, macro-level cycle will necessarily affect a specific micro-level sector or economic situation. To become preoccupied with cyclic thinking may inadvertantly lead to a conservative maintenance bias in strategic planning and snuff out the sparks of individual enthusiasm and risk-taking without which the entrepreneur is but a straw man blowing in the wind.

Corporate Strategy

Stepping into the shoes of the corporate manager who is responsible for strategic plans, which assure not merely the corporation's survival but also a significant return on investment for owners and shareholders, it becomes easy to understand why a conservative maintenance strategy is tempting in an era of erratic change and uncertainty. The timing of business cycles often appears to be inscrutable. International markets and sources of supply are politicized. Flexible exchange rates and money-market funds have revolutionized the international monetary system. Productivity growth is erratic. Technological breakthroughs often appear to be in capital-intensive rather than labor-intensive sectors. Future inflation hovers like a black cloud above the aspirations and indeterminacy of industrial democracies where most multinational corporate headquarters are based. It almost seems reasonable under such circumstances to think in terms of Social Darwinism—the strong survive, the weak go under. And it is tempting to adopt a defensive strategy to preserve the value of existing assets and investments, to shore up existing bulkheads in the structure, and to tighten up on efficiency controls within the organization.

An examination of corporate strategies that were employed to fight inflation in the 1970s in terms of four Weberian ideal types—the Defeatist, the Free-rider, the Maintenance Man, and the Entrepreneur—revealed that the maintenance strategy predominated. These four types of strategies were classified according to risk orientation, time horizon, guiding motive, consumption pattern, and characteristic portfolio mix as illustrated in Figure 6–2.[23]

Figure 6–2 is not meant to be exhaustive either in the number of strategy types or in the range of portfolio mixes. Weberian "ideal types" are just typical patterns or typifications of striking features in social reality, like the tips of icebergs that serve to indicate the massive structure that lies invisible beneath the surface. Actual corporate behavior patterns usually draw from more than one strategy type, and sometimes from all of them. Nevertheless, particular strategy types appear to be dominant in specific organizations at certain historical moments. Organizational survival in the past decade, for example, appeared to depend upon the company's ability to transcend defeatist and free-rider strategies. But the international climate of uncertainty did not stimulate healthy, risk-taking behavior, and concerns about losing because of change or inflation reinforced a normal conservative bias of organizations that favors maintenance strategies and penalizes the entrepreneur in an environment calling for the opposite.[24]

In seeking to understand the rationale for the defensive, risk-avoiding attitude that prevails in many corporations and institutions, it is helpful to recall economist Mancur Olson's thesis in *The Logic of Collective Action:* Unless the number of individuals in a group is small, or unless there is coercion or some other incentive to make individuals act in their common interest, rational, self-interested individuals will not act to achieve their common or group interests.[25] There has to be some principle or policy of motivation and deterrence that cuts through large organizations and corporations to constantly remind individuals to maximize the organization's interest, not just their own. In capitalist free-market systems or mixed economies, this is no easy task and management can never be sure of the effectiveness of efforts to assure company loyalty. Moreover, in the large, anonymous group context of the corporation, the individual is often tempted to become a free rider (or a defeatist), settling for mediocre group compromises in which strategies are targeted not for high gains (entrepreneurial strategies) but are rather spread to reduce risks and to keep things going as they are for the sake of job security or promotion (maintenance strategies). Thus the corporation in turbulent times appears to be caught in a double bind: For organizational survival certain "maintenance" rules and conventional loyalty codes must be established, but healthy organizational growth depends upon entrepreneurial risk-taking, which is obstructed by this very maintenance activity. Security and stable returns become the predominate concerns in an era of economic uncertainty. And stockholders in American firms reinforce the problem by

FIGURE 6-2 Corporate Strategies

Strategy Type	Risk Orientation	Time Horizon	Dominant Motive	Consumption Pattern	Portfolio Mix
DEFEATIST	Low	Past	Passive	Thrifty	*Security-oriented:* divest weak holdings insure areas of vulnerability consider declaring bankruptcy exploit cash cows/mature products
FREE-RIDER	High	Present	Active/Passive	High when others pay	*Cheap credit-oriented:* refinance at cheaper interest rate relocate where taxes are lower and public transportation and infrastructure can be exploited relocate abroad for cheap labor speculate in exchange markets
MAINTE-NANCE	Medium	Present short-term	Passive/Active	High	*Stable return and diversity-oriented:* maximize short-term profits reorganize business units within firm, targeting for specific markets buy back company's own stocks shorten reaction time within business units with limited computer planning develop better inflation indicators diversify in firm to cover risks mergers with large companies in similar fields
ENTREPRE-NEUR	High	Future long-term	Aggressive	All or nothing	*High return orientation:* acquire smaller companies to reduce resource dependence & increase innovation and technology R&D bring in outside consultants to plan better financing and R&D increase individual payoffs in company for those who create plans for long-term gains foreign expansion to follow or create customers, increase world market share, overcome international currency and tax fluctuations or government regulatory barriers lobby in government for tax subsidies for R&D, capital formation, and less regulation

annually pushing for short-term profits rather than cultivating long-term world market share and research and development (R&D).

There is one obvious way out of this corporate dilemma in theory, despite numerous variations in practice: The corporation must clearly define limited maintenance objectives for the sake of organizational and group stability (which in many cases may be centralized within the organization) and simultaneously select a number of entrepreneurial target areas and creative pilot tests aimed at high returns and adaptation to change in the long term (which may well be decentralized).

In looking at Figure 6–2 and comparing the portfolio mixes of the maintenance and entrepreneurial strategies, it is clear that maintenance thinking has a low or medium risk orientation, with a focus upon cutting costs and maximizing benefits *within* the firm, whereas entrepreneurial strategies focus on long-term planning and investment in new areas of greatest potential growth with a high risk orientation, seeking to maximize benefits or cut costs by investing *outside* the firm either nationally or internationally. This observation, based on the analysis of corporate strategies in the inflationary environment of the 1970s, is consistent with Peter Drucker's well-known (but often neglected) thesis in his book *Management* that *within* the organization the focus is upon *efficiency,* whereas *outside* the organization the focus is upon effectiveness, and that corporate strategies cannot be effective unless they go from the inside out.[26]

To survive and expand in the twentieth century, corporations require a maintenance base from which to take long-term entrepreneurial risks in the search for new technologies, markets, and sources of resource supply. The Japanese, for example, have become hypercompetitive on the world market in many sectors, such as automobiles, through a unique blend of maintenance and entrepreneurial strategies (or maintenpreneurial strategies). For example, according to the maintenance principle, about one-third of Japanese workers are guaranteed that once hired they will not lose their jobs until they are "retired" in their mid-fifties.* This and other conservative maintenance preconditions built into the Japanese culture give company managers a freer hand in times of change or crisis, permitting them to introduce radical reorganization and technical innovation—such as the introduction of robots on the assembly line.

In the mid-1970s when major automakers were threatened with bankruptcy, governments stepped in to bail out companies like Chrysler and

---

*At this point, they typically either accept more difficult (and usually less desirable) assignments abroad or live off of personal savings until their pensions start at 65 (thus stimulating the Japanese savings rate throughout the life-cycle). The earnings of Japanese are more conditioned by the number of dependents, age and seniority than those of American workers. See Arne Kalleberg and James Lincoln, "The Structure of Earnings Inequality in the United States and Japan," *American Journal of Sociology,* supp., 94: p. S149 (1988).

British Leyland with mixed results, whereas in Japan a maintenpreneurial culture integrating companies and banks permitted Toyo Kogya (the producer of Mazda cars) of Hiroshima to radically shift its strategy, restructure, double its productivity, cut its debt, and to fire no one for five years. The "maintenance base" was provided by the traditional loyalty of the Japanese local community, labor force (given job security), and private creditors. Thus, the Sumitomo Bank appointed six of its people to major management positions in the auto company, including chairman (a standard practice in Japan where banks usually own companies and supply managers). These personnel shifts together with worker-participation groups offering suggestions gave Mazda both the financial basis and flexibility needed for effective entrepreneurial adaptation to the changed environment. Parts inventories were cut back, even given the risks of stopping assembly lines; new equipment was purchased to improve efficiency (including robots); new hiring was frozen; workers agreed to accept smaller wage rises; and several thousand unneeded workers on the assembly line were rerouted to serve temporarily as Mazda car salesmen at distribution centers and from door-to-door.

Whereas the development of Western industrial societies involved the evolution of separate institutions with autonomous spheres of influence and it was assumed that the spiritual and social life of the individual should reside *outside* the workplace, this is not the case in Japan or China.[27] The Japanese company concerns itself with the worker's full range of social and spiritual needs, creating a maintenance base that is tightly knit and integrated with the culture. For example, Toyota Motor Company, Japan's largest automaker, has created an entire town ("Toyota City") to satisfy needs of its workers ranging from houses, dormitories, baseball fields, gymnasiums, swimming pools, tennis courts, and sumo rings, to a company stadium. This is perhaps the most efficient automobile production center in the world. Toyota managers long resisted the temptation to attempt to apply their manufacturing formula outside Toyota City before reluctantly setting up a plant with General Motors in California in the 1980s.[28] By strictly adhering to three manufacturing objectives, the efficiency of the maintenance base of Toyota allowed the company to manufacture and ship small cars to the United States for $1,300 to $1,700 (in 1982 figures) less than American automakers could produce a similar car. These three manufacturing objectives were: (1) keep inventories to a bare minimum, (2) ensure that all phases of the manufacturing process are completed correctly the first time even if it slows down the assembly line, and (3) reduce the amount of human labor expended on each automobile. This efficient maintenance base of Japan's incredibly effective entrepreneurship is grounded on a "shame culture." Kenichi Ohmae, managing director of McKinsey & Company in Tokyo, observes: "The Toyota system is based on shame culture—that it is shameful to stop the whole plant. It would be risky in the United States. One guy could sabotage the whole plant. A lot of Toyota's advantage is not directly transferable."[29] The resulting

Japanese advantage over American automobile manufacturers is sharply revealed in the statistics[30] contained in Figure 6–3 that compares all Japanese auto firms with U.S. companies.

FIGURE 6–3 Comparisons Between Japanese and American Automakers

		Japan	U.S.
MANUFACTURING: (Machine stamping operations)	Parts stamped per hour	550	325
	Manpower per press line	1	7–13
	Time needed to change dies	5 minutes	4–6 hours
	Average production run	2 days	10 days
	Time needed to build small car	30.8 hours	59.9 hours
PERSONNEL: (Average auto plant)	Total work force	2,360	4,250
	Average number of workers absent (vacation, illness, etc.)	185	500
	Average absentee rate	8.3%	11.8%

The ways in which a culture or society (such as Japan) is able to create such an efficient maintenance base, which permits such effective entrepreneurial strategies in the world market, remain somewhat mysterious, although an hypothesis can be suggested. When the samuri of Japan lost status in the disintegration of their feudal society, they turned to business to recover their sense of purpose.[31] A similar pattern of entrepreneurial reaction resulted from the downward mobility suffered by the Balinese aristocracy.[32] *The hypothesis is that acute downward mobility or outright disaster in a feudal society brings maintenance and security needs to the surface if the society is to survive, forcing upper-class elites into focused entrepreneurial patterns initially oriented toward reconstructing an efficient maintenance base.* This hypothesis (complemented with the investment of U.S. capital and technology) could explain the incredible Japanese and German economic reconstructions* after World War II.[33] A disturbing corollary to this hypothesis may be that societies that have skipped the feudal stage and have largely avoided acute downward mobility

---

*An alternative hypothesis is that of economist Mancur Olson who argues that the West German and Japanese "economic miracles" after World War II can be explained by the breakup of old distributional coalitions by totalitarian governments and foreign occupation, paving the way for economic growth. See M. Olson, *The Rise and Decline of Nations* (New Haven, Ct: Yale University Press, 1982), Chapter 4, pp. 75–117.

or wartime destruction on their own soil, such as the United States, may not be sufficiently motivated to reconstruct a modern, efficient maintenance base and will become increasingly less competitive against societies, such as the Japanese and German, which have succeeded in reconstituting a modern basis for effective entrepreneurial strategies.

However, despite its feudal past, the British case following World War II provides another contrast to the German and Japanese, given that most of the outdated British industrial plant was not destroyed during the war and so there was less incentive to reconstruct a modern and efficient maintenance base (meaning the British must now compete with old factories and equipment). Many of the British upper class were led to believe they could preserve their status without having to modernize their industries or to stoop to become merely upwardly mobile entrepreneurs.[34] The limits of Anglo-Saxon liberalism in Britain and the United States played a role in fragmenting domestic power.

If a society, because of downward mobility or destructive experience, "takes care of" creating and sustaining an efficient maintenance base (through, for example, the Japanese culture of shame or the German culture of order), the business sector is free to focus its energy upon export-oriented growth and entrepreneurial strategies (assuming that government policies permit the corporate flexibility they have in West Germany and Japan). In short, there are numerous cultural and maintenance-base preconditions to "the German economic miracle" and the efficiency of Japan's global "laser beam" market analysis. Such prerequisites also facilitate corporations from these countries in *hedging* and *positioning* strategies aimed at ensuring against the risk of downturns in the business cycle on the one hand, and at preparing them to be in the right place at the right time for upturns in the cycle on the other.

Thus, in terms of "hedging," in 1982 Toyota sought a more international stance by going into negotiations with General Motors Corporation concerning the possibility of jointly producing small cars in the United States. Although the negotiations succeeded, this was less important for Toyota than that they were held. For such cooperative gestures ease American protectionist pressures aimed at keeping Japanese cars out of the American market whether by tariff or "voluntary restraint." Other corporate hedging strategies include concentric and conglomerate diversification* and ensuring assets against loss due to exchange-rate fluctuations or high interest rates by buying foreign currencies or shares in money funds.

As for "positioning" strategies, an example *par excellence* is the Japanese strategy of shifting away from additional future investment in the politicized

---

*Concentric diversification is related to an organization's existing line of business (or "strategic fit"), whereas conglomerate diversification branches out into lines of business or markets unrelated to existing ones.

sector of automobiles and turning increasingly to microchips and other related high-tech sectors. (By 1982 the Japanese 64K RAM microcomputer chip had 70 percent of the world market share, and Japanese market share in microchip development has since increased.)

IMPLICATIONS

This analysis of corporate strategy suggests a multitude of reasons why corporations are tempted to adopt maintenance strategies to assure their survival. If a country does *not* have a secure and efficient maintenance base—the case of most countries in the world including most developed industrial nations—companies may be more tempted than otherwise to focus on a maintenance strategy rather than a high-risk entrepreneurial approach (indeed, companies in many countries may have to establish certain infrastructural maintenance prerequisites, which they cannot take for granted that their culture or government will provide*). Significantly, one cross-cultural study concluded that Japanese managers have a hierarchy that places social and security needs higher than self-actualization needs because these needs are less well satisfied than in British and American cultures.[35]

Another possibility is that at a certain stage of development, industrial societies with a maintenance or conservative set of value biases may socialize or indoctrinate managers and companies with maintenance strategies to such an extent that entrepreneurial long-term risks cannot break through. Such collective learning patterns and their effect on strategies of social planning have been substantiated cross-culturally by anthropologist Gregory Bateson, although much research remains to be done on how and why apperceptive learning habits vary in different cultural contexts.[36] Both the theorist and the corporate strategist would like to know what the role of big companies is compared to small business in this process of collective adjustment within particular cultures to the turbulent global economic process. For this last question, at least, some tentative answers have emerged that may be useful in future corporate and social planning.

Big-Business Buffers and Small-Business Flexibility

The trade-offs between big business and small business in a modern society involve extreme claims on both sides: "Bigger is better" versus "Small is beautiful." Let us assume that the survival of the business enterprise is a common value that all firms share, whether they be large or small. The

---

*This may explain why business interests in capitalist cultures ask the government both for subsidies (maintenance prerequisites) and freedom.

question is then whether large or small companies best assure survival in the late twentieth century. And further, which size firm has greater advantages in addition to mere survival?

Big business, ultimately incorporated in the multinational organization, is an organizational form that emerged from the Industrial Revolution, illustrated by enterprises such as the Hudson's Bay Company and British East India Company and later, in the 1890s, by American companies such as Singer, Standard Oil, and American Bell. The promise of bigness was the promise of combining maintenance and entrepreneurial strategies in an organization large enough to buffer its interests against the storms of creative destruction in the world economy on the one hand, and providing the base for research and development, and investment risk-taking on the other. In a famous chapter on "Monopolistic Practices" economist Joseph Schumpeter argues that the very imperfection of the world market creates conditions appropriate for large corporations since the big company can use its resources strategically, adapting to change through its research and development capacity while buffering against unexpected change with its very size and ability to set or control prices.[37] Economies of scale given corporate size and large world market share allow big companies to deter new competitors from entering the market, thus assuring the stability afforded by a limited number of suppliers of a goods or service. Investors are attracted by the security of bigness, particularly in an era when governments are reluctant to permit large corporations to go bankrupt because of the increase in the unemployment rate that would result or because of the strategic nature of certain industries in terms of the national interest (the steel industry, for example).

Paradoxically, as the world economy becomes more interdependent, mercantilist state philosophies are stimulated that view major corporations as critical arms of state economic objectives in the competition for world trade, resources, and development. Some have even gone as far as to claim the corporate era is an improvement over earlier eras since "corporate pluralism" is more viable and progressive than the rugged individualistic pluralism upon which democratic Western state ideologies were founded.[38] Many multinational corporations have the communications, technological, financial, and personnel capacity to have a global view of change and collective interests. Ultimately, some even have a corporate foreign policy that transcends that of any particular nation-state, ideology, or region. For example, Gianni Agnelli, head of Fiat, referred to the Soviet Union as a "neutral" country since Fiat has done business with the Soviets for the past several decades.[39]

However, not everyone is pleased with "the global bargain" struck by the multinational corporations abroad or the monopoly effects of the big corporation at home. The opposing viewpoint was elegantly expressed by economist E.F. Schumacher in his populist classic *Small Is Beautiful*. Schumacher argued that the "bigger is better" thrust of the corporate economies of advanced industrial states has contributed to the error of treating capital as income, particularly "natural capital" (such as fossil fuels) as if it were expendable without limits. Developing countries, accordingly, should not aim for this insatiable big business model of capitalist Westernization but wisely accept the limits of nature and the earth's resources and utilize "intermediate technologies" targeted for their own unique capacities and situation. Economic growth per se is not a higher priority for Schumacher than the dignity of man or the respect for the natural environment: "The substance of man cannot be measured by the Gross National Product. Perhaps it cannot be measured at all, except for certain symptoms of loss."[40]

On a philosophical level, who can deny that small is beautiful, that humans should "cultivate their gardens," that human dignity resides in the creation of one's own limited niche, and that in small, limited, but carefully targeted plans lie flexibility as well as independence?[41] The motivational allure of independent small business entrepreneurship is, of course, one of the classical seeds of the capitalist economic model. One "Eureka" or "ah ha!" experience transformed into a marketable product or niche and one has the future key to all individual happiness—is this not the New World dream of going into business for oneself, becoming independent of any boss, becoming free, and one day becoming rich (which is what "making it" means in capitalist society)?

Moreover, small young businesses are where most of the jobs are created in advanced stages of capitalist society, contrary to "bigger is better" mythology. The M.I.T. Program on Neighborhoods and Regional Change discovered where the net new jobs emerged in a sample of 5.6 million businesses in the United States between 1969 and 1976: Two-thirds were created by companies with twenty or fewer employees, and about 80 percent were created by companies with 100 or fewer employees! As David L. Birch observes: "Smaller businesses more than offset their higher failure rates with their capacity to start up and expand dramatically. Larger businesses, in contrast, appear rather stagnant."[42] In addition, the M.I.T. study indicated that 80 percent of replacement jobs are created by firms four years old or younger. So large companies are no longer the major providers of new jobs for Americans. Nor are old companies. And in Italy, where macroeconomists were surprised at the economic recovery and growth rate in the late 1970s, the basis for the growth was found to be in small- and medium-sized firms. Evidently, at a certain advanced stage of capitalist development, as a national economy shifts increasingly away from the manufacturing and toward the service sector, small young businesses become the engines of economic growth and job creation as large corporations seem to reach a point of stalemate or diminishing returns.

Centralization and Decentralization

Of course the *either-or* thinking behind the split between big and small business organizations is a Western habit or pattern of collective learning that may be more a part of the economic problem than of the solution. Not surprisingly, Schumacher saw through this in his chapter entitled "Towards a Theory of Large-Scale Organisation". Here he notes that while large-scale organisation is here to stay, the fundamental task is to achieve smallness *within* large organization. A large organization normally goes through alternating phases of *centralizing* and *decentralizing*, like swings of a pendulum: "Whenever one encounters such *opposites*, each of them with persuasive arguments in its favour, it is worth looking into the depth of the problem for something more than compromise, more than a half-and-half solution. Maybe what we really need is not *either-or* but *the-one-and-the-other-at-the-same-time*."[43]

This non-Western approach of simultaneously centralizing and decentralizing within the large organization, or as the Zen sage might put it, seeing the *yin* and *yang*, big and small, black and white, good and evil as interdependent, appears to be one of the reasons for the effectiveness of Japanese management in competing on world markets in spite of the turbulence of global change. For example, take the world's largest manufacturer of electrical appliances, Matsushita. In the 1930s, Matsushita combined four decentralized functions with four centralized functions within the organization. The four decentralized functions included independent managers and distinct product categories; strong consumer orientation on part of these self-sufficient managers; the flexibility of small companies; and the cultivation of specialized expertise among these managers to allow them to mature rapidly.

At the same time, Matsushita countered these characteristics with four centralized functions: controllers reporting to a centralized accounting system at headquarters; a company bank that took in divisional profits and gave out funds for capital improvements; centralized personnel recruitment; and centralized training. The managerial genius of Matsushita (the founder) resided in the fact that he refused to choose "once and for all" between decentralization and centralization (the trap of Western either-or rigidity) and accepted the uncertainty of an unresolvable conflict between these organizational alternatives. This allowed Matsushita to view centralization and decentralization as a kind of alternating spiral, and he could draw on one aspect or the other depending upon what each particular historical moment called for.

Thus, in the confusion following World War II, Matsushita replaced his decentralized divisional organization with strong centralization under himself, and he headed the advertising department personally to stimulate consumer confidence in his products. In the early 1950s, with greater need for flexibility to match increasing competition, he shifted the company back to a phase of decentralization, bringing back independent product groups. In the late 1950s he recentralized to adjust to the turbulence of an historical stage of growth and increasing interdependence in international markets. But when the business cycle in the early 1960s swung into recession and stagnation, he decentralized again to give his people in the field more flexibility and initiative. Following the oil crisis in the early 1970s, centralization was again instituted as a buffer against this disruptive rush of creative destruction.[44]

Thus the astute corporate manager can use centralization as a means to solidify maintenance objectives in times of historical crisis or disruptive change and can shift to decentralization to stimulate entrepreneurship among his people when the business cycle permits. Effective corporate strategies in the late twentieth century depend upon managers getting the feel for the relativity of unexpected change; upon sensing when to shore up the maintenance base and when to throw all energies toward entrepreneurial risk; upon knowing when to take a business cycle downturn or upturn seriously and how to react without overreacting: *both-and*, not either-or, *big-small*, not big or small, *long-short-term planning*, not long-term or short-term, *centralization and decentralization*, not centralization or decentralization. Governments can promote (or retard) such strategies of corporate adaptation by providing information, subsidies for sunrise industries, and protection for sunset industries. But from the corporate management perspective, rather than relying upon the uncertainty of government aid, it is usually best to try to reduce some of the uncertainty in planning by trying to anticipate business-electoral cycles that can have a significant impact upon economic growth and consumption.

The Politics of Business Cycles

Not only must corporate managers find a balance between long-term and short-term planning, between centralization and decentralization, between bigness and smallness, and between maintenance efficiency and entrepreneurial effectiveness, but they must develop an acute sense of political as well as economic timing in order to take advantage of business-electoral cycles. When asked in 1982 why he predicted a world economic recovery in 1984 given the global recession and widespread pessimism about the economic future, William W. Crouse, president of the Latin American Region of Revlon Health Care Group, answered: "Because a number of major countries have elections in 1984 and the economy picks up before elections."[45] In Western democracies, the dependence of corporate planning upon governmental policies takes on a certain wavelike form that usually follows the pattern of national elections.

In an analysis of electoral-economic cycles in twenty-seven countries between 1961 and 1972, Professor Edward Tufte discovered that in nineteen of them short-run accelerations in real disposable income per capita were more likely to occur in election years than in years without elections. Tufte concluded: "The politicians' economic theory of election outcomes gives great weight to economic events in the months before the election; thus the politicians' strategy is to turn on the spigot surely and swiftly and fill the trough so that it counts with the electorate."[46] And other studies have confirmed that upswings in real disposable income per capita are highly correlated with greater electoral support for incumbents.[47]

By using instruments of economic policy like tax cuts, money creation, and transfer payments, politicians up for reelection can stimulate spending, economic growth, and job creation in the months before the election. Managers of multinational corporations seeking to maximize corporate interests and to buffer themselves against unfavorable change can systematically use their "international election portfolio" in order to take advantage of these spurts of economic growth, spending, and credit availability. And they can disinvest or lower their vulnerability in the off-years between elections. Even if the presence of a multinational company in a country is more or less permanent, the management can shift its funds and tax vulnerability according to the electoral-economic cycle of democracy so as to maximize its financial interests.

Of course these general electoral-economic cycle schedules must be counterbalanced by the real possibility of government incompetence in the management of macroeconomic tools for its own interest. Such government incompetence has become more apparent as changes in the global economy narrow the options of state economic policymakers—such as the rise of OPEC and the Euro-credit market. The mismanagement of the U.S. economy in terms of the electoral economic cycle in the late 1970s and early 1980s is a striking example. President Jimmy Carter perfectly mistimed the recession his economic advisors had been coordinating, believing that Americans would stop spending once they anticipated hard times ahead, while in fact they kept spending out of an accurate sense that Carter's anti-inflation policy would prove ineffective in the short term and that dollars should be used up before they lost even more value. Thus, the belated recession preceding the 1980 presidential election was timed to the advantage not of the incumbent, as it should have been, but of the challenger, Ronald Reagan. President Reagan, however, initially appeared to be equally unable to manage the electoral-economic cycle. Waging an excessive battle against inflation, which resulted in record-high interest rates, the recessionary effect overwhelmed the stimulation provided by general tax cuts and tax advantages for high-income investors, and this dampened the electoral chances of Reagan's fellow Republicans up for election in the fall of 1982, who had been promised an economic recovery in time to lift their sinking boats. The Reagan recovery followed but at a high cost in federal deficits pushed up by Keynesian defense spending.

Neither President Carter nor President Reagan had enough knowledge of the global economy to anticipate accurately the limitations of their efforts to influence the timing of macroeconomic events. The overemphasis on anti-inflation policy through tight money and high interest rates caused the international value of the dollar to rise to such an extent that the resulting

U.S. trade deficit brought about a "structural recession" in 1981, which could no longer be easily arrested by short-term economic levers.[48] Both Carter and Reagan proved to be incapable of predicting the economic behavior of their fellow citizens: Carter overestimated the American propensity to save (even given a dismal past record) and Reagan overestimated the willingness of the rich to make long-term capital investments upon which his promised economic recovery depended.[49]

The failure of corporate strategists to appreciate the bias that electoral cycles can have upon business cycle projections in democracies such as the United States may help to explain the short-term motives and pressures for immediate results that have served to undermine American competitiveness in world markets in important sectors. Politically unwary, corporate planners too often take government projections at face value, which must necessarily be overly optimistic for the sake of reelection prospects. For similar reasons, corporate strategists may not take sufficient advantage of short-term economic boomlets that tend to occur before national elections, while simultaneously overstressing short-term *business* cycles, which appear to have been rendered more erratic by technological and global developments since the 1940s than they had been previously. Thus, the Hayes-Abernathy thesis of the Harvard Business School, which contends that American management has gone astray by drifting away from basics such as the factory floor and assembly line, focusing upon short-term financial management rather than long-term investment in technology and production facilities, may be more of a symptom than the root cause of American industrial decline.[50] Global changes in technology and finance have been revolutionary in the late twentieth century, making the long-term future so uncertain that the maintenance-oriented manager is tempted to stress the short-term and low-level risks out of insecurity. The contribution of Professors Robert Hayes and William Abernathy lies in pointing out the *abstract* nature of the short-term thinking of American management in contrast, for example, with the "zero-defect" objective of the Japanese production process. The entrepreneurial American culture is good at innovative beginnings, mass marketing and consuming the new. These very characteristics, however, mitigate against its ability to compete with the more conservative German and Japanese cultures in terms of systematic follow-through in managing programs, meeting perfectionist zero-defect standards and martialing and targeting resources for effective competitiveness.

But long-term thinking must be motivated by more than mere error-elimination and assembly-line efficiency. Investing in technology and plant capacity for the twenty-first century implies seeing through the red herrings provided by short-term electoral and business cycles, anticipating intermediate and long-term business waves, and choosing strategic areas for concrete development in which a particular national political economy or corporation is apt to be able to maintain a comparative advantage in the future. From the long-term perspective, it may be more of a time to cut the quick from the dead than a time to become preoccupied with reviving the dead on the assembly line. The maintenance base of industrial manufacturing in a country is best served by a maintenpreneurial culture in which the state targets growth areas for long-term economic support and helps to consolidate weak sectors essential to the national interest. The key is public management to create long-term conditions conducive to corporate competitiveness and low national unemployment through indirect means rather than direct intervention. As the Zen masters put it: "To point at the moon a finger is needed, but woe to him who mistakes the finger for the moon."

Finally, by turning to specific examples of state strategies, structures, and economic policies in the context of existing international institutions of the global economy, we may be able to derive some guidelines for collective learning in order to know "what is to be done."

ENDNOTES

1. Mira Wilkins, *American Business Abroad from the Colonial Era to 1914* (Cambridge, MA: Harvard University Press, 1970), p. 6. Wilkins serves as the basic source for this section on the American evolution.

2. Ibid., p. 70.

3. Mansel G. Blackford, *The Rise of Modern Business in Great Britain, the U.S. and Japan* (Chapel Hill: University of North Carolina Press, 1988), p. 35.

4. Ibid., p. 80.

5. See Georg H. Küster, "Germany," in Raymond Vernon, ed., *Big Business and the State: Changing Relations in Western Europe* (Cambridge, MA: Harvard University Press, 1974), p. 138.

6. Anonymous personal interview with manager in Mitsubishi, November 26, 1988.

7. Yoshi Tsurumi, *Multinational Management: Business Strategy and Government Policy*, 2nd edition (Cambridge, MA: Ballinger, 1984), pp. 107–20.

8. Hymer made the oligopoly-leading-direct-investment argument in his 1960 doctoral dissertation at the Massachusetts Institute of Technology. For the relation of this argument to the "Law of Uneven Development," see Stephen Hymer, "The Multinational Corporation and the Law of Uneven Development," in J. Bhagwati, ed., *Economics and World Order from the 1970s to the 1990s* (New York: Collier-Macmillan, 1972), pp. 113–40.

9. United Nations Centre on Transnational Corporations, *Transnational Corporations in World Development*, Third Survey (New York: United Nations, 1983), pp. 318–26.

10. See Y. Tsurumi, *Multinational Management*, pp. 193–96.

11. Theodore H. Moran, "A New United States Policy Toward Multinational Enterprises," a paper presented at the Faculty Seminar on International Political Economy at Columbia University, New York, November 19, 1975.

12. For initial efforts at forming such Third-World companies, see David A. Heenan and Warren J. Keegan, "The Rise of Third World Multinationals," *Harvard*

Business Review (Jan.–Feb. 1979): 102, 103; and Louis T. Wells, Jr., "Guess Who's Creating the World's Newest Multinationals?" *The Wall Street Journal*, December 12, 1983, p. 22.

13. See Raymond Vernon, "International Investment and International Trade in the Product Cycle," *Quarterly Journal of Economics* LXXX (May 1966): 190–207.

14. See James M. Lutz and Robert T. Green, "The Product Life Cycle and the Export Position of the United States," *Journal of International Business Studies* XIV, No. 3 (Winter 1983): 77–94, and Alicia Mullor-Sebastian, "The Product Life Cycle Theory: Empirical Evidence," *Journal of International Business Studies* XIV, No. 3 (1983): 95–106.

15. See Ian Giddy, "The Demise of the Product Life Cycle Model in International Business Theory," *Columbia Journal of World Business* (Spring 1978): 90–96.

16. Alvin H. Hansen, *Fiscal Policy and Business Cycles* (New York: W.W. Norton, 1941), pp. 18–24.

17. Alekandr Solzhenitsyn, *The Gulag Archipelago* (New York: Harper & Row, 1973), p. 50 fn.

18. N.D. Kondratieff, "The Long Waves in Economic Life," *The Review of Economic Statistics* XVII (November 1935). Also see George Garvy, "Kondratieff's Theory of Long Cycles," *Review of Economic Statistics* XXV (November 1943), and W.W. Rostow, "Kondratieff, Schumpeter, and Kuznets: Trend Periods Revisited," *Journal of Economic History* 35, No. 4 (December 1975). Also see W.W. Rostow, *Why the Poor Get Richer and the Rich Slow Down* (Austin: University of Texas Press, 1980), Chapters 1 and 2.

19. Jay W. Forrester, "A Great Depression Ahead?" *The Futurist*, December 1978, pp. 379–385.

20. Ibid., p. 380.

21. Federal Reserve Board statistics as cited in Leonard Silk, "The Great Depression," *The New York Times*, March 14, 1982.

22. Benedetto Croce, *History of Europe in the Nineteenth Century* (New York: Harcourt, Brace and World, Inc., 1963, originally published in 1933), p. 37.

23. Robert Isaak, "Modern Reactions to Inflation: Private and Public Strategies," Part II in Wilhelm Hankel and Robert Isaak, *Modern Inflation: Its Economics and Politics* (Lanham, MD: University Press of America, 1983). German version: *Die moderne Inflation* (Köln: Bund-Verlag, 1981). Also see R. Isaak, "Inflation Strategies in the 1980s," *The Adherent* 9, No. 1 (March 1982): 32–47.

24. Ibid. For the conservative bias of organizations, see Ruth Mack, *Planning on Uncertainty* (New York: Wiley, 1971); Robert Townsend, *Up the Organization: How to Stop the Corporation from Stifling People and Strangling Profits* (London: Michael Joseph Ltd., 1970); and Peter Drucker, *Managing for Results* (New York: Harper & Row, 1964). On being overenamored with the process of management stressing order, efficiency, and predictability (what I have referred to as the 'maintenance syndrome') see Abraham Zaleznik, *The Managerial Mystique* (N.Y.: Harper & Row, 1989).

25. Mancur Olson, *The Logic of Collective Action* (Cambridge, MA: Harvard University Press, 1965), p. 2.

26. Peter F. Drucker, *Management: Tasks, Responsibilities and Practices* (New York: Harper & Row, 1973).

27. Richard Tanner Pascale and Anthony G. Athos, *The Art of Japanese Management* (New York: Simon & Schuster, 1981), Chapter 1, pp. 19–27. For the global

implications from a Japanese perspective, see Takashi Inoguchi and Daniel I. Okimoto, *The Political Economy of Japan* (Stanford, CA: Stanford University Press, 1988).

28. For a critical view see Mike Parker and Jane Slaughter, "Behind the Scenes at Nummi Motors," *The New York Times*, December 4, 1988.

29. Steven Lohr, "The Company That Stopped Detroit," *The New York Times*, March 21, 1982, Section 3, p. 26.

30. Ibid., p. 1, Harbour & Associates statistics.

31. See Everett Hagen, *On the Theory of Social Change* (London: Tavistock Publications, 1964), Chapter 14.

32. See Clifford Gertz, *Peddlers and Princes: Social Development and Economics in Two Indonesian Towns* (Chicago: University of Chicago Press, 1963).

33. For the German case interpreted from this perspective see R. Isaak, *European Politics: Political Economy and Policy Making in Western Democracies* (New York: St. Martin's Press, 1980), Chapter 2, pp. 27–62.

34. Ibid., Chapter 4: "Great Britain: A Socialized Economy in Crisis," pp. 99–125.

35. Mason Haire, Edwin Ghiselli, and Lyman W. Porter, *Managerial Thinking* (New York: Wiley, 1966). But also see C.J. McMillan, "Social Values and Management Innovation: The Case of Japan," in *Management under Differing Value Systems*, edited by Günter Dlugos and Klaus Weiermair (Hawthorne, NY: Walter de Gruyter, Inc., 1981).

36. Gregory Bateson, "Social Planning and the Concept of Deutero-Learning," *Steps to an Ecology of Mind* (New York: Ballantine Books, 1972), pp. 159–76. It may be time to take one step backwards in order to take two steps forward and learn how non-human animals learn collectively. For example, big horn sheep transmit home range knowledge from generation to generation *if* individual lambs are not dispersed from their home range (see Valarius Geist, *Mountain Sheep: A Study in Behavior and Evolution*. Chicago: University of Chicago Press, 1971). And wolf pups raised without the social structure of a wolf pack adapt poorly to life in the wild (see Barry Holstun Lopez, *Of Wolves and Men*. New York: Charles Scribners' Sons, 1978). Individual freedom (that is, mobility) is not always the recipe for health, survival or collective adaptation to global change. The cultural constraints upon mobility in West Germany and Japan may help to explain their efficacy at collective learning.

37. Joseph Schumpeter, *Capitalism, Socialism and Democracy* (New York: Harper & Row, 1950), pp. 87–106.

38. See Neil H. Jacoby, *Corporate Power and Social Responsibility* (New York: Macmillan, 1973).

39. Gianni Agnelli's speech to the Foreign Policy Association, Hotel Pierre, New York City, February 24, 1977.

40. E.F. Schumacher, *Small Is Beautiful: Economics as if People Mattered* (New York: Harper & Row, 1973), p. 20.

41. See, for example, Kempe Ronald Hope, "Self-Reliance and Participation of the Poor in the Development Process in the Third World," *Futures*, Vol. 15, No. 6 (December, 1983), pp. 455–462. And Charles Hampden-Turner, *From Poverty to Dignity* (Garden City, NY: Anchor-Doubleday, 1974).

42. David L. Birch, "Who Create Jobs?" *The Public Interest* 65 (Fall 1981): 7.

43. Schumacher, *Small Is Beautiful*, pp. 242–43. International Management consultant Stanley Davis confirms the need to overcome false either/or, centraliza-

tion/decentralization dichotomies and to deal with the simultaneity of business opposites: see S. Davis, *Future Perfect* (Reading, MA: Addison-Wesley Publishing Co., 1987), p. 188.

44. Pascale and Athos, *Art of Japanese Management*, Chapter 2, "The Matsushita Example," pp. 28–57.

45. William W. Crouse, "Future Trends in International Business." Panel at conference on The Increasing Internationalization of Business, Pace University, White Plains, New York, March 6, 1982.

46. Edward Tufte, *Political Control of the Economy* (Princeton, NJ: Princeton University Press, 1978), pp. 10–11.

47. See Gerald Kramer, "Short-Term Fluctuations in U.S. Voting Behavior, 1896–1964," *American Political Science Review* 65 (March 1971): 131–43; and Edward Tufte, "Determinants of the Outcomes of Midterm Congressional Elections," *American Political Science Review* 69 (September 1975): 812–26.

48. See C. Fred Bergsten, "The Main Cause of the Recession," *The New York Times*, Op Ed, December 21, 1981. Also see interview with Bergsten in the March/April 1982 issue of *Challenge*, pp. 25–32.

49. See R. Isaak, "On Unstuffing the Turkey and Making Jobs from the Wishbone," *The Adherent* 9, No. 2 (Fall 1982).

50. Robert Hayes and William Abernathy, "Managing Our Way to Economic Decline," *Harvard Business Review* (July–August 1980). See Martin K. Starr, ed., *Global Competitiveness* (N.Y.: W.W. Norton, 1988) and Lester C. Thurow, ed., *The Management Challenge: Japanese Views* (Cambridge, MA: The MIT Press, 1985).

CHAPTER SEVEN

NORTH–SOUTH STRUCTURES AND STRATEGY

Despite crushing debt loads and depressed living standards, poorer countries are transferring their wealth to richer nations in amounts that will reach records this year, 50 percent above 1987 levels, a World Bank report released today says.

The New York Times, December 19, 1988

The global environment and domestic sources of multinational behavior both function like half of a pair of scissors in the collective learning process. But at the fulcrum where the two meet there is often an opportunity for an individual manager or collective management team to point the dynamic interaction in a particular strategic policy direction after taking specific political and economic structural constraints into account. This cognitive or strategic element of collective learning, where free will has its greatest running room, can be illustrated by contrasting North–South with East–West structures, strategies, and policies.

The most poignant human focus of international political economy is the "North–South structure"—the asymmetrical relationship between the developed and developing countries in the world economy. The shift toward a high technology/high information global economy has accelerated the widening of the gap in levels of development between rich and poor populations as money, technology, and skilled personnel flow to the secured, developed nations of the world and the poorest countries find themselves without the resources to even begin to catch up. The increasing speed of technological change thus works to the disproportionate benefit of the advantaged over the disadvantaged. Hence, movements on the part of lesser developed countries to slow the pace of technological transformations on their home ground should not be surprising: Their traditional way of life, the very cultural essence of their collective existence, becomes increasingly vulnerable to disruption if not eradication by foreign trends of modernity. From this perspective, resistance to technological change may be more rational than irrational as people desperately try to preserve the integrity of their indigenous culture.

From the perspective of the rich nations of the "North"* the initial temptation is to maximize the self-interest of one's own people regardless of the consequences for the poorer developing nations of the "South." But this short-term viewpoint has become increasingly problematic in an interdependent world economy in which exports from the North can only be purchased by customers in the South if the North helps to provide the South with money or credit to make such purchases. Moreover, many regions of the so-called rich countries of the North are as poor in some ways as the poor developing countries of the South, which, in turn, are often studded with their own rich elites or minor metropoles. Hence the asymmetry of the world economy is such that some analysts argue the North–South split is a myth—the figment of the polarizing logic of the Western imagination.

For instance, who is more "developed"—the man who dies at forty-five from a heart attack in a high-pressure, future-oriented, workaholic metropolitan center of the North or the man who dies at a similar age of a snake bite on a present-oriented, developing Pacific island of the South? The Northerner lives to work and has sacrificed his present for a future that never materializes. The Southerner lives each day to the hilt and dies as naturally as he lives—with neither the promise nor the hazards of modern technology or drugs. No doubt the technology and drugs will eventually make their way to the peripheries of the South, but will this really improve the quality of life and constitute a more meaningful level of human development?

Regardless of the meaning attributed to the process of Western modernization in the developing nations, one can identify dominant structures and strategies in North–South relations since World War II, highlighting Northern institutional efforts to "manage the economic problems of the South" and attempts by the developing countries to change the game rules in their favor. One paradox in this analysis is that Western industrial nations often assume that the leaders of developing countries are primarily after wealth whereas

---

*"North" usually refers to developed, industrialized nations of the Northern Hemisphere, while "South" designates developing countries of the Southern Hemisphere; however, many countries and regions have a North–South economic split *within* them (such as southern Italy, the rural south of the U.S., the EC's southern members).

they may in fact be aiming first for control and less vulnerability. Conversely, the Southern developing countries often assume the industrial North is seeking imperialistic control as a primary motive whereas the rich countries may actually be in pursuit of more wealth.* From the perspective of collective learning, the management of North–South relations is a chaotic, politically charged adventure in which ideological blinders often obstruct long-term blueprints, tempting both sides to give up on each other or to insulate themselves from the other's problems, whereas the interdependent political economy of the world demands constant communication, negotiation, and adjustment on all sides to keep the global economy healthy.

ORIGINS

While the origins of the relations between the developed and developing countries are deep and complex, some highlights are suggestive in terms of the collective learning approach used here and the notion of "modeling," which derives from it. Clearly the nation-states, which were first established in Europe—England and France, for example—had the advantages that all first arrivals enjoy. They had their choice of colonies, whereas nation-states united later—Italy and Germany—were forced to chose from leftovers (and even these colonial efforts were perceived as illegitimate given the tides of liberalism and parliamentary democracy that swept over Europe in the course of the nineteenth and early twentieth centuries). And even when France and England were eventually forced to give up their colonies in the course of the twentieth century, they left deeply rutted cultural and administrative traditions behind that would work in the favor of British and French trade: The former colonies usually preferred to do business with "the bastards they knew the best."

So by the end of the nineteenth century, most of the prime global real estate was tied up one way or another by established interests, dominated by European nations. They had the advantages, in addition, of relatively unregulated flows of trade, capital, and labor, thus allowing them to profit as efficiently as the state of technology would allow from their colonial investments. Moreover, with minor exceptions, this colonial business could be consolidated without any interruption from war. The colonial powers learned from each other how to set up colonies for power and business in such a way that benefits soon flowed to the home country.

Advocates of the Third World or developing country position argue that global economic opportunities have changed drastically since the nineteenth

---

*The pursuit of power and the pursuit of wealth, however, are often hard to distinguish from each other and may be flip sides of the same coin (as argued variously by political economists Jacob Viner, Robert Gilpin, and Stephen Krasner, and by historian Paul Kennedy).

century. Goods and labor cannot move as freely over borders as they did for Europeans and Americans a century ago. Protective tariff barriers and strict immigration quotas block Third-World goods and labor from moving freely to the developed industrialized world, thus hindering modernization processes of the poorer countries. Dr. Mahbub ul Haq, former Director of Policy Planning and Program Review at the World Bank, maintains that the poor countries are not asking for a massive redistribution of wealth, even though three-fourths of the world's income, investment, and services and most of the world's research facilities are in the hands of one-fourth of its population. Rather, the developing nations want greater equality of opportunity, which is made impossible by existing economic imbalances and international structures skewed toward the rich nations.[1]

Whether speaking for the rich nations or the poor, no one denies the asymmetry that exists between the economic structures of the developed and developing nations. The conflict of perspectives dwells not upon this basic fact of international political economy but upon whose fault it is and which means are most appropriate for ameliorating the situation. The international institution emerging from the Bretton Woods settlement which has been caught with most of the practical long-term consequences of this North–South gap is the World Bank.

The World Bank

The perspective of the developed countries toward the South, or Third World, developing countries was initially set forth by the American-dominated Bretton Woods philosophy after World War II. As noted in Chapter 2, this philosophy initially represented a partial resurrection of classical economic liberalism according to which international credit should be given only to countries or projects that were "economically sound" (that is, "hard banker terms," not "soft loans"). The exception which proved the rule was the Marshall Plan program of outright grants for European reconstruction, to which we will later return. But the ruling constitution for managing the economic problems of the developing countries in the postwar era was the "embedded liberalism" of the Bretton-Woods regime spearheaded by the International Monetary Fund (IMF) and the World Bank, or its formal name—the International Bank for Reconstruction and Development (IBRD).

While the IMF was founded to provide international liquidity and short-term credit to alleviate balance-of-payments problems of its member nations, the World Bank's major function has been to stimulate the flow of capital into long-term investment across national boundaries (although not always from the rich countries to the poor). At the time it came into being, on December 27, 1945, the International Bank for Reconstruction and Development was overshadowed by the IMF and was focused upon making loans to war-damaged countries in Western Europe, not to the underdeveloped countries where the credit risks were higher. As with the IMF, the site chosen for the headquarters of the World Bank was Washington, D.C.—to the dismay of John Maynard Keynes who preferred London or even New York but not a location "under the thumb of the U.S. government." Actually the IMF and World Bank headquarters are housed in the same building in Washington, sort of "Siamese twins" with representatives going to each other's meetings despite their different functions. The building could be considered a monument to U.S. hegemony in the Bretton Woods settlement. Membership in the World Bank has always been contingent upon membership in the IMF, and any nation expelled or withdrawing from the IMF automatically ceases to be a member of the World Bank.

With the adoption of the Marshall Plan or European Recovery Program (proposed in 1947 by U.S. General George Marshall), the World Bank was able to shift its priorities from reconstruction to development. However, the World Bank's role is not restricted to raising money in developed countries so it can lend to developing nations: The bank borrows from and makes loans to both groups. Loans are targeted for specific, viable economic projects— typically to build up the infrastructure of developing countries as a prerequisite to industrialization: highways, railroads, power and port facilities, irrigation and flood control (as contrasted with public health projects, schools, seeds, or houses). Normally loans by the World Bank cover only hard-currency import needs and have to be repaid in hard currency at long-term rates. Initially, the daily operations of the IBRD were steered by a group of executive directors, five appointed by the five member governments with the largest subscriptions to the bank, the rest elected biennially by the remaining members. A president was hired (and could be fired) by the executive directors, who, with their approval, could select a staff made up of as diverse a geographical representation as possible. Traditionally, the president of the World Bank has been American, and the president of the IMF a European. But this convention may change when a Japanese president is selected for one of these international bodies in an effort to draw Japan into more obligations in the management of a global economy from which the Japanese have benefitted most handsomely. Such an institutional development would be a natural outgrowth of the trilateralism that has emerged *de facto* in the management of the global economy.

In 1960 the *International Development Association* (IDA) was created as part of the World Bank Group in order to provide loans to developing countries on a more liberal basis than was permitted within normal IBRD guidelines—typically fifty-year, interest-free loans. Moreover, there is normally a ten-year grace period before loans must start to be repaid, and the repayment can be in local currency, provided that it is convertible. With resources of its own, the IDA loan projects go through the same World Bank evaluation process as do regular credit applications. The purpose is to provide liquidity on a more liberal, long-term basis to the poorest countries.

Another key organization within the World Bank Group is the *International Finance Corporation* (IFC), formed in 1956 to provide risk capital for productive private enterprises, to encourage the development of local capital markets, and to stimulate the international flow of capital. Loans by the IFC to private companies in developing countries are normally for seven- to twelve-year periods. Such loans can also be made for joint ventures between investors in developed and developing countries and cover a multitude of projects in such fields as mining, manufacturing, steel, textile production, food processing, machinery production, local development finance companies, and tourism.

Organizational "Modeling": Regional Development Banks

A key proposition of collective learning theory is that when one international organization is seen to have economic success, other countries or regions often view it as a model to shape their own economic organizations. With the World Bank model in mind, regional development banks were created: the Inter-American Development Bank (IDB) in 1959 to provide World Bank-type services to countries in the Western Hemisphere (particularly the United States and Latin America); the African Development Bank (ADB), organized by a group of newly independent African countries in 1963 under United Nations auspices; and the Asian Development Bank, which set up headquarters in Manila in 1966. Nor do the offspring stop there. The World Bank has been instrumental in helping to found more than fifty development banks (mainly national banks) in member countries.

As an illustration of how the regional development banks work, consider the African Development Bank, which has become Africa's premier source of credit. With fifty African members and an additional twenty-five from the industrialized world, the ADB is structured like a mini-World Bank, financing projects in most African countries and granting soft, long-term loans to the poorest among them. By 1987 the ADB had approved about $10 billion in loans, including $4 billion interest-free through the African Development Fund (ADF)—the soft-loan window of the ADB modeled after the International Development Association. The money for ADF comes from the rich developed members of ADB, while the operating funds for the ADB come from all its members in addition to the loans raised on the international markets where the ADB has the same blue-chip rating as does the World Bank. With more than $19 billion in capital, the ADB projects a doubling of its rate of lending to more than $10 billion from 1987 through 1991.[2] But what about the World Bank itself?

McNamara's Basic Human-Needs Orientation

When Robert McNamara became president of the World Bank in 1968, he shifted the bank's priorities away from focusing upon the modern sector of developing countries (usually cities) toward alleviating absolute poverty through direct action at the rural level. He defined "absolute poverty" as "conditions of deprivation that fall below any rational definition of human decency" in his speech at the Annual Meeting of the World Bank at Nairobi in 1973. In his first five-year term McNamara not only doubled the amount of lending by the World Bank (without losing its AAA-credit rating for never having anyone default on a loan) but he also changed bank policy, aiming to break the main constraints on development (such as population increase, malnutrition, and illiteracy) rather than limiting credit to conventional infrastructure projects. Thus, much more money went for agriculture, education, and the control of population growth (McNamara's original, controversial contribution to the mix) and to the poorest developing countries, particularly Africa. The basic human-needs orientation (not original with McNamara) focuses upon alleviating the needs of the poorest *individuals* in the world as the appropriate orientation to the North–South dilemma.

McNamara himself was somewhat of a Faustian figure as head of the World Bank, having learned the cold, efficient techniques of managerial decision-making theory at Harvard, applying his cognitive skills later at Harvard as an accounting professor, at Ford Motor Company as chief executive officer, and then at the Pentagon as Secretary of Defense during the Vietnam War where efficiently maximizing "body counts" was the indicator of success rather than the reduction of absolute poverty. The legendary Faust, it will be recalled, sold his soul to the devil in exchange for knowledge, which he knew to be worldly power. By 1966 McNamara realized the Vietnam War was morally wrong, even stating in a speech in Montreal that peace and stability in the world depended less on building up armaments than on raising the living standards of the poorer two-thirds of mankind.

Given his academic brilliance, prodigious energy, and arrogant efficiency in applying powerful decision-making models, McNamara, who left the Pentagon for the World Bank, discovered he was using technological means to the wrong ends, and in his new job he set about to improve health care for the world's poor rather than to wage war against the Vietcong. There may be a moral in this tale that can be applied to the asymmetrical balance in world markets in terms of payoffs for arms and war versus support for health care and the alleviation of world poverty. The North knows its Faust well....

While aware that four-fifths of the resources must come from the developing country itself, McNamara sought to use the other one-fifth to create a critical mass of financial and technical power through the World Bank so as to accelerate the process of development to a high but sustainable level. His purpose, using decision-theory methodology, was to maximize whatever small impact the World Bank funds had. He also expanded the research arm of the bank to make it one of the world's most authoritative centers for studies of key development problems and issues. Under McNamara's leadership the

IDA portion of IBRD loans became ever greater given the targeting of the poorest of the poor countries. While Nobel laureate and economist Arthur Lewis suggested separating the two organizations so that the IDA could focus solely upon development without the drag of banking orthodoxy, McNamara rejected this advice. Forced to choose between the two, he said he would select development over banking orthodoxy, but that this was a false choice that one did not have to make: By submitting all projects to the same procedures, development could be made more effective and the financial credibility of the World Bank preserved. McNamara pushed the IFC to select developmental projects benefitting the poor masses rather than more short-term profitable undertakings and to support local, home-grown enterprises instead of large multinational companies. Not surprisingly, the developed nations were split on their support of McNamara's policies, several OECD nations observing that the IBRD poverty program was less than helpful in their export of capital goods.[3] But the Scandinavian countries and the Dutch strongly stood behind the new stress on poverty-oriented projects: It is no accident that these are generally neo-corporatist nations that are known for contributing more than the average share of their GNP in foreign aid.

From OPEC to the New International Economic Order

As modeling goes, the most influential pro-Southern example in the world economy is OPEC, which other less successful would-be commodity cartels have tried to mimic. As documented in Chapter Three, OPEC's successes stem to a large extent from its oligopolistic roots in the oil industry, which has a history and structure different from the organization of other commodity businesses.[4] Of course the efficacy of managerial structure cannot be separated from cyclic trends in the sectoral market: Since 1890, roughly every decade the dollar price of oil in real terms appears to go from trough to peak and then from peak to trough in the following decade. With a peak in oil prices in real terms reached in 1981 (a 225 percent increase over the previous decade), if the pattern is extended, a long price decline should bottom out in the early 1990s.[5] After each trough in this twenty-year boom-and-bust pattern, the oil industry tends to reorganize. The collective learning and cooperation at this critical juncture set the stage for the relative efficacy of the cartel as demand again begins to outstrip supply. *Thus the efficiency of the maintenance learning base is prerequisite to the effectiveness of the collective, entrepreneurial bloc demand for certain prices and production quotas.* As the coordination or efficiency breaks down, OPEC's power is undermined.

The success of OPEC had great impact upon Third-World countries, some of whom attempted to form other commodity cartels—in copper and bananas, for example—without much success.[6] The OPEC situation was unique. Even given the development of other energy sources and oil discoveries in the world, by 1980 OPEC still accounted for two-thirds of the world's petroleum reserves and for over 40 percent of the world's petroleum production. OPEC's success was contingent upon high demand, inelastic oil prices, tight supplies, a small number of producing countries, common political interests, a tradition of cooperation or "collective learning," and a sufficient supply of financial reserves. The falling prices of other commodities and great number of alternative suppliers did not make them likely candidates for successful commodity cartels.

Nevertheless, the OPEC model inspired developing countries to band together to demand the establishment of a New International Economic Order (NIEO) at the United Nations' Sixth Special Session in 1974. Observing that between 1952 and 1972 per capita real income in developed market economies went up from about $2,000 to $4,000 (1973 prices) while in developing countries per capita income rose from $175 to $300, the developing countries concluded that the international economic system was skewed against them. Rather than catering only to the improvement of standards of living in the developed countries, the objective of the NIEO was to make the basic needs of developing countries a priority as well by restructuring the world economy to allow greater Third-World participation and effectiveness.[7]

The call for a New International Economic Order also pressured for a change in financial flows, beginning with a target of 0.7% of industrialized countries' GNP for aid to the developing countries. While the North resisted NIEO pressures, they served to changed global consciousness on economic matters, leading Secretary of State Henry Kissinger to reverse his policy of benign neglect in 1975 and the European Economic Community (EEC) to sign the first Lomé Convention with forty-six developing countries from Africa, the Caribbean, and the Pacific to stabilize their export earnings and to make EEC capital and technical assistance available to them through a Center for Industrial Development. This was a seminal breakthrough in the Northern establishment for the sake of Southern interests.

The Lomé Strategy: A Model for North–South Economic Ties?

The world's largest regional agreement linking over 500 million people in industrialized European and developing countries was signed on February 28, 1975, as the result of hard bargaining inspired by the NIEO movement. The African, Caribbean, and Pacific states (the ACP nations) began from a maximal position in negotiations, demanding that export and import prices should be indexed in a stabilization system to guarantee the purchasing power of the developing countries based upon their major export products. The European Community (EC) opposed this indexation of export and import prices on two grounds: (1) such indexation could hurt some of the

ACP states since trade took place not only between industrialized and developing states but also between developing states themselves, and (2) interference with the market mechanism could have negative, bottleneck effects such as the EC had experienced in the expensive subsidies for the EC's Common Agricultural Policy.[8] The European Commission did a study of the major ACP exports and discovered that variations in quantities of key exports as well as price changes were responsible for the instability of ACP export earnings.[9] Partly because of this study, the EC agreed to stabilize export earnings instead of focusing upon prices, and it proposed a list of key exports from the ACP countries: groundnuts, cocoa, coffee, cotton, coconut products, and bananas. The ACP states responded with tough bargaining, which resulted in a list of twelve major products plus seventeen more derived from them. The twelve: groundnut products, cocoa products, coffee products, cotton products, coconut products, palm (palm nut and kernel) products, rawhides (skins and leather), wood products, fresh bananas, tea, raw sisal, and iron ore. With sugar, the stabilization guarantees go even further than with these dozen products. *Southern bloc unity at a propitious historical moment with a negotiating partner with long-term economic interests in the bloc were the main ingredients of the Lomé success.* The European Community, for its part, assured itself privileged access to the resources and markets of an important bloc of developing countries, which could become invaluable in the event of any future all out protectionist trade war in the global economy. Indeed, the potential power of the agreement could serve as a deterrent to exactly such a trade conflict.

By the mid-1980s, sixty-six ACP states had signed the Lomé Convention, which was renewed in 1979 and again in 1984. These include all the former French colonies, suggesting once again the shrewdness of French diplomacy within the European Community. The Lomé Convention frees ACP members from all customs duties on 99.5 percent of their exports to the EC with no reciprocal concessions required. Also, the EC grants the ACP countries technical and financial aid (including grants, loans, and low-interest agreements for risk-capital transactions). When the export earnings of the major ACP products listed above fall below the average of preceding years, the EC compensates them in repayable advances for the more prosperous ACP nations and in nonrepayable grants for the rest. An agreement was reached in 1979 to cover support for a certain level of production or export potential for key ACP minerals as well. A 1985 agreement expanded cooperation in areas of rural development, energy, industry, fisheries, and social and cultural problems.[10]

The Lomé Convention has been praised as a model of relations between industrialized and developing nations. It is sector and product specific and aimed toward "win-win" arenas that benefit both the European and developing countries in the long run. The STABEX system, for example, is limited to *sta*bilizing the *ex*port earnings from products that affect employment and induce a deterioration in the overall terms of trade in ACP countries. Given the high unemployment among the largest growing category of the population in the Third World—youth—the Lomé Convention provides concrete, strategic solutions. Such positive models are the basis of collective learning, breaking beyond defensive, risk-shy maintenance strategies or defeatist pessimism. Collective learning is a strategy of adapting to the world economy in a way that targets effective economic growth while supporting social equity and cultural integrity.

UNCTAD and UNIDO: Trade and Industrial Pressure Groups

The focus provided by the demand for a New International Economic Order in the 1970s motivated new efforts by existing international economic pressure groups for the developing countries, sponsored by the United Nations. As described in some detail in Chapter 4, UNCTAD, or the United Nations Conference on Trade and Development, had been organized to promote the interests of the countries disadvantaged by the asymmetrical world trading system. Recall the structuralist Raul Prebisch of Argentina, first head of UNCTAD, who argued that the Northern center of world trade was so structured as to keep the South on the periphery and to increase the North–South gap. Southern countries typically produce commodities and basic resources with prices that tend to fall, whereas developed countries specialize in finished manufactured goods with rising prices. Only by providing import substitutes for Northern goods could the South catch up. Prebisch concluded that the North was preoccupied with a maintenance strategy concerned with furthering the well-being of industrialized countries in the status quo. The concerns of the South were not even on the agenda of the North, which increasingly squeezed the poor countries out of the world trade system into poverty and despair. GATT had become a *de facto* rich man's club—a commercial treaty organization that best served those who could afford its terms. UNCTAD, then, was the economic pressure group for the poor countries.[11]

The NIEO helped to promote the implementation of UNCTAD's Integrated Program for commodities and the establishment of its Common Fund.[12]

On the industrial side, the United Nations Industrial Development Organization (UNIDO) was established in 1966 to help the developing countries in the private industrial sector. Headquartered in Vienna, UNIDO has set a target of at least 5 percent economic growth in gross domestic product for the developing countries, advocating that by the year 2000 25 percent of all industrial output should be by the developing countries. Nations must come to UNIDO, which uses its Industrial and Technology Bank (established in 1976) to help them with marketing and capital financing strategies. In addition, there is a Special Industrial

Services program (SIS) to provide specific project help in industrial development through, for example, a fellowship program for technological and managerial training for key personnel.

The Industrial Development Board, which governs UNIDO, is made up of forty-five seats elected from the General Assembly of the United Nations: fifteen seats for developed countries, eighteen seats for Africa, Asia, and Yugoslavia, seven seats for Latin America and the Caribbean, and five seats for socialist countries. Industrialization is not seen as an end in itself by UNIDO, but as a means to economic growth in developing nations. Projects are analyzed for visibility, cost-benefit ratios, and the promotion of financing. UNIDO encourages a focus initially upon agricultural and then other projects. At its 34th Conference in New Delhi in 1980, UNIDO proposed that a $300 billion fund be established by the year 2000 for industrial financing, which should become long term rather than short term in nature. However, countries usually prefer short-term financing, and these financial goals proved to be utopian in terms of the power realities of the 1980s. Still, as a targeted organization for Southern economic unity, the collective learning potential of UNIDO should not be underestimated in the long term.

But such frail international economic organizations were no match for the debt crisis of the 1980s—a crisis resolved by commercial banks as surrogates for governments and international organizations, a role for which they were not designed.

The Debt Crisis

The seeds of the debt crisis in the world economy were planted with the quadrupling of oil prices in 1973: Transfer of wealth to the oil-producing Third-World countries amounted to a "tax" equivalent to 2–3 percent of the GNP (on average) of the industrialized countries. And this economic cost of some $30 billion was soon recycled from the North to the non-oil-producing South—those poorer countries that produced no oil and were least able to cope with the price increases.

Meanwhile, the OPEC nations, most of which were sparsely populated, found themselves with more wealth on their hands than they could absorb domestically. So they deposited their funds in "safe," short-term accounts in banks of the North—in Europe, the United States, and Japan. This game of "hot capital" (same rules as hot potato) was then continued by the commercial banks of the North who wanted so desperately to get rid of this abundance of cash that they hired hundreds of young graduates to fly around the world to sell loans to developing countries. And given that the economic growth rates in the oil-importing developing countries between 1973 and 1980 averaged 4.6 percent annually compared to a mere 2.5 percent in the industrialized countries, one can understand why the bankers were attracted.[13]

Citibank, the Bank of America, Chase Manhattan, the First National Bank of Chicago, the Bank of Tokyo, and other world-class banks (and some smaller ones who should not have been in the game at all) acted as turntables, recycling the petrodollars deposited by OPEC to provide liquidity in the non-oil-developing countries who needed cash to pay for their higher oil bills. Because some of these banks actually calculated that they probably would *not* get the principal back on the loans, planning to live a long time on high rates of interest, this massive commercial loan program has been referred to as "the third redistribution" (the first two redistributions from wealthy to disadvantaged nations being the Marshall Plan and OPEC's success in raising oil prices). Since both industrialized governments and the international organizations they supported (the IMF, for instance) were under great financial pressures in the 1970s, they applauded the action of commercial banks without attempting to discern the long-term consequences. The outstanding debt of developing countries shot up from $161 billion in 1974 to $599 billion in 1982, and by 1982 debt-service payments claimed 24 percent of the export earnings of developing countries compared with 14 percent in the mid-1970s.[14]

Nevertheless, in the late 1970s the Marxist-oriented Cambridge School of economics in England sent advisors to Mexico who recommended that the Mexicans borrow all they could as long as North Americans were willing to lend. The loans would indirectly be insured by the U.S. government and even if the loans went bad, Mexico would have the Americans by their debt.

By 1982 some forty developing countries found themselves in a cash squeeze: Interest rates on their variable-rate loans were skyrocketing in tandem with the Paul Volcker tight-money, anti-inflation policy of the United States at the same time that their export earnings were falling because of a recession in the industrial world and because of plunging commodity prices. As economist John Maynard Keynes observed, if you owe your bank a hundred pounds, you have a problem; but if you owe your bank a million pounds the bank has a problem. And in a global economy, if a number of countries owe banks billions of pounds, everybody has a problem.

Poland, with $27 billion in debts, was the first casualty. Because of the imposition of martial law in Poland, the United States pushed for calling the loans in default, but was dissuaded from doing so by West European allies whose banks had large stakes in Poland.

In Latin America the debt stakes were even higher—$90 billion in Brazil, close to the same amount in Mexico, and $38 billion in Argentina. But it was not Poland but the Mexican debt crisis that shocked the financial markets severely in August 1982. The advice of the Cambridge School had come home to roost.

The Mexican Case and the Debt Trap

Commercial banks had been particularly anxious to lend money to developing countries where new oil had been discovered, as in Mexico, assuming that oil prices would continue to rise and back up the loans. And since the Mexican economy grew an average of 8 percent annually between 1978 and 1981, all looked well on the surface. But a structural crisis resulted when the oil price forecasts by the banks proved to be wrong. The demand and price for oil began to go down, not up.

Underlying this structural crisis we discover the hegemony of Anglo-Saxon economic theory at work (see the Introduction). Most policymakers from the developed world accept the assumptions of Keynesian economics that savings always equals investment, that whatever is not consumption is defined as savings, and that whatever is not consumption is defined as investment. While these assumptions might work in the economy of a closed domestic system (which does not exist in a global world economy), in an open economy imports and exports have to be worked into the definition of savings equalling investment. In the daily practice of balance-of-payments statistics, a current account deficit (or the total export of goods and services that is less than the total import of goods and services) goes down as a deficiency of domestic savings vis-à-vis investment. Since foreign savings (that is, foreign debt) can be tapped to supplement a shortfall in the domestic savings rate, according to this economic philosophy or set of assumptions the growth process for developing countries cannot help but be associated with foreign indebtedness. Current account deficits are perceived to be the normal way of life in this formulation, and no great collective learning motivation exists for developing economies to concentrate upon suitable production for exports to balance foreign-exchange requirements. While initially Mexican President Luis Echeverria used foreign commercial bank loans in the early 1970s to back up state enterprises and public credit agencies for loans to small and medium-sized businesses, the Mexican economy became overheated in the late 1970s and unduly dependent upon foreign sources of financing to repay both its old debt and to keep the hyped-up economic growth going.[15]

From the late 1970s onwards, Mexico's President José López Portillo pretended as if all was well until the election was won in July 1982. But in one week in August 1982, the peso lost half its value and the Mexican government declared it could not pay the $20 billion in principal repayments due on government debt through 1984. Mexico was broke and $10 billion was owed to the banks within a few months. The money borrowed by Portillo was to be used ostensibly for an ambitious industrial development program based on greatly expanded petroleum production. However, a large amount of the money lent—perhaps as much as half of it—was never invested in Mexico but wound up in the Swiss bank accounts of corrupt government functionaries or was used by businessmen for secure investments and real estate purchases in the United States and Europe. Portillo's own assets and summer villas flourished. By August 1982 Mexico had only $200 million remaining in its central bank; it suspended commercial debt principal payments and requested a three-month moratorium on its debt. Mexico's decision to suspend payments on its foreign debts and to request $10 billion from the United States to bail itself out shocked the world and functioned as a model: Other Latin American countries followed suit in acknowledging their unserviceable debts publicly, igniting the world debt crisis.

Following an exhaustive weekend of negotiations, the United States agreed to purchase $1 billion of Mexican oil at $25 to $30 a barrel to go to the Strategic Petroleum Reserve and the Pentagon, and the Federal Reserve was willing to put up $750 million for Mexico through the Bank for International Settlements if the Swiss, German, and British central banks would together put up the same amount. Nearly $4 billion was provided in emergency credit, almost $3 billion by the United States, and the rest by other central banks of the North. Another credit of about $4 billion was then granted by the IMF after negotiations with Mexico; the credit was contingent on stringent austerity measures that Mexico would enact.

A major Mexican problem was capital flight—Mexico was the largest of any debtor nation. Some $60 billion left the country between 1977 and 1984, and about $5 billion flowed out in the first half of 1985.[16] Such capital flight depleted foreign-exchange reserves, reduced the tax base, and eliminated investment resources, thus undermining economic growth. Also, the Mexicans have traditionally tried to keep foreigners from acquiring a majority share of stock in a Mexican company (despite exceptions made for IBM and the *maquiladora** plants on the American border), deterring high-tech companies from investing a great deal or transferring technology to a situation they cannot control. The class structure of Mexico makes traditional wealthy families jealous of foreign competition, thus reinforcing this trend of cultural resistance.[17] Such a class structure appears to be compatible with the corruption of the Institutional Revolutionary Party, which has ruled Mexico for over half a century. By 1986 Mexico's total debt stood at $99 billion, most of the $25 billion U.S. share being held by the ten largest American financial institutions.[18]

Brazil and Argentina soon mimicked Mexico's behavior in seeking aid from the IMF and a rescheduling of their debts. By 1982 the Third World and Eastern European countries combined had foreign debts totaling $626 billion—three times as much as in 1976.[19] The key international economic organizations that the North used to attempt to manage or analyze the world economy—the OECD and World Bank—both initially underplayed the debt crisis, focusing upon the largest debtor country problems, hoping to prevent a general loss of confidence in the Western financial markets. For if the commercial loans could not be rescheduled and were officially declared in default and written off as losses, the stocks of the large banks involved could

---

Maquiladora industry plants just below the U.S. border assemble parts from abroad and export the finished products. By 1988 they employed 350,000 workers in some 1,500 plants and had grown 14 percent annually since 1978.

plummet, risking a run on the banks or, at the least, a great crisis in confidence in the stability of world finance. A comment made in 1982 attributed to Arthur Burns, former Chairman of the Federal Reserve Board, summed up the situation: "The international banks have made many foolish loans and now we can only pray they will make some more of them."

However, to receive IMF-sponsored loans, which permit developing countries to reschedule their debts with lower interest rates spread out over a longer time period, the debtor governments usually were forced to agree to austerity conditions that initially cut economic growth and caused unemployment, lower living standards, and domestic political unrest. Mexico, for example, had to agree to cut government subsidies and employment, curb imports and inflation, and permit the peso to float against the dollar. Between 1982 and 1987 real income in Mexico fell 40 percent and annual inflation reached 160 percent. Thousands of workers lost their jobs.

The following year, preceding the national election, the government's six-year-old austerity plan finally slowed the inflation rate and foreign trade surpluses doubled to $8.4 billion. Mexico also followed the advice of Ronald Reagan's Treasury Secretary, James Baker, to start selling state enterprises, reduce tariffs, ease restrictions on foreign investment, and encourage non-oil exports. To make the economy look good before the election, the government negotiated a wage-and-price pact with workers and manufacturers and increased the availability of consumer goods. But the successful political strategy, which barely gave the incoming president over 50 percent of the vote in a contested election, caused chaos in Mexico's balance of payments, already suffering from a drop in oil prices. Capital flew the coop for safer havens abroad.

Mexico illustrates the "debt trap" situation of debtor developing countries caused by economic policies of the Reagan administration: A nation can either aim for an external balance-of-payments policy or it can try to meet the population's demand for a higher quality life—but not both. Most of the resources needed to service Mexico's external debts come out of domestic investment. Between 1982 and 1988 the investment rate within Mexico fell 6 percent and Mexico's GNP shrank even though the population grew by 13 percent.[20] About 4 percent of Mexican GNP goes to foreigners for debt servicing. So the $3.5 billion loan given to Mexico by the United States in 1988 paradoxically sank Mexico deeper into the debt trap.[21] Nor did the landmark deal completed in 1990 with American bankers under the Brady plan, under which most banks reduced the value of Mexico's debt by 35 percent (by lowering the principle on existing loans or accepting lower interest payments) change this structure of dependence. Further debt reduction on the part of the creditors, combined with an increased focus upon internal Mexican growth led by tourism and the dynamism of the *maquiladora* plants, appear to be necessary prerequisites to restructuring the Mexican economy to become more self-sufficient. Such positive reforms are consistent with the policy shift at the IMF under Managing Director Michel J. Camdessus stressing increasing economic growth rather than austerity in the debtor nations.[22]

INTERPRETATIONS

In contemplating the 1960s, 1970s, and 1980s one cannot help but note that the tempo of global economic change and technological innovation has speeded up and has put increased psychosocial and financial pressures upon both rich and poor alike. It is self-evident that the rich have the resources to create more buffer zones between themselves and socioeconomic change, that is if they choose to do so. Nevertheless, Swedish economist Staffan Linder has argued in his biting book *The Harried Leisure Class* that the higher one is on the class scale, the more harried one's "leisure" time becomes as the goods and opportunities to be consumed grow geometrically while the time one has in the day is still finite—24 hours for the rich as well as for the poor. Or, as poet Antonio Machado put it: "Speed kills the soul."

Whether this increase in speed has increased the gap between the rich and poor nations is less often asked than this question: How great has the gap become and how fast is it increasing? Still, among economists based in the classical liberal school, such as W.W. Rostow, it has appeared that the poor have gotten richer while the rich have slowed down.[23] Growth rates among the developing countries, particularly those in the newly industrializing category (the NICs), have certainly exceeded those of the developed countries in many cases.

On the other hand, developing countries start with much less so there is more room for growth (or the numbers are easier to double). From the reformist liberal perspective, world capitalism can be made to work for the poor if it is better targeted for economic growth in the less developed regions—as in the case of Michael J. Camdessus's policy at the IMF.[24] The basic human needs perspective represented by the philosophy of Robert McNamara at the World Bank focuses upon helping the poorest of the poor individually.[25] Such a target seems unrealistic to the realist school variously represented by Hedley Bull, Robert Tucker, and Stephen Krasner: The power, security, control, and vulnerability of the nation-state make up the dominant reality for these analysts.[26]

The interdependence school of Robert Keohane and Joseph Nye stresses the increasing global dependency of rich and poor nations upon each other.[27] Finally, the neo-Marxists perceive global capitalism as a system headed for self-destruction.[28] A brief look at how such various perspectives conflict in their interpretation of foreign aid as a means to ameliorate the gap between rich and poor nations may serve as a useful illustration of the main theme of international political economy: the asymmetry of power and wealth in the relationship of rich nations to the poor ones.

Foreign Aid: Partial Solution, Drug, or Panacea?

The success of OPEC and demands for the New International Economic Order set the stage for an expansion of multinational financial aid for the developing countries in the 1970s. The focus upon bilateral foreign aid,* which dominated the discussion concerning economic relations between developed and developing countries in the 1950s and 1960s, had come to be viewed with skepticism by not only the poor nations but also by the mass publics of the industrialized world. The widely read book *The Ugly American* told the tale of the United States donating thousands of sacks of wheat to malnourished countries only to have Soviet agents stamp the sacks upon arrival as gifts from the USSR. The American share of total Western financial aid fell from 59 percent in 1961 to 27 percent in 1980, when the United States ranked only thirteenth among the top seventeen Western aid donors in terms of percentage of aid relative to GNP.[29] In terms of absolute quantity, Japan in 1989 surpassed the United States as the number-one giver of foreign aid. Given the pressures in the 1980s for budget reductions in U.S. domestic programs, foreign aid bills had a difficult time getting through Congress.

The neo-corporatist nations of Scandinavia and the Netherlands, on the other hand, have continued to support foreign aid strongly. So have Japan and West Germany, beginning in the 1970s after their postwar reconstruction and economic successes were assured. In 1989 Japan surpassed the United States as the world's largest aid donor and targeted $65 billion for recycling to indebted countries from 1990–1993. China more or less stopped its foreign-aid program in the late 1970s, while aid from the Soviet Union and Eastern bloc countries declined.

Although foreign aid or economic assistance typically makes up only 10 percent of the cash received by developing countries (compared with some 70 percent for export receipts), this 10 percent can be more easily targeted by governments for specific projects than can commercial money, giving foreign aid more influence on national economic development than its percentage weight might suggest. Clearly, foreign aid cannot be more than a partial solution to the North–South economic asymmetry, but as Robert McNamara was well aware, aid can be carefully targeted as a strategic tool to greatly influence national policies.

While McNamara used foreign aid via the World Bank to target the poorest individuals in the poorest countries, others have found this nonstructural approach too diffuse to have anything but a short-term effect. McNamara's focus on individuals is a typical example of the humanism of Western culture. Taking more the viewpoint of the power realists, the Soviet

---

*Defined as official financial assistance, excluding military aid, private philanthropy, and private investment.

Union and Eastern European countries targeted long-term strategic states for aid—Cuba, North Korea, and Vietnam—as did OPEC in targeting Islamic states—Syria, Jordan, and Egypt—and the United States in shoring up Middle Eastern allies—Israel and Egypt. According to the realist perspective, foreign economic assistance becomes a form of political war fought by means other than force. For the realist the national security of the nation and its allies becomes the criterion for granting aid—a criterion that may better serve the interests of one-party, authoritarian economies than of multiparty, factional democracies.[30] The cold war motivation of Marshall Plan reconstruction of Western Europe, for example, served as a defense against Soviet influence only in the short-term, while at the same time building up the economies of future competitors in the world economy. Opposing the dispensing of foreign aid as a gift (except when the beneficiary is a developing country with deep structural problems) as unnecessary, unnatural, and unwise, structuralist economist Gunnar Myrdal noted: "The whole international exchange situation would have been more wholesome now and in the past decade if the United States could have called for repayments of loans from West European governments—gradually and with due considerations."[31] Myrdal went on to note that aid policies cannot be morally neutral: From a realist's state-centered focus, the Swedish government's criterion for aid is to promote political democracy and social equality, not to preserve anti-progressive social structures (too often the case in using shortsighted cold war realism as an aid criterion).

As a structuralist (see Chapter 3), Myrdal agrees with the reformist school of liberalism to the extent that he suggests the capitalist world economy can be fixed to be more human and less asymmetrical. And while somewhat belonging to a category all of his own, Myrdal has much in common with what has been called the "interdependence school": the stress upon the mutual dependency of developed and developing countries. This school of thought grew out of the momentum of the NIEO movement and the growing consensus that the decision-making framework of international organizations gave more bargaining leverage to developing countries in *multilateral* aid negotiations where norms and rules are more clear than they would in the *bilateral* negotiations (between two states) preferred by the realists, where asymmetry is likely to be the dominant perception.[32]

The interdependence school rejects the realist's state-centered focus of international political economy in the late twentieth century, arguing that this form of analysis cannot capture the reality of many transnational flows that have little to do with the nation-state—the transactions of multinational companies, for instance. State sovereignty, in short, has become as leaky as a sieve, and the global political economy can only be understood in terms of a network of domestic, business, cultural, political, and economic linkages that perforate the pretentious control of the nation-state. Technology and financial flows are cited as evidence of the need for an interdependence perspective.

Perhaps the ultimate example of this approach is the initial report of the Independent Commission for International Economic Cooperation chaired by Willy Brandt of West Germany—the well-known *Brandt Report* of 1980.[33] Using a vision of global Keynesianism, the Brandt Commission argued that the Third World must carry the main share of its own burden but cannot be left alone to the world markets or haphazard nature of the liberal or basic-human-needs perspectives. Rather, aid must be shifted from bilateral to multilateral forms and focus, for the sake of the South, upon the automaticity of an international tax on armaments, the trade of luxury goods, the use of the global commons (that is, the international seabed), and so forth. Without general increases in aid levels based on these and other policies, economic forces left to themselves tend to produce growing inequalities.

From the radical or neo-Marxist perspective, foreign aid is a tool for imperialism and social control, aiming to undermine the independence of developing countries.[34] In *The Debt Trap*, Cheryl Payer, for example, implies that the solution to this dilemma of becoming dependent upon the debt trap cultivated by foreign-aid donors from the industrialized world and the growth-dampening austerity measures of the IMF is to try going it alone as much as possible. The North Korean constitution is cited as a model.[35] In the postwar period Albania tried this strategy only to face ever-greater poverty until reluctantly the Albanians rejoined the world economy.

On the other hand, the People's Republic of China successfully modernized its agricultural base largely in isolation, joining the world economy officially as it was becoming a net exporter of food, thus giving the country a less dependent bargaining position. From the contemporary radical perspective, models of the ideal socialist society must be established to be ready to take over when global capitalism breaks apart from its own contradictions.

Marxism and Dependency Theory

Marx himself, however, believed that the role of capitalist or bourgeois imperialism was revolutionary and would transform all traditional societies until they used the same mode of commodity production. In his *Communist Manifesto* of 1848, Marx wrote: "It compels all nations, on pain of extinction, to adopt the bourgeois mode of production...compels them to introduce what it calls civilization into their midst,...creates a world after its own image." But in going beyond the Continent, Marx discovered that his European theory of development did not seem to apply. In Asia and the Middle East, precapitalist stages did not appear to exist. These societies were stuck in what Marx termed the "Asiatic mode of production," based on the unity and autarchy of agriculture and manufacturing at the village level and an autonomous, parasitic state split from the rest of society at the top. Since nothing existed internally to change such a conservative social structure, Marx thought the external force of Western imperialism would be the agent of change.[36] Thus, nineteenth century-England's role in India was both the destruction of the old Asian society and the laying of the groundwork for the material basis of Western society in Asia. Lenin extended this thinking to conclude that the inherent contradiction of capitalism was that it developed, not underdeveloped, the world, spreading its technology and industry to lesser-developed nations, thus undermining its position, preparing the competitive basis for its own destruction.[37]

Picking up Marx's theory of capitalist imperialism and Marx's concern for the domestic distribution of wealth, dependency theory arose in the mid-1960s, adding a strong dose of economic nationalism to its recipe. Disenchanted with the inadequacy of the structuralists' strategy of import substitution as a means to wealth for the developing countries, dependency theorists were convinced that the failure lay in the inability of this strategy to change the traditional social and economic conditions of peripheral states. Whereas the Marxist-Leninist thesis of capitalist imperialism suggests the necessity of foreign aid as part of the process of inevitable capitalist development, dependency theory argues that dependency causes underdevelopment and is apt to be critical of aid.

In the often-cited definition of Brazilian scholar Theotonio Dos Santos, *dependence* is "a situation in which the economy of certain countries is conditioned by the development and expansion of another economy to which the former is subjected."[38] Whereas liberals perceive underdevelopment as a *condition* of countries that have not kept up with the leaders in the world economy, dependency theorists view it as a *process* inherent in an asymmetrical system that continually restructures developing countries into underdeveloped positions compared to developed countries.[39] Rather than the liberal vision of developing countries as split between modern sectors well integrated into the national and international economies and backward sectors that have not yet adapted, the dependency school sees the developing countries locked into a backward position on the periphery of an integrated global economy. This position of "negative self-fulfilling prophecy" is characterized typically by an overdependence upon raw materials with unsteady prices; inequitably distributed national income catering to the tastes of the elite and not targeted toward the needs of the masses; distorting investments by multinational companies that stymie local entrepreneurship and technological innovation as profits are recycled abroad; an undermining of the local labor market as foreign firms pay higher salaries, creating structural unemployment; and dependence upon foreign capital that fosters authoritarian governments, which provide multinational companies with the stability they require.[40] The underdevelopment of dependent countries is caused, according to dependency theorists, by transnational class linkages between the metropolitan international centers of world capitalism and a parasitic, feudal clientele class dominating the political system of the country at the periphery. True nationalists must rise up against this international class hegemony and pursue the welfare of the entire society, not just of the class in which they find themselves. The aim is to create an autonomous, industrialized state characterized by equality, not parasitic dependence. As this goal is achieved, foreign aid presumably becomes less and less necessary.

While dependency theory describes certain cases of poor, exploited, commodity-producing states—such as the Philippines of Ferdinand Marcos—it cannot account for the higher growth rate characterizing lesser-developed countries as a group over that of the developed countries in the recent past.[41] Rather than systematically underdeveloping the developing countries, the global economy appears inadvertently to have helped many of them, although in a sporadic way that no doubt has worked to help the least advantaged nations the least (such as those of sub-Sahara Africa). Other theories, such as the *world-system* perspective, fault dependence theory for neglecting the implications of the *global* division of labor.

The World-System Perspective

From the viewpoint of sociologist Immanuel Wallerstein's world-system perspective, foreign aid is no more than a transitory epiphenomenon, distracting one from the essential structural transformations and macro-cycles and trends of global capitalism. In his book *The Modern World System II* (1980), Wallerstein argues that the modern world system emerged from the transformation of European feudalism and mercantilism into a capitalist world economy colored by Europe's particular redistributive or tributary mode of production. This transformation originated in the economic expansion of the sixteenth century (phase A) and subsequent contraction, depression, or "crisis" in the seventeenth century (phase B). Ever since then, the capitalist world economy has expanded to cover the entire globe, manifesting a cyclical pattern of economic expansion and contraction (François Simiand's phases A and B) with shifting geographic locations of economic roles (the rise and fall of hegemonies and hierarchical displacements of particular core, peripheral, and semi-peripheral zones), and has continued to undergo a process of secular transformation (that is, of technological advance, industrialization, proletarianization, and of the emergence of structural resistance to the system itself).

According to Wallerstein, the French Revolution and its Napoleonic continuation catalyzed the ideological transformation of the capitalist world economy *as a world system*, creating three new sets of cultural institutions central to this system: the ideologies (conservatism, liberalism, and Marxism), the social sciences, and the social movements.* The antisystemic

---

*Wallerstein argues that the French Revolution did not change France very much but did change the world system very much: Immanuel Wallerstein, "The French Revolution as a World Historical Event," *Social Research* 56, No. 1 (Spring 1989): 33–52.

national and social movements are created by growing economic constraints at those cyclical moments when world economic production is in excess of world demand, precipitating stagnation (or phase B—contraction). Labor unions, socialist parties, and other kinds of workers' organizations are examples of social movements, emphasizing the growing polarity between successful bourgeois groups and the proletariat caught in the economic squeeze. Paradoxically, according to Wallerstein, these worker movements turn to the state to maximize their collective interests, further strengthening the governmental structural supports of the bourgeois classes against whom they feel the sting of increasing inequality.

While in the nineteenth century the process of the social movement spread from core to periphery in the world economy, the national movement going from periphery to core, in the late twentieth century, Wallerstein argues, they are no longer ideological rivals: "Today there is scarcely a social movement which is not nationalist, and there are few national movements which are not socialist."[42] This questionable supposition (given national conservative movements in the United States and Great Britain, as well as in France, West Germany and Eastern Europe) permits Wallerstein to project that we are living in a global transition from capitalism to socialism that may take more than a century to complete given capitalism's tendency to reemerge in cyclic ways. Such a transformation would presumably bring more equity to a world system now flawed by the absence of an overarching international political authority to match the global scope of the world economy.

* * *

Curiously, there appears to be a meeting of the minds in the rejection of foreign aid on the part of the extreme, socialist perspective to the left and the extreme capitalist viewpoint on the orthodox, liberal right. Orthodox liberal economists Peter T. Bauer and Basil S. Yamey argue that foreign aid serves to reify and politicize the state in a developing country, giving power to corrupt leaders who have their own personal and political interests in mind rather than the interests of the poorest people in their nation. Thus Dr. Julius K. Nyerere of Tanzania used aid to force millions of people to move from their homes into socialist villages, devastating food production. And President Mobutu of Zaire, who received a great deal of aid, expelled traders, bringing the society back to subsistence production and widespread deprivation. Aid, according to this perspective lowers international competitiveness of a developing country by permitting governments to disguise the worst aspects of their economic policies—such as creating or maintaining overvalued exchange rates or increasing the domestic money supply, often leading to inflation, a lack of confidence, and a flight of capital.[43] Indeed, economists Bauer and Yamey observe: "The concept of the Third World and the policy of official aid are inseparable. Without foreign aid there is no Third World."[44] In other words, foreign aid is a drug that corrupts the economic competitiveness of a country, rendering it dependent upon the aid-giving North as long as the drug is consumed.

IMPLICATIONS

From a collective learning perspective, the role of foreign aid or financial assistance must be structured and targeted for the economic interests of the countries involved at that historical moment according to a model that links short-term help to long-term rewards and mutual benefits. Leaving the world markets alone to run their own course—an orthodox liberal policy—amounts to a *de facto* maintenance strategy that leaves existing inequalities between the North and South in place, causing the gap between rich and poor to widen as the high technology and information revolutions speed up economic transactions, leaving the underequipped or less informed further and further behind.

　　The North–South gap widened in the 1980s because of the debt crisis, which discouraged commercial banks from lending any new money to debtor nations (a negative trend reinforced by new banking regulations). Money was granted for interest repayments on outstanding loans. But this causes increasing political unrest in Latin American democracies, which see such a large share of their scarce export earnings going to pay interest on debt rather than being reinvested in their own economies to stimulate economic growth and employment.

　　By 1989, Latin American governments had paid $160 billion in interest on their $420 billion foreign debt, and to avoid default many of them cut back essential imports, reduced government spending, and watched economic growth and political support evaporate.[45] The largest Latin American debtors see themselves as caught in a vicious circle or debt trap in which the banks just grant them enough money to tide them over until the next payment is due to avoid having to formally write off the loans and cause a crisis in world financial markets: This sense of running in place and never catching up with their collective economic problems led to a widespread political and economic malaise throughout Latin America.[46] Thus, in terms of change in per capita gross domestic product from 1981 to 1989: Mexico: −9.2, Venezuela: −24.9, Colombia: 13.9, Brazil: −0.4, Ecuador: −1.1, Peru: −24.7, Bolivia: −26.6, Chile: 9.6; and Argentina: −23.5. In the 1990s Chile and Bolivia will benefit from tough austerity and free market measures taken (although at significant social cost—particularly for the poor). Meanwhile, Argentina started the decade reeling from a 3,700 percent inflation for 1981, while Peru's inflation was 2,775 percent for the same year (statistics from Economic Commission for Latin America and the Caribbean).

The 1985 plan of U.S. Treasury Secretary James Baker—to encourage more World Bank and commercial lending to debtor countries in return for privatization and opening up of their economies to foreigners—did not work. Nevertheless, as Baker was appointed Secretary of State under President George Bush, the ideology behind the Baker Plan will continue, broken down on a case-by-case basis as a reformist liberal tries to head off political and economic crises in key countries (starting with Mexico) in terms of U.S. national interests on a cost-effective basis. Since the United States itself ran up debts amounting to nearly four times that of the greatest Latin American debtor (Brazil) by the end of the 1980s, there are financial constraints on how far the United States can go on its own to help alleviate Third-World debt. Europe and Japan have become increasingly involved, whether they like it or not.* Indeed, the Lomé Convention provides one model that has worked quite well in targeting aid to a large number of developing countries—sector-specific support of benefit to donors and recipients alike in the long run. Rather than short-term, put-out-the-fire crisis management, the American government might be well advised to create its own form of Lomé Convention for Latin American countries, letting the Japanese do the same in the Asian region.

But in addition to such targeted, sector-specific plans, commercial banks may have to be persuaded to cut their interest rates by half on outstanding debts to create the preconditions for sustained economic recovery in Latin American democracies.

Perhaps the greatest threat to global economic adjustment in the last decade of the twentieth century is the ascendency of the ideology of neorealism in some American government circles and academic establishments at a time when East–West conflicts recede and new liquidity must be forthcoming from the North to finance the South not only for interest repayments on debt but also for purchases of imports and for investment in economic development. As a reaction against the forecasts of the demise of the nation-state on the one hand, and as a counter to the naiveté of earlier American aid policies on the other, the neorealistic perspective attributes the loss of control by national governments in the 1970s to a power vacuum resulting from decline in U.S. hegemony (dating particularly from the American defeat in Vietnam). But as implied in Chapter 2, a focus upon existing reality in terms of power calculations, national interest, and hegemonic stability theory plants the seeds for its own destruction. As Martin Rochester has noted, the hegemon is inevitably inclined to carry an excessive demand load in sacrificing itself for "the common good" (look at the U.S. sacrifice of

---

*The Japanese organization in charge of lending to the developing countries is the Export-Import Bank of Japan with four decades of experience in promoting corporate interests with low-cost loans. However, the majority of loan recipients are no longer tied to buying from Japanese companies.

its national budget for military security spending for NATO). Rochester has observed: "With few exceptions, the current generation of scholars, compared to earlier generations, has been so concerned about accurately and soberly observing reality that they have lost a sense of vision."[47]

To move beyond what sociologist C. Wright Mills called "crack-pot realism," industrialized nations need to look beyond short-term economic and power interests to long-term regional and global strategies that integrate idealism and realism in mutual benefit packages. From Myrdal and the Swedes one learns not only that foreign aid is not morally neutral but that it can also further national ideological objectives to the extent these are long term and exportable. The key prerequisite here for successful long-term support and success is not to mix kinds of aid just to get one bill through a parliament or Congress but to clearly distinguish humanitarian aid, development or modernization aid, and military assistance for national security from each other; and, as one moves from the humanitarian to the military, also shift from multilateral to bilateral organization for financing.[48] It is unrealistic to expect governments of developed countries to give foreign aid without targeting it to be consistent with their national interest. But those nation-states with long-term visions of global strategy and a *positive*, community-oriented rationale for foreign aid will reap the benefits of solidarity with allies, while those with short-term, defensive, national security Band-Aid policies will find themselves lining the pockets of corrupt authoritarian leaders, who, in turn, generate more animosity toward the donor than good-will.[49] Collective models of equality of economic opportunity should be cultivated as the rule in targeting aid, not the exception. Apart from aid, developing countries look to Newly Industrialized Countries (NICs) for models of successful *internal* development—longing for more independence.

East Asian "Models": Beyond "Disembedded" Liberalism

Between 1965 and 1986, Taiwan went from being the twenty-eighth biggest exporter of manufactures to tenth and Korea jumped from thirty-third to thirteenth. The assumption that the successful East Asian NICs—Hong Kong, Singapore, Taiwan, and South Korea—are models of classical liberal economic efficiency that can be adopted by others with a little help from the recently disembedded liberal guidelines of the IMF and World Bank ("disembedded" or brought to the surface by the thrust of the Reagan, Thatcher, and Kohl governments of the 1980s, which pushed for deregulated market incentives) has proved to be oversimplistic. While Karl Marx was probably wrong in his negative prognosis for the "Asian mode of production" (Japan, after all, represents an Asian corporatist success that seems often to transcend the Western economic model of liberal capitalism), both he and Lenin were no doubt correct that state managers of developing countries

would only succeed if they used capitalist tools and adapted to the technological change diffused by capitalist metropoles or hegemonies (symbolized
by London and New York).

While not wrong in the need for distinctive forms of economic nationalism, the dependency school on the other hand goes too far in advocating
attempted autonomy from the world economy (as the cases of Albania, Cuba,
and Rumania illustrated all too clearly in economic terms). And despite the
danger of macro-abstraction and determinism implicit in world-systems
theory, this perspective teaches the managers of nation-states the importance
of positioning oneself carefully in the international division of labor if
unique, national factor endowments are to be brought into fruitful combination for competitiveness in the interdependent system of global capitalism.

As economist Colin Bradford has demonstrated, the East Asian NICs
are not simple models of pro-market, neoclassical liberalism, but are complex
mixes of market forces, public policies, and government intervention—that
is, successful development based *both* upon import substitution (state) and
export promotion (market) forces working together consistently.[50] The Western polarization of thought and ideology between pro-market (liberalism)
and pro-state (economic nationalism) does not fit here anymore than it does
in the corporatist political economies of Northern Europe (see Chapters 4 and
5). Rather, the terminology of collective learning and positioning theory is
useful here in distinguishing between the "stabilization" policies critical for
an effective maintenance base (consensual agreements among government,
labor, and corporate management) and the export promotion and innovative
sector targeting and adaptation policies that make up the entrepreneurial
side of the dynamic NIC economy (forming a "maintenpreneurial" synthesis,
the most advanced form of which is no doubt the Japanese example).

For instance, South Korea's success in increasing its exports of highly
capital-intensive goods (the entrepreneurial side of the strategy mix) during
the 1970s can only be explained by the extensive subsidies on capital use
amounting to at least 10 percent of the country's GNP annually (the maintenance base targeting side of the strategy mix).[51] Taiwan used import substitution to accompany, not merely precede, export promotion, with the
government selectively managing the volume and composition of imports
and fiscal incentives for new export sectors.[52] This represented a dynamic
maintenpreneurial strategy consistent with traditions in Taiwan and with
factor endowments.

One of the most market-driven of the East Asian NICs (after Hong
Kong), Singapore, relied heavily on private enterprise for its development.
Nevertheless, some analysts have found that the targeted structuring of the
maintenance base—in this case the state—was the most important factor
behind Singapore's success with middle-range (five- to ten-year) tax relief for
specified pioneer industries, heavy tax deduction incentives for new fixed
investment in plant, machinery and factory buildings (up to 50 percent), and

tax incentives and long-term, low-interest loans for research and development in the manufacturing sector.[53] Economist Ralph Bryant has identified a similar set of gradual maintenance-base targeted incentives and lifting of constraints in the financial sector of Singapore.[54]

Paradoxically, Hong Kong, the East Asian NIC where the neoclassical, liberal market model comes closest to fitting, is apt to end the twentieth century with massive disinvestment, given the People's Republic of China's announcement following the repression of the 1989 democratic rebellion that China will exercise her option in 1997 to base Chinese troops in Hong Kong—the state or maintenance base gone so heavy-handed that it crushes the confidence of foreign investors in the stability and future freedom in the oasis of entrepreneurship in Asia.

Using the high growth 1960s as a staging ground and Japan as an inspiration and model for outward or export-oriented development in the 1970s (in contrast to the inward-oriented Latin American development strategies), the East Asian NICs provide examples of successful maintenpreneurial strategies combining state and market forces consistently for targeted growth—*provided* that the global environment remains benign, if not positive. Without such a positive global background, developing countries will have to continue to rely upon external aid to get export-oriented growth started. The drive for external support becomes even more obvious when one looks at East bloc socialist states aiming for more market-oriented, democratic political economies.

ENDNOTES

1. Mahbub ul Haq, "The New International Economic Order," paper presented at the Faculty Seminar on International Political Economy at Columbia University, December 17, 1975. See Haq's *The Poverty Curtain: Choices for the Third World* (New York: Columbia University Press, 1976).

2. Fiametta Rocco, "ADB Becomes Premier Source of Credit," *International Herald Tribune*, September 28, 1987, p. 10.

3. William Clark, "Robert McNamara at the World Bank," *Foreign Affairs* (Fall 1981): 171–74.

4. See Stephen D. Krasner, "Oil Is the Exception," *Foreign Policy* 14 (Spring 1974): 68–84.

5. Edward L. Morse, "After the Fall: The Politics of Oil," *Foreign Affairs* 64, No. 4 (Spring 1986): 793.

6. On prerequisites for successful producer cartels, see C. Fred Bergsten, "The Threat from the Third World," *Foreign Policy* (Summer 1973): 102–24; and Benson Varon and Kenji Takenchi, "Developing Countries and Non-Fuel Minerals," *Foreign Affairs* 52 (1974): 497–510.

7. See Karl P. Sauvant and Hajo Hasenpflug, eds., *The New International Economic Order: Confrontation or Cooperation between North and South?* (Boulder, CO: Westview Press, 1977).

8. Ibid., pp. 165–66.

9. Commission of the European Communities, "The Lomé Convention: The Sta-bilization of Export Earnings," *Information Development and Cooperation* No. 94 (1975): 2–3.

10. "The European Community in the World," *European File,* Commission of the European Communities (Brussels, Belgium, October 1986), pp. 9–10.

11. Michael Zammit Cutjar, *UNCTAD and the North-South Dialogue: The First Twenty Years* (Oxford: Pergamon Press, 1985).

12. See Donald J. Puchala, ed., *Issues Before the 35th General Assembly of the United Nations 1980–1981* (New York: United Nations Association of the United States, 1980), pp. 73–104.

13. Christopher A. Kojm, ed., *The Problem of International Debt* (New York: H. W. Wilson Co., 1984), p. 14. See also Philip A. Wellons, *Passing the Buck: Governments and the Third World Debt* (Cambridge, MA: Harvard Business School Press, 1987); Miles Kahler, "Politics and International Debt: Explaining the Crisis," *International Organization* 39, No. 3 (Summer 1985): 357–82; and Michael Palmer and Kenneth R. Gordon, "External Indebtedness and Debt Servicing Problems of Developing Countries," *Columbia Journal of World Business* (Spring 1985): 37–43.

14. C. Bogdanowicz-Bindert, "Financial Crisis of 1982: A Debtor's Perspective," in *International Banking and Global Financing,* edited by S.K. Kaushik (New York: Pace University, 1983), pp. 203–204.

15. Luis Catan, "The Future of Debtor Countries in Latin America," in *The Debt Crisis and Financial Stability,* edited by S.K. Kaushik (New York: Pace University, 1985), pp. 17–31. Also see Jorge I. Dominquez, *Mexico's Political Economy* (London: Sage Publications, 1982) and C.W. Reynolds and C. Tello, *U.S.–Mexico Relations* (Stanford, CA: Stanford University Press, 1983). On money going into Swiss accounts, see Curtis Skinner, "The Next Earthquake," *Commonweal* (July 11, 1986), p. 397.

16. Ibid., p. 398.

17. Brian O'Reilly, "Doing Business on Mexico's Volcano," *Fortune* (August 29, 1988), p. 74.

18. House of Representatives, Committee on Foreign Affairs, "Global Debt Crisis: Mexican Debt Situation" (Washington, DC: U.S. Congress, July 30, 1986), p. 58. See also "U.S. Senate Committee on Finance, Subcommittee on International Debt, Hearings on Third World Debt," April 6, 1987, 100th Congress, 1st session, U.S. Superintendent of Public Documents, 1987.

19. Kojm, *Problem of International Debt,* p. 38.

20. Karin Lissakers, "More Funds for Mexico, More Debt Trap," *The New York Times,* November 8, 1988. For alternative views, see Benjamin J. Cohen, "International Debt and U.S. Policy," *International Organization* 39, No. 4 (Autumn 1985): 699–727, and Henry S. Bienen and Mark Gersovitz, "Economic Stabilization, Conditionality, and Political Stability," pp. 729–754 in the same issue.

21. For a neo-Marxist interpretation of the debt trap, see Cheryl Payer, *The Debt Trap: The IMF and the Third World* (New York: Monthly Review Press, 1974).

22. "Michel Camdessus Is Making the IMF Less of a Scrooge," *Business Week* (October 5, 1987), p. 32. Also see Steven Greenhouse, "I.M.F. Leader Assails Rise in Dollar," *The New York Times,* September 22, 1988; Bahran Nowzad and Tony Killick, "The IMF's Role in Developing Countries," *Finance and Development* 21 (September 1984): 21–27; John Williamson, *IMF Conditionality* (Cambridge, MA:

MIT Press, 1983); and Rudiger Dornbusch, "How to Turn Mexico's Debt and Inflation into Growth," *Challenge*, January–February 1989, pp. 4–10.

23. W.W. Rostow, *Why the Poor Get Richer and the Rich Slow Down* (Austin: The University of Texas Press, 1980).

24. For an example of the reformist liberal perspective, see Albert Fishlow, "A New International Economic Order: What Kind?," in A. Fishlow et al., *Rich and Poor Nations in the World Economy* (New York: McGraw-Hill, 1978). Also see Robert E. Wood, *From Marshall Plan to Debt Crisis: Foreign Aid and Development Choices in the World Economy* (Berkeley: University of California Press, 1986).

25. See Robert S. McNamara, *Address to the Board of Governors*, International Bank for Reconstruction and Development, October 2, 1979 (Washington, DC: IBRD) and R. McNamara, "The Population Problem," *Foreign Affairs* 62 (Summer 1984).

26. See Hedley Bull, *The Anarchical Society* (New York: Columbia University Press, 1977); Robert W. Tucker, *The Inequality of Nations* (New York: Basic Books, 1977); and Stephen D. Krasner, *Structural Conflict: The Third World Against Global Liberalism* (Berkeley: University of California Press, 1985).

27. Robert Keohane and Joseph Nye, *Power and Interdependence* (Boston: Little, Brown, 1977).

28. See, for example, André Gunder Frank, *Latin America: Underdevelopment or Revolution?* (New York: Monthly Review Press, 1969); Arghiri Emmanuel, *Unequal Exchange: A Study of the Imperialism of Trade* (New York: Monthly Review Press, 1972); and Samire Amin, *Accumulation on a World Scale: A Critique of the Theory of Development*, 2 vols. (New York: Monthly Review Press, 1974).

29. Organization for Economic Cooperation and Development, *Development Cooperation 1980 Review* (Paris: OECD, 1980), p. 99.

30. See Robert S. Walters, *American and Soviet Aid: A Comparative Analysis* (Pittsburgh: University of Pittsburgh Press, 1970), p. 240.

31. Gunnar Myrdal, *The Challenge of World Poverty: A World Anti-Poverty Program in Outline* (New York: Random House, 1970), p. 338.

32. See Leon Gordenker, *International Aid and National Decisions* (Princeton, NJ: Princeton University Press, 1976), pp. 57–58, 67.

33. Willy Brandt and Anthony Sampson, eds., *North–South: A Program for Survival* (Cambridge, MA: MIT Press, 1980).

34. See, for example, Steven Weisman, ed., *The Trojan Horse: A Radical Look at Foreign Aid* (San Francisco: Ramparts Press, 1974) and Teresa Hayter, *Aid as Imperialism* (Middlesex, England: Penguin, 1971).

35. Payer, *The Debt Trap.*

36. See Shlomo Avineri, ed., *Karl Marx on Colonialism and Modernization* (Garden City, NY: Anchor Books, 1969).

37. V.I. Lenin, *Imperialism: The Highest Stage of Capitalism* (New York: International Publishers, 1917, 1939), p. 65.

38. Theotonio Dos Santos, "The Structure of Dependence," *American Economic Review* 60 (May, 1970): 231.

39. Robert Gilpin, "The Issue of Dependency and Economic Development," Chapter 7 in *The Political Economy of International Relations* (Princeton, NJ: Princeton University Press, 1987), p. 282.

40. Ibid, pp. 285–86. See, for example, Peter Evans, *Dependent Development: The Alliance of Multinational, State and Local Capital in Brazil* (Princeton, NJ: Princeton University Press, 1979).

41. Krasner, *Structural Conflict*, pp. 97–101.

42. Immanuel Wallerstein, "The Future of the World-Economy," in Charles Kegley and Eugene Wittkopf, eds., *The Global Agenda* (New York: Random House, 1984), p. 279. For a critical view of Wallerstein, see Theda Skocpol, "Wallerstein's World Capitalist System: A Theoretical and Historical Critique," *American Journal of Sociology* 82 (March, 1977): 1075–90.

43. See Hans O. Schmitt, "Development Assistance: A View from Bretton Woods," *Public Policy* (Fall 1973).

44. Peter T. Bauer and Basil S. Yamey, "Foreign Aid: What Is at Stake?," in W. Scott Thompson, ed., *The Third World: Premises of U.S. Policy* (San Francisco: Institute of Contemporary Studies, 1983), p. 117.

45. Alan Riding, "Latins Want Bush to Help on Debts," *The New York Times,* November 29, 1988.

46. Sarah Bartlett, "A Vicious Circle Keeps Latin America in Debt," *The New York Times,* January 15, 1989.

47. Martin J. Rochester, "The Rise and Fall of International Organization as a Field of Study," *International Organization* (Autumn 1986): 801.

48. See "Public Opinion, Foreign Policy Making and Foreign Aid," Chapter 6 of R. Isaak, *American Democracy and World Power* (New York: St. Martin's Press, 1977).

49. Or, as economist Barbara Ward put it: "In all this welter of Western insistence upon self-interest and self-defense, one looks in vain for any consistent exposition of a *positive* policy of foreign aid, some general political philosophy to match the Communist confidence in world brotherhood based on Socialist production, some framework of solidarity between givers and takers of aid, some aspect of human concern beyond the narrow limits of common fear." In B. Ward's "For a New Foreign Aid Concept," in Robert A. Goldwin and Harry M. Clor, eds., *Readings in American Foreign Policy* (New York: Oxford University Press, 1970), p. 582.

50. Colin I. Bradford, "East Asian 'Models': Myths and Lessons," in John P. Lewis and Valeriana Kallab, eds., *Development Strategies Reconsidered* (Overseas Development Council Publication) New Brunswick, NJ: Transaction Books, 1986, pp. 115–28. And see: Robert Wade, "What Can Economics Learn from East Asian Success?," in *The Annals*, 505, Sept., 1989, pp. 68–79.

51. Wontack Hong, "Export Oriented Growth and Trade Patterns of Korea," in Colin I. Bradford and William H. Branson, eds., *Trade and Structural Change in Pacific Asia* (Chicago: University of Chicago Press, forthcoming).

52. See Robert Wade, "Dirigisme Taiwan-Style," in Robert Wade and Gorden White, eds., *Development State in East Asia: Capitalist and Socialist, IDS Bulletin,* Vol. 5, No. 2 (Sussex, U.K.: Institute of Development Studies, 1984) and Chi Schive, *A Measure of Secondary Import Substitution in Taiwan* (Cambridge, MA: Harvard–Yenching Institute, 1985).

53. Chung M. Wong, "Trends and Patterns of Singapore's Trade in Manufacturers," in Bradford and Branson, *Trade and Structural Change.*

54. Ralph C. Bryant, "Financial Structure and International Banking in Singapore," *Brookings Discussion Papers in International Economics,* Washington, DC, May 1985.

CHAPTER EIGHT

EAST–WEST STRUCTURES AND STRATEGY

Today, the economic basis of American primacy is clearly much weaker and is likely to become weaker still in relation to the growth of other economic centers. At the same time, however, the Soviet Union has clearly failed as an economic rival. It has been revealed to be at best a one-dimensional power, a challenger in the military realm alone but not a serious rival socially, economically or ideologically.

Zbigniew Brzezinski, *Foreign Affairs* (1988)

There is no doubt that regarding the outer shell or container of civilization, which is the state, all our efforts tend against aggregation and toward disintegration. Yearning and action alike are moving us toward the small, self-contained unit that can be "free."

Jacques Barzun, *The Culture We Deserve* (1989)

Traditionally, to be an "intellectual" in the United States in the late twentieth century has come to be synonymous with having a clear-cut, grounded opinion of the Soviet Union and of the conflict between the ideologies of capitalism and socialism. The East–West struggle has been so predominant in the American mind that individual freedom was routinely defined in contrast with the "monolithic" state socialism of the USSR. And American governments have been adamant in attempting to persuade foreigners— particularly their European allies—that this vision of positive freedom contrasted with the Soviet threat should be the universal one of the West. But the "new thinking" of Mikhail Gorbachev (not to mention the rise of Asian economic power) has undermined this traditional perspective. By the end of the 1980s, the Soviet threat was perceived to be more latent than real by an increasing number of Americans; socialism was widely viewed as economically bankrupt; and Gorbachev's own policies were often interpreted as a desperate effort on the part of the Eastern bloc to get an infusion of capital and technology from the West just to keep it above water.[1]

Could it be that the West has won? (Which West?) Or that the East has lost? (Which East?) With the breakdown of superpower dominance at the end of the twentieth century, some have speculated that the East–West struggle has become as much of an anachronism as the possibility of a socialist or capitalist utopia. In 1989 the American intellectual debate was marked by the publication of two controversial articles—one in *The National Interest* (summer) by former U.S. State Department official Francis Fukuyama suggesting "the end of history" and victory by the West; the other, an argument in *Daedalus* (winter) by "Z" (a pseudonym) that Gorbachev's reform policies served only to speed up "Communism's terminal crisis" caused by the Soviet Communist Party, rather than to alleviate it. The economic evidence in the twentieth century suggests that free-market-oriented economic systems perform better than do socialist state-controlled economies. But the opportunity costs in terms of the spread of personal income (that is, the maldistribution of economic wealth) and social obstacles to equal economic opportunity given equal merit are usually high in these market-oriented systems. Nevertheless, the 1980s projected a spreading fashion of deregulation (or, at least reregulation) and privatization, away from state control (just consider developments in the USSR, Hungary and Poland).

To understand the meaning of this tendency, it is useful to look briefly at the structure and strategies of traditional "control economies" of the socialist bloc and the international economic organizations that affected their management. Typically, such states have been highly centralized; they have been hierarchically structured political economies with a lack of differentiation between state-governmental and economic-productive institutions; they have been one-party Marxist-Leninist systems with a power monopoly, and a sovereignty penetrated by party rather than economic interests that set economic and foreign policy—policy more determined by shortages than by principles of comparative advantage.[2] The desire for hard currency, the need for Western technology, the longing for ethnic autonomy and freedom of self-expression are prime reasons for the revolutionary shift away from an increasingly archaic Stalinesque economic model toward opening socialist economies to OECD economies, a prerequisite to membership in and help from the IMF and World Bank, not to mention Western commercial banks. East–West relations, in short, have become North–South relations with an ideological, geopolitical strategic twist: As détente set in between the superpowers on the military security "chessboard," state managers of the East bloc found the room for maneuver on the economic and industrial chessboard. And the peoples of Eastern Europe used Gorbachev's policy of not intervening with force to stage revolutionary, democratic mass movements.

ORIGINS

"Imperialism is capitalism at that stage of development in which the domination of monopoly and finance capital has taken shape, in which the export of capital has acquired pronounced importance, in which the division of the world by international trusts has begun, and in which the partition of all the territory of the earth by the greatest capitalist countries has been completed."[3] So wrote Lenin in 1916 in *Imperialism, the Highest Stage of Capitalism.* A year later he took over the Bolshevik Revolution, establishing the Soviet Union on the Marxist-Leninist principle of leadership by an elite, secretive vanguard— a party dictatorship of the proletariat and peasantry for the sake of a revolutionary society. The Communist Party assumed total political control, nationalizing industry, organizing the Soviet Youth Movement (Komsomol), proclaiming atheism, making marriage unnecessary, and totally redirecting education. According to Lenin, although the political process decides "what is to be done," state structure specifies "who can do what to whom" (*kto/kovo*) in the state and the economy. Convinced that England and Germany had reached the point of capitalist concentration when their disintegration would begin according to his theory of imperialism, Lenin instructed the Comintern—a network of Communist parties directed secretly by the Soviet Communist Party—to help speed up this process.

While a number of Western intellectuals were attracted by the Russian experiment, the overwhelming majority of Americans and Western Europeans feared the "Red Terror." Diplomatic relations were broken off with the Soviet Union, which was soon isolated in the world community. By 1920 neither the nationalization of factories nor Marxian economic principles helped salvage a Soviet economy that was in desperate shape. Lenin realized that his country could not afford to put through revolutionary principles at home and simultaneously expand the Communist movement into world revolution. Ever the pragmatist, Lenin announced the principle of taking one step backward in order to take two steps forward and postponed the global revolutionary effort. He announced the New Economic Policy, which denationalized industries, praised native millionaires, and invited foreign investment. The West was relieved, believing that the Soviet Union had matured into a normal player in the game of nations. A Soviet non-aggression and mutual trade pact was signed with Germany in 1922 at Rapallo.

But then Lenin died in 1924 and was replaced by Communist Party strongman Joseph Stalin, who advocated "socialism in one country," based upon a demanding Five-Year Plan. Industry was nationalized and agriculture was collectivized in the 1930s. Stalin believed that the Soviet Union had to build up its economic and political power in order to become a fortress for future world revolution, and he used whatever authoritarian means necessary to crush political opponents, such as Leon Trotsky, who advocated simultaneous world revolution.

The Stalinist Model: Collective Learning through Shortages

Stalin argued that in a period of rapid national modernization, the Soviet Union must exist in peaceful coexistence with the rest of the world, avoiding war and seeking trade until Russia became a great military-industrial power. Moreover, he stressed the total subordination of agriculture to the rapid development of heavy industry, using whatever authoritarian methods were required by the state. Although the Eastern bloc countries have not always subordinated agriculture to heavy industry (Bulgaria, for example, attempted to specialize in agricultural production as its competitive "niche"), the basic structures of the East European hegemony of the USSR have largely mimicked the Stalinist model (with the exception of Yugoslavia, which has a market-type of socialism and was only in the shadow of Soviet hegemony). Moreover, recent studies suggest that the domestic structure of East European states is so similar that it was not a determining variable in accounting for the different economic strategies these states adopted in the 1970s and 1980s.[4] What remains of the Stalinist model in Eastern Europe is thus the commonality that must be understood in order to assess the meaning of specific national economic reforms that depart from this model. The institutions of Soviet hegemony and similar status as small-resource or capital-poor economic systems in the world economy work to reinforce this commonality.

Apart from the state ownership of the means of production, the key difference between Communist and capitalist economic mechanisms is that Communist systems rely upon direct controls in the allocation of resources, whereas for most purposes capitalist systems depend upon markets.* Until the revolutionary reforms of the late 1980s, the central planning authority or board established output goals for major commodities of Eastern nations, including individual input targets for firms or groups of companies and supply plans specifying where the enterprises were to obtain their nonlabor, material inputs and to whom they were to ship their outputs. The coordination problems in such a regional, collective system of centralized planning

---

*Exceptions to this in the United States include government interventions of the Federal Reserve (Central) Bank in the money markets and of the Pentagon in the government procurement contract markets.

were staggering, not to mention the adjustments that eventually had to be made if errors or misjudgments emerged in the planning process (which was inevitable). Given the high priority allocated in socialist systems to full employment (or what some analysts term "overfull" employment), plans tend to be drawn too tightly (with few margins for error or lack of productivity) and projected output targets cannot be achieved with the proscribed inputs. Demand is thus chronically greater than supply, much as with the case of inflation in free-market economies.[5]

Because there is a lack of markets for land and capital in Stalinist political economies, rent, interest and profits are not accurately accounted for, and the pricing system for commodities is called "irrational" by Western economists.[6] This is partly due to the fact that direct controls rather than decentralized markets are used in resource allocation with all the errors and inertia that bureaucratic administration implies. Specifically, both ministries and enterprises are evaluated on the basis of output performance over time according to the central plan, thus motivating managers of ministries and enterprises to conceal from their superiors both capacity and overorder inputs and to avoid new technology. The Stalinist model is also characterized by *commodity incovertibility*, meaning that foreigners are not permitted to spend either their own currency or the native currency on commodities within the socialist state (that is, mass intermediate products like coal or machinery, not consumer products purchased by tourists and embassies). Such commodity inconvertibility has the effect of stimulating rigid bilateralism in foreign trade between countries within the socialist bloc. Each socialist country must keep a balance in trade with every other socialist nation, for to run a surplus would raise the problem of how to spend it given the restrictions of the Stalinist structure.

Thus the Stalinist model has a dampening effect on interbloc socialist trade, although it has no such effect necessarily on East–West trade where the socialist countries are in hot pursuit of "hard" (convertible) Western currencies.

Finally, the uncertainties involved in expanding the Stalinist nation's trade in terms of rendering it more vulnerable to shortages given unpredictable downturns lead socialist planners into a behavioral pattern of trade aversion, thus dampening growth.[7] *The Stalinist model overemphasizes maintenance strategy by rewarding risk-reduction rather than entrepreneurial growth. Resource shortages and bureaucratic bottlenecks determine economic policy, not prices. And the single-party elites, not producers and consumers, create and manage the shortages.*[8]

Stalinist economies result in chronic hard currency deficits. This occurs because the full employment policy drives managers to protect firms rather than letting weak enterprises go bankrupt, reducing their competitiveness through a permanent "greenhouse" treatment or "tenure." The full employment policy yields a seller's market, for there is always surplus demand given endemic shortages. Thus, goods are distributed according to a central plan rather than sold, and "salesmanship" is so unnecessary as to be irrelevant. Tariffs on international goods are redundant given centralized state control and planning, although they can work as implicit quotas discriminating against countries that do not have most-favored-nation status.[9] From a collective learning perspective, the lack of practice or irrelevance of "selling" leads to poor packaging, poor product quality, and a difficulty in adapting products to fit the consumers in specific foreign markets. With the exception of homogeneous raw materials (with which few Stalinist economies are well endowed), international competitiveness is hard to come by given such maladaptive learning patterns.

COMECON: Council for Mutual Economic Assistance (CMEA)

Comecon, or the Council for Mutual Economic Assistance (CMEA), is the international economic organization Soviet leaders use to manage the political economic coordination of East bloc economies based on the Stalinist model. It was formed in 1949 to assist in the economic development of member nations. However, it was more or less dormant until Stalin's death in 1953, meeting only three times in his lifetime. Stimulated by the Western success of the European Coal and Steel Committee (founded in 1952), which became the basis of the most successful regional economic organization in the world, namely the European Economic Community (EEC), an effort was made to strengthen CMEA in the late 1950s. The initial members were Bulgaria, Czechoslovakia, the German Democratic Republic, Hungary, Poland, Rumania, Albania, and the USSR. Albania dropped out in 1961 (seeking to isolate itself entirely from the world economy), and Mongolia, Cuba, and Vietnam later joined in 1962, 1972, and 1978, respectively. Yugoslavia became an "associate observer" participating in "affairs of mutual interest." North Korea also became an observer, while CMEA made cooperation agreements with Finland, Iraq, and Mexico.

In 1962 the CMEA Executive Committee was set up composed of deputy premiers from each Comecon nation and a charter, "Basic Principles of the International Socialist Division of Labor," was ratified. The following year The International Bank of Economic Cooperation for Comecon members was established.

Until 1968 the Comecon was largely a passive organization preoccupied with bookkeeping and the distribution of information. Inter-CMEA trade was declining and no consensus had been reached among the members on how to achieve the economic integration of Eastern Europe. By 1969, however, collective learning and rapprochement in the thinking of the members was manifested in a 15- to 20-year program made up of proposals for multilateral joint forecasting in technology, population, and other statistical areas, as well as in central planning. Each member country would specialize its production, concentrating upon their leading industrial sectors, in order to advance well-rounded community development. Joint multilateral investment plans were also made. The economic integration of Eastern Europe proceeded systematically, based upon central planning using a series of five-year plans. Since each member country specialized in particular products, intra-Comecon trade was induced by the structure. The impressive size of the CMEA regional grouping is somewhat deceptive, however, since the Soviet Union accounts for 60 percent of the population and for some 70 percent of the GNP of the group. In no other regional economic organization is one member so dominant. Concretely, this has translated into a rigid bilateral barter trading system in which the Russians sell (subsidized) raw materials in exchange for food and shoddy East European manufactures. Exchange transactions have been done in so-called "transferable" rubles which are not transferable.

At the Comecon meeting at Sofia, Bulgaria in January, 1990, the Czechs, Poles and Hungarians proposed radical change immediately to free trade in convertible currencies (stimulated by their own radical politico-economic reforms at home). This radical "collective learning bloc" was slowed down, however, by a cautionary, step-by-step reform group—the Soviet Union backed by Bulgaria, East Germany and Rumania. Silence was the response by Vietnam, Cuba and Mongolia. Russian policy was to continue trade in bilateral fashion, converting accounts into hard currency once annually. This will not satisfy the fast movers who will make their own arrangements.

Trade with the West is bilateral. There is no multilateral trade with Comecon members. And as a part of "the South," the Eastern bloc has significant debts owed to Western banks since World War II. Between 1983 and 1987 alone the net borrowing of Comecon countries increased by roughly half: some $35 billion (one-third accounted for the USSR, one-third by Poland, and almost one-quarter by Hungary). As Table 8–1 indicates, by 1988 the Polish debt was not only the highest in absolute terms ($37.5 billion out of the 1987 Comecon total of $102 billion), but had not improved the country's economic growth significantly as indicated by the amount of Polish debt the banks had written off.[10]

The Soviet debts are not regarded as alarming since no problems in debt funding are known to have arisen—in stark contrast with the Polish debts. But in this case, the integrity of cultural values represented by the resistance of the once banned Solidarity Union in Poland contributed to the sociopolitical disintegration that undermined the smooth functioning of the old Stalinist model until a revolutionary restructuring of the maintenance base of Poland's political economy occurred in 1989–1990. The integrity argument, of course, cuts several ways: While Poland's economy was disrupted by "anti-Stalinist" rebellion against centralized authority (at least until Solidarity was elected into the pathbreaking coalition government of

TABLE 8–1   The Pressure of Comecon Debt

	Net debt of Comecon countries in convertible currency (shown here in billions of dollars)		Net debt as a % of export earnings in convertible currency		Debt servicing (principal and interest as a % of export earnings in convertible currency)*	
	1983	1987	1983	1987	1983	1987
Bulgaria	1.3	5.1	46	149	24	30
GDR	9.1	10.4	103	115	36	33
Poland	25.4	37.5	427	465	138	71
Rumania	8.1	4.6	134	83	37	32
USSR	14.2	26.1	39	87	14	23
Czech	2.6	3.5	64	81	21	18
Hungary	6.7	14.9	139	297	36	47
Totals	67.4	102.1	96	143	34	33

*Figure would be a third higher if short-term repayment obligations were included.

Source: OECD as appeared in The German Tribune, No. 1353, (Hamburg) January 1, 1989.

1989), economic growth in Rumania had been undermined by a pro-Stalinist clinging to centralized, arbitrary power by a nepotistic family regime until a massacre of demonstrators late in 1989 sparked a revolutionary overthrow of the regime. Blind adherence to Stalinist ideology in times of economic flux represented integrity to some, while uncompromising rebellion against the Stalinist model for the sake of human rights and economic reform symbolized integrity to many others.

Post-Stalinist Economic Growth and Strategies

While Stalin was still alive, the Soviet Union used its centralized power to redirect East European trade from the West (where most of its trade had gone before the war) to the USSR (the Soviet share of East European trade rising from 25 percent in 1947 to 82 percent in 1954). This was a period of Soviet extractions from its East European "satellites": $1 billion each from Rumania and Hungary in goods, 6.5 million tons of coal from Poland, and so on. The value of this extraction by the Soviet Union has been estimated to equal the value of Marshall Plan aid given by the United States for West European reconstruction.[11]

After Stalin's death, Soviet leaders realized they had reached a point of diminishing returns in extractions from their CMEA allies and would have to invest in their growth or be obligated to subsidize them in the future. Some of this investment had already been made in the form of "mixed" companies founded in the East bloc with some of the extracted wealth. But these had caused great local resentment given Soviet control and the disproportionate share of the proceeds that seemed to flow back to the Soviet Union. Some scholars have referred to this pattern as the "ghettoization" of Eastern Europe.[12]

In reversing policy, the Soviet Union was motivated by the Eastern European riots of 1953 to cancel debts and extend credits—as long as the CMEA allies continued to buy Soviet goods. This shift in strategy resulted in economic growth in the Comecon countries that outstripped the national income growth in the European Common Market between 1950 and 1980 (7 percent for CMEA excluding the USSR versus 5 percent for the EEC).[13] Thus the Soviets managed to have their hegemonic ghettoization and a pattern of dependent economic development in the East bloc too.[14]

Within the CMEA countries, different foreign policy and economic strategies evolved despite the similarities in domestic structure stemming from the Stalinist model. For example, there was a sharp break even among the most Stalinist of East European states—Rumania and East Germany—in 1968 when Rumania established official diplomatic relations with West Germany without informing any of its East bloc allies. For a quarter of a century (before his violent overthrow in 1989) Nicolae Ceausescu, Secretary General of the Rumanian Communist Party, was able to use an extreme conservative version of the Stalinist model at home to give him the leeway to take independent foreign policy stands—as France did within the NATO alliance (without the Stalinist model at home of course). The East German government was extremely upset by the 1968 development and was disappointed to find the Soviet Union (which had had diplomatic ties with West Germany since 1955) so tolerant of the Rumanian–West German tie: It was the first step to the success of Chancellor Willy Brandt's *Ost-politik* of the 1970s in which West Germany tacitly recognized World War II boundaries in exchange for widespread political and economic cooperation with Comecon countries.[15] Given the desire of the West German people for integration or "unification" with East Germany, the state strategy of West Germany has always been different from that of any other NATO member country, tilting heavily toward détente and economic, if not political, integration with East European states. It is no accident, for example, that West German banks more than the banks of any other Western country are "held hostage" by Polish debt.

COCOM and Technology Transfer

West Germany's unique position geopolitically between East and West was underscored by the controversy in the early 1980s concerning a West German contract to build a West Europe–Soviet gas pipeline. Anticipated to fill one-third of West Germany's energy needs, the United States feared that the West Germans would become too energy dependent upon the Soviet Union and that the West European, Japanese, and U.S. firms subcontracted in the project would transfer technology with potential national-security implications in the process.

Thus, the Reagan administration prohibited American firms from participating in the project and appealed to the principles of the Coordinating Committee on Multilateral Export Controls (Cocom) as a basis for stopping Japan and European NATO allies from exporting to the USSR as well. In addition to the United States, Japan and all members of the NATO alliance except Iceland are members of Cocom, an organization set up in the cold war atmosphere of 1949 (operating out of a wing of the U.S. consulate in Paris) which coordinates a list of strategic technology prohibited for export to communist countries. However, led by West Germany, the Europeans and Japanese refused to prevent their companies from participating in the gas pipeline project, and the American government was forced to back down and let its firms participate or face the economic costs of losing business to international competitors.[16]

In 1984, the tables were turned when West Germany and France complained about American trade liberalization with the People's Republic of China.[17] Cocom members often circumvent the restrictions by exporting technological goods (such as digital computers) to countries were they are legal and then reexporting them to countries on "the blacklist." Such efforts cause great strains between governments and businesses *within* NATO countries, particularly the United States, as well as conflicts between Cocom member countries. Difficulties in coordination emerge because the export controls in the United States are more stringent than the Cocom list and stricter than the domestic controls of other NATO countries (particularly West Germany). These differences were made clear in the late 1980s when the U.S. government protested the sale of technologies and chemicals that enabled Libya to construct a chemical weapons plant: American export restrictions (coordinated by the State, Defense, Energy, and Commerce departments) kept American firms from being involved in such sales, while European countries had much looser restrictions letting such sales sift through. From a global standpoint of legitimacy, it is difficult to prohibit other countries from selling the elements of potential chemical weapons plants when the United States has stockpiled so many chemical weapons itself. By 1990 the Soviet-American detente, the transformation of Eastern Europe and pressures from the business community led the Bush administration to ease up on Cocom restrictions on high tech sales to the Eastern bloc.

Technology transfer refers to the movement of knowledge or techniques that contribute to the production process across national borders. In a high-tech/high-information, service-sector-dominated age Benjamin Franklin's principle of sharing all knowledge and techniques with all human beings for the benefit of mankind is a notion considered naive, if not archaic, by leaders of modern nation-states. So technology gaps grow between countries of the North and the South, increasing the gaps in economic production and growth.[18] And, in this sense, often the countries of the East bloc have been twice discriminated against: as economic members of the South and as strategic risks of the East.

INTERPRETATIONS

From the economic reforms in Hungary and multiparty systems toppling Communist Party monopolies throughout Eastern Europe to the market experiments of the People's Republic of China to the worldwide reverberations of *glasnost* (openness) and *perestroika* (restructuring) in the USSR, socialist movements are being radically transformed by new interpretations of what communism means in the socioeconomic circumstances of the late twentieth century. An underground joke in the Communist nations indicates how far these interpretations have gone in transforming how people of "the Second World" (the socialist bloc) see themselves. In responding to the question "What is communism?" comes the reply: "Communism is the longest and most painful route from capitalism to capitalism."[19] Communists are confused about the meaning of their ideology in a world economy in which capitalism has refused to be overturned by its own contradictions, as Marx anticipated it would be, and in which socialist leaders are turning heavily toward market incentives, capitalist techniques, and multiparty democracy in order to catch up with the quality of life of the industrialized West. The question that is inescapable: Is this just a tactical adaptation or phase of collective learning by socialist countries at this historical moment—"one step backward in order to take two forward"—or is it a permanent transformation of socialist states in the direction of the capitalist model? Perhaps a brief sketch of some of the reforms in Hungary, China, and the USSR will provide clues to this enigmatic question.

The Hungarian Reforms

Seen in global perspective, one could say on the one hand that the Soviet Union has intervened with force (or the threat of force) every decade to establish its authority over its empire, and to clarify the limits to political and economic reform in its client states: In 1956 the USSR put down the revolt in Hungary; in 1968 it crushed the reform movement in Czechoslovakia; in 1979 the Soviets invaded Afghanistan; and in 1990 Gorbachev ordered troops into Azerbaijan. Paradoxically, after these interventions by force, instead of a reversion to Stalinist models the consequence was a slow political economic sea-change toward more liberalization of economic, if not political, structures.

Hungary is the example *par excellence* of this CMEA collective learning pattern of one iron-and-steel step followed by a small tide of market-oriented economic reforms and a shift to a multiparty system. In the early 1950s, guided by the shortage-oriented strategy of the CMEA bureaucracy, Hungary modeled itself after the Stalinist model: a centrally planned, one-party state with brutal collectivization of agriculture (which ruined the well-endowed Hungarian agricultural system), investment at the expense of consumption, and a shift toward heavy industry and away from light industry at all costs. CMEA targeted Hungary to become "a nation of iron and steel" despite the fact that Hungary lacked the energy resources and raw materials for such industrial development (its strength being agriculture in the Danube Basin). So the oil, iron ore, and much of the materials Hungary needed had to be imported from the Soviet Union, making the Hungarian satellite ever more dependent.

After Stalin's death in 1953, the United States promoted a policy of liberating Eastern Europe, stirring discontent there. In February 1956 Soviet Premier Nikita Khrushchev publicly denounced Stalin, opening the way for reformist demands in Eastern Europe. Poland tried to mimic the Yugoslav movement toward independence, demanding removal of the Soviet secret police and military rule, acceptance of the Catholic Church, and the right to follow its own national route to socialism. Patterned after the Polish demands, the Hungarians revolted against the Soviets, seeking to reject communism totally. The Hungarians were crushed with Soviet tanks.[20]

The shock of the Hungarian revolt undermined the legitimacy of Soviet hegemony over Hungary's economy. The one-sided emphasis upon heavy industry was modified to adapt collective goals to the natural conditions of Hungary's resource base. The collectivized farm effort was loosened up with voluntary contracts replacing compulsory production. Agriculture was no longer neglected as a mainstay of the Hungarian economy. After several years of planning, in 1968 the Hungarian government launched a major set of economic reforms called the New Economic Mechanism. The program was designed to integrate the market mechanism into the centralized planning structure. Managers were no longer bound by compulsory production targets and product mixes; the materials allocation system by the government was abolished; and managers were almost totally free to decide what to invest in, what supplies to buy, and other questions regarding production and employment of labor. However, the foundation of centralized planning remained: government control over strategic industries such as banking, communications, public utilities, and transportation. However, prices were decontrolled for most producer's goods, an attempt was made to bring domestic prices more in line with world prices, and the bonuses of managers were based upon the profits earned by their enterprises.[21]

The initial improvements made possible by the Hungarian reforms were disrupted by the global economic dislocations of the 1970s. And, of course, the authoritarian management of firms by state-appointed managers had never changed. Nevertheless, the 1968 reform stimulated the creation of a new form of semiprivate enterprises in which private entrepreneurs would pay agricultural cooperatives 60 percent of the venture's income after taxes in return for running plants and shops autonomously involved in repairs, construction, and small-scale industry. The reforms also stimulated widespread growth in the second or moonlighting economy. Workers were permitted to take public factory tools home after hours. Soon the profit motive was in full swing as workers put more energy into their moonlighting efforts than they did at their official jobs (also cultivating their own private garden plots more productively than the collectively run farms—as happened also in the Soviet Union).[22]

The trial-and-error nature of the Hungarian reforms (so closely watched by other socialist states for their lessons) was triggered somewhat by Hungary's pre-Stalinist experience as a market-oriented economy on the one hand and frustrated by the Stalinist habits picked up more recently on the other. Hard-line party ideologues and well-placed bureaucrats had control and prestige to lose if reforms and decentralization went too far. And they saw to it that many controls remained after the 1968 reforms. Companies, for example, had to allocate profits to separate funds for wages, investments, and reserves—each of these taxed at different levels. Even major firms were not allowed to amass enough profits to make large investments, which might have created a "critical mass" in terms of competitiveness. And if the authorities deemed that products which had become unprofitable were still necessary in the society, enterprises were not permitted to stop producing them. Moreover, decades of administrative protectionism and restrictions on currency convertibility for the sake of the balance of payments stymied the liberalization of imports, making international competitiveness difficult to achieve for a small country like Hungary.[23]

Domestic economic reforms of the 1980s aimed to overcome the tradition of domestic and CMEA supply constraints, which blocked Hungary's attempts at adaptation to the turbulence of the global economy in the 1970s. And the Soviet policy of *glasnost* and *perestroika* served to strengthen the hand of the reformists in the government bureaucracies.

By the end of the 1980s, ten opposition groups to the governing Socialist Workers Party had emerged and the Hungarian Parliament passed legislation calling for a general multiparty election in 1990. This radical political change overwhelmed efforts of Hungarian hardliners who tried to make sure that Hungarian control was not lost to Soviet initiatives and that Gorbachev's stimulus did not push Hungary's significant reforms in the direction of a market economy too far. The Hungarian dilemma was how to graft effective market-oriented reforms onto a state-controlled Stalinist base. This problem was illustrated with the difficulties in founding the Hungarian stock market in 1989.

The reforms in the 1980s resulted in a small number of private businesses with somewhat competitive prices, the introduction of bankruptcy laws and the cultivation of the only bond market in Eastern Europe. Despite a high rate of inflation and a heavy per capita national debt, by the late 1980s Hungary was able to run a trade surplus of between $300 million and $500 million a year based largely upon selling electronics and industrial equipment to the Third World. Badly in need of investment capital, the Hungarians decided to try to go back to an old tradition of combining a nascent entrepreneurial culture with a stock market.

The Hungarians had a stock exchange from the 1860s until the Communist Party shut it down in 1948—an exchange which stimulated an economic boom until World War I. Moreover, the Hungarian reformists can cite Lenin's New Economic Policy of the 1920s as a precedent that permitted Soviet stocks to be traded in Latvia in order to help rebuild the economy. At the beginning of 1989, Hungary allowed foreigners to buy shares in Hungarian companies for the first time, even to the point of owning 100 percent of certain public and private businesses. While the stock exchange was small (initially listing only ten to twenty companies to choose from) and limited (starting out with weekly trading), it represented an important symbolic piece of a plan of Communist Party leader Karoly Grosz to privatize large sections of Hungarian industry, reduce bureaucracy, free-up entrepreneurs, and attract badly needed investments from abroad.

The Hungarian government worked out ambitious joint-venture agreements with major American firms to help fulfill these plans: Bear, Stearns and Company, the New York stock brokerage company, and Peat Marwick and Price Waterhouse—large U.S. accounting firms. However, the realization of such optimistic plans depends upon changing conditions that are not totally within Hungary's control: transforming the Hungarian forint into a fully convertible currency; overcoming the skepticism of Western investors who have a hard time knowing what profits mean in a partially irrational national price system and fear that it may be difficult to disinvest given limited Hungarian markets; and, the constant possibility of a fall in worldwide stock markets, which would make Hungarian investments seem to be even more precarious than those in more established markets.[24]

U.S. President George Bush's visit to Hungary in 1989 resulted in a promise of American financial support provided that Hungary permitted the Iron Curtain to lift a bit on its borders. That summer thousands of East German citizens used the atmosphere of détente to take extended summer vacations, many going first to Hungary, then over the Hungarian border to Austria and from there to West Germany for permanent asylum.[*] From 40,000 in 1986 and 200,000 in 1988, in 1989 well over 300,000 ethnic German immigrants from the Soviet Union, Poland, and Rumania flowed into West Germany in addition to tens of thousands from East Germany. By 1990 two

---

[*]To enable this to happen the Hungarian government chose to disregard a treaty between Hungary and East Germany, which prohibited either country from letting citizens of the other travel to a third country without the appropriate visa.

thousand East Germans per day flowed into West Germany. Internal reforms within East bloc national boundaries, which led to a loosening of those boundaries, inspired increasing numbers of people to vote with their feet. As if to hedge this kind of collective learning, Hungary's Polish neighbors managed to negotiate to become the first Communist country to get a government led by a non-Communist coalition in 1989 (although granting the Communists the head of the police and army, as well as other unusual privileges)—a culmination of the Solidarity union movement led by Lech Walesa, the Nobel Peace laureate. The Eastern bloc is undergoing an historical transformation, which is proving to diffuse status quo or maintenance power balances (dating back to the Hitler–Stalin Pact of 1939) and which will further undermine simplistic distinctions between socialist and capitalist systems in the global economy (perhaps making the very term "Eastern bloc" obsolete). Nor is socialist transformation limited to the East European bloc. The People's Republic of China is undergoing more change than either its managers or its people can easily digest.

Market-Oriented Reforms in China

Unlike the Hungarian case, the People's Republic of China was not constrained in its *economic* experiments with the possibility of hegemonic intervention by a superpower (although there were times in its *political* revolution when Chinese leaders no doubt were concerned with a Soviet invasion as the Chinese turned radically to their own route to socialism). After his victory in the civil war and his establishment of the People's Republic of China in 1949, Mao Tse-tung turned first to the Stalinist model as a basis for Chinese modernization: politicalization of the economy by the state and an emphasis upon heavy industry at all costs. However, by 1956 widespread famines in China had convinced Mao that the Stalinist model was not appropriate for the Chinese situation. In the Hundred Flowers Campaign Mao emphasized the importance of agriculture given China's large rural areas as well as light industry, thus taking the focus away from heavy industry as the core of China's modernization. After the Revolution, control was Mao's concern. Now it turned to feeding his people and creating a stable agricultural system. People, not machines, were his priority, he announced (he had more of them, after all) and the modernization of the rural areas became primary, not the Soviet stress on urban centers.[25] Mao initiated the Great Leap Forward, which in many ways established the triumph of the Maoist approach over Soviet modes.[26] The subtle pragmatism of Mao's strategy was not to break entirely with the Stalinist emphasis in the heavy industrial sector of the economy, but to concentrate on organizing human energy for the agricultural and light-industrial sectors without diverting material capital from heavy industry. Attention was paid to producing fertilizer, improving seeds, and developing irrigation and farm equipment.

But in opposition to some of the Chinese elite who argued for the necessity of material incentives, Mao denounced capitalist tendencies that developed among small producers as in agriculture. Ultimately, he sacrificed economic progress for the sake of his goal, which was the internationalization of Communist values through social education and he established the Cultural Revolution of 1966: He sent university students throughout China to spread his ideological doctrine, arresting capitalists and sending intellectuals out to work the fields. Pragmatist Deng Xiaoping, a former friend of Mao's in the leadership, was made a waiter.

Economic growth slowed in China and party unity was undermined as the political struggle between economic-growth-oriented technocrats and Maoist social revolutionaries polarized opinions in the society. Two years after Mao's death in 1976, following a period of understated "de-Maoification," Chinese leaders launched an ambitious investment program in industry and agriculture, depending upon imported technologies and loans from abroad. The self-sufficient maintenance base of agriculture established by Mao became the launching pad for a series of market-oriented political and economic reforms that shook the socialist camp and impressed the industrialized West. China's annual average GNP growth rate went from 5.5 percent in the 1971–1975 period to 6.1 percent between 1976 and 1980, to top 9 percent throughout the 1980s.[27]

In the late 1970s, however, problems arose due to some of the consequences of the reforms: imbalances in industrial supplies, deterioration of consumption, higher state deficits, and inflation. In 1979 the Chinese took a step backward—called the policy of readjustment—in order to go ahead later with their major economic reform plans. Incentives in the farming sector were improved, permitting part of the farmland collectively owned by a state production team to be assigned to specific individuals, families, or groups who could keep the proceeds from any surplus production in excess of the contracted quota that went to the production team.

Gradually the distinction between "readjustment" and "reform" faded as more innovations were carefully introduced. Industrial firms were given more freedom in their production and marketing decisions and their managers became responsible for profits and losses. Bonuses and fringe benefits (such as company housing) could be used as incentives. And managers of such state-owned companies could sell or barter surplus products (after meeting their production quotas) and borrow funds from banks.

Beginning in 1981 small businesses were permitted to be opened in urban areas (if approved by government authorities) in fields like repairs, restaurants, or retailing. These entrepreneurs could hire one or two workers, or up to five apprentices in the case of skilled craftsmen. In 1984 a large private company was allowed to operate outside the state-planning system for the first time as a pilot experiment—the Minsheng Shipping Company.[28] As the largest Chinese conglomerate before the Revolution one has a sense here of the "restoration of an old maintenance base" to give it a better chance to succeed in an extremely competitive world economy—much as large German firms re-emerged after a superficial effort at breaking them up after World War II or the Japanese *zaibatsu* were reborn in their postwar reincarnation as *sogoshosha* or trading companies. *Political economic managers in times of structural stalemate attempt to breathe new life into their national economies by taking calculated entrepreneurial risks in support of the maintenance of old industrial champions from the past. Such maintenance-entrepreneurial strategy mixes are used as pilot experiments loaded toward re-creating past success in new, competitive organizational forms.*

The collective learning strategy of the Chinese government before the 1989 rebellion was to call upon capitalists of former times to apply their skills to economic productivity. Thus the son of the founder of the Minsheng Shipping Company was put in charge. Stockholders shared in profits and losses and paid taxes to the government on the company's profits. And the manager was free to hire and fire workers at will and to set business targets without interference by centralized planning. Should the experiment prove successful it may be repeated in other regions and serve as a model.[29]

Similarly, in 1978 Zhao Ziyang, first secretary of the Communist Party in Sichuan Province, permitted six factories to keep a part of their profits for reinvestment in plant or distribution to the workers. Productive workers could be given bonuses and lazy ones punished. Within two years this pilot experiment spread to 6,600 enterprises, producing 45 percent of China's industrial output.[30] Such carefully planned and well-targeted pilot experiments in entrepreneurship could have helped to transform China into one of the world's great competitive nations in the twenty-first century.[31] Or, to paraphrase Mao, little sparks can set off forest fires. But fires have a way of suddenly springing out of control....

To superimpose entrepreneurial market mechanisms on top of a Stalinesque centralized and control economy inevitably results in contradictions, confusion, and corruption. As permission to fire workers in China spread, state budget deficits escalated since the commitment to full employment must remain the top priority in a socialist state. Some entrepreneurs were obnoxiously successful, raising questions about the state's ability to keep the range of competitive inequalities in check. Workers soon learned to go after larger bonuses as a value rather than to produce or meet production targets as a social obligation above all others. Managers of refrigerator plants were subsidized with bonuses for producing a surplus much beyond the existing demand on the market, while less expensive items not as favorably targeted were underproduced although they were badly needed.

Such economic distortions and widespread reports of corruption on the part of selfish individuals led Chinese leaders to retrench and restore centralized planning where it had lapsed in the late 1980s. This retrenchment delayed plans to free prices of most goods and services, reimposed price controls that had been lifted, and cancelled construction projects and brought Beijing more actively back into managing the economy. While some feared that the retrenchment would slow down the initiative of restructuring in the Chinese economy, others thought the double-digit inflation rate, panic buying in anticipation of shortages, and reckless capital spending called for a reining in of the forces released by the decentralizing reforms.[32]

But typical of China's multiphase (as opposed to the West's polarized modes of either/or) policies, while some reforms were being pragmatically cut back, other forms of restructuring were being introduced such as the transfer of ownership of homes from the state to private individuals. The pragmatism of China's reformist program is caught in the aphorism of the leader Deng Xiaoping: "It doesn't matter whether a cat is black or white; it matters only whether it can catch mice." And one new "mouse-trap" that China was experimenting with was the introduction of a more widespread stock market system. In 1988 the Communist Party adopted a plan to turn state-owned companies into stock-issuing enterprises. And stock markets were set up in Beijing, Shenyang, and Shanghai, which mostly operated as do the Western bond markets, paying a fixed interest rate and not bringing ownership rights to shareholders. Initially, the stock system spread quite rapidly with between 7,000 and 10,000 firms having issued shares by 1989, one company on Hong Kong's border even trading stock to foreigners.[33] But then came the great democratic revolt and repression of 1989.

Capitalist Reform Minus Democracy Equals Raised Expectations and Rebellion

In *The Old Regime and the French Revolution* (1856) Alexis de Tocqueville wrote that it is not always when things are going from bad to worse that revolutions break out, but rather when an oppressive rule over a long period without protest suddenly finds the government relaxing its pressure. So it was in the People's Republic of China where Deng thought capitalist reforms without political liberalization would modernize the Chinese state without difficulty. Even with economic growth and personal incomes expanding, the people found their raised expectations frustrated by inflation, political corruption, and the lack of freedom of speech. Resentment had also built up over market-oriented reforms near the coast by those in state-run firms inland.

In April of 1989, thousands of students, later joined by workers, marched through the capital of Beijing demanding more democracy and an end to government corruption. Defying a ban on public protests, they camped in Tiananmen Square, set up tents, and began a hunger strike. In the middle of this, Mikhail Gorbachev, on a state visit to China, arrived to formally reconcile the antagonism between the two Communist countries. Both the demonstrators and the government initially showed great restraint toward each other until a government split between hard-liners and those sympathetic with the students was resolved by the victory of the hard-liners. In early June, they ordered troops from outlying parts of China unfamiliar with the meaning of the protests to come in and take over the center of Beijing with force. Hundreds of people were killed or wounded by the soldiers and tanks as Deng (who feared another student cultural revolution would do him in again) and hard-liner Prime Minister Li Peng consolidated their power. General Party Secretary Zhao Ziyang, who was sympathetic to the students, was stripped of power. Intellectuals and leaders of the democratic rebellion were imprisoned in a flashback to the repressions under the Cultural Revolution of the 1960s.

Until the 1989 rebellion, the Chinese economy ranked approximately seventh in the world in terms of economic growth rate potential, awakening visions of the economic progress of Japan, South Korea, and Hong Kong.[34] Since both the hard-liners and the democrats support the economic reforms, they are apt to be continued. But the government crackdown badly damaged the infrastructure in Chinese cities, affected the psychology of the Chinese people with uncertainty, and caused a mass exodus of foreigners. The $3.5 billion in U.S. direct investment in China, $9.3 billion in imports to the United States from China, and $5.3 billion in U.S. exports to China in 1988 are figures not easily apt to be surpassed given the criticism of Chinese repression by the American government, the halt of weapons and technology transfers from the United States to China, and the political and economic uncertainty in a polarized Chinese society. The recentralization of the Chinese economy and tough anti-inflation austerity measures will take their toll in economic growth.

Mikhail S. Gorbachev was careful not to criticize what was going on within China, as the American government was doing, in order to consolidate later ties with the Chinese government, hoping to woo the Chinese away from the United States back into the Soviet camp. Previously, Gorbachev had noted that the wrong countries from his perspective were running off with the initiative, claiming to be "model" political economies for others. And whether out of a desire to counter these ideological threats or out of a profound recognition of the dire straits of his own economy (or both), he decided to do something about the situation. Working in the brain trust of former Party Secretary Andropov, Gorbachev and his followers had prepared the way intellectually for a major political economy shift.

Perestroika and the Democratization of Russia

Perestroika (restructuring) and related political and economic reforms announced by Mikhail Gorbachev in the late 1980s represent the most innovative domestic and foreign policy changes in the Soviet Union since the death of Lenin. Soviet experts agree that these ideas did not spring spontaneously from the head of one man, but that they were carefully developed by a reformist team who patiently kept their blueprints in the drawer until the timing was ripe. Such planning evolved in recognition of the failure of a stalemated socialist economy heavily rooted in the Stalinist model. The 5 percent annual average growth rate in the GNP in the late 1960s fell to 2 percent by the late 1970s and approached zero growth in the late 1980s.[35]

While the USSR's structural economic problems were obvious by the late 1970s, many Western observers did not clearly take their consequences into account until the turnover of a series of aging Soviet leaders in the 1980s. Again, a dark joke circulating in the USSR symbolized the ossification which the Soviet political economy had come to represent: In answer to the question—What is the difference between a crocodile and the Politburo?—comes the reply: The former has forty teeth and four legs, while in the latter the numbers are reversed.

Failures were not only rampant in the economic system but also in the political system. Although the share of the GNP claimed by defense spending had reached 15 to 25 percent (compared to 1 percent in Japan, 3 percent in West Germany and 6 to 7 percent in the United States), Soviet security policy could not prevent a Cessna 172 (piloted by a young West German) from landing in Red Square or the Afghan rebels from defeating the Soviet army. Moreover, flaws in the Soviet health care system had actually led to *reductions* in average life expectancy, unlike any other industrial nation.[36] A series of poor harvests entailed billions of dollars of purchases of grain and food from the West. And since some 80 percent of Soviet export earnings came from the sale of primary energy, when the price of oil unexpectedly dropped and the dollar exchange rate (in which most energy is priced) plummeted, the USSR was suddenly faced with shortfall in annual earnings of hard currency exports of between $8 billion and $10 billion.[37] Since Soviet policy was not to import more than it exports to avoid difficulties with obtaining hard currency for exchange, Soviet trade volume with the West sank about 40 percent. The technological gap between the Soviet Union and leading Western European countries was great, not to mention the gap with Japan and the United States, whose technology in a number of sectors was significantly ahead of that of the Europeans.

Gorbachev was elected Secretary General of the Communist Party of the Soviet Union at the beginning of 1985. There are three key concepts that make up the core of the reforms Gorbachev has since advocated: *glasnost* (openness), *perestroika* (restructuring), and *uskorenie* (acceleration). Statistics indicate that the first two of these are now among the best-known foreign-language terms in the world.[38] Gorbachev uses these notions as the basis of what he calls "the new thinking."[39]

The debate as to whether these key terms are conceptual breakthroughs for a radical transformation of the Soviet system or are merely new, sophisticated permutations of Soviet propaganda will not be resolved for some time (and will depend on to what extent the USSR truly becomes a multiparty system). In all likelihood, the terms are both: instruments of an effort at radical adaptation of the Soviet political economy to international competitiveness and marketing symbols capable of making the new thinking in the USSR easy to pick up as a model for influencing other states in the socialist camp. *Glasnost*, for example, advocates open admission of the faults of the Soviet system at the local and regional level, a philosophy of "transparency" and seeing things objectively for what they really are in order to improve them.

But seeing things for what they really are can also be a way of lowering popular expectations and of becoming more comfortable with a status quo that is open for discussion: a progressive and popular terminology that may lead to a realistic acceptance of social facts that would be unacceptable in Western industrialized democracies. This latter interpretation is perhaps more typical of those inside the Soviet Union (who have seen lots of slogans and leaders come and go but little improvement in the waiting lines to buy simple goods) than those on the outside—Soviet citizens who have adopted a wait-and-see attitude in regard to the Gorbachev rhetoric. Another dark joke summed this up: What has Gorbachev moved in his first year in power?—His lips.*

Perestroika is a strategy of decentralization that aims to increase the personal responsibility of key managers in Soviet economic organizations and to make them more easily accessible to those in the region which they service. A significant portion of the top economic administrators were dismissed when Gorbachev came to power—particularly hard-liners whom he wanted to replace with people who understood his new thinking. But given this philosophy of increased personal responsibility for what goes wrong in the system, there is apt to be more turnover of personnel in economic organizations than in the past, when party loyalty and seniority often led to what amounted to lifetime tenure. Moreover, these shifts are apt to shake up the complacency of managers of large corporations from abroad who have quietly counted upon their "old buddy" ties with comrades in the national bureaucracy, who have now been replaced or who often have to share authority with newly created regional economic institutions. These economic institutions, in turn, are expected to become "independently

---

*An example of the rhetoric that evokes such skepticism (from Gorbachev's "revolutionary" speech of February 5, 1990 to the Central Committee of the Communist Party calling for the Party to eliminate its monopoly on power): "Yes, there are shortages of resources and technology. Yes, social transformations must be conducted on a different scale at different rates. All this is true. But primary importance should be assigned to restructuring relations of production in the village. And the crux of the matter now is the position of our cadre at the center and localities. This is a political rather than an economic question. All obstacles should be removed in the way of the farmer, he should be given a free hand." (Cf. "Excerpts from Remarks by Gorbachev Before Central Committee of Party," *The New York Times*, February 6, 1990, p. A16.)

operating economic entities" with flexibility and the power to make entrepreneurial decisions. Business firms that operate successfully are no longer
to be penalized by having profits skimmed off or by having their production
quotas increased (typically in Stalinesque economies managers with political clout measure success by their ability to reduce their production quotas,
giving their workers a better working life).

However, according to the same logic, subsidies will not necessarily
be forthcoming for firms that fail: Bankruptcy has become a threat that
leads to efficiency. Whether Soviet citizens can get used to the possibility
of losing a job in a state that has guaranteed them employment (up to this
point) is another question. Functional and regional decentralization
moved so quickly in some sectors that by 1988, 170 Soviet firms were
authorized to make business deals directly with foreign partners in contrast to the old "foreign trade monopoly" system of having all deals go
through the Foreign Trade Ministry.

From the viewpoint of collective learning, the acid tests or ultimate
models of *perestroika* are supposed to be joint ventures with foreigners which
attract capital, transfer technological and organizational know-how, teach
Soviet managers sales marketing skills, and illustrate day-to-day operations
(*glasnost*) as well as the more rapid pace of Western business (*uskorenie*). From
the time the Joint Venture Act came into force in January 1987 to March 1988,
thirty joint venture deals were approved with Western partners. These joint
ventures are supposed to serve as models of international cooperation for the
1990s, having a signal effect for the rest of the Soviet economy and the world.
In this sense, they appear to be similar in some ways to the "pilot-business
experiments" in the People's Republic of China.

Another form of cooperation under the *perestroika* program initiated in
the late 1980s is the "consortium"—groups of sometimes heterogeneous
Western companies coordinated by one general enterprise that work on large
industrial projects or develop specific regions in the USSR. This is somewhat
like the extension of the Western "turnkey project"* or of the Turkish Build-
Operate-Transfer (BOT) model.

The final, least-known, and in some respects perhaps most critical of
Gorbachev's three key concepts of reform is *uskorenie* (acceleration). Given
the slow temperament that often has characterized the Russian people since
the czars and the cultural pride the Russians take in their extensive view of
time (which permits the depth of cultivation of the Russian spirit and that
matches the vast expanses of Russian territory), widespread resistance to the
concept of *uskorenie* surfaced as expected, slowing the *perestroika* process
down immensely. *The increasing tempo of international competitiveness in the
global economy demands that traditional cultures radically transform their notions*

---

*Turnkey projects involve constructing operating facilities that are then trans-
ferred to the national owner when operable.

*of time if they are to adapt effectively as collective units; but the cultural and spiritual
integrity of the people calls for strong resistance to such changes in their way of life
out of a legitimate concern that the cultural distinctiveness of their community may
be lost for the sake of dubious secular gains.*

Gorbachev's desire to speed his people up to the competitive tempo of
the Japanese or Americans runs up against deeply ingrained Russian adages
such as "The slower you travel, the further you'll get" and "Measure seven
times before cutting the cloth."[40] No wonder that Gorbachev's reforms often
appear more popular abroad than they do at home. Whether he will be able
to reeducate his people to adopt *uskorenie* in time to bring them enough
consumer goods to keep them from rising up is the ultimate Russian question. The Russian people have good historical reasons to be skeptical of the
efforts of non-elected Soviet leaders who try to force modernization plans
down their throats from above.

By the 1990s it became clear that while Gorbachev had largely succeeded with his political and ideological reforms, his economic reforms had
yet to begin to take effect. The concept of *uskorenie* had faded from discourse
since 1987, although its spirit drove Gorbachev's rhetorical requests for
change. The mistakes of seventy years of a mechanical, centrally planned
economy had been openly admitted and Stalin's crimes condemned. March
1989 introduced the first competitive Russian elections for the national
parliament (albeit among different members of the Communist Party). A
year later at Gorbachev's controversial request, the Communist Party voted
to support a platform denouncing its monopoly role on power, agreeing to
seek influence by democratic political means. As Soviet Economist Elena
Ivanova of Moscow's Institute of USA and Canada Studies noted, the top of
the pyramid of the Soviet power structure was shaking and the base, which
had been preserved, was finally shaken by the spring regional elections of
1990, putting human values ahead of class interests.[41] For Gorbachev's had
been a revolution from above, stimulated by foreign policy shifts to the
principle of non-intervention in Eastern Europe and Soviet respect for the
sovereignty of other nations.

But while the people had been excited by the successes in freedom of
expression and democratization of *glasnost*, after five years they were frustrated that the promises of *perestroika* had not been met. The peasants had
no land of their own. The workers owned no factories. And the Soviet policy
of 1989 aiming to reduce the number of centrally planned enterprises from
100 percent to 80 percent was dropped. The new five-year plan did not
introduce a wholesale market until 1993; no market reforms were to be
introduced for two years.

Meanwhile, there was a great surplus of savings and nothing to buy
with it. Before, although commodities were scarce in the periphery of the
country, Moscow always was well provided for. But now, even in Moscow
there was nothing to buy. And in the periphery there were open revolts. In

the industrial center of Volgograd there were no vegetables to buy; meat, butter, sugar and sausage were carefully rationed; and one had to wait ten years for housing. When the local Communist chief gave a choice apartment to his daughter, the people revolted and threw him out. Other party leaders were thrown out in the Syberian city of Tyumen, in the Soviet Far East and in the western Ukranian territory of Chernovtsy.[42] Anarchy in the countryside caused some to demand strong leadership, even dictatorship. The Soviet republics began to demand secession from the USSR, for which there was no legal mechanism. Gorbachev accelerated political reforms to cope with the growing crisis and moved up the meeting of the expanded Parliament of People's Deputies to strengthen the powers of the president (himself). As ethnic violence spread throughout the country, Gorbachev knew it was vital to replace the declining power of the Communist Party with an increase of power in the executive branch of the democratically elected Supreme Soviet.

Although political reforms look positive, the outlook for Soviet economic recovery in the 1990s appears to be dim. While the Chinese were able to fulfill their promise of returning land to the peasants (through a leasing scheme) given the undermining of the Chinese Communist Party and government bureaucracy in the villages since the time of the Cultural Revolution, the opposition to reform is much stronger in local and regional centers in the Soviet Union where the party bureaucracy is entrenched.[43] Hardliners against the concept of private property, such as Yegor Ligachev who headed the Ministry of Agriculture, slowed down Gorbachev's restructuring efforts. And the Soviet compromise of accepting the concept of *individual property* as long as it covers small things like cars, summer houses and bank accounts, but not *private property*, which implies larger systems of exploitation in the Marxist mind, seems unlikely to provide sufficient individual motivation to allow *perestroika* reforms to take off as planned.

East Bloc Revolution

Philosopher Sören Kierkegaard told the story of a flock of geese kept in a wire cage by a farmer. One day one of the geese looked up and saw there was no top, telling the others excitedly: "Look, there is no top, we may leave and become free!" Few listened or turned their heads to the sky. So he flew away alone. When it became clear that Gorbachev would not use force to put down revolutionary change in his Eastern European satellites in 1989, one Eastern European people after another looked up and saw they were free to express themselves and to throw over their keepers. The top was off the cage and the birds just started to fly.[44]

The politico-economic revolutions in the Eastern bloc are examples *par excellence* of collective learning: one group mimicked another, revolting in domino series until not a single Communist Party monopoly was left standing intact. Within the first six months of 1990 all the nations of Eastern Europe held free elections in one form or another. Actually, the 1989–1990 transformation was just the beginning of a collective learning process in which Eastern Europeans started to unlearn forty years of obedience to Communist one-party rule, of job security in state-run enterprises, and of working along as opposed to working hard given the absence of meaningful individual economic incentives. The revolutions brought widespread social uncertainty, skyrocketing inflation, devalued currencies, rising unemployment and lack of confidence that newly elected leaders, who often had little experience, could manage the politico-economic crises.

Just consider the quantity and intensity of change the Eastern Europeans had to digest in 1989 alone:

In Poland, the Communist Party agreed to talk with the formerly outlawed Solidarity union movement in January, agreed to legalize Solidarity and schedule elections for a partly representative parliament in April; and, while keeping control of the military and internal security, permitted Solidarity's Tadeusz Mazowiecki to become Prime Minister and to form a coalition Cabinet with non-Communists directing social and economic policy in August.

In Hungary, Communist Party leaders made assurances that a multi-party system would be allowed in January and February; in May the barbed-wire barrier on the border with Austria was partly torn down; Imre Nagy of the uprising of 1956 was given a hero's burial in June; in September, the Hungarians opened the Hungarian border with Austria and permitted thousands of East Germans to escape to the West; by October the Communist Party changed its name to the Socialist Party and the parliament revised the Constitution to permit a multiparty system and free elections; and in November, a free referendum blocked the dominant party from holding a presidential election before the parliamentary election (which would have given them an advantage against the barely organized opposition).

In East Germany Communist Party leader Erich Honecker permitted East German refugees from Czechoslovakia and Poland to go by train to the West through his state in October and then unsuccessfully attempted to slow down those leaving by requiring visas for travel to Czechoslovakia; by month's end thousands were demonstrating on the streets of major cities and Honecker was replaced by Egon Krenz, who eased travel restrictions. In November hard-liners were removed from the Politburo, the government pleaded with East Germans to stay, protests grew, the politburo resigned, free travel was permitted and the Berlin Wall was opened (on November 9). Krenz promised free elections only to be replaced by Communist reformist Hans Modrow, who became Prime Minister, and, by Gregor Gysi as head of the Communist Party (in December). Since the monthly rent for a two-bedroom apartment in East Berlin was equivalent to the cost of a middle-class meal at a West Berlin restaurant and the East German currency nosedived compared to the West German market, East Germany began to disintegrate economically. By year's end an average of two thousand East Germans were leaving for West Germany daily (particularly young skilled workers, doctors and nurses). Free elections were scheduled for the spring and the stage was set for East Germany's economic integration with West Germany to be followed eventually by political unification.

In Czechoslovakia, playwright Vaclav Havel's arrest (among others) in October led to a protest by 10,000 people, broken up by police. Communist Party leader Milos Jakes unsuccessfully tried to prohibit protests and keep party control in November. Travel restrictions were lifted; thousands of people demonstrated on the streets of Prague; Jakes was replaced by Karel Urbanek; Havel emerged as chief opposition leader (head of Civic Forum) destined to become President and to govern with Prime Minister Marian Calfa, a Communist reformer overseeing a Cabinet with only ten of twenty-one members from the Communist Party; free parliamentary elections were set for June 1990. Mimicking Poland's example, the Czech currency was sharply devalued against the dollar and the new government made plans to follow Poland's lead in permitting the private ownership of businesses (collective learning at work). President Havel declared a New Year's amnesty for prisoners, bringing the Skoda automobile works to a stop since it lost more than 1,500 of its involuntary labor force. Havel later called the Czechoslav transformation "the velvet revolution," which sought to position the country as a modern bridge between East and West.

In Bulgaria, an October protest rally led orthodox Communist leader Todor Zhivkov to promise reform. By November, Zhivkov was replaced by Foreign Minister Petar Mladenov, who promised free elections by May 1990 and started talks with opposition groups, which would lead the parliament to drop the party's guarantee of a leading role in society. But Mladenov's reform plans were threatened when he decided to end the forced assimilation of Bulgaria's ethnic Turks, allowing them to use their own names and language. This decision would provoke a virulent backlash among Bulgarians who remembered the 500 years of Turkish occupation, and, more concretely, who feared they might have to give back apartments and cars they bought for bargain prices from Turks expelled or encouraged to leave under the Zhivkov regime.

In Rumania a crackdown against protests in December by hard-line dictator President Nicolae Ceausescu left 4,500 bodies in open graves (including many women and children) and led to a violent overthrow of his regime by a combination of army generals, veteran Communist politicians who had been placed under detention and student leaders. The result was a quick trial and execution of Ceausescu and his wife for genocide and the formation of a Council of National Salvation, made up of Communists and non-Communists, that formed an interim government headed by Ion Iliescu (a Ceausescu official who had fallen out of favor) until elections in April 1990. While Rumania had no foreign debt given Ceausescu's decision to deprive his people of decent food, heat and electric lighting in order to export enough to pay loans off, the industrial infrastructure was outdated and chaos prevailed. The provisional government abolished the secret police, legalized abortion (prohibited by Ceausescu to increase the labor force) and canceled "system-ization" in the countryside, which dictated that thousands of villages be destroyed for the sake of modernization and peasants be forced to move into high-rise apartment complexes. It also made it illegal to refuse medical treatment for the elderly (reversing Ceausescu's policy designed to keep the population young) and canceled food exports and tried to improve distribu-tion to feed the hungry. The perversion of Rumania's maintenance base (a potentially prosperous agricultural economy) since World War II was stag-gering, but the people struggled to recover their cultural integrity and human dignity in the chaos.

In the Baltic states of the U.S.S.R., Lithuania, Latvia and Estonia, as well as in the republics of Moldavia, Georgia and Azerbaijan to the south, independence movements blossomed, stimulated by Eastern Europe's generally peaceful revolutions. Armenians amended their republic's constitution to give them-selves a veto over national laws that went against Armenian interests and defied Moscow by voting to include the disputed Nagorno-Karabakh region in Azerbaijan in their budget. Azerbaijanis reacted with weapons, attacking Manashid, a village in the disputed area and a shift in political economy became the grounds for civil war, which Gorbachev felt obliged to put down with Soviet tanks (particularly given the militant nationalist demands of Azerbaijani Shi'ite Muslims for freedom to mix with the Shi'ite Iranians across the border). The Lithuanian Communist Party broke with Moscow, demanding independence, and in early 1990, Gorbachev acknowledged the possibility of secession if sufficiently supported by a Lithuanian referen-dum. Gorbachev's reforms had come home to roost. On February 7, 1990 the Soviet Central Committee of the Communist Party voted to suggest an amendment to Article 6 of the Soviet Constitution, which grants the party a monopoly on rule. The way was prepared for the evolution of a multiparty system in the Soviet Union.

The Political Economy of German Reunification

While political and economic reform may have been orchestrated to some degree by Gorbachev when he visited orthodox Communist leader Erich Honecker (just as the other East bloc revolutions may have been orchestrated as well as inspired by the Soviet leader) for the 40th anniversary celebration of the East German state in October 1989, Gorbachev had no idea that just four months later he would be asked for approval for the reunifica-tion of Germany and watching the West Germans initiate a common German currency. Even for a leader identified with the concept of *uskorenie*, accelera-tion, the pace of change seemed too fast.

Specifically, Honecker fell soon after Gorbachev's visit given widespread protests the police were unable to contain. By November 1989, free travel was permitted for East German citizens and the Berlin Wall was opened. The Politburo had resigned and Communist reformist Hans Modrow headed a transitional government until free elections could be held in the spring of 1990. Chancellor Helmut Kohl of West Germany proposed a ten-point German federation plan for integrating the two Germanies. This political initiative mobilized all other political factions in West Germany to offer their own reunification ideas so as not to be outmaneuvered before the December 1990 West German election. Kohl's plan was soon countered with a proposal by Modrow (with Gorbachev's approval) for a neutral, demilitarized united Germany without ties to either the NATO or Warsaw Pact alliances (consistent with Soviet policy on the issue since Stalin ruled). Kohl and his Western allies turned down this proposal.

Meanwhile, over 2,000 East Germans per day were permanently migrating over the border to West Germany, leaving the East German economy (which already had a labor shortage before the exodus) in shambles. The East German currency fell like a rock. East German-made portable stereos in East Berlin, selling for twenty times the price of their better-made West German counterparts just a subway stop away, piled up on the shelves unsold. Color T.V. sets in spacious East German apartments cost a hundred times as much as the monthly (subsidized) rent. By February, warnings seeped out of the West German capital of the imminent financial collapse of East Germany. Elections had been moved up from May to March 18, 1990. And in a political move without the Bundesbank's approval, Chancellor Kohl proposed to substitute the West German mark for the East German currency, hoping this symbolic gesture would give East Germans confidence and would stem the tide of people coming into his country and putting severe strains on a social system already suffering from unemployment and a housing shortage. Despite the warnings of Karl Otto Pöhl, president of the West German Bundesbank, that a rapid currency union would involve serious risks of rising inflation, higher interest rates and deepening budget deficits, Chancellor Kohl's government went ahead with plans for monetary unification. The political component thus preceded the economic one in the decision-making process. One of the key factors was the exchange rate to be used in the reform: While the 1-to-1 rate chosen did not reflect the disastrous state of the East German economy, a 1-to-3 rate would have cut the already low income of East German pensioners by a third. And had one West German mark been exchanged for five East German marks, economists estimated there would have been a three percent increase in the West German economy's money supply, confirming the inflationary fears of the head of the Bundesbank.[45]

While relatively independent (and with an inflation-fighting priority, like the U.S. Federal Reserve Bank), the Bundesbank is forced by law to carry out West German government policy. Pöhl quickly adapted and became a leader in the monetary reform given certain prerequisites the West German government demanded: complete freedom of commercial activities, the recognition of private property, unlimited rights of investment and tax and price reforms, and last, but not least, East Germany's acceptance of the Federal Republic's Bundesbank as an autonomous institution for the securing of monetary stability.[46]

In the shortterm, higher inflation, higher interest rates, greater unemployment, larger public deficits and higher taxes appeared to be inevitable in West Germany as East and West German monetary and economic integration proceeded. However, as the world's largest exporter, with a record trade surplus of $81 billion in 1989 (exceeding Japan's for the first time since the 1970s), the booming West German economy was well-positioned to take on the responsibilities of subsidizing the East German economy and integration process. Many West German banks and industries, such as Siemens (electronics), Zeiss (optical equipment), Dresdner Bank, and Volkswagen had already revived ties with East German firms with the market openings made possible under *perestroika* and were ready to expand East German operations. And East Germany, after all, ranked second only to the Soviet Union among the East bloc's industrial powers. Given the common language, culture, and even educational structures—such as the apprenticeship system—the longterm prospects of a reunified Germany becoming an economic powerhouse (with a population of some 78 million) rivaling the United States and Japan appeared to become a self-fulfilling prophecy.

However, for some East Germans, such as novelist Christa Wolf, who were proud of the socialist cultural integrity of their own forty-year old society and who believed that the creative destruction of capitalism would destroy this cultural integrity through the over-bearing hegemony of West German business and government, these prospects were dark rather than bright. Social jealousy became pronounced as "the poor cousins" from the East experienced how far behind they were and as some of the established West Germans had second thoughts about overloaded social services, higher taxes and increased competition for jobs and housing. The East Germans found it difficult to adjust to a social situation in which their apartments were not subsidized and in which work was not guaranteed as they had been used to under socialism.

Both superpowers accepted the inevitability of German reunification. By February 1990, 75 percent of the East Germans supported reunification according to a Leipzig polling organization; since both the Soviet Union and the United States had committed themselves to the "self-determination" of the East German people they could do little but go along with the historical momentum. This momentum appeared to be speeded up deliberately by Chancellor Helmut Kohl's foreign policy advisor, Horst Teltschik, who spoke of East Germany's imminent economic collapse in a press briefing before Kohl went to Moscow for talks, stoking alarmist fears that could only accelerate the pace of union. In his February 1990 visit to Moscow, U.S. Secretary of State James Baker suggested that a reunified Germany might have some sort of loose association with NATO (perhaps on the French model, since the French are not involved in the military arm of NATO), a shift in American policy that had previously required a Germany firmly anchored in NATO. In Ottawa, Canada on February 13, 1990, the foreign ministers of the four major Allies—the United States, Britain, France and the Soviet Union—agreed with the foreign ministers of the two Germanies to a two-phase process of negotiating German unification: First, internal unification measures worked out by the two Germanies after the March 18 East German elections; and, second, external security measures negotiated with the four Allies. The fall, 1990 meeting of the 35-nation Conference on Security and Cooperation in Europe would confirm the conditions of the unification of the German state. The next step on the agenda was the negotiation of a peace treaty by Germany with the eighty countries that had declared hostilities by the end of World War II.

German reunification can be viewed as an example of "quick study" collective learning—a restructuring of an expanded maintenance base, speeded up immensely by Gorbachev's *perestroika* policy. The Soviet Union will gain in being able to import higher quality industrial and technological goods from a united Germany than would have been received from the East German economy and in partially neutralizing West Germany, but ultimately will lose influence over Germany and Central Europe as Soviet troops are withdrawn. The process of European Common Market integration and monetary union will accelerate given the stimulus of German unification and the fears of the French of being declassed and pushed to the periphery as Germany again becomes the major Central European power. And the influence of the United States is apt to decline in Europe as American troops are withdrawn and the cultural commonality of "Europe's Common House" finds its own new integrity in differentiation from the American (and, to some extent, Anglo-Saxon) culture.* From a global perspective, one could say that Anglo-Saxon hegemony has succeeded so well in creating prosperity that it has subsidized European and Pacific Rim counter-cultures destined to undermine some of its basic assumptions while pragmatically adopting others. Multipolarity in power breeds multicultural renaissance and the protectionism this implies in terms of preserving cultural identities from the creative, destructive dynamic of world capitalism.

------

*In his book, *Perestroika* (N.Y.: Harper & Row, 1987, p. 208), Gorbachev, for example, is explicit about the anti-American ingredient in the noble phrase "the Common House of Europe": "A serious threat is hovering over European culture too. The threat emanates from an onslaught of "mass culture" from across the Atlantic. We understand pretty well the concern of West European intellectuals. Indeed one can only wonder that a deep, profoundly intelligent and inherently humane European culture is retreating to the background before the primitive revelry of violence and ᐁornography and the flood of cheap feelings and low thoughts." (See Fritz Stern, "The ᐁmon House of Europe," *The New York Review of Books*, Dec. 7, 1989, pp. 9–10).

IMPLICATIONS

Some observers, such as Sovietologist Jerry Hough at Duke University, believe that the coming of Gorbachev and his policy announcements signify the end of the post-World War II world. The USSR, in this view, is never going to invade the United States, nor the United States the USSR. This implication was reached after Gorbachev announced in late 1988 that in the coming two years he would cut Soviet tanks in Europe in half and reduce the Soviet armed forces numbering 5.1 million men by 10 percent. Moreover, he maintained that "The use or threat of force no longer can or must be an instrument of foreign policy."[47] Clearly, in order to make room in his domestic economy budget, Gorbachev wanted to lower the heavy defense spending in the Soviet Union to give *perestroika* a chance.

After Gorbachev returned home suddenly after making his announcement in Washington, D.C., to oversee relief efforts for the devastating earthquake in Armenia, Gorbachev's popularity continued to soar in the Western world. For example, in early 1989 an opinion poll conducted in extremely conservative Orange County, California, put approval of Gorbachev at 70 percent, above the 68 percent of the newly elected Republican President George Bush. Gorbachev seized the initiative, leaving Western countries in disarray. His foreign policy retreats and ideological and political successes with *glasnost* and democratization appeared to be aimed to create a demilitarized, neutral zone in Europe (centered in reunited Germany) independent of NATO, which will cut Soviet security costs, provide access to Common Market technology and hard currency and increasingly isolate continental Europe ideologically from the United States.

If the superpowers in the East and West continue to cut back heavily on defense spending, this will have major implications for the world economy in the 1990s. The unilateral reduction strategy of Gorbachev put pressure on the United States to do the same or to continue to be outmaneuvered by Gorbachev's peace initiative in world opinion. By sensing that disarmament is the inevitable global trend for the superpowers and by placing himself on the cutting edge of this trend, if the Americans fail to match the Russian's initiatives (as President Bush tried to do in announcing major troop cuts in Europe in his 1990 State of the Union address), they lose in the propaganda war. And even if they meet the Russians step for step, they are placed in the defensive, reactionary position of following the Russian lead toward world peace. Just as the United States lost its "great communicator" or "propagandist" for world capitalism—President Ronald Reagan—the Russian version of a great socialist communicator, Mikhail Gorbachev, was coming into his own in a political system where (at least initially) he could not easily be voted out of office.

Moreover, with the largest share of the U.S. budget going to defense, 25 percent in 1989, the United States finds itself in danger of being outpositioned on the global economic chessboard, having put too many chips in the wrong basket. Despite so-called "defense cuts," the Bush administration actually *increased* defense spending (to just under *$300 billion*) in its proposed budget of 1990. Its main economic rivals, Japan and West Germany, target state investment to bolster commercially applicable research and development while the United States is stalemated in the debate over how much the Strategic Defense Initiative (SDI) and other Pentagon projects should be subsidized. The United States, in short, has specialized in a declining industry (strategic defense) while Japan has typically spent no more than about 1 percent of its GNP on defense, specializing in sunrise industries (such as microelectronics).[48] And German reunification involves a clear reduction of troops and weapons in Germany and socio-economic restructuring for competitiveness.

Nor does Gorbachev's "New Politics" end in Soviet relations with the United States and its industrial allies. Following a conservative, pragmatic policy line adopted by Andropov in 1982, Gorbachev has focused his Third-World initiatives upon large, important geopolitical states, such as India, turning away from the left-oriented policy of supporting Marxist-Leninist vanguard parties throughout the developing world typical of the 1973 to 1982 period. This strategic, nonideological realism recalls the right-oriented New Economic Policy of Lenin that was used to help to revive a devastated Soviet economy at that time.

Indeed, Francis Fukuyama has identified a cycle of alternation between right-oriented and left-oriented policies in the Soviet Union since the Revolution, Gorbachev's being merely the most recent right-oriented manifestation.[49] Gorbachev seems to have adopted former U.S. National Security advisor Zbigniew Brzezinski's focus upon "new influentials"—countries apt to have an increasingly important position in the future geopolitical strategy of the superpowers (Brzezinski identified India, Indonesia, Iran, Venezuela, Nigeria, and Saudi Arabia).

However, Gorbachev's successful foreign policy initiatives cannot disguise grave economic disorders and ethnic movements for autonomy at home for which the *perestroika* therapy may be too little too late. There is an emerging consensus that the USSR may not begin to show real improvements in economic growth until the mid-1990s. In 1990, for example, the Russians ran out of feed grain and had no money to buy more: as meat supplies dwindled so did the people's confidence in *perestroika*. The Soviets will have tremendous difficulty in decontrolling their price system. And if they do succeed, the odds are they will release a level of price inflation that will be almost impossible to check. Rents in Russia, for example, were last raised in 1928. The price of bread was set in 1954. And meat prices have held steady since 1962. With bread selling for something like 7 percent of its price of production, it is cheaper for farmers to feed their cattle bread than grain.[50] ...d since farmers do not get a financial payoff for much of what they grow, up to 40 percent of Russian grain rots on the fields. And the USSR continues to have to import grain and foodstuffs from abroad.

Meanwhile, pent-up demand is growing, along with high savings and large government deficits (7 to 8 percent of GNP compared with 3.5 percent for combined federal and state deficits in the United States)—a perfect recipe for inflation, which just needs to be set off with price decontrol. The Russian citizens, in short, have more money in many cases than goods to purchase—a situation that can lead to widespread discontent unless consumer goods start showing up in Soviet stores soon and the waiting lines become shorter. But to produce such goods takes years of lead time to create the industrial and marketing infrastructure—time that is running out for Gorbachev.

Stalin's solution to high inflation was simple enough: In 1947 he took away the people's money by forcing them to turn in their old currency for a new one, eliminating savings and inflation with one blow. West Germany was able to decontrol prices with its overnight currency reform of 1949: But this was under American occupation and with the help of Marshall Plan funds and long-term soft loans—all elements that are not likely parts of a Soviet solution. Japan was also able to move successfully from a tightly controlled "command economy" to a market-oriented one after World War II, but again with American occupation to keep order (and take the blame), American financial support, and cheap American technology to make the transition possible. The effort in the 1980s to decontrol some prices in China led to an inflation rate officially admitted to be 50 to 60 percent, but which was probably much higher in reality. The Chinese were forced to back-pedal with their reforms. And Soviet economic advisors have suggested to Gorbachev to slow down the schedule for decontrolling prices in order to keep inflation down and full employment in place. Meanwhile, (despite the Soviet movement towards a multiparty system) what is to become of *uskorenie* or "acceleration"?

COLLECTIVE LEARNING: WHAT IS TO BE DONE?

Collective learning is concerned with cognitive and behavioral patterns of either adapting to environmental change or of resisting such change. In most cases, first comes the environmental crisis, then the cognitive intention or strategic plan, and finally (if at all), the follow-through collective behavior. If a Soviet leader initiates a cognitive strategy of acceleration in adaptation to radical world economic shifts, collective learning is measured by the extent to which the Russian people adapt within the context of their tradition by successfully differentiating core integrity values from more passing or superficial motivators, *or* by the extent to which they continue to behave as if their cultural integrity depends upon their *slowness* to adapt for the sake of their traditional values and life-style. *Collective learning is a process of differentiation of legitimate patterns of adaptive behavior from sacrosanct cultural values in order to manage environmental change without losing group identity.*

When Gorbachev called leaders of striking miners on the telephone to ask them to ease off he was implicitly acknowledging the legitimacy of their resistance for the sake of traditional group values while yet calling on them to separate their integrity from this particular strike action for the sake of the nation's need to adapt to change. The successful political leader or manager has to move people toward his announced strategy while breaking down their incentives to resist by identifying with their specific economic plight. But he alone cannot make all the necessary telephone calls. Ultimately, success or failure will depend upon his ability to co-opt scores of others with his strategic plan so that they will help to break down resistance to collective learning.

There are several advantages of the collective learning approach to international political economy over others: (1) Its ability to differentiate between different strategies and contexts in terms of an objective standard of making progress; (2) its identification of a collective process that is potentially measurable, which transcends the individual (social learning) while not discounting the efficacy of individual free will (learning vicariously from models rather than learning by burning); (3) a universal vocabulary that transcends ideological fixations despite its bias toward entrepreneurship and innovation from a stable, equity-oriented maintenance base, and which permits one to translate strategies (that is, the free-rider, the maintenance, and the entrepreneurial) from one organizational level or level of analysis to another; and (4) a comprehensive theoretical synthesis of cognitive, behavioral, and environmental factors that has the virtues of social learning theory but goes beyond it in its concern with collective gestalt or the organizational pattern that delimits the schemata for learning or for resistance to change (such as, the proud Russian tradition of endless time).

But what is to be learned (or, as Lenin would have put it, What is to be done?)—whether from a North–South or East–West perspective? As a manager of a developing state (or of a multinational firm based in such a state), how can one restructure the maintenance base to be both more efficient and equitable within and more effective in terms of exports and competitive positioning without? Some specific guideline questions that indicate what is to be learned for such adaptation or adjustment include the following:

Guidelines for Collective Learning

1. Each individual has a *maintenance base* of home living expenses. If each is told to cut these in half (for instance) in order to provide savings to be used for voluntary investment in an entrepreneurial undertaking that can ᵃad to individual wealth and economic growth (positioning the collectivity ⟶reater competitiveness), and the individual is willing and able to do this,

an entrepreneur is born and the maintenance base is made more efficient. If the individual is able but not willing to do so (the maintenance syndrome), the organization or state may have to provide incentives if the collective objective is to increase economic growth through an entrepreneurial strategy. And if the individual is willing but not able, the collectivity must provide cash (from a loan, grant or taxes) for that purpose. If successful with a critical mass of individuals who work together, the effect is to radically restructure the maintenance base of the society towards efficiency and savings and to free capital and target funds for entrepreneurial investment.

2. Similarly, if the corporation or state cuts expenditures *within* the collectivity and automatically shifts this savings into *strategically targeted* investments *outside* the collectivity according to comparative advantage in terms of return on investment, economic growth and jobs will be created. Social equality demands the maximum participation of the members of the collectivity in both the process of strategic targeting and in the jobs and rewards stemming from economic growth.

3. In looking for savings and strategic targets, it helps to view the local economy as Jack McCall does in his *Small Town Survival Manual* (1988): as a bucket where much is poured into the top but the bucket never overflows until the leaks are plugged in the bottom—plugged by *import substitutions, market analysis* and *focused community organization* in order to *add value* to products, services and raw materials in order to *keep money and jobs at home* that otherwise leak out. This recipe has saved many poor rural towns in the South of the United States from extinction given the creative destruction of world economic change and could do the same for what is often called the South (or developing countries) in the rest of the world.

4. The motivated community organization required to transform collective participation into a consensus of teamwork that makes for an efficient maintenance base is stimulated by grassroots democratic organization. In an authoritarian state, the citizen has but "one boss" and must go underground psychologically for autonomy and creative freedom (with work often going underground in the black economy as well). Democracy presupposes a choice between at least two potential "bosses" or alternative parties, allowing the individual's energy to shine forth above ground and in community and market efforts in which she or he feels a part "owner". To limit the factional instability of "too many bosses" (one strong opposition party is better than two weak ones), a rule can be adopted requiring a party to receive five percent of the vote to have representation in parliament. And by always defending human rights, and particularly the rights of minority groups and factions, the community will coopt the energies of all individuals to work enthusiastically towards collective goals.

As development of the community progresses, the following collective learning questions should be asked.

5. Which collective behavior patterns need to be changed to modernize the agricultural sector, making it productive enough to release surplus capacity for the manufacturing and service sectors?

6. Which mature, standardized industries should the state subsidize *directly* and protect to assure resource availability and national security independence (water, electricity, and so forth). To what extent can joint ventures in these sectors transfer the cost of maintaining them to other states, firms or organizations (a systematic free-rider strategy)? How can entrepreneurial innovations be targeted for the sake of modernization and rationalization to further reduce costs? *For the reduction in costs at the maintenance base is the basis for the increase in the quality of life:* eliminations of variations, economies of scale and strategic import substitutions increase competitiveness and quality by creating savings for investment and retooling. Such "cold shower" restructuring of the maintenance base is also required periodically of advanced welfare states that come to take their subsidies and standard of life for granted at the cost of non-competitive tax rates and bureaucratic regulation that stifle entrepreneurial growth.

7. Which emerging, high growth "sunrise" industries should the state stimulate through tax incentives and *indirect* subsidies to sharpen national competitiveness in the longterm—microelectronics? machine tools? software? fiber optics? What timetable and market share will enable the state to step out of the way of firms in these sectors once the infant industry stage has been passed (with the exception of research and development support)? Many of the initial import substitutions may also be set for self-destruct as comparative advantage shifts with development (but only provided that core community and cultural integrity can be kept). Is the moment ripe in terms of economic cycles and changing value structures for the quick, sharp break that may be required to shift the society from a vicious to a virtuous economic circle (by cutting inflation through wage controls, stabilizing money, postponing foreign debt repayment, soliciting foreign loans, grants and investment, privatizing state-run firms, stimulating small-business entrepreneurship)?

8. Which educational and knowledge structures should the state and companies cultivate to train future workers in the agricultural, mature and emerging economic sectors? Which models of social and collective learning will increase this adaptation while preserving a sense of equity and the integrity of core cultural values? Have vocational training and apprenticeship systems targeted for key economic sectors of comparative advantage been sufficiently differentiated from general education, on the one hand, and from high tech and professional development, on the other? Which companies, states or international organizations can help to support these long-term educational and training strategies?

9. How can international credits be restructured to increase collective independence rather than dependence in the longterm? How can a monetary reform be introduced that assures a stable national currency? Which free rides, if any, are available to ease the transition? Which partners are apt to be most benign given collective objectives? Which foreign policies support this strategy?

10. Or, to make the overall collective-learning objective clear: *How can a maintenpreneurial harmony be achieved, which increases efficiency by reducing unnecessary variations and costs in the maintenance base while yet maximizing equal participation and preserving core cultural integrity, while also promoting the effectiveness of entrepreneurial targeting and export-oriented growth with fast feedback and systematic follow-through?*

ENDNOTES

1. On the fundamental attitude shifts toward the Soviet Union in the United States, see Daniel Yankelovich and Richard Smoke, "America's 'New Thinking,' " *Foreign Affairs* 67, No. 1 (Fall 1988).

2. See Ellen Comisso, "Introduction: State Structures, Political Processes, and Collective Choice in CMEA States," *International Organization* 40, No. 2 (Spring 1986):195–96.

3. V.I. Lenin, *Selected Works* (Moscow: Lenin Institute, 1963–1969), Vol. 2, p. 709. For a summary of Lenin's development, see "Lenin: Elites, Imperialism and Revolution," Chapter 2 in R. Isaak, *Individuals and World Politics*, 2nd edition (Belmont, CA: Duxbury Press of Wadsworth Publishing Co., 1981).

4. Ellen Comisso and Laura Tyson, "Preface" to special issue on "Power, Purpose and Collective Choice: Economic Strategy in Socialist States," *International Organization* Vol. 40, No. 2 (Spring 1986):189.

5. Franklyn D. Holzman and Robert Legvold, "The Economics and Politics of East–West Relations," in C. Fred Bergsten and Lawrence B. Krause, eds., *World Politics and International Economics* (Washington, DC: The Brookings Institution, 1975), p. 284. On "overfull" employment planning, see Franklyn D. Holzman, "Overfull Employment Planning, Input-Output, and The Soviet Economic Reforms," *Soviet Studies* 22 (October 1970):255–61

6. See Ludwig von Mises, "Economic Calculation in the Socialist Commonwealth," in *Collectivist Economic Planning*, edited by F.A. Hayek (London: Routledge & Kegan Paul, Ltd., 1935), pp. 87–130.

7. Holzman and Legvold, "East–West Relations," pp. 285–286.

8. See János Kornai, *Economics of Shortage*, 2 vols (Amsterdam: North Holland, 1980), and Paul R. Gregory, "The Stalinist Command Economy," in *The Annals*, 507, January, 1990:18–25.

9. Holzman and Legvold, "East–West Relations," pp. 286–87.

10. Wilhelm Nölling, "Moulding New Economic Links with East Bloc," *The German Tribune*, No. 1353, January 1, 1989, p. 2.

11. Glen Alden Smith, *Soviet Foreign Trade* (New York: Praeger, 1973), pp. 81–83.

12. Edward Weisband, Robert Rosh, and Scott Rosenthal, "Dual Ghettos and Dependent Development: The Economic Consequences of Superpower Hegemony in Eastern Europe and Latin America," paper presented at the Annual Meeting of the International Studies Association, Atlanta, Georgia, March 27–30, 1984.

13. J. Wilcyznski, *The Economies of Socialism*, 4th edition (New York: George Allen and Unwin Press, 1982), p. 53.

14. Weisband et al., p. 17.

15. R.A. Isaak, "International Integration and Foreign Policy Decision-making," an unpublished doctoral dissertation (New York: New York University, 1971), pp. 232–42.

16. See D. A. Loeber and A.P. Friedland, "Soviet Imports of Industrial Installations under Compensation Agreements: West Europe's Siberian Pipeline Revisited," *Columbia Journal of World Business* 18, No. 4 (Winter 1983):51–62. One observer has noted that the key rule operative in Cocom is that "In America everything is banned that is not expressly permitted, while in most of Europe the opposite is true." See Jürgen Klotz, "Not Everyone Believes Cocom Can Stop Technology Transfer to East Bloc," *The German Tribune*, No. 1289, September 1987, p. 7.

17. Frederick Kempe and Eduardo Lachica, "Cocom Feuds over Trade to East Bloc," *The Wall Street Journal*, July 17, 1984, p. 27.

18. See UNCTAD Secretariat, report of the Secretariat, *Towards the Technological Transformation of Developing Countries* (New York: United Nations, 1979) and Bruce R. Guile and Harvey Brooks, eds., *Technology and Global Industry: Companies and Nations in the World Economy* (Washington, DC: National Academy Press, 1987).

19. See the excerpted remarks of interviews with 50 Communists from 23 countries in *The New York Times*, January 22, 23, and 24, 1989.

20. See Paul Zinner, *Revolution in Hungary* (New York: Columbia University Press, 1962).

21. István Friss, ed., *Reform of the Economic Mechanism in Hungary* (Budapest: Akadémai Kiadó, 1969).

22. Kanji Haitani, "Market and Planning," Chapter 12 in Haitani, *Comparative Economic Systems: Organizational and Managerial Perspectives* (Englewood Cliffs, NJ: Prentice-Hall, 1986), pp. 354–59.

23. Ellen Comisso and Paul Marer, "The Economics and Politics of Reform in Hungary," *International Organization* 40, No. 2 (Spring 1986): 427.

24. Tim Stone, "Wall St. on the Danube," *The New York Times*, December 18, 1988.

25. See "Mao: Charisma, Limited Warfare and Modernization," Chapter 3 in Isaak, *Individuals and World Politics*, pp. 44–61.

26. Benjamin Schwartz, "China's Developmental Experience 1949–1972," in Michel Oksenberg, ed., *China's Developmental Experience* (New York: Praeger, 1973), p. 22. Also see Michel Oksenberg, "Policy Making under Mao Tse-tung 1949–1968," *Comparative Politics* 3, No. 3 (1971):323–60.

27. *The Wall Street Journal*, January 23, 1989, p. A8.

28. Haitani, "Market and Planning," pp. 359–60.

29. See Vigor Fung, "China Allows the Rebirth of Some Private Corporations," *The Wall Street Journal*, August 10, 1984, p. 22.

30. "China Walks the Edge of the Capitalist Road," *Business Week* (October 18, 1982), pp. 80–86.

31. See Dwight H. Perkins, *China—Asia's Next Economic Giant*. Seattle: University of Washington Press, 1986; and N.J. Wang, *China's Modernization and Transnational Corporations* (Lexington, MA: D.C. Heath and Co., 1984).

32. Nicholas Kristof, "China's Big Lurch Backward Theory Is Now Seen as Study in Pragmatism," *The New York Times*, January 3, 1989.

33. Nicholas Kristof, "Selling China on a 'Public' Privatization," *The New York Times*, January 8, 1989. On events leading up to the 1989 policy reversal, see John P. Burns, "China's Governance: Political Reform in a Turbulent Environment," *The China Quarterly* (Special Issue: The People's Republic of China after 40 Years), Sept. 1989, pp. 481–518.

34. Nicholas Kristof, "China Celebrates 10 Years Along the Capitalist Road," *The New York Times*, January 1, 1989.

35. Statistics from the *CIA Handbook of Economic Statistics; International Institute for Strategic Studies: The Military Balance: 1988–1989; OECD Economic Outlook, December 1988* as reported in *The Wall Street Journal*, January 23, 1989.

36. Graham T. Allison, Jr., "Testing Gorbachev," *Foreign Affairs* 67, No. 1 (Fall 1988):20. For an analysis of the stalemated Soviet economy see Marshall I. Goldman, *U.S.S.R. in Crisis: The Failure of an Economic System* (New York: W.W. Norton, 1983).

37. Axel Lebahn, *Politische und wirtschaftliche Auswirkungen der Perestrojka auf die Sowjetunion sowie auf ihre Beziehungen zu Osteuropa und zum Westen, Aussenpolitik*, Jg. 39, No. II, 1988, p. 114.

38. Ibid., p. 109.

39. See Mikhail Gorbachev, *Perestroika: New Thinking for Our Country and the World* (New York: Harper & Row, 1987).

40. Lebahn, *Politische und wirtschaftliche Auswirkungen*, pp. 115–16.

41. Lecture by Elena Ivanova at Pace University, Pleasantville, New York on February 14, 1990. Member of Academy of Sciences of the U.S.S.R.

42. See Esther B. Fein, "Angry Politics in the Soviet Heartland," *The New York Times*, Feb. 15, 1990, p. A20.

43. Lecture by Alexander Parkansky, Senior Research Fellow at the Institute of USA and Canada Studies in Moscow, given at Pace University, Pleasantville, N.Y. on February 14, 1990. Member of Academy of Sciences of the U.S.S.R.

44. For background on the Eastern European events, see Hoyt Gimlin, "Balkanization of Eastern Europe (Again)," *Congressional Quarterly Editorial Research Reports*, Volume 2, No. 17, Nov. 3, 1989, pp. 618–630; and, "East of Eden: A Survey of Eastern Europe," *The Economist*, Aug. 12, 1989, p. 11 and following.

45. Ferdinand Protzman, "Bonn's Point Man on Currency," *The New York Times*, February 12, 1992, p. D4. Also: *The Week in Germany* (New York: The German Information Center, February 9, 1990), pp. 1–5. For background on German reunification, see Mary H. Cooper, "A Primer on German Reunification," *Congressional Quarterly Editorial Research Report*, 2, No. 23 (Washington, DC: Congressional Quarterly Inc., Dec. 22, 1989, pp. 714–726; and R. Isaak, *German American Trends: 1984–1989* (New York: The German American Institute of Pace University, 1990).

46. Ferdinand Protzman, "Bonn's Point Man on Currency," *The New York Times*, February 12, 1990, p. D4.

47. Andrew Rosenthal, "Gorbachev in Motion: Asking for A New World, He Leaves Bush Tough Choices," *The New York Times*, December 11, 1988.

48. See John H. Cushman, "The Coming Crunch for the Military Budget," *The New York Times*, November 27, 1988.

49. Francis Fukuyama, "Gorbachev's New Politics: Soviet Third World Policy," *Current* 303 (June 1988):15–24.

50. Joel Kurtzman, "Of Perestroika, Prices and Pessimism," *The New York Times*, November 6, 1988. For a variety of views on long-term trends, see Seweryn Bialer, ed., *Politics, Society and Nationality Inside Gorbachev's Russia* (Boulder, CO: Westview Press, 1989).

CHAPTER NINE

SUMMATION AND ANTICIPATION

In social manipulation our tools are people, and people learn, and they acquire habits which are more subtle and pervasive than the tricks which the blueprinter teaches them.

Gregory Bateson, *Social Planning and the Concept of Deutero-Learning*

When it comes to the future, the task is not to predict it, but simply to enable it.

Antoine de Saint Exupéry

A collective learning approach to international political economy assumes that a people's competitive behavior on the one hand and sense of participative fair play on the other are not just individual or abstract phenomena but result from a social learning pattern with a specific organizational context and cultural gestalt. We learn not just from the teacher but from the milieu in the classroom. Our values are shaped not just by the ends or objects obtained by those to whom we grant deference, but by the rules of the game or means which our leaders use to get to their ends. Collectively, the Japanese would not epitomize such a well-navigated, tight ship in the turbulent storm of the global economy without the backdrop of a neo-Confucian, hierarchical culture. Nor would the Swedes be so generous with foreign aid and willing to sacrifice great ranges of personal income if the neo-corporatist culture of their society did not place equality of economic opportunity before individual self-aggrandizement.

This book started with the analogy of a tale by O. Henry in which the political authority of a society broke down not because of the economic asymmetry itself but because of the collective learning by the people when foreign goods were introduced in a situation of high demand and structured scarcity. The asymmetry was the fuel; but the recognition that desired goods were being arbitrarily withheld was the match. This book ends with a similar moral: While capitalist models of political economy may win in the short and medium term as means to maximize economic growth, standards of living and individual freedom, the legitimacy of elites in such societies is apt to be undermined to the extent wealth gaps or ratios between high and low incomes become too extreme. Or, as Lord Overstone put it, "No warning can save a people determined to grow suddenly rich." It was not without reason that Aristotle argued that stable democracy presupposes a large middle class. Extremes of wealth and poverty and of economic opportunity serve to undermine the legitimacy of democratic societies—*and* the stability of global political economic systems.

For if an undemocratic world economy is envisioned as one large, *potential* democratic society in the future, extremes of rich and poor and blatantly unequal economic opportunities in different nations threaten to undermine the legitimacy of the existing world order, thereby destabilizing it. Transnational terrorism is motivated, in part, by a sense of being declassed and marginalized by the existing system, the rules of which appear to be heavily loaded not only against one's self but against one's people. While this general diagnosis of the consequences of extreme asymmetry seems obvious, effective political economic recipes to do something about the situation are not. Perhaps some conclusions or principles drawn from this exploratory survey of international political economy from the collective learning perspective (in contrast with other viewpoints) may be of some help in clearing the way.

* * *

DEFINING THE SITUATION

International political economy is the study of the inequality or asymmetry between nations and peoples and of the collective learning and positioning patterns that either preserve or change this asymmetry.

Anglo-Saxon ideology has structured the institutional context of international economic exchanges during the nineteenth and twentieth centuries through a *pax Britannica* followed later by a *pax Americana*. The socialist antithesis to this hegemony—whether in its Soviet or Chinese or nonaligned manifestations—has failed. However, the cold war struggles during the twentieth century did serve to undermine the legitimacy and financial soundness of the Anglo-Saxon order.

Great Britain was already financially crippled by the end of World War II. But U.S. military spending, hyped-up to fever pitch during that war, led the way to push the Americans into becoming the world's greatest national debtor (four times that of Brazil) in absolute terms by the end of the 1980s, mitigated only by the fact that the U.S. debt was in its own currency and that currency happened still to be the world's key reserve currency.

As the superpowers realized they could no longer afford their strategic arms race (which could, after all, prove to be suicidal), the bipolar world became increasingly multipolar and international change became increasingly unpredictable: The greater the number of major players, the greater the uncertainty in global outcomes. Not only did a number of other nations obtain nuclear weapons, but Japan, Western Europe, and newly industrializing countries became world-class economic competitors in a number of fields. Ideologically, First, Second, Third, and Fourth Worlds proliferated. And *within* these "Worlds" the trend was toward disintegration within states for the sake of the ethnic autonomy of small, self-contained units. Those used to viewing world affairs with *binoculars* now discovered that they were looking through a kaleidoscope.

With the spread of multipolarity—militarily, technologically, economically, and ideologically—the primacy of global logic became self-evident as the twentieth century wound to a close. For example, the managers of Shell Oil Company were so concerned about global warming trends (due to the destruction of the world's ozone layer) that they ordered all of their oil drilling platforms in the North Sea to be built a full meter higher. The asymmetry between nations and peoples became more pronounced as technological developments and socioeconomic change accelerated both the tempo of life and the collective adaptations necessary to remain internationally competitive.

THE MAINTENANCE THESIS: MANAGING ECONOMIC RISK

The more dependent a country is in the world economy, the more its managers usually tend to seek control and stability, or at least the appearance of equilibrium, which keeps them in power and makes their domestic situation seem predictable enough to outsiders to attract foreign aid and investment. Managers in wealthier or more independent countries, in contrast, can take this equilibrium or *maintenance base* for granted, using it as a springboard for entrepreneurial risk and technological innovation. Financial credit, too, flows more automatically to such stable collectivities to support their risks.

Many managers in such a well maintained milieu, however, do not take advantage of this dynamic management potential inherent in their privileged position and prefer to minimize their risks for the sake of preserving a comfortable routine and a status quo friendly to their interests (falling into the maintenance syndrome). Thus, there are distinctive but understandable conservative tendencies on the part of managers in both rich and poor countries to embrace stability and to optimize existing equilibria rather than to make policies aimed at radical change or long-term risk for the sake of adjusting their collectivities to the condition of competitiveness required in the rapidly changing global economy.

The maintenance base is a boundaried social system or organization oriented toward internal stability, security, efficiency, and risk-reduction. The "inside" perspective of the maintenance base contrasts with the "outside" efforts at entrepreneurial innovation, risk-taking, adaptation, and effectiveness in terms of changing external markets in the global environment. Effective collective learning in the world economy involves going from the inside out once the efficiency of the maintenance base can be taken for granted and can help to target entrepreneurial risks in new global markets. To become too self-preoccupied within the maintenance base is soon to be passed by as global competitors aggressively pursue new global opportunities from their home bases.

On the other hand, to diffuse oneself in too many risk-taking ventures at once at the expense of neglecting the maintenance base is similar to having too many irons in the fire or to attacking with too many figures at once in a chess game without backing them up with protection. All risks need not be hedged, but they need to be collectively thought through and targeted after careful positioning and follow up. Extraordinary economic success over time demands a flexible yet tightly coordinated institutional infrastructure capable of backing up collective entrepreneurial targeting.

In the late twentieth century, economic advantages have been seen to accrue to nations with a feudal, hierarchical tradition and taken-for-granted maintenance base of order that have experienced an entrepreneurial break from this order as their security needs are covered by others and they find ready access to finance and technology in a growing world economy: West Germany, Japan and South Korea—for example. The past hierarchical traditions of these countries underscore the importance of education and respect for those older and wiser with more experience. In short, a deep-seated social consensus exists at the maintenance base that permits such societies to concentrate their collective energies on adapting to opportunities and innovations abroad. Indeed, there is a pattern in feudal societies of the past in which elites, whose landed status and legitimacy has been displaced by modernization and democracy, attempt to recover their status through entrepreneurial efforts, thus bringing new economic life to the maintenance base of their countries as well as to their families. Recall the cases of the Balinese aristocracy, the samuri of Japan, or, more recently, the restoration of the Minsheng Shipping Company family as the first large private company allowed to operate outside the state-planning system in the People's Republic of China. The resurrection of large German firms after World War II and the reincarnation of the Japanese *zaibatsu* as *sogoshosha* in postwar Japan are other cases in point. In times of economic crisis or structural stalemate, political economy managers call on the support of old elites and successful economic organizations of the past, taking calculated entrepreneurial risks to breathe new life into their national economies.

Whereas nations with "industrialized" feudal or hierarchical pasts often represent tight ships of order in the international chaos of global political economy, the United States represents the maintenance of domestic disorder or chaos for the sake of individual freedom and dynamic markets. This stable chaos keeps the Americans from being "ordered" around by hierarchical authorities and stimulates innovative creativity as people cast off relationships, careers, businesses, homes and life-styles like unfashionable clothing in a restless, nonstop environment of mobility. Small wonder that savings rates are low, consumption high, markets innovative, and debt mushrooming in a country whose basic behavioral ground rules are freedom of action and the individual desire to freely choose to do well that which others in the society tell them is fashionable or appropriate. The possibility of exporting this consumer-led, democratic chaos of innovative mobility to other countries seems remote, despite American foreign policy efforts to the contrary. The absence of a feudal experience in American history sets the nation apart from many others, making it as hard for Americans to understand those with feudal pasts as it is for citizens of countries with former feudal ties to understand a nation without them. It should come as no surprise that the United State should have become the dynamic source of global innovation, security, and credit in the twentieth century for other nations constrained by feudal/hierarchical pasts and defeats given the different resource bases and cultural heritages.

SPEED LIMITS AND INFORMATION OVERLOAD: ACCELERATION VERSUS RETARDATION

Although hard to measure, the tempo of socioeconomic and technological change has greatly speeded up in the atomic century, and peoples all over the earth have found themselves future-shocked and overloaded with information. The Russian scientist Pavlov discovered that animals could be driven crazy if given too much stimulation or choice. The tempo of socioeconomic change threatens to have this Pavlovian effect upon the human animal. There are clear limits to how much information a human being or group of human beings can absorb and how fast a human being or group of human beings can be asked to think or to move without making irrational choices or breaking down.

In a high-technology, high-information global economy information has become power, but not just any information. The key to collective learning for economic and political effectiveness is to slow the information flow down, analyze it, select only the salient data for a clearly defined purpose, and to act on this targeted information, getting as much feedback as quickly as possible once action has been taken. Significant information is that "ah ha" phenomenon which radically changes how we see the world and shakes us out of old routines or beliefs. Such a meaningful "information storm" (like brainstorm) or breakthrough causes the socialist to realize one cannot stimulate economic growth without creating explicitly unequal material incentives, or causes the capitalist to see that the social control of violence or maintenance of social harmony depends upon explicit limitations upon human freedom and limitations on extreme income disparities. Clearly it is more comfortable for such socialists and capitalists to maintain their conventional worldviews without having such information-storm breakdowns (or lighting ups). But the tempo of global economic change and the pervasiveness of international communications is such that data overloads and information storms are inevitable for those who continue to function as fully rational human beings capable of learning.

Speed control is perhaps the most underestimated phenomena in international political economy. Speeding up and slowing down are equally important strategic concepts, which can sometimes be used simultaneously in different sectors. Gorbachev is trying desperately to get the Russian people to accept the concept of *uskorenie* (acceleration) in order to bring collective learning up to speed in furthering his *perestroika* (restructuring) program.* But the integrity of the Russian soul depends upon an extensive view of time, as eternal patience for the sake of eternal values, if you will. The unhurried pace of life, which was the charm of Russian culture in the nineteenth century (the Chekhov *cachet*), has become a stumbling block for Gorbachev's desire for acceleration. Local ethnic communities want autonomy for their cultural way of life first, distrusting state-sponsored programs of modernization.

On another front, no insignificant part of the success of the Japanese political economy is its ability to slow down the decision-making process by use of *nemawashi*, or the informal shaking down of ideas among those who will be affected by them in order to prepare the ground or consensus for effective innovation. This slowing down process permits each individual in the company to make suggestions and point out weaknesses before a change becomes official, refining and targeting adaptations before they are instituted and getting everyone on board before innovation is launched. Such a slowing-down-in-order-to-follow-through-with-all-on-board process would be a good one for Americans to learn from: The traditional U.S. chief executive

------

*Another example of deliberate acceleration is West German Chancellor Helmut Kohl's policy of speeding up the pace of German unification in February, 1990 in order to outmaneuver the domestic political opposition and to present the world with a fait accompli.

officer typically rams changes down the throats of subordinates in memos from the top of the hierarchy, thus putting his status on the line before the flaws are removed or before the soil has been properly prepared for change among his subordinates. On the other hand, in the same organization there are no doubt individuals who have to be motivated to accelerate their work processes—indeed, people whose slowness may be a hidden protest against the arbitrary authority represented by impulsive orders from the top.

To take a positive example of the use of strategic *retardation* (or slowing down), during the 1987 stock market crash the head of the New York Stock Exchange prohibited computer programming for a few hours, requiring brokers to make buy or sell orders by hand. Slowing down the system meant that it did not have to be shut down, cooling off panic. The international manager can use a deliberate policy of retardation not only as a cooling off device, but also to focus attention upon the quality of results. On the other hand, the strategy of *acceleration* speeds up the process of change by identifying with it and positioning oneself on the cutting edge (as did Gorbachev) or pushing through fait accompli policy (such as German unification by West Germany).

COLLECTIVE LEARNING AND CULTURAL RESISTANCE

Information overload implies that collective learning is most effective when it is arbitrarily delimited and targeted but in a way that breeds consensus and high morale rather than polarization and resistance. If knowledge is the orderly loss of information, the critical prerequisite to collective learning is to create a consensus upon the criteria for sorting the wheat from the chaff. Ideology is only an abstract and imperfect criterion in this regard as those who tried to apply the Stalinist model of political economy have discovered. What we are dealing with here is a dynamic link between the micro and macro levels of analysis, which enables groups of people to learn things efficiently and to apply them effectively in the context of a rapidly changing global economy.

Collective learning is social learning with a specific organizational context and cultural gestalt: It is a process of differentiating legitimate patterns of adaptive behavior to manage environmental change without losing cultural integrity. The concept gets beyond the overly psychological notion of social learning theory—the result of reciprocal interactions among person (cognition), behavior, and environmental situation. While accepting these elements of social learning theory, and particularly its assumption that individuals can learn from others vicariously or from modeling their own behavior after others whom they have observed, collective learning emphasizes the collective gestalt or organizational pattern that delimits the schemata for learning or for resistance to change. Such a collective gestalt or cultural context presupposes the legitimacy of specific learning models, structures, and paradigms and the exclusion of others. It emphasizes deutero-learning or how people learn learnings, what they pick up from the learning process and milieu, not just the content of learning.

For example, in Bulgaria the successful manager of the state-owned company has traditionally been the one with enough clout with his superiors in the party hierarchy to get a *reduction* in the annual production quota for his factory, even though this behavior contradicts the functional purpose of the enterprise. For the socialist manager has learned that lower quotas are easier to reach, meaning bonuses for himself and his workers. Less work also means more free time and a higher quality of life. The collective gestalt in such a political economy encourages the most "successful" individuals to reduce their output—a learning pattern picked up fast but not exactly a recipe for increasing international competitiveness.

To take another example, the American worker is often stimulated to dance the Olsonian rag: Behavior is guided by the assumption that the interests of one's self and one's own small group are different from the interests of the larger organization.* The worker quickly learns to maximize his or her own personal interests, income, and job prospects regardless of the costs to the organization or firm since in any case he or she will cut and run and take a job soon with another firm. The job mobility built into the cultural context of the system means that large organizations get left holding the bills for the opportunity costs left behind by workers whom they have trained and nurtured.

The Japanese and, to some extent Europeans, have often avoided such opportunity costs by assuring core workers of formal or informal lifetime job security. This breeds an atmosphere of trust and social community in the organizational and cultural context, which often serves to nip labor disputes in the bud and encourages management to invest in lifetime training programs for workers who will be with them a lifetime. However, the drawback in this motivational milieu is that once again the worker will catch on to the tricks or real rules behind the formal commitments: Lifetime security may dampen the enthusiasm for extraordinary achievement or taking innovative risks. In a culture like that of the Japanese, "where the nail that sticks up gets hit," consensus can mean complacent followership and a deterrent to creativity. Even the remarkably effective Japanese quality circles (originally modeled on W. Edwards Deming's criterion of quality being the reduction of variation) may best serve the function of improving processes already in place by cutting costs, reducing hazards, eliminating defects, rather than nurturing the "anti-system" mentality that leads to creative, technological breakthroughs.

---

*Refers to Mancur Olson's *The Logic of Collective Action* (Cambridge, MA: Harvard University Press, 1965).

The two German scientists who won the Nobel Prize in physics in 1988, for example, did so with research work conducted secretly in their IBM laboratory in Zurich, unannounced to their scientist manager whom they feared might stop them from putting time into such an heretical idea. The most successful innovative organizational contexts appear to be those that select the right people to start with and then let them run free in a semi-controlled, highly motivated environment with broad targets.

Of course the right people presupposes a cultural as well as a functional selection that may leave the majority outside the system or even systematically discriminate against the most brilliant individuals. A person who believes that *Ogni mattina io rinasco* (Each morning, I am born anew) may have to work for himself or herself to find a superior willing to put up with this first principle. Yet firmly held first principles are essential to individual and cultural integrity. A person with "character" is one willing to fight the fashionable trends or repressive laws even to the death if necessary for some higher value. Antigone thus insisted on the right to bury her brother, despite the law forbidding it. And Lech Walesa, the leader of the once-outlawed Solidarity trade union in Poland, took his stand so firmly and persistently that by 1989 the Polish government reversed itself and opened talks with him, recognizing Solidarity's right to exist and Solidarity moved front and center into government power.

Throughout Eastern Europe there is a caldron of national movements to defend the cultural, if not political, rights of autonomy for ethnic minorities—from Estonia, Latvia, and Lithuania in the USSR to the Turks in Bulgaria to the uniting of the Serbs and Montenegrins against the Albanians in the region of Kosovo in Yugoslavia. Cultural resistance to collective learning patterns directed from party officials and government leaders may be the key to the existential integrity of many peoples, even though their struggles have high collective costs.

Finally, the successful national manager of a political economy must read through the unmovable schemata of resistance scattered throughout the culture and give those marginal people of integrity a legitimate part in the process of collective economic transformation or watch desired reforms die of inertia. "Weimar Russia" in the 1990s is a case in point.

CLOSURE VERSUS AMBIVALENT BELIEF SYSTEMS

Effective collective political economy strategies depend upon anticipating the tendency of the human mind toward closure and countering it, or unlocking it before it is too late. Collective organizational efforts can take on a life of their own and continue to the point of self-destruction unless they are derailed or side-tracked. An example of this "edge effect" gone mad, the momentum for the sake of aesthetic completion regardless of human consequences, is the World War II Manhattan Project, which developed the atomic bomb in the United States. Participants in the project found that they were so caught up in the collective learning process after three years of night-and-day struggle to achieve the breakthrough that even though they knew Nazi Germany had surrendered they had to continue to completion. The result was the dropping of two atomic bombs on Japan. Once "group think" gets rolling and is stimulated with patriotism, money, honor, status, and wartime frenzy, the temptation for closure becomes almost irresistible.

Moreover, closure is often a much more attractive political style in a highly uncertain world situation that an ambivalent belief system. Stalin knew this. So did Mao Tse-tung. President Ronald Reagan benefitted from this effect in the simplicity of his creed, although thankfully he turned out to be a pragmatic compromiser in practice. People want their great communicators to have simple, firmly held beliefs. Closure, in short.

Not that all closure is necessarily a bad thing. If one considers those few modern cases of success in transforming authoritarian state-controlled economies to market-oriented, democratic economies one finds a moment of closure in historical time in which things are suddenly reversed, the price system decontrolled. Such was the case in the spring of 1948 in West Germany when the Reichsmark was almost without value, long lines surrounded stores, and black markets proliferated. German Economic Minister Ludwig Erhard with the cooperation of the American occupation forces (in Operation Bird Dog) obtained a few wagonloads of paper money printed in the United States and declared "the Currency Reform" overnight. Each German citizen was at first permitted to receive forty new Deutsche Marks (DM) in a 1:1 exchange for the next to worthless Reichsmark. No one was to receive either more nor less than forty DM. A little later, each citizen was permitted to receive twenty more. Thus began the Social Market Economy and West German economic miracle. And all done with a simple act of closure.*

Other forms of closure, however, are incompatible with collective adaptation for either the sake of international competitiveness or for the sake of more widespread economic opportunity or social justice. This form of closure, for example, closes off the opportunity of becoming a U.S. Senator unless one has already been elected to that office and happens to have raised an average of $4 million. The closure of thinking against truly democratic election financing in the United States is turning a democracy quickly into an oligarchy with over 90 percent of those elected to the Senate and House

---

*Of course it must be recalled that this currency reform was done under a military government that could force the people who lost their savings to swallow it—not exactly a democratic recipe. Poland's 1990 "shock therapy" policy of removing price controls while keeping wage controls, ending subsidies for goods and services, privatizing state-owned companies, postponing foreign debt repayment and getting aid from the World Bank, IMF and friendly governments is another alternative bordering on short-term closure that bears watching.

of Representatives being incumbents (a sort of informal lifetime tenure). Or the closure of unions, which refuse to compromise with management even given the greater competitiveness and flexibility of workers abroad in the same industry. Or the closure of management in not granting the union workers meaningful lifetime security and health benefits. Or the closure of protectionism bills passed in Congress to put such managers and workers in a "greenhouse" until they use their time to become competitive.

But with the exceptions of infant industries, short-term import substitution, strategic and high-tech sectors, the greenhouse strategy often backfires in its collective learning effects. By putting their electronics companies in a state-subsidized greenhouse program, the French in the 1950s, for example, encouraged managers and workers alike to believe the comfortable support would go on forever. So they grew complacent and when the subsidies were withdrawn the French electronics industry went into a major crisis: It could not compete in real terms on the world market. And East Germans, used to guaranteed jobs and subsidized housing under the closure of a Communist Party state up until the fall of 1989, found the "cold shower" of market uncertainty and competition painful as they joined the West German collective learning process in the reunification of the 1990s. Closure, in short, can lull one into thinking uncertainty and risk have been licked and that one has it permanently made (despite the positive sense of social security which this provides). Closure is usually too comfortable to work for long.

The opposite of closure is targeted, strategic openness. As composer John Cage put it in *A Year from Monday* (1967): "In music it was hopeless to think in terms of the old structure (tonality), to do things following old methods (counterpoint, harmony), to use the old materials (orchestra instruments). We started from scratch: sound, silence, time, activity. In society, no amount of doctoring up economics/politics will help. Begin again, assuming abundance, unemployment, a field situation, multiplicity, unpredictability, immediacy, the possibility of participation." Not the cynical closure of Stalin nor the naive openness of democratic reformist ideology of the 1960s, but a yin/yang rhythm between the closure of necessary semi-control and targeting and the openness of spontaneous innovation and options for widening participation. The 1990s bring with them a realization of the systemness of the global economy, an in-house Keynesian system where international demand and supply can be stimulated or depressed with consequences for everyone on the earth. But within this realization of the earth's closure and delicate ecological shield is the serendipity of chaotic markets, opening and closing markets depending upon innumerable liberating uncertainties and repressive structural obstacles, the rise and fall of petty protectionisms and heuristic innovations. If the Western markets continue to be partially closed to the exports of the South and the East, the South and the East will have less currency to pay for goods from the West and the global economy will slow down. As the domestic economies of the South and the East work beyond temporary greenhouse and import substitution strategies to restructure and compete with Western industries, the world economy will grow and more people will be employed. The radical restructuring in Eastern Europe towards market economics and multiparty democracy in 1989 and 1990 bodes well for world economic growth. East-West German economic integration, accelerating the restructuring of the European Common Market, will lead the way.

MODELS AND MODELING

The late twentieth century can be characterized as the Era of the Non-automatic Pilot Experiment. The scientific method and techniques of social learning have spread throughout the globe, including the notion of vicarious learning, modeling, and the pilot experiment. What characterizes the economic organizational models that have succeeded? On the national level these include the Japanese and the Swedish political economies. On the regional or international level, the European Economic Community and OPEC come to mind. None of these political economy organizations succeeded over night and all are imperfect still today (note the austerity policy with which Sweden began the 1990s). All have in common a long history of frustrated consensus-building.

The dream of European unification goes back to Julius Caesar's conquests of France, England, and the Lowlands, which were added to the Roman territories of Italy, Spain, and the Balkans. The first book on European federation was Pierre Dubois's *On the Reconquest of the Holy Land* in 1306. Later both Edmund Burke and Immanuel Kant argued for the necessity of cultural similarity, if not homogeneity, for successful European integration (a strategy of exclusion). In the twentieth century progressive business leaders actually led the way to the formation of the European Economic Community, which could not, however, have been born without the cold, strategic calculations of French and German leaders when they joined forces in the European Coal and Steel Community. A history of collective action, a striving for homogenity to the point of a strategy of exclusion, geopolitical strategic calculation, members with economic clout and leadership by both business and government leaders are behind the success of the European Common Market—not to mention a benign American hegemony which not only let the bloc form, but helped to finance it. The 1989 expansion of the European Community (EC) of twelve nations to include six European Free Trade Association (EFTA) countries in a "European Economic Zone" provides a model for accepting Eastern European countries (such as Poland and Hungary) into a European bloc without having to admit them to the more exclusive EC club.

OPEC, too, represented a coming together of members with economic clout (based on oil), a strategy of exclusion, hard strategic calculations, and an assumption that American hegemony would not stand in their way. And OPEC, too, created loose joint ventures with other oil producing nations to expand its influence without diluting its core. The timing of both the EC and OPEC ventures was perfect and the leaders sophisticated enough politically to suggest that such timing was no accident. Both were no doubt motivated to some extent by the desire for regional independence from the influence of the American hegemon. Other commodity cartels inspired by the OPEC model were based upon more diffuse membership, a less scarce or demanded commodity (bauxite, bananas and copper), and inappropriate timing and were not successful. The prerequisites for successful economic organizations (such as market share, organizational leadership and timing) must be studied before they can be applied effectively as models.

Both the Japanese and Swedish models represent deep-rooted traditions of neo-corporatist consensus (the Japanese "without labor" and Sweden almost labor-dominated), homogeneous populations, small states, and geographical locations on the periphery of American hegemony (that is, more protected by it than contributing to it). The literacy rate of both countries is high, and both are committed to maintaining a high level of intelligent participation by citizens in the economy (although the Japanese tendency to exclude women versus the Swedish tendency to include them is notable). Very little is left to chance when it comes to organizational networks in these countries. Control over population growth is also a similar characteristic. The extreme hierarchical nature of influence and information processing distinguishes Japan from the extreme focus upon egalitarianism, particularly when it comes to economic opportunity, present in Sweden. Both countries have maintained legitimate roles for traditional, noble families, who are expected to contribute in the form of public service. Both cultures stress limiting the range of incomes between those earning the most and those earning the least as a principle necessary for social harmony and consensus (in marked contrast with the United States, for example). Both target the industries they specialize in with great care and use government institutions and subsidies extensively in this task, thus maintaining international competitiveness while yet preserving the integrity of their national cultures, social commitments, and some modicum of security at home.

In terms of the critical modeling phenomenon in the collective learning approach to international political economy one must also highlight the heavy reliance upon the strategy of the pilot experiment in the socialist bloc—the capitalist zones and privatized factories near Hong Kong in the People's Republic of China, the Soviet companies designated by the government to be permitted to make trade deals directly with Western firms in order to create "model" joint ventures (the cutting edge of *perestroika*), the experiments with stock markets in Hungary and China, and so forth. The initial aim in all cases appeared to be to graft market mechanisms on an outdated Stalinesque economic structure in order to make the political economy more competitive, attract Western hard currency and technology, and still not lose their integrity as socialist states.

Given the ability of Hungary and China to transcend the Stalinist focus on heavy industry and to become self-sufficient in agriculture, China and Hungary seem likely to be more successful in their economic reforms sooner than the Soviet Union, even given China's 1989 authoritarian crackdown. However, all three countries have benefitted in economic growth by carefully targeting key industries in strategic regions for pilot experiments, which are designed to serve as models or "signals" for the rest of the country should they succeed.

One deutero-learning problem here is that it may always be more motivating to be part of a pilot experiment than it is to be a secondary copy of someone else's experiment making the initial experiments more successful than their clones. On the other hand, to the extent bugs are worked out, going second may be better than going first (as Japan has illustrated to the West in many industries).

STRATEGIES AND CYCLES

The success of political economy models in terms of economic growth depends upon the ability of their managers to launch or adapt them using appropriate strategic mixes at opportune moments in short-term, medium-term, and long-term business cycles. The key strategies associated with the maintenance thesis or maintenance model used in this book are the defeatist, the free-rider, the maintenance, and the entrepreneurial. One reason why so few successful economic models emerge from the developing world is that the global economy is structured to give them a choice between the least desirable of these two strategies: the defeatist and the free-rider. This is one reason why managers in developing countries dream of being able to pursue a maintenance strategy—that is, dream of being able to keep control of a self-sustaining system of equilibrium in which economic growth keeps up with the business cycle and the nation does not fall further behind. So if a country such as Mexico opts for a free-rider strategy in taking on as much debt as it can (as it did in the 1970s under the advice of the Cambridge School), one must understand this decision as one of the few choices realistically available to Mexico at the time. Bolivia's suspension of payments on its international debt in the 1980s is another free-rider variation.

The dilemma of advanced industrialized countries is markedly different. They can more or less take the maintenance of their existing political economy and its legitimacy for granted and have a choice between different risk-portfolios—or entrepreneurial strategies—depending upon whether they prefer maximizing the objectives of economic growth and job creation, or prefer the objectives of more equal distribution of economic opportunities and increasing the quality of life for those in the present generation. To a certain extent these are future versus past and savings/investment versus consumption trade-offs from the economist's viewpoint, but the cases of Sweden and West Germany illustrate that for fairly long periods (between periodic maintenance base restructurings for efficiency) it is possible for political economies to be able to have their cake and to eat it too (at least as long as the American protector protects).

No matter where one stands on these issues, however, they can be described in terms of various maintenance-entrepreneurial (mainten-preneurial) strategy mixes. The economic threat to advanced industrial countries is more apt to come from risk-aversion or risk-shy behavior (or the maintenance syndrome) than it is from overdoing entrepreneurial risk-taking.

A case in point is the failure of West European countries to develop their own microchips in time to compete with the Japanese and Americans in the microelectronics business globally, making them dependent for some time to come on foreign chips (the Americans seem to be intent upon mimicking their European forefathers in this regard as they become increasingly dependent upon Japanese chips). We can conclude that the optimum strategy is a maintenance-entrepreneurial mix heavily loaded toward the entrepreneurial *if* the tempo of socioeconomic and technological change continues at the same rate as in the 1980s or speeds up in the 1990s. Gorbachev realized this and sought to orchestrate radical economic and political restructuring of the maintenance bases of nations in the East bloc (including his own) in part to increase their capacity to absorb Western technology and investment in order to make them more competitive.

The cycles that all managers must face whether in the public or private sector are short-term, medium-term, and long-term. Since political economy strategies depend upon future assumptions concerning global economic growth or recession, energy prices, exchange rates and so forth, competent managers of international economic change must master the global cycles that will affect all their decisions and pay particular attention to the medium-term cycles specific to their own industry or national comparative advantage. Long-term, one must decide whether to side with those who believe the twentieth century will end with a bust—or with a boom—or with a wash between bust and boom. The depression scenarios tend to highlight a gap between existing technological developments and the ability commercially to apply and to sell these technologies, or a scarcity of liquidity given a debt-load melt-down globally, or both.

While it is true that from our collective learning perspective the infor-mation-overload, risk-shy maintenance thesis suggests that there are defi-nite limits to the ability of people globally to absorb existing technology (that is until people start throwing out computers every year like an old-fashioned pair of shoes), it is important to recall that the markets tend to discount this absorption problem well in advance, giving Silicon Valley its own private recession (in 1984) without necessarily contributing to a massive cyclical downturn.

The boom hypothesis, of course, has its own flaws, but perhaps not so many as the depression scenario. The optimists believe, for example, that the world's public and private financial institutions will ease the global debt crisis by informally writing off most of the developing country loans from the 1970s through longer terms and lower interest rates (which seems probable). They also argue that although the disinflationary trend may reverse, the rise of inflation will be gradual, thus providing the perfect elixir for global economic growth—stable growth with increasing liquidity. International peace seems to be breaking out throughout the world (led by Soviet and American weapons cut-backs and troop withdrawals), giving the stability argument further plausibility. But there are some drawbacks to this rosy scenario when one looks at specific sectors of the global economy (leaving the overcapacity problem in technology aside). If peace really succeeds, fewer weapons will be produced and sold, dampening these parts of the economy in those countries specializing in the weapons business. With well over half of the aerospace military market in the world, the U.S. economy may be struck hard with readjustment problems, followed by European countries. (This, however, assumes that the United States and Europe put peace before economic growth, which is an open question.) The majority of oil analysts project a significant rise in oil prices in the mid-1990s, which could undermine the moderate inflation assumption of the boom hypothesis.

When one descends from the level of the long-term, Kondratieff boom-or-bust genre of cycle projections (fifty years) to middle-range Kuznets cycles (fifteen to twenty-five years) or short-term "business cycles" (seven to nine years), the need for the manager of global economic change to be up-to-date in key sectors becomes even more compelling. If the manager should have corporate or national stakes in the global construction business, for example, it becomes important to know that the Hansen/Kuznets cycle projects that every other short-term business cycle will be a real boom in the construction cycle in the United States, whereas alternating recessions are apt to be particularly deep when they coincide with the construction slump (the construction cycle being seventeen to eighteen years in length, about twice the length of the normal business cycle). When the manager anticipates a short- to medium-term recession coming on in a specific sector, he or she should adopt a maintenance strategy of consolidation or efficiency cutbacks, while an anticipation of boom might well trigger a higher risk, entrepreneurial strategy of expansion. Another option is to ignore market timing altogether, like Peter Lynch, manager of the most successful (long-term) stock mutual fund, Fidelity Magellan, and to invest systematically in concrete situations that one is closely familiar with (which also seems to be the Japanese Research and Development investment strategy). This systematic, close-to-the-ground entrepreneurial strategy permits one to gain from economies of scale (as one's investment portfolio becomes ever larger), while simultaneously maintaining quality (by reducing variations by limiting oneself to industries one knows) and experiencing higher growth than average macro investment cycle returns by focusing upon the micromanagement of undervalued situations.

Since public managers are presumably responsible for forecasting levels of unemployment and for attempting to encourage workers to shift from areas of low demand to areas of growing demand, such sector-specific short- to medium-term economic cycle research and micro-management analysis becomes invaluable to them as well. Mikhail Gorbachev could do worse in planning targets for *perestroika* than employing some Western cycle researchers in specific, promising economic sectors to work together with Russian economists in joint-venture cycle projections and investment planning. As indicated in the guidelines of "What Is to Be Done?" (pp. 258–261 of Chapter Eight), the aim of collective learning is to restructure the maintenance base of the organization or state with efficiency, cultural integrity and equal participation in order to position and target the collectivity for entrepreneurial niches and export-oriented growth.

SHIFTS IN HEGEMONY

Even if an economic boom should mark the beginning of the twenty-first century, the key question for international political economy is how it is likely to be distributed. While straight-line projections of past trends tend to be misleading (for reasons which Karl Popper documented in *The Poverty of Historicism*), they do identify the major players in the game of global hegemony and give one plausible projection of the global situation in the year 2000.

Let us take the following figures for data through 1987 as reported by the *CIA Handbook of Economic Statistics* to illustrate such a straight-line projection. Between 1970–1980 and 1980–1987 the average annual growth rate of real gross national product in the USSR shrank from 3 percent to less than 2 percent, in the European Community it shrank from 3 percent to less than 2 percent, in the United States it rose from just 2 percent to 3 percent, in Japan it shrank from over 4.5 percent to under 4 percent, in China it rose from under 6 percent to almost 9 percent. According to this important indicator of global economic power, Soviet hegemony would be projected to continue to decline, European Community clout would also decline (although this may well be reversed when the 1992 transformation of the EC is completed), United States economic power will increase (despite academic fashions of decline portrayed by Paul Kennedy, Lester Thurow, J. Forrester, and others), Japanese economic strength will fall off (a trend that may be countered by heavy Japanese investment), and Chinese economic growth will continue—albeit dampened by the 1989 polarization, centralization and repression. The same source of data demonstrates what this means in terms of shares of the World GNP: The United States: 26 percent; the European Community: 22.2 percent; the Soviet Union: 13.9 percent; Japan: 9.4 percent; Eastern Europe: 5.3 percent; China: 1.7 percent; the others: 21.5 percent. What this indicates is that although China's growth is apt to continue at a high rate, it is so far behind in global market share that it will take generations to catch up with the big economic players. Japan will be able to expand its share of the pie but not enough to surpass either the European Community or the United States (although Japan is apt to pass the Soviet Union in this and most other economic indicators).

Finally, if the Europeans do get their act together economically as a bloc as expected, they alone have the breadth of economic power to give the United States a run for its money in the year 2000, followed close behind by the cash-swamped Japanese.

These trends are reinforced when the implications of the likely trend toward trade bloc mercantilism are taken into account. The European Community regional bloc (extending to the European Free Trade Association and Eastern Europe) is apt to be facing down the United States–Canadian Free Trade bloc on a number of issues with both blocs running frequently into GATT conflicts with Japan as well. But Japan is apt to remain isolated, despite its effort to build up its Asian ties and relations with developing countries. In fact, strong Japanese–American ties are likely to be more significant than any other bilateral economic tie Japan may have, reinforcing American economic hegemony with a heavy influx of Japanese investment and skilled management personnel. The profound economic dislocations within the USSR and the Eastern European bloc and the strategic shift toward disarmament on the part of the Soviets free American energies to focus more intensely on commercial applications of research and technology, rather than military applications. Perhaps the most important aspect of the "peace dividend" is not the freeing up of capital as much as it is the providing of psychological space for the Americans to concentrate on their own socio-economic restructuring at home.

Moreover, the American "limelight effect" will continue, giving the United States more economic power globally than meets the eye. High tech, deregulation, management training and entrepreneurship are all American-generated trends that illustrate the demonstration power of the American economy: Once the limelight is focused there, other countries follow suit and mimic American innovations (for better or for worse). In the low-tech entrepreneurial sector, the McDonald's hamburger chain (or, more precisely, real estate franchise) is perhaps the ultimate example. Not only is a new

McDonald's fast-food restaurant created in the world every eighteen hours, but the government of Singapore encourages families to have children's birthdays there in order to stimulate an appetite for consumption to mimic the consumption-driven dynamism of the American economy. For while the cultural context of "stable, free-wheeling chaos" cannot be exported abroad, specific mass consumption trends and fashions can be.

Academically it is fashionable to dwell upon the fact that compared to 50 percent of the world GNP after World War II, the U.S. economy now makes up only about half that percentage, meaning that the United States alone can no longer serve as the locomotive when the world economic growth rate slows down. But just as it is not necessary to own 51 percent of the shares of a company to have effective control, the United States still has enough economic power and attractive, flexible investment opportunities to skew the lion's share of world capital to flow in its direction in order to help pay for its deficits and innovations. And the deregulating, job-creating entrepreneurial efforts of European governments in their desire to mimic the positive economic aspects of the Reagan era are widespread enough even among so-called socialist governments (East and West) to quiet all doubts about the latent power of the United States to serve as a model for other countries.

This is not to say that the Reagan model was "fair" in the sense of serving the interests of the disadvantaged to the same extent as those of the advantaged (clearly it did not). The point is just that the demonstration or limelight effect of the American example is still potent enough to cause major shifts in the policies of many countries, as illustrated in the 1980s by the reversal of French public opinion from an anti-American to an almost pro-American economic and high-tech position (despite continuing French skepticism concerning American culture). The entrepreneurial restructuring in the United States has yet to be fully appreciated by Europeans and other countries. Just as Sputnik shocked the Americans into getting their technological house in order to land on the moon before the Russians, the Japanese challenge economically has stimulated them into a massive economic restructuring: The American *perestroika* is well under way, as Gorbachev is all too much aware. The West Europeans may be too comfortable with their welfare-state maintenance strategies to go through the pain such readjustment requires quickly (the 1992 transformation not withstanding). Rapid East-West German economic integration may have more of a "Sputnik shock effect" upon Common Market leaders and bureaucrats than upon the people of Western Europe who are living well. And a common European currency will come more easily than the integration of proud, national institutions. While many business people in Europe envy the economic dynamism that springs from the entrepreneurial culture of the United States, few are in favor of cutting back on the social welfare nets of European states to the extent that would be necessary to mimic the free markets that stimulate American entrepreneurship. And one of the great problems of economic reform in

Eastern Europe is that you cannot have free market capitalism without capitalists and there may not be enough capitalists in the East to really get it going soon. The likely prospect in Europe in the 1990s is a stalemated pushing towards adjustment to world economic competitiveness as national interest groups try to hang on to their cultural traditions, union prerogatives and individual freedoms.

Apart from reunited Germany, only the four dragons—Hong Kong, Taiwan, Singapore, and South Korea (which alone accounted for up to 20 percent of the American trade deficit in the late 1980s)—appear to have the collective motivation to try to keep pace with the fast-moving Japanese and American (and possibly Canadian) economic examples. Other developing countries will have higher economic growth rates than the United States during the 1990s, but like China, it is because they are so far down in global market share to start with. Nevertheless, developing nations represent major investment opportunities for advanced industrialized nations and will have increasing bargaining power in international economic organizations.

Such investment could be stimulated by "insurance policy" stability provided by an International Monetary Fund expanded into a World Central Bank (leaving the World Bank as it is for long-term development) and by a General Agreement on Tariffs and Trade transformed into a World Trade Organization—both with greater funding and powers. A conservative but dynamic restructuring of this "maintenance base" of international institutions could provide a refurbishing of the legitimacy of the Bretton Woods framework and a technical clearing house which would help to overcome risk-shy hesitations blocking investors and entrepreneurs from commitment in an uncertain world economy.

As for the truly "academic" myth of the great decline in American hegemony, a simple straight-line projection from economic data at the end of the 1980s combined with the American limelight effect and entrepreneurial cultural dynamism tend to confirm the prediction of political scientist Seizaburo Sato, advisor to former Japanese Prime Minister Nakasone: "The twentieth century was the American century. And the twenty-first century will be the American century." Diffuse power pluralism and traditional values suggest that revolution or radical change is unlikely in the United States, which is a positive factor for investors. As the world's key currency country, the United States does not appear to have to worry about sources of liquidity to cover its debts—unlike almost all other nations. Americans have got their foreign investors by the huge amount of equity they own in dollar-denominated assets. Where else would the great flow of conservative cash go? To a changing but uncertain Europe where taxes are often higher than returns on investment? To a possibly overvalued and more politically dependent Japan with its own sophisticated regulations? Or to the world's largest, unified entrepreneurial cafeteria with low top tax rates, an old-fashioned political stability of infinite checks and balances and never a hint of nationalization? And as long as the rest of the world sells more to the United States than it buys from the Americans, it has little choice but to lend back the excess dollars to the United States.

Certainly American domination has declined somewhat and will not approach the peak circumstances following World War II, even if recent frustrated efforts to make the educational and socio-economic infrastructure more equitable and competitive should ultimately succeed. Key global economic decisions will be shared in an expanding coalition including nations in the Common Market (led by united Germany), Canada and Japan. But these countries will find it in their best interest to let the United States carry the greatest burden of global responsibility: the twenty-first century will most likely be the century of "embedded hegemony" for the United States.

SELECTED
BIBLIOGRAPHY

Agmon, Tamir. *Political Economy and Risk in World Financial Markets*, Lexington MA: Lexington Books, 1986.

Alt, J.E., & K.A. Chrystal. *Political Economics*, Berkeley, CA: Wheatsheaf Books, 1983.

Amin, S. *Imperialism and Unequal Development*, New York: Monthly Review Press, 1977.

Anderson, James E. *The Relative Inefficiency of Quotas*, Cambridge, MA: MIT Press, 1988.

Anderson, L., & D.M. Windham, eds. *Education and Development: Issues in the Analysis and Planning of Postcolonial Societies*, Lexington, MA: Lexington Books, 1982.

Aron, Raymond. *Progress and Disillusion: The Dialectics of Modern Society*, New York: Praeger, 1968.

Aronson, J.D. *Money and Power: Banks and the World Monetary System*, Beverly Hills, CA: Sage Publications, 1978.

Ashley, R.K. *The Political Economy of War and Peace: The Sino-Soviet-American Triangle and the Modern Security Problematique*. London: Francis Pinter, 1980.

Avery, W.P., & D.P. Rapkin, eds. *America in a Changing World Political Economy*, New York: Longman, 1982.

Balassa, B., ed. *Newly Industrializing Countries in the World Economy*, New York: Pergamon Press, 1981.

BALL, GEORGE W. *Global Companies: The Political Economy of World Business*, Englewood Cliffs, NJ: Prentice Hall, 1975.

BANDURA, ALBERT. *Social Learning Theory*, Englewood Cliffs, NJ: Prentice Hall, 1977.

BARNETT, D.A. *China's Economy in Global Perspective*, Washington, DC: Brookings Institution, 1981.

BATES, R.H. *Rural Response to Industrialization: Study of Village Zambia*, New Haven, CT: Yale University Press, 1976.

BATES, ROBERT A. ED. *Toward a Political Economy of Development: A Rational Choice Perspective*, Berkeley: University of California Press, 1988.

BATESON, GREGORY. *Steps to an Ecology of Mind*, New York: Ballantine Books, 1975.

BAUER, P.T. *Equality, the Third World, and Economic Delusion*, Cambridge, MA: Harvard University Press, 1983.

BECKER, J.F. *Marxian Political Economy: An Outline* Cambridge: Cambridge University Press, 1977.

BELL, DANIEL. *The Coming of Post-Industrial Society: A Venture in social forecasting*, New York: Basic Books, 1976.

———. *The Cultural Contradictions of Capitalism*, New York: Basic Books, 1978.

BELL, DANIEL, & IRVING KRISTOL. *Crisis in Economic Theory*, New York: Basic Books, 1982.

BERGER, SUZANNE, & MICHAEL PIORE. *Dualism and Discontinuity in Industrial Societies*, New York: Cambridge University Press, 1980.

BERGSTEN, FRED, ED. *Global Economic Imbalances*, Washington, DC: Institute for International Economics, 1986.

BERGSTEN, FRED, & LAWRENCE B. KRAUSE, EDS. *World Politics and International Economics*, Washington, DC: The Brookings Institution, 1975.

BERRY, R.A., & W.R. CLINE. *Agrarian Structure and Productivity in Developing Countries*, Baltimore: Johns Hopkins University Press, 1978.

BHAGWATI, JAGDISH N. *New International Economic Order: The North–South Debate*, Cambridge, MA: MIT Press, 1977.

BIENEN, HENRY, & RICHARD BUTWELL, EDS. *Foreign Policy and the Developing Nation*, Lexington: University of Kentucky Press, 1969.

BLACK, J.E., & K.W. THOMPSON, EDS. *Foreign Policies in a World of Change*, Salem, NH: Ayer Co., 1975.

BLOCK, F.L. *Origins of International Economic Disorder: Study of United States International Monetary Policy.* Berkeley: University of California Press, 1979.

BONN, MORITZ JULIUS. *The Crumbling of Empire: The Disintegration of World Economy,* London: 1938.

BORNSTEIN, M.Z.GITELMAN, & W. ZIMMERMAN, EDS. *East-West Relations and the Future of Eastern Europe,* Boston: George. Allen Unwin, 1981.

BOTKIN, JAMES, DAN DIMANCESCU, & RAY STATA. *Global Stakes: The Future of High Technology in America,* Cambridge, MA: Ballinger Publishing Co., 1982.

BOULDING, KENNETH. *Conflict and Defense: A General Theory,* New York: Harper and Row, 1962.

BOULDING, KENNETH E. *Economy of Love and Fear,* Belmont, CA: Wadsworth Publishing Co., 1973.

———. *The Image: Knowledge in Life and Society,* Ann Arbor: University of Michigan Press, 1956.

BRADFORD, COLIN I. & WILLIAM H. BRANSON, EDS., *Trade and Structural Change in Pacific Asia* (Chicago: University of Chicago Press, 1987).

BRANDT, WILLY, ET AL. *North–South: A Program for Survival,* London: MIT Press, 1980.

BRAUDEL, F. *Capitalism and Material Life,* New York: Harper & Row, 1973.

———. *The Structures of Everyday Life: The Limits of the Possible,* London: Collins, 1981.

BROWN, MICHAEL BARRATT. *The Economics of Imperialism,* London: Penguin Press, 1974.

BRUNDENIUS, C., & M. LUNDAHL, EDS. *Development Strategies and Basic Needs in Latin America: Challenges for the 1980s,* Boulder: Westview Press, 1982.

BUCHANAN, J.M., & G. TULLOCH. *Calculus of Consent: Logical Foundations of Constitutional Democracy,* Ann Arbor: University of Michigan Press, 1962.

CALLEO, DAVID, & BENJAMIN ROWLAND. *America and the World Political Economy: Atlantic Dreams and National Realities,* Bloomington: Indiana University Press, 1973.

CAPORASO, JAMES A. *A Changing International Division of Labor,* Boulder: Lynne Rienner Publishers, 1987.

CASTANEDA, J., & E. HETT. *El Economismo Dependentista,* Mexico City: Siglo XXI, 1978.

CAVES, RICHARD E. *Multinational Enterprise and Economic Analysis*, Cambridge: Cambridge University Press, 1983.

CHENERY, H.B., M.S. AHLUWALIA, C. BELL, J.H. DULOY, & R. JOLLY. *Redistribution With Growth: Policies to Improve Income Distribution in Developing Countries in the Context of Economic Growth*, London: Oxford University Press, 1974.

CHILCOTE, R.H. ED. *Dependency and Marxism: Towards a Resolution of the Debate*, Boulder: Westview Press, 1982.

CIPOLLA, CARLO M. *The Economic Decline of Empires*, London: Methuen, 1970.

COHEN, BENJAMIN. *Organizing the World's Money: Political Economy of International Relations*, New York: Macmillan, 1978.

COLE, R. *The Japanese Automobile Industry: Model and Challenge for the Future*, Ann Arbor: Center for Japanese Studies, University of Michigan Press, 1981.

CORNWALL, JOHN. *Modern Capitalism: Its Growth and Transformation*, Oxford: Martin Robertson and Co., Ltd., 1977.

DAHRENDORF, RALF. *Lebenschancen*, Frankfurt: Suhrkamp Verlag, 1979.

DELAISI, FRANCIS. *Political Myths and Economic Realities*, Port Washington, NY: Kennikat Publications, 1971.

DEMING, W. EDWARDS. *Quality, Productivity and Competitive Position*. Cambridge, MA: M.I.T. Center for Advanced Engineering Study, 1982.

DENISON, E.F. *Accounting for United States Economic Growth, 1929–1969*, Washington, DC: Brookings Institution, 1974.

DEO, SOM. *Multinational Corporations and the Third World*, Columbia, MO: South Asia Books, 1986.

DE SILVA, S.B.D. *The Political Economy of Underdevelopment*, London: Routledge Chapman & Hall, 1982.

DIAZ-ALEJANDRO, C.F. *Less Developed Countries and the Post-1971 Inernational Financial System*, Princeton, NJ: Princeton University Press, 1975.

DRUCKER, PETER. *Innovation and Entrepreneurship*, New York: Harper & Row, 1985.

DUCHENE, FRANCOIS, & GEOFFREY SHEPHERD. *Managing Industrial Change in Europe*, London: Francis Pinter, 1987.

EELLS, RICHARD, introd. by GEORGE W. BALL. *Global Corporations: the Emerging System of World Economic Power*, New York: Free Press, 1976.

ENGLAND, GEORGE W., ET AL. *Organizational Functioning in Cross-Cultural Perspective*, Kent, OH: Kent State University Press, 1974.

FELD, W.J., ED. *Western Europe's Global Reach: Regional Cooperation and Worldwide Aspirations*, Elmsford, NY: Pergamon Press, 1980.

FLEMING, SPENCER. *Power Anatomy of the Economic Forces Dominating the Business and The Political World*, Albuquerque, NM: Institute for Economic and Political World Strategic Studies, 1983.

FLORA, P., & A.J. HEIDENHEIMER, EDS. *The Development of Welfare States in Europe and America*, New Brunswick, NJ: Transaction Books, 1981.

FOSTER, JOHN. *Energy for Development: An International Challenge*, New York: Praeger, 1981.

FRANK, ANDRE. *Crisis in the World Economy*, New York: Holmes & Meier Publishers, 1980.

FREY, BRUNO S. *International Political Economics*, Oxford: Basil Blackwell, 1986.

FRIEDEN, JEFFREY A., & DAVID A. LAKE, EDS. *International Political Economy: Perspectives on Global Power and Wealth*, New York: St. Martin's Press, 1986.

FRIESEN, CONNIE M. *The Political Economy of East-West Trade*, New York: Praeger, 1976.

FROHLICH, N., & J.A. OPPENHEIMER. *Modern Political Economy*, Englewood Cliffs, NJ: Prentice Hall, 1978.

GALTUNG, J. *The True Worlds: A Transnational Perspective*, New York: Free Press, 1980.

GARDNER, RICHARD. *Sterling-Dollar Diplomacy in Current Perspective: The Origins & Prospects of our International Economic Order*, New York: Columbia University Press, 1980.

GEIGER, THEODORE. *The Future of the International System: The United States and the World Political Economy*, Boston: George, Allen & Unwin, 1988.

GEORGESCU-ROEGEN, NICHOLAS. *The Entropy Law and the Economic Process*, Cambridge, MA: Harvard University Press, 1971.

GERTZ, CLIFFORD. *Peddlers and Princes: Social Development and Economies in Two Indonesian Towns*, Chicago: University of Chicago Press, 1963.

GHOSH, PRADIP K. *Multi-National Coporations and Third World Development*, Westport, CT: Greenwood Press, 1984.

GILPIN, ROBERT. *The Political Economy of International Relations*, Princeton, NJ: Princeton University Press, 1987.

GILPIN, R. *War and Change in World Politics,* New York: Cambridge University Press, 1984.

GOUREVITCH, PETER. *Politics in Hard Times: Comparative Responses to International Economic Crises,* Ithaca, NY: Cornell University Press, 1986.

GRIEVES, FOREST L. ED. *Transnationalism in World Politics and Business,* Elmsford, NY: Pergamon Press, 1979.

GUNBERG, L. *Failed Multinational Ventures: The Political Economy of International Divestments,* Lexington, MA: D.C. Heath, 1981.

HAGEN, EVERETT. *On the Theory of Social Change,* London: Tavistock Publications, 1964.

HAITANI, KANJI. *Comparative Economic Systems: Organizational & Managerial Perspectives,* Englewood Cliffs, NJ: Prentice Hall, 1989.

HALL, EDWARD. *Beyond Culture,* Garden City, NY: Anchor Press, 1976.

HAMPDEN-TURNER, CHARLES. *Gentlemen and Tradesmen: The Values of Economic Catastrophe,* London: Routledge Chapman & Hall, 1984.

HANER, FREDERICK THEODORE. *Global Business Strategy for the 1980's,* New York: Praeger, 1980.

HANKEL, WILHELM, & ROBERT ISAAK. *Modern Inflation: Its Economics and Its Politics,* Lanham, MD: University Press of America, 1983.

HANKEL, WILHELM. "The Financial Crisis Between North and South," in *Economics: A Biannual collection of Recent German Contributions to the Field of Economic Science,* vol. 29, Tubingern: Institut fur Wissenschaftliche Zusammenarbeit, 1984.

HANKEL, WILHELM. *Weltwirtschaft,* Dusseldorf: Econ Verlag, 1977.

HANSEN, ROGER D. *Beyond the North-South Stalemate,* New York: McGraw-Hill, 1979.

HANSEN, ROGER D. ED. *The Global Negotiation and Beyond: Toward North–South Accommodation in the 1980's,* Austin, TX: Lyndon B. Johnson School of Public Affairs, 1981.

HANSSON, GOTE. *Social Clauses and International Trade: Economic Analysis of Labour Standards in Trade Policy,* London: Croom Helm, 1982.

HARDIN, GARRET, & J. BADEN, EDS. *Managing the Commons,* San Francisco: W.H. Freeman & Co., 1977.

HAWKINS, ROBERT G., ED. *The Economic Effects of Multinational Corporations,* Greenwich, CT: Jai Press, 1982.

HAYEK, F.A. *Monetary Nationalism and International Stability,* New York: Macmillan, 1937.

HEKHUIS, DALE J., CHARLES G. MCCLINTOCK, & ARTHUR L. BURNS. *International Stability: Military, Economic and Political Dimensions*, New York: Wiley, 1964.

HEWLETT, S.A. *The Cruel Dilemmas of Development*, New York: Basic Books, 1980.

HICKS, J.R. *Monetary Theory and History: An Attempt at Perspective*, Oxford: G.B. Clarendon Press, 1967.

HIGGINS, B., & J.D. HIGGINS. *Economic Development of a Small Planet*, New York: W.W. Norton, 1979.

HIRSCH, FRED. *Social Limits to Growth*, Cambridge, MA: Harvard University Press, 1976.

HIRSCH, FRED, & JOHN GOLDTHORPE, EDS. *The Political Economy of Inflation*, Cambridge, MA: Harvard University Press, 1978.

HIRSCHMAN, ALBERT O. *National Power and the Structure of Foreign Trade*, Berkeley and Los Angeles: University of California Press, 1980.

HODGES, MICHAEL. *Multinational Corporations and National Government*, London: Saxon House/Lexington Books, 1974.

HOLLIS, W., & F. LaMOND TULLIS, EDS. *An International Political Economy: International Political Economy Yearbook*, vol. 1, Boulder: Westview Press, 1985.

HOOD, NEIL, & STEPHEN YOUNG. *The Economics of Multinational Enterprise*, White Plains, NY: Longman, 1979.

HOPKINS, R.F., & D. J. PUCHALA. *The Global Political Economy of Food*, Madison: University of Wisconsin Press, 1979.

HOPKINS, TERENCE K., & IMMANUEL WALLERSTEIN, EDS. *Processes of the World-System*, Newbury Park, CA: Sage Publications, 1980.

ISAAK, ROBERT. *European Politics: Political Economy and Policymaking in Western Democracies*, New York: St. Martin's Press, 1980.

INOGUCHI, TAKASHI & DANIEL I. OKIMOTO. *The Political Economy of Japan*. Stanford, CA: Stanford University Press, 1988.

JACOBSON, HAROLD K., & SUSAN SIDJANSKI, EDS. *The Emerging International Economic Order: Dynamics, Processes, Constraints & Opportunities*, Beverly Hills, CA: Sage Publications, 1982.

JOHARI, J.C. *International Relations and Politics: Theoretical Perspective*, New York: Apt Books, Inc., 1986.

JOHNSON, CHALMERS. *MITI and the Japanese Miracle, The Growth of Industrial Policy, 1925–1975*, Stanford, CA: Stanford University Press, 1982.

JONES, R.B. *Perspectives on Political Economy,* London: F. Pinter, 1985.

KATZENSTEIN, PETER J., ED. *Between Power and Plenty: Foreign Economic Policies of Advanced Industrial States.* Madison: University of Wisconsin Press, 1978.

KATZENSTEIN, PETER J. *Small States in World Markets: Industrial Policy in Europe,* Ithaca, NY: Cornell University Press, 1985.

KAUSHIK, S.K. *The Debt Crisis and Financial Stability: The Future,* New York: Pace University Press, 1985.

KEOHANE, ROBERT O. *After Hegemony: Cooperation and Discord in the World Political Economy,* Princeton, NJ: Princeton University Press, 1984.

KEOHANE, ROBERT O., & JOSEPH S. NYE. *Power and Interdependence,* Boston: Little Brown, 1977.

KEYNES, JOHN MAYNARD. *General Theory of Employment, Interest and Money,* New York: A Harbinger Book, 1965.

———. *Laissez-faire and Communism.* New York: New Republic, Inc.: 1926.

KIM, KYUNG-WON. *Revolution and International System,* New York: New York University Press, 1970.

KINDLEBERGER, CHARLES. *Power and Money: The Economics of International Politics and the Politics of International Economics,* New York: Basic Books, 1970.

KINDLEBERGER, CHARLES. *The World in Depression, 1929–1939,* Berkeley: University of California Press, 1986.

KORNAI, JANOS. *Economics of Shortage,* vol. 1, Amsterdam: North Holland, 1981.

KRASNER, STEPHEN D. *Structural Conflict: The Third World Against Global Liberalism,* Berkeley: University of California Press, 1985.

KUZNETS, SIMON. *Modern Economic Growth,* New Haven, CT: Yale University Press, 1966.

LINDBLOM, CHARLES. *Politics and Markets: The World's Political-Economic Systems,* New York: Basic Books, 1980.

LINDER, STAFFAN B. *The Harried Leisure Class,* New York: Columbia University Press, 1970.

LINK, WERNER. *The East-West Conflict: The Organization of International Relations in the Twentieth Century,* New York: St. Martin's Press, 1986.

LOMBRA, RAYMOND E., & WILLIAM E. WITTE, EDS. *The Political Economy of International and Domestic Monetary Relations,* Ames: Iowa State University Press, 1982.

MAKIN, JOHN H. *The Global Debt Crisis: America's Growing Involvement,* New York: Basic Books, 1984.

MACRIDIS, ROY C. *Foreign Policy in World Politics,* Englewood Cliffs, NJ: Prentice Hall, 1985.

MARRIS, PETER. *Loss and Change,* New York: Pantheon, 1974.

MARX, KARL, & FREDERICK ENGELS. *Communist Manifesto,* Chicago: Charles H. Kerr, 1946.

MAZRUI, ALI A. *The Moving Cultural Frontier of World Order: From Monotheism to North-South Relations,* New York: World Policy Institute, 1982.

MCCALL, JACK. *Small Town Survival Manual,* Columbia, Missouri: University of Missouri, 1988.

MCCLELLAND, DAVID C. *Roots of Consciousness,* New York: D. VanNostrand, 1964.

METRAUX, R., ET AL. *Some Hypotheses about French Culture,* New York: Research in Contemporary Cultures, Columbia University, 1950.

MILL, J.S. *Principles of Political Economy,* New York: Penguin, 1986.

MODELSKI, GEORGE, ED. *Transnational Corporations and World Order: Readings in International Political Economy,* New York: W.H. Freeman & Co., 1979.

MUIR RAMSAY. *Interdependent World and Its Problems,* New York: Associated Faculty Press, Inc., 1971.

MUNDELL, ROBERT A. *Monetary Theory: Inflation, Interest and Growth in the World Economy,* Pacific Palisades, CA: Goodyear Publishing Co., 1971.

NEWFARMER, RICHARD. *Transnational Conglomerates and the Economics of Dependent Development,* Greenwich, CT: Jai Press, 1980.

NISBET, ROBERT. *The Present Age: Progress & Anarchy in Modern America,* NY: Harper & Row, 1988.

NOHLEN, DIETER, & FRANZ NUSCHELER, EDS. *Handbuch der Dritten Welt,* Band 2: *Sudamerika: Unterentwicklung und Entwicklung,* Ludwisgberg, W. Germany: Hoffman und Campes, 1985.

NURKSE, RAGNER. *Equilibrium and Growth in the World Economy,* edited by Gottfried Haberler and Robert M. Stern, Cambridge, MA: Harvard University Press, 1961.

NYILAS, JOZSEF. *World Economy and Its Main Development Tendencies*, The Hague: Martinue Nijhoff, 1982.

OECD. *Technology on Trial: Public Participation in Decision-making Related to Science and Technology*, Paris: Organization for Economic Cooperation and Development, 1979.

OHLIN, BERTIL, PER OVE HESSLEBORN, & WIJKMAN PER MAGNUS. *The International Allocation of Economic Activity*, New York: Holmes & Meier, 1978.

OLSON, MANCUR. *Logic of Collective Action: Public Goods and the Theory of Groups*, Cambridge, MA: Harvard University Press, 1971.

———. *The Rise and Decline of Nations: Economic Growth, Stagflation and Social Rigidities*, New Haven, CT: Yale University Press, 1982.

PACKENHAM, ROBERT A. *Liberal America and the Third-World: Political Development Ideas in Foreign Aid and Social Science*, Princeton, NJ: Princeton University Press, 1987.

PANIC, M. *National Management of the International Economy*, New York: St. Martin's Press, 1988.

PARKIN, FRANK. *Class Inequality and Political Order: Social Stratification in Capitalist and Communist Societies*, New York: Praeger, 1975.

PATTERSON, ERNEST M. *Economic Bases of Peace*, New York: Associated Faculty Press, Inc., 1971.

PERKINS, DWIGHT H. *China—Asia's Next Economic Giant?* Seattle and London: University of Washington Press, 1986.

POLANYI, K. *Great Transformation: The Political & Economic Origins of our Time*, Boston: Beacon Press, 1957.

POLLARD, ROBERT A. *Political Economy of International Change*, New York: Columbia University Press, 1987.

PUTNAM, ROBERT D., & NICHOLAS BAYNE. *Hanging Together: The Seven Power Summits*, Cambridge, MA: Harvard University Press, 1984.

RADICE, H., ED. *International Firms and Modern Imperialism*, Harmondsworth, U.K.: Penguin, 1975.

RAVENHILL, JOHN. *Collective Clientelism: The Lome Convention and North-South Relations*, New York: Columbia University Press, 1985.

RICARDO, DAVID. *Works and Corresponce of David Ricardo: Principles of Political Economy and Taxation*, London: Cambridge University Press, 1981.

ROSECRANCE, RICHARD. *The Rise of the Trading State: Commerce and Conquest in the Modern World*, New York: Basic Books, 1987.

ROSTOW, W.W. *Stages of Economic Growth.* London: Cambridge University Press, 1971.

—————. *Why the Poor Get Richer and the Rich Slow Down: Essays in the Marshallian Long Period,* Austin: University of Texas Press, 1980.

ROTHSTEIN, ROBERT L. *Global Bargaining: UNCTAD and the Quest for a New International Economic Order,* Princeton, NJ: Princeton University Press, 1979.

ROWLAND, BENJAMIN, ED. *Balance of Power or Hegemony: The Interwar Monetary System,* New York: New York University Press, 1975.

RUGGIE, JOHN GERARD, ED. *The Antinomies of Interdependence: (The Political Economy of International Change),* New York: Columbia University Press, 1983.

SANDLER, TODD, ED. *The Theory and Structures of International Political Economy,* Boulder: Westview Press, 1980.

SAUVANT, KARL P., & HAJO HASENPFLUG, EDS. *The New International Economic Order: Confrontation or Cooperation Between North and South,* Boulder: Westview Press, 1977.

SCHELLING, THOMAS C. *Micromotives and Macrobehavior,* NY: W.W. Norton, 1978.

SCHUMACHER, E.F. *Small Is Beautiful: Economics as if People Mattered,* New York: Harper & Row, 1975.

SCHUMPETER, JOSEPH. *The Theory of Economic Development: An Enquiry into Profits, Capital Interest & the Business Cycle,* Cambridge, MA: Harvard University Press, 1984.

SIMONDS, FRANK H., & BROOKS EMENY. *The Great Powers in World Politics: International Relations and Economic Nationalism,* New York: American Book Company, 1935.

SMITH, ADAM. *An Inquiry into the Nature and Causes of the Wealth of Nations.* New York: Modern Library, 1937.

SMITH, TONY. *The Pattern of Imperialism: The U.S., Great Britain, and the Late-Industrializing World Since 1815,* New York: Cambridge University Press, 1981.

STRANGE, SUSAN, ED. *Paths to International Economy,* London: George Allen & Unwin, 1984.

STRANGE, S. & R. TOOZE, EDS. *The International Politics of Surplus Capacity: Competition for Market Shares in the World Recession,* London: George, Allen & Unwin, 1981.

TARROW, SIDNEY, PETER KATZENSTEIN, & LUIGI GRAZIANO, EDS. *Territorial Politics in Industrial Nations,* New York: Praeger, 1978.

TRIFFIN, ROBERT. *Gold and the Dollar Crisis: The Future of Convertibility,* New Haven, CT: Yale University Press, 1960.

TSURUMI, YOSHI. *Multinational Management: Business Strategy and Government Policy,* 2nd ed., Cambridge, MA: Ballinger, 1983.

TUCKER, ROBERT W. *The Inequality of Nations,* New York: Basic Books, 1979.

TUFTE, EDWARD R. *Political Control of the Economy,* Princeton, NJ: Princeton University Press, 1980.

VARGA, EUGEN. *The Great Crisis and Its Political Consequenses:* New York: H. Fertig, 1974.

VERNON, RAYMOND. ED. *Big Business and the State: Changing Relations in Western Europe,* Cambridge, MA: Harvard University Press, 1974.

———, ED. *The Promise of Privatization: A Challenge for U.S. Foreign Policy,* New York: Council on Foreign Relations, 1988.

VON BEYME, KLAUS. *Ökonomie und Politik im Sozialismus,* Munich: Piper, 1977.

———. *Der Vergleich in der Politikwissenschaft,* Munich: Piper, 1988.

WADE, ROBERT. *Governing the Market: Economic Theory and the Role of Government in East Asian Industrialization,* (Princeton: Princeton University Press, forthcoming).

WALLERSTEIN, IMMANUEL. *The Capitalist World Economy,* Cambridge, MA: Cambridge University Press, 1979.

———, ED. *World Inequality: Origins and Perspectives on the World System,* Montreal: Black Rose Books, 1975.

WALTZ, KENNETH. *Theory of International Politics,* Reading, MA: Addison-Wesley, 1979.

WEBER, MAX. *Economy and Society: An Outline of Interpretive Sociology,* 2 vols., Berkeley: University of California Press, 1978.

WEISBAND, EDWARD, ED. *Poverty Amidst Plenty: World Political Economy and Distributive Justice,* Boulder: Westview Press, 1989.

WHITE, ROBERT W. *The Study of Lives,* Chicago: Aldine-Atherton, 1971.

WICKSELL, KNUT. *Lectures on Political Economy,* 2 vols., London: Routledge & Kegan Paul Ltd., 1934.

WILDENMANN, RUDOLF, ED. *The Future of Party Government*, vol. 3: *Managing Mixed Economies*, ed. by Francis G. Castles, Franz Lehner, and Manfred G. Schmidt, New York/Berlin: Walter de Gruyter, 1988.

WILKINS, MIRA. *The Maturing of Multinational Enterprise: American Business Abroad from 1914–1970*, Cambridge, MA: Harvard University Press, 1974.

WILSON, GRAHAM K. *Business and Politics: A Comparative Introduction*, Chatham, NJ: Chatham House, 1985.

WOODBY, SYLVIA, & MARTHA COTTAM. *The Changing Agenda: World Politics Since 1945*, Boulder: Westview Press, 1988.

ZYSMAN, JOHN. *Government, Markets and Growth: Financial Systems and the Politics of Industrial Change*, Ithaca, NY: Cornell University Press, 1983.

INDEX